The Transformation of Agri-Food Systems

Globalization, Supply Chains and Smallholder Farmers

Edited by
Ellen B. McCullough, Prabhu L. Pingali and
Kostas G. Stamoulis

Published by
The Food and Agriculture Organization of the United Nations
and
Earthscan

publishing for a sustainable future

London • Sterling, VA

First published by FAO and Earthscan in the UK and USA in 2008

Paperback ISBN: 978-92-5-105962-3 (FAO)
Paperback ISBN: 978-1-84407-569-0 (Earthscan)
Hardback ISBN: 978-1-84407-568-3 (Earthscan)
Typeset by MapSet Ltd, Gateshead, UK
Printed and bound in the UK by MPG Books Ltd, Bodmin
Cover design by Susanne Harris

For a full list of publications please contact:

Earthscan
Dunstan House
14a St Cross Street
London, EC1N 8XA, UK
Tel: +44 (0)20 7841 1930
Fax: +44 (0)20 7242 1474
Email: earthinfo@earthscan.co.uk
Web: **www.earthscan.co.uk**

22883 Quicksilver Drive, Sterling, VA 20166-2012, USA

Earthscan publishes in association with the International Institute for Environment and Development

A catalogue record for this book is available from the British Library

Library of Congress Cataloging-in-Publication Data

The transformation of agri-food systems : globalization, supply chains and smallholder farmers / edited by Ellen B. McCullough, Prabhu L. Pingali and Kostas G. Stamoulis.
     p. cm.
   Includes index.
   ISBN 978-1-84407-569-0 (pbk.) – ISBN 978-1-84407-568-3 (hardback) 1. Food supply–Developing countries–Case studies. 2. Farms, Small–Developing countries–Case studies. 3. Food industry and trade–Developing countries–Case studies. I. McCullough, Ellen B. II. Pingali, Prabhu L., 1955- III. Stamoulis, Kostas G.
   HD9018.D44T726 2008
   338.109172'4–dc22

                                                                      2008011461

Contents

Part One: Transformation of Food Systems and the Small Farmer: Key Concepts

Part Two: The Changing Structure of Food Systems

Part Three: Implications of Food Systems Transformation for Smallholder Farmers

List of Figures, Tables and Boxes

Figures

Tables

Boxes

List of Contributors

Belem Avendaño is a professor at the Faculty of Economics and International Relations of the University of Baja California. Her experience in research is focused on the impact of food safety standards on Mexican fresh produce exports. She has collaborated as an adviser to the produce industry in Baja California, Mexico since 1995. Email: belem_avendano@yahoo.com

Julio Berdegue is president of the Latin American Center for Rural Development (RIMISP) in Santiago, Chile. RIMISP has far-ranging activities in Latin America focused on issues of sustainability, rural territorial development, food industry transformation, poverty alleviation and agri-food policy and programme design. Email: jberdegue@rimisp.org

Kevin Z. Chen is currently director of the China Canada Small Farmers Adapting to Global Market Project based in Beijing, China. Formerly, he served as an associate professor at the University of Alberta, Canada. He has a PhD in agricultural economics from the University of Guelph, Canada, and his main interests include agricultural and agribusiness policy and rural development. Email: kevin.chen@ccag.com.cn

Jacques de Graaf holds an MSc in Tropical Agricultural Development, Economics and Management from the University of Reading, UK. He is currently employed by the Ministry of Agriculture, Nature and Food Quality of The Netherlands. For more than 10 years, he worked on agricultural development projects in sub-Saharan Africa. Afterwards, he worked with the United States Department of Agriculture on international agricultural trade. Between 2003 and 2005, he was seconded to the office of the assistant director-general of the Agriculture Department in the Food and Agriculture Organization. His interests include agricultural economic and trade issues between developed and developing countries. Email: degraafjacques@gmail.com

Martine Dirven has an undergraduate degree in applied economics from the State University of Antwerp, a Master's Degree in development planning from the College for Developing Countries in Antwerp, and has completed postgraduate studies in project evaluation (Bradford, UK), marketing (Brussels, Belgium) and applied econometrics (Santiago, Chile). She has worked in the field with the United Nations since 1977, in Colombia, Bolivia, Congo, Mozambique, the

United Arab Emirates and the Maldives, as well as in headquarters offices in Vienna, New York and, presently, Santiago. Since 1988, she has served in the Agricultural Development Unit of the UN-Economic Commission for Latin America and the Caribbean, with a focus on the socio-economic aspects of agricultural and rural development. Since 2003, she has been chief of the Agricultural Development Unit. She was born in Antwerp, Belgium. Email: Martine.Dirven@cepal.org

Liesbeth Dries has been a lecturer in agribusiness at Lincoln University in New Zealand since 2007. Previously, she was employed as an assistant professor in agricultural and food policy at the Katholieke Universiteit Leuven in Belgium, where she completed her PhD in Economics in 2003. Her research focuses on issues of vertical coordination in agri-food supply chains. Email: driesl@lincoln.ac.nz

Sergio Faiguenbaum is an agricultural economist at the Regional Office for Latin America and the Caribbean (in Santiago, Chile) of the FAO. He is currently a doctoral candidate in American Studies at the Instituto de Estudios Avanzados in the Universidad de Santiago de Chile. He has worked both in public and non-governmental organizations in Chile, and as an international consultant in the field of agri-food systems and rural development. Email: Sergio.Faiguenbaum@fao.org

Hyde Haantuba holds a PhD from Washington State University in the United States. For 20 years, he was the director of the Marketing Department of the Ministry of Agriculture in Zambia (Lusaka). He is currently director of the Agriculture Consultative Forum in Zambia. Dr Haantuba's research interests are in the areas of marketing, food chain analysis and agricultural policy analysis. Email: ACFS@microlink.zm

Jon Hellin works at the International Maize and Wheat Improvement Center (CIMMYT) in Mexico. He has 15 years of experience in research and rural development from Latin America, South Asia and East Africa. After completing a cross-disciplinary PhD on smallholder land management in Central America, his research has focused on farmers' livelihood security and access to markets. Email: j.hellin@cgiar.org

Jikun Huang is the founder and director of the Center for Chinese Agricultural Policy (CCAP) of the Chinese Academy of Sciences (CAS), as well as a professor in the Institute of Geographical Sciences and Natural Resources Research. He received a BSc from Nanjing Agricultural University in 1984 and a PhD in economics from the University of the Philippines at Los Baños in 1990. His research covers a wide range of issues surrounding agricultural and rural development in China, including work on agricultural R&D policy, water resource economics, price and marketing, food consumption, poverty and trade liberalization. Email: jkhuang.ccap@igsnrr.ac.cn

Thomas Jayne is a professor of international development, in the Department of Agricultural Economics and a member of the core faculty of the African Studies Center at Michigan State University. He received his PhD in agricultural economics from Michigan State University. His research interests focus on agricultural marketing, smallholder farm productivity and response strategies to combat HIV/AIDS in Africa. Jayne sits on the editorial boards of two development journals and received a 2004 top paper award from the International Association of Agricultural Economists. His work has been recognized at the 1996 World Food Summit in Rome, the Secretariat of Global Agricultural Science Policy for the Twenty-first Century and the 1999 World Food Prize Conference. Email: jayne@msu.edu

Mark Lundy is a researcher at the Centro Internacional de Agricultura Tropical (CIAT), in Cali, Colombia. His work on rural enterprise development focuses on pro-poor business models, knowledge management and multistakeholder platforms for innovation in Central America and elsewhere. He holds a Masters in both community and regional planning and Latin American studies from the University of Texas at Austin. Email: m.lundy@cgiar.org

Ellen McCullough coordinated a multinational research project on the transformation of food systems between 2005 and 2007, while she was based in the Agricultural Development Economics division of the Food and Agriculture Organization. In 2008, Ellen joined the Agricultural Development Division at the Bill and Melinda Gates Foundation, where she is working with the Agricultural Policy and Statistics team. She received a BSc and MSc from Stanford University in earth systems. Her research interests include market linkages for smallholders, sustainable resource management and the policy enabling environment. Email: Ellen.McCullough@gatesfoundation.org

Madelon Meijer is currently a policy adviser on agriculture at Oxfam Novib in The Netherlands. Previous work at FAO included research on changing food systems and smallholder farmers and contribution to *The State of Food Insecurity*, one of FAO's flagship publications. She worked over four years in Latin America on rural economic development, strengthening farmer organizations and facilitating market linkages. She holds a Masters in agricultural development economics from the University of Reading in the UK and a Masters in economics from the University of Amsterdam in The Netherlands. Email: madelon.meijer@oxfamnovib.nl

Clare Narrod is a research fellow in the Markets Trade and Institutions division of the International Food Policy Research Institute (IFPRI), which she joined in August 2005 to lead a programme in food and water safety. Before coming to IFPRI, Clare worked for the United States Department of Agriculture (USDA) in the office of the chief economist, where she reviewed food safety and animal and plant health rules for departmental clearance as a risk assessor and regulatory economist. She also has worked at the Food and Agriculture Organization, where she led a number of livestock projects focused on the policy, technology and environmental determinants and implications of scaling up livestock production. From 1998 to 2000, she served as an American Association for the Advancement of Science Risk Fellow at the USDA. She received her PhD in energy management and environmental policy and her Masters Degree in international development and appropriate technology, both from the University of Pennsylvania. Email: C.Narrod@cgiar.org

David Neven is an agri-food marketing economist providing technical assistance to projects in agriculture and agribusiness. Previously a cooperant for a Belgian development organization and an academic at Michigan State University, he has over 10 years of experience in food marketing, including extensive fieldwork in agricultural market development in sub-Saharan Africa, the Caribbean, Southeast Asia and Eastern Europe. He holds a PhD in agricultural economics from Michigan State University. Email: david_neven@dai.com

Timothy Osoro Nyanamba is a graduate student in the department of Agricultural Economics and Agribusiness Management at Egerton University, Kenya. While completing the research contained in this volume, he served as a research associate at the Kenya Institute for Public Policy Research and Analysis (KIPPRA). His research interests include rural agricultural development and agricultural policy. Email: nyanambat@yahoo.com

Julius J. Okello is a lecturer in the Department of Agricultural Economics at the University of Nairobi, Kenya and an adjunct scientist at the International Crops Research Institute for the Semi-Arid Tropics (ICRISAT). Julius earned his PhD from Michigan State University in 2005 with specialization in international agricultural development, agricultural marketing and resource and environmental economics. His current research focus is on the role of collective action, public–private partnerships, and information and communication technology in linking smallholder farmers to high-value domestic and international markets. Other research activities are centred on soil and water management and the management of beneficial and invasive animal species. Email: J.Okello@cgiar.org

John M. Omiti holds a PhD in agricultural economics and is a senior policy analyst with the Kenya Institute for Public Policy Research and Analysis (KIPPRA) in Nairobi. He also has worked with a number of national and international agricultural research centres (e.g. Institute of Policy Analysis and Research (IPAR), International Livestock Research Institute (ILRI), International Crops Research Institute for the Semi-Arid Tropics (ICRISAT)). He has a keen interest in the analysis of policy issues affecting the agricultural sector, food security, poverty alleviation and institutional development at the macro- and sectoral levels. Email: jmomiti@yahoo.com

David Jakinda Otieno is a tutorial fellow in the Department of Agricultural Economics at the University of Nairobi, Kenya. He was a research associate at the Kenya Institute for Public Policy Research and Analysis (KIPPRA) at the time of this research work. David holds an MSc in agricultural economics from the University of Nairobi and a BSc in agricultural economics from Egerton University, Kenya. His research interests include market access, international trade, policy and institutional reform. Email: jakinda1@yahoo.com

Prabhu Pingali recently joined the Agricultural Development Division at the Bill and Melinda Gates Foundation to lead the Agricultural Policy and Statistics Team. Prior to joining the Gates Foundation, he directed the Agricultural and Development Economics Division of the Food and Agriculture Organization. He served as president of the International Association of Agricultural Economists (IAAE) between 2003 and 2006 and co-chaired the Millennium Ecosystem Assessment Panel's working group on Future Scenarios. In 2007, Pingali was elected to the US National Academy of Sciences as a foreign fellow. He has over 25 years of experience in assessing the extent and impact of technical change in developing country agriculture in Asia, Africa and Latin America. An Indian national, he earned a PhD in economics from North Carolina State University in 1982. He also directed the Economics Program at CIMMYT, worked at the International Rice Research Institute, and at the World Bank. Email: Prabhu.Pingali@gatesfoundation.org

Thomas Reardon is a professor of agricultural economics at Michigan State University. He is co-director of the International Food Policy Research Institute/Michigan State University Joint Program on Markets in Asia. His work focuses on how food industry transformation (particularly that of supermarkets, fast-food chains, processors, wholesalers and input companies) affect small-scale food industry firms and farmers in developing regions, mainly in Asia and also in Latin America. Email: reardon@msu.edu

Iván Rodriguez holds an MBA and a degree in agronomy and has field experience working in agricultural value chains. He currently works for the Swiss Agency for Development and Cooperation (SDC) as the Swiss contact in Honduras, and has also worked as fresh products manager for a supermarket chain and manager of a coffee roasting company. He has conducted studies for USAID in Nicaragua and Guatemala, and worked for a rural micro enterprises development programme founded by the Inter-American Development Bank. Email: swisscontact_ivan@cablecolor.hn

Devesh Roy joined the International Food Policy Research Institute in 2004 as a postdoctoral fellow, and he conducts research on international economics with a focus on product standards in international trade. His other areas of research include development economics, economic geography, institutions for firm–farm linkages and the impact of trade liberalization on food security in poor countries. Before coming to IFPRI, he received a PhD from the University of Maryland. Roy also holds a BA in economics from Delhi University and a MA from the Delhi School of Economics. He is a citizen of India. Email: D.Roy@cgiar.org

Scott Rozelle holds the Helen Farnsworth Endowed Professorship at Stanford University and is a senior fellow and professor in the Shorenstein Asia-Pacific Research Center, Freeman Spogli Institute (FSI) of International Studies. His research focuses on agricultural policy, the emergence and evolution of markets and institutions and the economics of poverty and inequality. He is also the chair of the Board of Academic Advisors of the Center for Chinese Agricultural Policy in Beijing. Email: rozelle@stanford.edu

Sukhpal Singh holds a PhD in Economics and, since 2004, has been an associate professor at the Centre for Management in Agriculture (CMA) in the Indian Institute of Management (IIM), Ahmedabad (Gujarat). Before assuming this position, he worked with the Institute of Rural Management (IRMA) in Anand (Gujarat) for 12 years. His research and teaching interests are in vertical coordination of agribusiness chains and their governance, especially regarding small producer participation in global food and fibre chains. Email: sukhpal@iimahd.ernet.in

Kostas Stamoulis is chief of the Agricultural Sector in Development Economics service in the Food and Agriculture Organization. Before joining the FAO, he taught agricultural economics at the University of Illinois in Urbana Champaign. His research has focused on the role of agriculture in growth and poverty reduction, the effects of stabilization on agricultural performance, the role of the non-farm rural sector on growth and food security, and the impact of urbanization and globalization. A Greek national, he has a PhD in agricultural and resource economics from the University of California at Berkeley. Email: Kostas.Stamoulis@fao.org

Johan F. M. Swinnen is professor of development economics and director of LICOS Center for Institutions and Economic Performance at the Katholieke Universiteit Leuven in Belgium. He was lead economist at the World Bank from 2003 to 2004 and economic adviser to the European Commission from 1998 to 2001. He has been adviser to many international institutions and governments. His research focuses on institutional reform and development, globalization and international integration, media economics, and agriculture and food policy. His latest books are *Global Supply Chains, Standards, and the Poor* and *From Marx and Mao to the Market*. He is also a senior research fellow at the Centre for European Policy Studies (CEPS), Brussels; coordinator of the European Network of Agricultural and Rural Policy Research Institutes (ENARPRI); member of the Advisory Committee of the Regoverning Markets Global Project; and of the Programme Committee of the International Agricultural Trade Research Consortium (IATRC). He holds a PhD from Cornell University. Email: Jo.Swinnen@econ.kuleuven.be

C. Peter Timmer has held tenured positions at Stanford, Cornell and Harvard Universities, and was the dean of the Graduate School of International Relations and Pacific Studies at the University of California, San Diego. He is currently visiting professor in the Program on Food Security and Environment at Stanford University, where he is pursuing his teaching and research interests in food policy in developing countries and pathways out of rural poverty. He is also a non-resident fellow at the Center for Global Development. Email: ptimmer@cgdev.org

Sonam Tobgay has a Masters Degree in business administration and a Bachelors Degree in agricultural economics. He served the Royal Government of Bhutan under the Ministry of Agriculture as a senior policy analyst and later as a chief agricultural negotiator in Bhutan's accession to the World Trade Organization. Between 2005 and 2007, he worked as a consultant to the Food and Agricultural Organization (FAO) and the United Nations Conference on Trade and Development (UNCTAD). The author's primary research interests include food security and poverty alleviation, agricultural trade policy and small farmer studies. Email: sktobgay@druknet.bt

John Wilkinson is a senior lecturer at the Graduate Center for Development, Agriculture and Society at the Rural Federal University, Rio de Janeiro, Brazil. He has served as a consultant to the Organisation for Economic Co-operation and Development (OECD), the European Economic Community (EEC), the Economic Commission for Latin America and the Caribbean (ECLAC) and the FAO on a variety of issues relating to agriculture and the food system. He has authored/edited 12 books, including *From Farming to Biotechnology* (co-author), and *Fair Trade: the Challenges of Transforming Globalization* (co-editor), together with some 50 articles published in reviewed journals in Europe, the US and Latin America. Email: jwilkins@uol.com.br

Yunhua Wu is a graduate student and PhD candidate in the Center for Chinese Agricultural Policy and associate professor at the Inner-Mongolia Agricultural University. She received a BSc in mathematics from Inner-Mongolia Normal University in 1993 and an MSc in agricultural economics from Inner-Mongolia Agricultural University in 1999. Her major research focus is on food markets and agricultural policy. Email: wuyh.04b@igsnrr.ac.cn

Foreword

As countries go through the development process, agriculture's share in the economy and the work force decreases in favour of other sectors. This basic characteristic of the development process, along with a new set of factors – globalization of diets, liberalization of investment and trade, and technology – shapes the organizational transformation of food systems. Modern retail chains are growing fast, drawing in new sources of investment and opening new, reliable markets for higher value products. Participation by agricultural producers in modern chains involves a different set of costs and skills relative to traditional market outlets and raises questions of how such requirements are shaping the landscape for smallholder farmers.

The rapid expansion of supermarkets in Latin America and Central and Eastern Europe has raised questions as to the extent and the pace at which other developing regions will follow trend and, more broadly, how retail concentration impacts smallholder farmers, rural communities and the poor overall. This book presents evidence that smallholders can and do participate in modern chains, but to varying degrees and with mixed results in terms of improving household welfare.

Despite the rapid rise of modern retail, for countries at the lower end of the transformation process, traditional market structures still account for the majority of food retail. In most of Africa, modern retail chains are not expected to capture a substantial share of food retail within the next decade. Furthermore, lucrative opportunities to access high-value export markets are quite limited in scope. The real danger for African smallholders is that they are excluded from larger agricultural markets due to high transportation and transaction costs and competition from imports.

For many smallholders throughout the world, and particularly in sub-Saharan Africa, the challenge of participating in modern, organized chains is eclipsed by the more fundamental challenge of participating in any market. Market linkages for smallholders can be improved by lowering transaction costs, investing in market and transport infrastructure, boosting productivity, improving access to inputs and building their capacity in meeting the standards of safety and quality demanded by the market.

This book fills a fundamental need for focusing on organizational changes in domestic markets, bringing a valuable cross-continent perspective of an important emerging issue. Part One sets the context with an overarching synthesis, a review of historical experience, and an analysis of important concepts. Parts Two and Three contain a rich set of case studies addressing contemporary examples of food systems transformation. Part Three is focused specifically on how farmers integrate with markets, while Part Four documents changes beyond the farm gate.

The analysis presented in this book was part of the work programme of the Agricultural Development Economics Division at the Food and Agriculture Organization of the United Nations. It was supported, in part, by the Netherlands through the FAO-Netherlands Partnership Programme and by Norway through a similar partnership. At the time of preparation, the book's editors were all part of the Agricultural Development Economics Division. Prabhu Pingali was director of the division, and Ellen McCullough was a staff member. Kostas Stamoulis continues to be chief of the Agricultural Sector in Economic Development Service. Andrea Stoutland provided editorial assistance, and Simran Kaur provided research assistance.

Hafez Ghanem
Assistant Director-General
Economic and Social Department
FAO

List of Acronyms and Abbreviations

AEZs	agro-ecological zones
AFC	Agricultural Finance Corporation (Kenya)
AMS	Agricultural Marketing Services (Bhutan)
APMC	Agricultural Produce Marketing Committee
ASEAN	Association of South East Asian Nations
BIMSTEC	Bay of Bengal Initiative for Multi-sectoral Technical and Economic Cooperation
BRC	British Retail Consortium
BSE	bovine spongiform encephalopathy
CAADP	Comprehensive African Agriculture Development Programme
CAFTA	Central American Free Trade Agreement (now DR-CAFTA)
CARHCO	Central American Retail Holding Company
CEE	central and eastern Europe
CEEC	central and eastern European countries
CIAA	Confederation of the Food and Drink Industries (EU)
CIAT	International Center for Tropical Agriculture
CII	Confederation of Indian Industry
CIRAD	*Centre de coopération internationale en recherche agronomique pour le développement*
COMESA	Common Market of Eastern and Southern Africa
DACO	District Agricultural Co-ordination (Zambia)
DAOs	District Agriculture Officers (Bhutan)
DC	distribution centre
DECDG	Development Economics, Development Data Group (World Bank)
EAP	economically active population
ECR	efficient consumer response
ETI	Ethical Trading Initiative
EU	European Union
EurepGAP	Euro-Retailer Produce Working Group on Good Agricultural Practices (now GLOBALGAP)
FAIDA	Food and Agriculture Integrated Development Action
FAO	Food and Agriculture Organization (of the UN)
FCB	Food Corporation of Bhutan
FDA	Food and Drug Administration (US)
FDI	foreign direct investment
FFV	fresh fruit and vegetables
FHIA	Honduran Foundation for Research in Agriculture
FNPP	FAO–Netherlands Partnership Programme

FPEAK	Fresh Produce Exporters Association of Kenya
FTAA	Free Trade Area of the Americas
GAPs	good agricultural practices
GDP	gross domestic product
GMPs	good manufacturing practices
GoI	Government of India
HACCP	hazard analysis and critical control point
HCDA	Horticultural Crop Development Authority (Kenya)
HEBI	Horticultural Ethical Business Initiative (Kenya)
HPHC	Horticultural Produce Handling Company
ICAE	International Conference of Agricultural Economists
IDS	Institute of Development Studies
IFAD	International Fund for Agricultural Development
IFPRI	International Food Policy Research Institute
IFSS	international food safety standards
ILRI	International Livestock Research Institute (Kenya)
IMF	International Monetary Fund
IPAR	Institute of Policy Analysis and Research (Kenya)
IPGRI	International Plant Genetic Research Institute
ISAE	Indian Society of Agricultural Economics
KACE	Kenya Agricultural Commodity Exchange
KCC	Kenya Cooperative Creameries
KCCs	Kisan Credit Cards (India)
KEPHIS	Kenya Plant Health Inspectorate Service
KIPPRA	Kenya Institute for Public Policy Research and Analysis
LDCs	least developed countries
MIGA	Multilateral Investment Guarantee Agency
MIS	market intervention schemes
MSP	minimum support price
MVA	manufacturing value added
NABARD	National Bank for Agriculture and Rural Development
NAFTA	North American Free Trade Area
NCPB	National Cereals and Produce Board (Kenya)
NGCs	new-generation cooperatives
NGO	non-governmental organization
NSBC	National Bureau of Statistics of China
NWP	North-Western Province (Zambia)
OECD	Organisation for Economic Co-operation and Development
PACS	Primary Agricultural Co-operative Societies
PRA	participatory rural appraisal
PRSP	poverty reduction strategy paper
RGOB	Royal Government of Bhutan
RNR	Renewable Natural Resource
RRA	rapid rural appraisal
SADC	Southern African Development Community

SAFTA	South Asian Free Trade Area
SAPs	structural adjustment programmes
SENASICA	Secretariat of Agriculture and Rural Development (Mexico)
SHG	self-help group
SMEs	small and medium enterprises
SPS	sanitary and phytosanitary
TBT	Technical Barriers to Trade
TNCs	transnational corporations
UN	United Nations
UNCTAD	United Nations Conference on Trade and Development
UNEP	United Nations Environment Programme
UNIDO	United Nations Industrial Development Organization
USDA	United States Department of Agriculture
WFP	World Food Programme
WTO	World Trade Organization
ZEGA	Zambia Export Growers Association
ZIC	Zambia Investment Centre
ZNFU	Zambian National Farmers Union
ZPA	Zambia Privatization Agency

Part One

Transformation of Food Systems and the Small Farmer: Key Concepts

Chapter 1

Small Farms and the Transformation of Food Systems: An Overview

Ellen B. McCullough, Prabhu L. Pingali and Kostas G. Stamoulis

Introduction

By making a strong case for the importance of agriculture in poverty reduction, even in developing countries with largely urbanized populations, the 2008 World Development Report has continued the renewed interest in agriculture as a force for poverty reduction (World Bank, 2008). Research has shown that rural poverty reduction, resulting from better conditions in rural areas and not from the movement of rural poor into urban areas, has been the engine of overall poverty reduction (Ravallion et al, 2007). Organizational changes that are currently underway in developing-country food systems necessitate a new look at agriculture's role in poverty reduction with an eye on the changing rural economy. The reorganization of supply chains, from farm to plate, is fuelling the transformation of entire food systems in developing countries. With the changing rural context in mind, we revisit prospects for poverty reduction in rural areas, particularly in the small farm sector. The transformation of food systems threatens business as usual but offers new opportunities for smallholder farmers and the rural poor.

The purpose of this volume is to take stock of important trends in the organization of food systems and to assess, with concrete examples and case studies, their impacts on smallholder producers in a wide range of contexts. This volume brings together relevant literature in a consistent manner and examines more holistically the issue of changing food systems, moving beyond the focus of supermarkets, which has been a dominant concern in recent literature. We focus on domestic markets as well as exports, and on a wide range of sub-sectors, not just fresh fruits and vegetables and dairy. This chapter begins with a description of changing consumption patterns in developing countries. Then we highlight organizational changes that have taken place along the food chain, recognizing important differences between countries, and exploring interactions between traditional and modern chains in countries where food systems are transforming. We present a framework for evaluating impacts at the household level, pulling together empirical evidence in support of the framework. We close with a policy discussion on managing the transition for smallholder households, which focuses on linking smallholders into modern food chains, upgrading traditional markets and providing exit strategies for those who are marginalized by the transformation process.

The transformation: An overview

In this chapter, we lay out three different typologies for food systems that correspond roughly with the development process. The first is a traditional food system, characterized by a dominance of traditional, unorganized supply chains and limited market infrastructure. The second is a structured food system, still characterized by traditional actors but with more rules and regulations applied to marketplaces and more market infrastructure. In structured food systems, organized chains begin to capture a growing share of the market, but traditional chains are still common. The third type is an industrialized food system, as observed throughout the developed world, with strong perceptions of safety, a high degree of coordination, a large and consolidated processing sector and organized retailers.

Major global shifts in consumption, marketing, production and trade are brought about, above all, by four important driving forces associated with economic development: rising incomes, demographic shifts, technology for managing food chains and globalization. As these changes are played out, modern chains capture a growing share of the market, and food systems transform. The variable that differs most strikingly between food system typologies is the share of the food market that passes through organized value chains. We identify economic factors that explain how modern chains capture a growing share of food retail over time, and we explore specific differences between organized and traditional chains. Then we examine the implication of the spread of modern chains from the perspective of chain participants and with respect to the entire food system. In practice, the boundaries between these food system typologies are not easily discernible. Nor is the path from traditional to structured to modern a linear one. A mix of different types of chains can be found within one country depending on the commodity involved, the size of urban centres and linkages with international markets (Chen and Stamoulis, this volume).

Understanding how different types of chains relate to each other is important for predicting future opportunities for smallholder farmers as food systems reorganize. In developing countries, the food system is typically composed of domestic traditional chains, domestic modern chains and export chains, which are usually exclusively modern. When traditional marketing systems fail to meet the needs of domestic consumers and processors, modern retailers develop mechanisms for bypassing the traditional market altogether. Modern food chains in developing countries advance rapidly due to global exposure, competition and investment, while traditional chains risk stagnation due to underinvestment. As the gap between traditional and modern food chains grows ever wider, the challenge of upgrading traditional chains becomes more pronounced. The entire food system's transition from traditional to structured is hindered as resources and attention are diverted from upgrading traditional markets in favour of bypassing them.

Assessing the full implications of changes for rural communities and, in particular, smallholder agriculture, requires an analysis of how risks and rewards are distributed both in traditional food systems and modern ones. As production and marketing change, there are obvious implications for smallholder farmers via changes in production costs, output prices and marketing costs. But changes in processing, transport, input distribution and food retail also impact rural households via household incomes (e.g. labour markets, small enterprises) and expenditures (e.g. food prices).

From farm to plate, one overarching trend is the rising need for coordination in modern food systems relative to traditional ones, and the transaction costs that are introduced as a result. Coordination helps to ensure that information about a product's provenance travels downstream with the product. It also helps to ensure that information about consumer demand and stock shortages/surpluses is transferred upstream more efficiently to producers (King and Phumpiu, 1996). Improving coordination along the supply chain reduces many costs but introduces new ones (Pingali et al, 2007). We explore and evaluate different strategies for coordination later in the chapter.

Towards dietary diversification

Brought about by rising incomes, demographic shifts and globalization, dietary change is sweeping the developing world. Consumers are shifting to more diverse diets that are higher in fresh produce and animal products and contain more processed foods. Shifts in food consumption parallel income growth, above all, which is associated with higher value food items displacing staples (Bennett's Law). The effect of per capita income growth on food consumption is most profound for poorer consumers who spend a large portion of their budget on food items (Engel's Law). A sustained decline in real food prices over the last 40 years has reinforced the effect of rising incomes on diet diversification.

Per capita incomes have risen substantially in many parts of the developing world over the past few decades. In developing countries, per capita income growth averaged around 1 per cent per year in the 1980s and 1990s but jumped to 3.7 per cent between 2001 and 2005 (World Bank, 2006). Growth rates have been most impressive in east Asia and slightly less spectacular in south Asia. Declining growth rates have been reversed since the 1990s in Latin America and since 2000 in sub-Saharan Africa. Income growth has been accompanied by an increase in the number of middle class consumers in developing countries, particularly in Asia and Latin America, whose consumption patterns have diversified (Beng-Huat, 2000; Solamino, 2006).

Beyond income growth, dietary diversification is also fuelled by urbanization and its associated characteristics, rising female employment and increased exposure to different types of foods. Globally, urban dwellers outnumbered rural populations during 2007 (Population Division of UN, 2006). Feeding cities is now a major challenge facing food systems.

Female employment has at least kept pace with population growth in developing countries since 1980 (World Bank, 2006). Female employment rates have risen substantially in Latin America, east Asia, and the Middle East and north Africa since the 1980s.

Urban consumers typically have higher wage rates and are willing to pay for more convenience, which frees up time for income-earning activities or leisure. Therefore, they place a higher premium on processed and pre-prepared convenience foods than do rural consumers (Popkin, 1999; Regmi and Dyck, 2001). Rising female employment also contributes to this phenomenon (Kennedy and Reardon, 1994). Smaller families are typical of urban areas, so households can afford more convenience in terms of processed and prepared foods.

Globalization has led to increased exchanges of ideas and culture across boundaries through communication and travel, leading to a tightening of the global community which is reflected in dietary patterns, such as increased consumption of American style convenience foods. Urban consumers are exposed to more advertisements and are influenced by the wide variety of food choices available to them (Reardon et al, this volume).

Dietary changes have played out differently in different regions and countries, depending on their per capita incomes, the degree of urbanization and cultural factors. The most striking feature of dietary change is the substitution of traditional staples for other staple grains (i.e. rice for wheat in east and southeast Asia) and for fruits and vegetables, meat and dairy, fats and oils (Pingali, 2007). Per capita meat consumption in developing countries tripled between 1970 and 2002, while milk consumption increased by 50 per cent (Steinfeld and Chilonda, 2006). Dietary changes are most striking in Asia, where diets are shifting away from rice and increasingly towards livestock products, fruits and vegetables, sugar and oils (Pingali, 2007). Diets in Latin America have not changed as drastically, although meat consumption has risen in recent years. In sub-Saharan Africa, perhaps the biggest change has been a rise in sugar consumption during the 1960s and 1970s (FAOSTAT, 2006). Cereals, roots and tubers still comprise the vast majority of sub-Saharan African diets, and this is expected to continue into the foreseeable future (FAO, 2006). Total food consumption in developing countries is projected to increase in coming decades, so dietary diversification does not necessarily imply that per capita consumption of any food products will decline in absolute terms (Figure 1.1). However, by 2030, absolute decreases are expected in per capita consumption of roots and tubers in sub-Saharan Africa

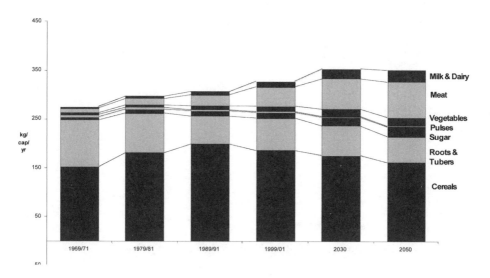

Source: Data from FAO, 2006

Figure 1.1 *Trends and projections for dietary diversification in east Asia*

and of cereals in east Asia (FAO, 2004). Since cereals are used as inputs in animal production, total cereal demand will not decrease due to indirect consumption.

Trends in food systems organization

Consumption of higher value products is on the rise in developing countries, and supply chains are ready to meet these demands. But which chains will reach dynamic consumer segments in developing countries, and which farmers will supply these chains? From farms to retail, technology and 'globalization' are the most important drivers of reorganization of the chains linking producers and consumers. Innovations in information and communications technology have allowed supply chains to become more responsive to consumers, while innovations in processing and transport have made products more suitable for global distribution. Technological innovation in food supply chain management has arisen in response to volatility in consumer demand (Kumar, 2001). New communication tools, such as the Universal Product Code, which came on line in the 1970s, have improved the efficiency of coordination between actors along the supply chain to shorten response times to demand fluctuations (King and Venturini, 2005). Packaging innovations throughout the second half of the 20th century continued to extend food products' shelf lives (Welch and Mitchell, 2000). Meanwhile, a downward trend in transportation costs and widespread availability of atmosphere-controlled storage infrastructure have made it cost-effective to transport products over longer distances. Crop varieties have been tailored specifically to chain characteristics, for example to meet processing standards or to extend shelf life. Conventional breeding and, more recently, biotechnology, have allowed these shifts.

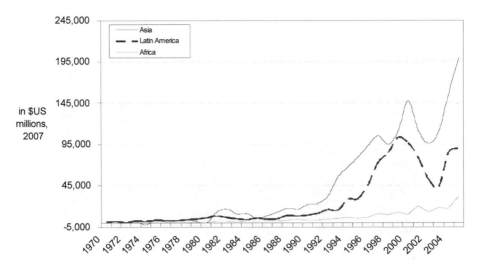

Source: Data from OECD, 2007

Figure 1.2 *Annual FDI net inflows into developing countries by region from 1970*

'Globalization' in retail and agribusiness is marked by liberalization of trade as well as of foreign direct investment (FDI). Trade has maintained a constant share in global food consumption but is shifting towards higher value products, such as processed goods, fresh produce and animal products (Hallam et al, 2004). Flows in capital can impact food systems as profoundly as flows in products. Rising FDI flows into developing countries have been linked with concentration throughout the food industry, boosts in productivity and innovation, and an increase in non-traditional agricultural exports (Wilkinson, this volume). Foreign direct investment in agriculture and the food industry grew substantially in Latin America and in Asia between the mid-1980s and mid-1990s, although investment remained very low in sub-Saharan Africa (FAO, 2004). In Asia, FDI in the food industry nearly tripled, from $750 million to $2.1 billion between 1988 and 1997. During that same period, food industry investment exploded in Latin America, from around $200 million to $3.3 billion. There is a limit in the availability of sector-specific FDI data since 2001, but economy-wide data through 2005 show a similar pattern: with long-term increases in developing countries in Asia and Latin America, with 2002–2003 slumps in both cases, and with Africa lagging behind but growing somewhat steadily since the 1970s (Figure 1.2). FDI flows into Africa have lagged behind those into Asia and Latin America because of structural and institutional constraints. The world's least developed countries (LDCs) receive only 2 per cent of global foreign direct investment.

The transformation of food systems is not something that occurs overnight. While many of the factors that affect food systems can change rather quickly, their reorganization involves large investments in specialized infrastructure, institutional change and regulatory reform. Often, these components are jointly determined rather than one causing the others. Institutions evolve as modern systems expand and infrastructure is built to accommodate the needs of the evolving markets and players. As mentioned above, multiple typologies can be observed simultaneously in the same country. Within one country, organizational change may take place earlier in chains for products that are prone to safety violations, such as meat and dairy (Chen and Stamoulis, this volume). International concerns over trans-boundary diseases (e.g. avian flu) place pressure even on non-exporting countries to upgrade supply chains in order to reduce the incidence of outbreaks and allow for better response when outbreaks occur. When a country does export food products, the onus is on the exporters to demonstrate that their products (and/or the production and post-harvest systems that give rise to them) meet the importers' safety standards.

Country typologies by stage of transformation

Organizational changes in food systems vary in speed and extent across contexts (national, sub-national, type of product and chain), and impacts vary across households and household typologies. At the country level, perhaps the most important determinant of the transition is the country's position in the agricultural development process. This is the path by which, over time, per capita incomes rise as the share of agriculture in a country's work force and economy declines (Figure 1.3) (Pingali, 1997, 2006).

Countries at the low end of the transformation process are characterized by low per capita incomes, with the agricultural sector accounting for more than 30 per cent of the national GDP and over 50 per cent of the work force (FAOSTAT, 2006). In these countries, which are mostly located in sub-Saharan Africa and

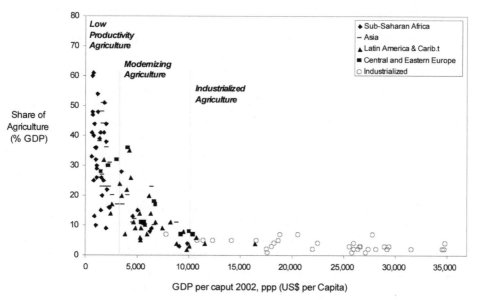

Source: Data from World Bank's World Development Indicators (World Bank, 2006)

Figure 1.3 *Falling share of agriculture in the economy as GDP rises*

Table 1.1 *Characteristics of food systems by country typology*

	Traditional	Structured	Modern / Integrated
Share of agriculture in GDP	High	Medium	Low
Urbanization	Rural	Urbanizing to varying degrees	Urbanized
State of the agricultural economy	Traditional	Modernizing	Industrialized
Rural income sources	Few opportunities outside agriculture (farming or ag. wage labour), high migration	More diversified opportunities, dualistic	Agriculture and manufacturing, dwindling rural population
Agriculture's role in poverty reduction	Agriculture growth stimulates mass poverty reduction via market linkages and labour for traditional export commodities	Ag. growth reduces rural poverty and manages the urban transition. Opportunities in processing and high-value crops in domestic markets	Ag. growth promotes rural income parity, agribusiness provides employment, provision of ecosystem services
Institutions	State boards	Transitioning	Regulatory
Examples	Bhutan, Kenya	India, China, Honduras, Mexico	US, EU

include, for example, Zambia, Kenya and Uganda, agriculture is mainly oriented towards the production of non-marketed staples, and cropping systems are often diversified at the farm level with inputs generated on the farm (Table 1.1). Some of the surplus production is marketed, but production systems are mainly subsistence-oriented. Staple crop productivity growth remains the primary engine of overall economic growth. In traditional agricultural economies, the transformation of food systems has been slow to take off. High-value, organized retail establishments may cater to a limited, often expatriate, clientele in capital cities, but most supply chains for most crops are still traditional in nature. Developing modern, vertically integrated supply chains is difficult and expensive in countries with poor road infrastructure and failed institutions.

In Africa, there is a high degree of dualism between traditional domestic food chains and organized chains, whether domestic or export-oriented. Food safety standards for poor consumers, who frequent traditional markets, are quite low as those markets are largely informal. Another major problem is the vicious cycle of low surplus volumes constraining market development, which then reinforces the subsistence nature of low-input production systems. In sub-Saharan Africa, continued underinvestment of public goods supporting smallholder agriculture is likely to further widen the gap between traditional domestic markets and the formal processing and retail sector (Jayne, this volume). Transforming consumer demand, particularly in urban areas, will be met with imports for products that domestic supply chains cannot provide competitively. In sub-Saharan Africa, urban demand is increasingly met with imports rather than by domestic producers. According to urban consumer surveys in Mozambique, Kenya and South Africa, expenditures on wheat and/or rice were higher than those on maize (Jayne, this volume). Without proper linkages between rural producers and urban consumers, economic growth in urban areas cannot spur widespread rural poverty reduction.

In modernizing economies, the agricultural sector accounts for a 10–30 per cent share of the economy and a 15–50 per cent share in the work force. Modernizing economies, which are mostly located in Asia, Latin America and central and eastern Europe, vary greatly with respect to urbanization rates and income.[1] Countries in Asia, such as Vietnam and Bangladesh, typically have lower urbanization rates, while those in Latin America and central and eastern Europe, such as Mexico and Honduras, have higher urbanization rates. In modernizing economies, the majority of farmers produce for domestic markets; but both subsistence- and export-oriented systems are present. Food systems in modernizing economies are neither traditional nor industrialized but somewhere in between. The more urbanized economies of central and eastern Europe and Latin America will be marked by more opportunities for marketing high-value products domestically. High rural poverty rates underscore the importance of agricultural growth for improving rural incomes in many Asian countries with lower urbanization rates. Meeting urban food demands can be the new source of growth for these economies. Further improving diversification into higher value agriculture to meet domestic urban demand is an important goal.

In industrialized economies, such as the US, the EU, Australia and New Zealand, agriculture usually accounts for less than 10 per cent of GDP and less than 15 per cent of the work force. Markets are domestically and internationally oriented; output mixes are highly diversified with a well-developed processing sector providing opportunities for value addition. Typically, industrialized agricultural systems are highly mechanized and scale economies are quite pronounced. Differentiated products flow through well organized value chains, and commodity markets maintain basic safety standards through regulation (Kinsey and Senauer, 1996).

Apart from the phase in which a country finds itself in the agricultural development process, several other factors can influence the speed and nature of the transformation of food systems (although such factors usually correlate highly with the transformation process and a country's attractiveness to outside investors). It is important to remember that capital is mobile and policies at the national level are important determinants of the investment climate, which is affected by institutions, infrastructure, capacity and transaction costs (Globerman and Shapiro, 2002; Bénassy-Quéré et al, 2007). Stable governments and institutions provide a better environment for large capital investments; widespread graft and excessive bureaucracy can discourage investment. Agribusiness firms looking to vertically integrate their supply chains will prefer countries where the regulatory environment is transparent and easy to negotiate. They will seek places where arbitration costs are low and coordination is easy to manage. All of these factors, which could be considered transaction costs, influence the cost of developing and managing supply chains, and therefore the competitiveness of their final products.

Organizational trends along the value chain

Acting at once and often reinforcing each other, driving forces have exacted and continue to exact major changes on food distribution systems. A wide body of literature, particularly from the last decade, describes the reorganization that has taken place in food chains, with implications for chain participants and for the broader economy (Table 1.2). Much of the evidence available is focused on retail,

Table 1.2 *Trends in the organization of food systems from farm to plate*

	Traditional	Structured	Industrialized
Consumption	Rising caloric intake, diversification of diets	Diet diversification, shift to processed foods	Higher value, processed foods
Retail	Small scale, wet markets	Spread of supermarkets, less penetration of FFV	Widespread supermarkets
Processing	Limited processing sector	Processing offers employment and value addition opportunities	Large processing sector for domestic and export markets
Wholesale	Traditional wholesalers, with retailer bypassing for exports	Traditional and specialized wholesalers, some retailer bypassing	Specialized wholesalers and retailer bypassing through distribution centres
Procurement	Via traditional markets	Via structured (regulated) markets	Via managed chains, advance arrangements
Production systems	Diversified, low input systems	Intensive input use, specialization of cropping systems	More focus on conservation
Safety in food system	No traceability	Traceability in some chains with private standards	HACCP system, private safety standards and public accountability (liability)
Vertical coordination	Relationships	Relationships/rules	Binding agreements, ICT systems for efficient consumer response

Notes: FFV = fresh fruit and vegetables

HACCP = hazard analysis and critical control point

ICT = information and computer technology

particularly supermarkets. Many of the procurement and marketing studies focus on fresh fruits and vegetables grown for export to consumers in developed countries. The dairy sub-sector has also garnered a fair amount of attention. While not all locations, crops or stages in the supply chain have received interest proportional to their importance for rural poverty, there nevertheless exists a robust set of documented studies from which to draw conclusions about the implications of the reorganization of supply chains and resulting transformation of food systems for food security, and in particular, rural poverty.

Retail consolidation trends

The proliferation of supermarkets in developing countries is one of the most widely cited elements of food system transformation. Trends in consumption pave the way for consolidation in the retail sector, which then reinforces dietary changes. Demand for safe food and for processed food products provides an entry point for organized, larger scale retail outlets in urban markets. By offering a wide variety of products, supermarkets can stimulate new demand through availability and exposure. Families who own refrigerators and vehicles are able to make fewer, but higher volume, trips to purchase food, which explains the strong link between the spread of supermarkets and the rise of the middle class. Income growth is closely linked with ownership of durable goods, like refrigerators and vehicles (Filmer and Pritchett, 1999).

The spread of supermarkets has been documented in a variety of studies specific to countries and regions (see Reardon and Berdegue, 2002; Weatherspoon and Reardon, 2003; Dries et al, 2004; Hu et al, 2004). Structural transformation of the retail sector took off in central Europe, South America and east Asia outside China in the early 1990s. The share of food retail sales by supermarkets grew from around 10 per cent to 50–60 per cent in these regions. By 2002, in central America and southeast Asia, the shares of food retail sales accounted for by supermarkets reached 30–50 per cent. Starting in the late 1990s and early 2000s, substantial structural changes taking place in eastern Europe spurred growth in supermarkets, which now comprise 30–40 per cent of food retail (Dries et al, 2004). So far, supermarkets have failed to capture a large portion of food retail in south Asia (1–2 per cent), China (11 per cent), and Africa (with the exception of South Africa, 5–10 per cent), despite the high growth rates that have been reported in the organized retail sector (Traill, 2006). There are indications of a rapid rise in supermarket growth rates in China and India over recent years.

A recent study by Traill (2006) involved compilation of a cross-country dataset on supermarket penetration in developing and developed countries (Figure 1.4). Using a multivariate regression, differences between countries were explained by per capita income, urbanization rates, female participation in the work force and income inequality. All of these factors were positively correlated with the share of food retail captured by supermarkets. It is important to stress that, in most developing countries with traditional food systems, supermarket share in retail is still limited to the 10 per cent range, even lower for the fresh

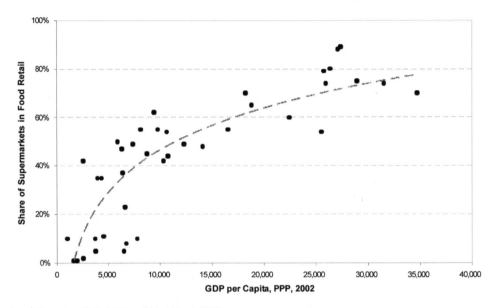

Source: Data from Traill, 2006 and World Bank, 2006

Figure 1.4 *Rising GDP per capita is associated with a larger share of supermarkets in food retail*

produce market segment. Low-penetration countries are unlikely to become high-penetration ones in the coming decade, even though supermarkets in developing countries have sustained impressive growth rates (Traill, 2006).

The methodology for collecting data on supermarket penetration differs from country to country, but supermarkets are usually defined as single, self-service retail outlets which exceed a threshold number of cash registers (e.g. 2–3) or floor space (e.g. 150m^2) (see the definition used in Neven and Reardon, this volume). Some important changes in the retail sector could go undetected in estimates based on such definitions, such as shifting procurement patterns among small-scale, traditional retailers of fresh and processed foods, which would have implications for the producers who supply them. Also, estimates of average retail share mask differences between sub-sectors. Supermarkets' share of fresh produce retail, for example, is consistently 25–50 per cent of supermarkets' share of total food retail (Berdegue et al, 2005).

Implications of consolidating retail

The implications of retail transformation on producers have been explored through a wide range of studies. Ultimately, small farmers are impacted through changing points and terms of sale and changing safety and quality requirements for products that are purchased. Two questions pertain: Which farmers participate? What happens to those who cannot or do not? The clearest mechanism by which retail transformation impacts farmers is through changing procurement standards, particularly with respect to quality and safety of products (see

Balsevich et al, 2003; Berdegue et al, 2005; Swinnen, 2007; Reardon et al, this volume). In order to ensure year-round availability of produce, private retailers may specify delivery standards for minimum monthly shipments throughout the growing season. The delivery requirements can serve as a barrier to smallholders directly supplying retailers (Dolan and Humphrey, 2002). Other retailer standards relate to the products themselves or the methods by which they are produced, for example, the EurepGAP[2] programme (McCluskey, 2007).

When possible, supermarkets have procured through regional distribution centres with the capacity to receive shipments from farmers, bulk up orders, sort products and ship to retail locations. Since supermarkets' distribution centres perform wholesale functions, they are discussed in the next section.

The practice of farmers selling directly to retailers is more common in fresh fruit and vegetable chains than in others. Evidence shows that supermarkets are more likely to procure directly from farmers or farmer groups in countries where supermarket penetration is still quite low, such as Thailand (Chen and Stamoulis, this volume). Relatively few farmers, small or large, supply supermarkets directly, so quality and safety standards are transmitted to farmers via processors, wholesalers and traders. The transmission of consumer preferences and retailer standards to producers depends on a number of factors, including the structure of the wholesale market.

Retail concentration in developing countries has implications for retail-related employment and for consumers. It is likely that at least some traditional retailers will be displaced by growth in the supermarket sector, leading to a net job loss in the retail sector. This hypothesis is based on the assumption that supermarkets are more capital intensive (with respect to labour) than are traditional retailers (Dries, 2005). Transformation of retail may cause consumer prices to go up or down, depending on the competitiveness of the sector, but the availability of more variety and more quality differentiation will improve consumers' welfare as long as prices are competitive. Consumers are likely to benefit from competition between organized and traditional retailers, as well as that within the supermarket sector, which can lead to improved services overall. In India, there is concern among the public that a change in FDI policy will drive small retailers out of business by offering low prices, initially at a loss. Predatory pricing patterns have been documented in many developed countries, with impacts borne by small retailers who must compete for customers and for suppliers (Foer, 2001; Reardon and Hopkins, 2006). Across Asia, there is evidence that consumers still prefer to buy their produce in traditional markets, where it tends to be fresher (see Chen et al, 2005; Maruyama and Viet Trung, 2007; Dirven and Faiguenbaum, this volume; Singh, this volume). In Latin America, the small-scale retail sector has relied on responsiveness to consumers to maintain some resilience in the face of competition with large retailers (D'Andrea et al, 2006). Supermarkets may earn lower profit margins on fresh produce relative to other items, but offering it is important for improving loyalty among customers who place a premium on one-stop shopping.

The size of the urban middle class determines the nature of the retail clientele (Wilkinson, this volume). The more 'mainstream' domestic supermarket chains become, the more they must compete among themselves on price, product safety and quality, and with traditional wholesalers on price and freshness. Price and convenience have been common entry points for supermarkets in developed countries. The consumer base will determine customers' willingness to pay for quality, and how retailers should handle the trade-off between quality and price (Maruyama and Viet Trung, 2007). Modern retailers can out-compete traditional chains on food safety because they can implement traceability and communications technology. It appears, for now, that traditional chains can compete with organized ones on freshness and price. As the middle class grows, so will the number of organized retailers that cater to them, offering different combinations of quality, safety and economy based on consumer preferences. Asian consumers appear to be willing to tolerate a lack of traceability in modern chains, but a big public safety scare could boost demand for safe food. In the absence of a marketing opportunity posed by changing public perceptions or a regulatory shift, supermarkets will continue to procure through the traditional wholesale system.

More processing and trade in processed products

Processed products are capturing a growing value share in global agricultural production and trade at the expense of bulk commodities (Regmi and Dyck, 2001). Some higher income developing countries match or surpass global trends, but most least developed countries have not shared in opportunities to expand agricultural processing for domestic consumption or for export (FAO, 2006; World Bank, 2008). While the LDCs comprise 10 per cent of the world's population, they account for only 0.4 per cent of global manufacturing value addition in all sectors (Wilkinson, this volume). Yet in these LDCs, the food industry often accounts for the largest share of manufacturing value addition. In 17 of Africa's LDCs, over 80 per cent of the manufacturing is in the agri-food sector. In most of Africa's other LDCs, the share is over 50 per cent.

This points to the opportunity to expand food manufacturing for domestic and export markets using domestically grown raw materials. Furthermore, quality standards for raw materials to be used in manufacturing are often not as strict as those for fresh produce. Because of lower costs of compliance, and less seasonal price variability, scale economies have been shown to be less prohibitive, and so processing channels may be more accessible to smallholders than fresh produce channels. Quality standards for green bean canning firms are much lower than those for fresh green beans in Kenya, even though both products are destined for export. As a result, the green bean processing chain has sustained smallholder participation much better than the fresh green bean chain has (Narrod et al, this volume).

With the transformation of food systems there has been a trend of upgrading and consolidation in agri-processing firms in developing countries. A shake-out of domestic processing firms has been observed with the entry of foreign firms, facilitated by the liberalization of FDI and trade (Chen and Stamoulis, this volume; Wilkinson, this volume). Competition to meet retailers' standards cost-effectively has led to consolidation among the remaining domestic processing firms in developing countries. Consolidation of retail in developing countries has been most pronounced in sub-sectors whose processors are smaller, more independent and less advanced technologically (Chen, 2004). Small processors in developing countries reported difficulties selling to supermarkets because the retailers applied large stocking fees (Chen and Stamoulis, this volume). For example, in southeast Asia, supermarkets have catalysed major changes in the fresh fruit and vegetable packing industry but not on chicken packers, who had already adopted internationally accepted standards by the time domestic supermarkets became important buyers.

Bypassing of traditional wholesalers

By assembling large volumes of produce from a 'marketshed', wholesalers are better positioned to meet retailers' and processors' requirements than are individual farmers, particularly smallholders. In traditional chains, which are still widely prevalent in agriculture-based economies, farmers and traders supply traditional wholesalers, who then sell to individual retailers and processors, many of whom are small in scale. In modern chains, farmers and traders supply specialized wholesalers or distribution centres, who then sell to organized retailers and processors. In countries with modernizing food systems, both chains may exist side to side, with some exchange between them as conditions allow (Figure 1.5).

When organized retailers first enter a country, they typically set up their own direct procurement systems. Specialized regional distribution centres are constructed to serve their wholesale needs when traditional and even specialized wholesale markets cannot, and once sufficient economies of scale are present. To justify the cost of a regional distribution centre for fresh produce with the savings generated, it is estimated that a retailer needs a minimum of 20 supermarkets

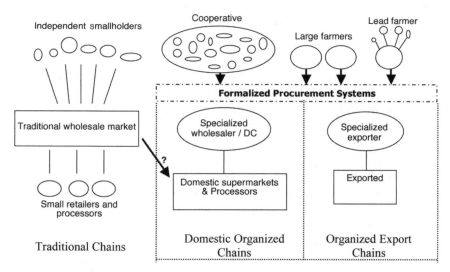

Figure 1.5 *Interactions between traditional and organized chains in modernizing food systems*

(Chen and Stamoulis, this volume). In the developing world, there are few regional distribution centres for fresh produce outside of Latin America. In the US and Japan, major retail distribution centres began to displace wholesalers by the 1960s (Chen and Stamoulis, this volume). More recently, there is evidence in developed countries of a shift back towards direct procurement, at least in niche markets where consumers place a premium on fresh, local and seasonal produce.

Wholesalers assemble, grade and sort produce, bridging the scale gap between producers and retailers. Traditional wholesalers can differentiate products on the basis of basic functions, like size, colour and other easily observable characteristics. But product information that is not readily observable does not transmit well through the traditional system. Specialized wholesalers are better positioned to keep track of quality information and meet more exacting demands from retailers and processors (Unnevehr and Roberts, 2002; Golan et al, 2004). For this reason, specialized wholesalers have captured important market segments in developing countries (Reardon and Berdegue, 2002; Coe and Hess, 2005; Reardon et al, this volume). For organized retailers, bypassing traditional wholesalers affords better quality control and can lower costs if savings from reduced spoilage offset the costs of managing the distribution facility. High spoilage rates in traditional wholesale markets in developing countries give retailers strong incentives to bypass traditional wholesalers.

To date, evidence of bypassing has been limited in developing countries outside Latin America (Chen and Stamoulis, this volume). With fresh fruits, vegetables and many bulk commodities, traditional wholesale markets remain vibrant, even in Latin American where supermarket penetration is high. In southeast Asia, specialized wholesalers have a small market share but play an important part in quality segmentation (Caldhilon et al, 2006). The traditional market system can accommodate some quality differentiation, but it is inefficient if quality-differentiated prices are not transmitted to producers and quality information is not transmitted to consumers (Digal, 2004). There is evidence that traditional wholesalers are responding to the spread of specialized wholesalers and distribution centres by investing in upgrades to improve quality and safety. In Chile, public and private investments were made to improve traditional wholesale markets serving Santiago, with the goal of helping wholesalers compete with private chains on quality, safety and customer service (Dirven and Faiguenbaum, this volume). Traditional markets may not be able to compete with specialized markets cost-effectively with regard to quality and safety.

From the perspective of the small-scale farmer, an important question is: who will the specialized wholesalers buy from, given the choice? And in order to compete with specialized wholesalers, will traditional wholesalers impose standards that lead to exclusion of smallholders? As retailers begin to pull a meaningful share of the wholesale market into distribution centres, what are the implications for smallholder farmers? The degree of duality between the traditional and specialized wholesale systems will determine, in part, whether the transformation of food systems threatens to squeeze smallholders out of the system altogether or just to prevent them from taking part in the most lucrative opportunities, thus imparting distributional effects. The more permeability between traditional and organized chains in the domestic food system, the lower the barriers to participation for smallholders (Figure 1.5). The differences between traditional and specialized wholesalers with respect to prices and standards will affect farmers' decisions on where to market their produce, along with other aspects of the point of sale that are explored below. There is evidence that specialized wholesalers can offer higher prices than traditional ones for produce that meets their standards (e.g. Schwentesius and Ángel Gómez, 2002), but as discussed below, the cost of complying with standards can eat into this price differential. Furthermore, the price differential may decrease over time as more and more producers in a location are capable of meeting exacting standards.

In Asia, many farmers are participating in organized retail chains serving domestic supermarkets without knowing it. Supermarkets in China and India have been shown to procure at least some fresh produce from the traditional wholesale market (Huang et al, this volume; Singh, this volume). In fact, small-holder fruit farmers in China's Shandong province were found to be supplying supermarkets in Russia and central and eastern Europe via the traditional market-ing system (Huang et al, this volume). To date, many Asian supermarkets have been able to scale up quickly by sourcing in traditional chains. This has been an effective strategy because there have not been major safety scares, or they have been sufficiently downplayed to avoid scandal. In China there has been a recent public backlash against the shortcomings of the public safety regulation system (Barboza, 2007). Retailers may come under greater pressure to introduce trace-ability into their sourcing systems in the near future.

Formalization of procurement and marketing

As the organization of retail leads to the specialization of wholesale, there is an expansion of formalized procurement systems designed to improve the efficiency of procurement. Formalized procurement systems facilitate the transmission of information upstream and downstream, allowing for differentiation of products based on quality and safety, and reducing the costs of coordination between buyers and sellers (Barry et al, 1992; Pingali et al, 2007). Procurement models are changing as marketing systems shift from traditional to structured to modern. Transactions in traditional markets are characterized as being 'spot' in nature, although relationships between farmers and traders are likely to be important in any market. Traditional markets may be regulated by institutions, such as govern-ment commodity boards, which require farmers to sell in certain channels (Jayne, this volume). Above all, traditional markets are characterized by informality, with farmers bearing many of the costs associated with poor market performance. Farmers may be charged irregular fees by various intermediaries, for example, and traders may depress prices through collusion (Omiti et al, this volume; Singh, this volume).

Structured markets are characterized by more rules and regulations set by government overseers, although not necessarily by heavy-handed direct involve-ment. The Agricultural Produce Marketing Committee (APMC) system in India is an example of a well-regulated auction where farmers can expect certain basic rules of engagement. Rules are meant to standardize transactions and make the market a fairer place to do business (Singh, this volume). Governments may publish price information to reduce farmers' information asymmetry. To some extent, farmers can access channels for arbitration when they feel that regulations have been violated. Traditional and structured markets often contain many intermediaries. When there are more intermediaries in the chain linking producers and consumers, each intermediary earns lower margins, and the overall marketing efficiency of the chain is lower (efficiency is based on the difference between producer and retail prices). Farmers and consumers lose when markets are inefficient, so, in a competitive market, both stand to gain if margins are reduced.

Modern supply chains are characterized, above all, by coordination, which usually reflects some pre-arranged agreement of the price and non-price terms of a transaction. Fewer intermediaries are found in modern chains, and upstream and downstream linkages are tighter. Improved coordination, horizontally and vertically, is an effective strategy for reducing transaction costs in modern chains. Costs associated with poor transmission of information are certainly lowered. More efficient consumer response systems reduce costs associated with the bullwhip effect which arises from delayed transfer of information about stocks from retailers to wholesalers, traders and producers (Fransoo and Wouters, 2000). When there is a disease outbreak in a food system with improved traceability, responses can be more efficiently targeted to the source of the outbreak, reducing total losses (McKean, 2001). Product traceability provides a mechanism for retailers to gain a competitive advantage on the basis of specific product attributes and for producers to gain price recognition for providing these attributes (Opara, 2003). At the same time, improved coordination introduces new transaction costs along the chain which can diminish or even completely offset the gains from coordination (Pingali et al, 2007). There are fixed, direct costs associated with building the necessary infrastructure for product differentiation and traceability. Initializing and developing more formal relationships between buyers and sellers can be a costly process, as buyers and sellers must be matched and then must negotiate terms of sale.

It is not undifferentiated commodities but products, characterized by specific attributes such as size, shape and colour, that flow through modern supply chains. Modern retailers and specialized wholesalers often use preferred supplier lists to lower their transaction costs. The buyers decide which farmers appear on the preferred supplier lists, and they often prefer larger farmers because of the fixed costs of transacting with each supplier (Pingali et al, 2007). Buyers may pass these transaction costs on to smallholder farmers or they may otherwise exclude them from contract opportunities by opting to procure from larger suppliers. There are also many reasons for and evidence of modern retailers and processors procuring regularly from smallholders. Smallholder farmers may be able to provide better quality assurance at a lower cost of enforcement. Thai Fresh United relies on many small producers, who use labour-intensive techniques to supply high quality herbs, spices, vegetables and fruits that meet their company's strict requirements (Boselie et al, 2003). Purchasers can also diversify their supply base and stabilize their supply stream by sourcing from smallholder farmers (Kirsten and Sartorius, 2002; Dries et al, 2004). When there are not enough larger farmers willing or able to produce the required volume and quality, buyers must turn to smallholders.

Major retailers and processors with a wide sourcing base have the ability to move goods among domestic markets, regionally or internationally at low cost given their economies of scale. Therefore, they can afford to be more price sensitive than firms with a smaller procurement base and to be more mobile in their procurement practices. Given the potential mobility of retailers with regards to sourcing, it is unrealistic to expect them or their procurement agents to pay prices that are higher than they would pay elsewhere, or to tolerate high transaction costs in the procurement process. For this reason, sustainable inclusion of smallholders in modern chains must rely on cost-effective models for bridging the scale discrepancies between individual smallholders and modern buyers.

As organized retailers and wholesalers capture a growing market share, they must assume the challenge of expanding procurement. Some must buy outside their managed chains to fill orders (Singh, this volume). Farmers and intermediaries who sell from traditional into formal chains must demonstrate, or be accountable for, the quality and safety of their produce. There are incentives for independent traders to bring produce into organized chains from the traditional market in order to take advantage of higher margins and the stability of organized outlets. These intermediaries can assume the quality risk themselves (by procuring from the traditional marketplace without paying a premium, sorting as necessary, and reselling) or they can pass the quality risk on to producers (by offering a price premium and imposing informal quality standards).

Implications and impacts for smallholder agriculture

A useful way for policy makers to conceptualize the impacts of current and future trends in the organization of food systems on smallholder farmers is to identify the incentives, opportunities and constraints they pose, now and in the future, from the small farmer perspective. The transformation of consumption and restructuring of supply chains have created new market opportunities for many agricultural producers. These opportunities may still hold fringe status relative to traditional marketing systems, but they are typically growing much faster. Rapid shifts to capital- and knowledge-intensive production technologies and the importance of scale are likely to exert pressure on smallholders to adjust, though they may lack the means to do so. If widespread 'exclusion' is, in fact, being observed, it could foretell difficult times for smallholder farmers as dynamic, high-value market outlets take over more of the market share. The speed of adjustment is important because it impacts the ability of smallholders to adapt to new changes and the possibility for an 'orderly exit' from agriculture. The latter involves building the appropriate human capital for employment in the off- or non-farm rural sectors or for migration. It is important to note that the migration of rural poor to urban areas does not reduce poverty but rather transfers it to cities (Ravallion et al, 2007).

Smallholder opportunities should arise from areas where smallholders are able to sustain a competitive advantage, such as low supervision costs when household labour is used. Similarly, constraints relate to aspects of production and marketing that prevent small farmers from exploiting their competitive advantages, such as financial capital or lack of experience coordinating with buyers. Once situation-specific opportunities have been identified, policy makers can facilitate efforts to pursue opportunities and overcome constraints. These efforts need not require chain-specific investments, but rather broader steps and strategic investments to create the conditions that encourage others to invest, and also to create alternative opportunities for income generation by smallholders outside production.

Here we lay out key direct and indirect pathways by which the restructuring of food systems impacts both smallholder farmers and the rural poor. We discuss concepts and evidence surrounding participation, terms of sale received, costs of participation and their broader impacts on production systems and interactions with the rural non-farm economy. We focus on the links between the reorganization of food systems and smallholder agriculture, while drawing on the work of others who have emphasized the importance of smallholder agriculture for rural poverty reduction. In an economy where there are market failures, household consumption and production decisions are not separable (Singh et al, 1986), and the transformation of food systems affects both production and consumption.

Why the small farm focus?

As of 2007, the world's population shifted from one that was mostly rural to one that is mostly urban, but for developing countries the majority of the population is still rural. Since poverty rates in rural areas exceed those in urban areas, most of the world's poor are still found in rural areas (World Bank, 2008). Although most rural households have diversified income sources, the majority of rural poor earn their income in agriculture (Davis et al, 2007). Even though farming households are highly diversified with respect to income sources, agricultural production and marketing remain important determinants of household welfare, especially those with lower incomes. Among farming households, smallholders are more likely to be poor than those with larger land holdings (Davis et al, 2007). Smallholder farmers, thus, comprise a substantial part of the rural poor demographic and are therefore a logical entry point for an analysis of how the reorganization of food systems affects rural poverty.

Furthermore, smallholders form the 'structural backbone' of the rural economy because of their linkages with small-scale input and service providers, traders, backyard processors and hired labourers (Ashley and Maxwell, 2001). Smallholder productivity and income gains are translated into demand for labour-intensive consumption goods produced in rural areas and also into investment in non-farm rural activities, thus creating multiplier effects in rural economies. Smallholders are also of interest because, in many instances, they are known to use land more productively than farmers with larger landholdings (Berry and Cline, 1979; Helfand and Levine, 2004). The inverse productivity relationship underscores the importance of pursuing growth in the smallholder sector, since gains can be shared broadly. Furthermore, it is posited that the transformation of food systems creates new opportunities for smallholders arising from aspects of production that are not scale sensitive. For instance, labour market imperfections, which result in a low opportunity cost of household labour, allow for cost-effective supervision of production systems (Heltberg, 1998).

Despite the strong linkages between the small farm sector and rural poverty, it is important to understand the distinction between farms and farming households. Rural households show a high degree of diversification in their activities, with income from agriculture and livestock supplemented by farm and non-farm wages, remittances and income from small enterprises. The vast majority of rural households in developing countries have some form of participation in agriculture. Despite diversification, farm income is the backbone of the income structure of poorer households (Anriquez and Stamoulis, 2007). A broad look at the changing structure of food systems, and rural economies must incorporate the different modalities by which households can be affected by a changing rural economy. Farming is but one entry point, albeit a very important one. To date, there has been little broad-based analytical work addressing the changing income patterns of rural households and composition of rural economies. The analysis shows that expansion of modern forms of retail organization has wider impacts in rural economies, on both farm and non-farm activities (Reardon et al, 2007).

Transformation of production systems

As retail becomes more organized, wholesale more specialized, and procurement more formalized, the management and composition of production systems is being transformed. As a general rule, production systems are becoming more commercialized in developing countries. Commercialized systems are characterized by specialization at the farm level, greater dependence on purchased inputs and more marketing of outputs (Pingali, 1997). Typically, commercialized systems use more labour and inputs per unit of land than subsistence systems. Input use remains low in production systems that are not closely linked with markets (Heisey and Mwangi, 1998; Omiti et al, this volume; Tobgay and McCullough, this volume). As urban centres demand higher value products, and as market structures respond to urban demand, we observe diversification of cropping systems at the meso- and macro-levels, even as they become more specialized at the farm level to take advantage of economies of scale. In Bhutan, areas closer to road points exhibit more market-oriented specialization of their cropping systems and a greater likelihood of participating in output markets (Tobgay and McCullough, this volume).

Particularly in areas where land holdings are small and arable land is limited, smallholders begin to specialize in higher value enterprises, such as horticulture and livestock, as opposed to lower value cereals. At the meso-level, diversification into higher value cropping systems is limited by agroclimatic potential, water resource development and the strength of market linkages. At the farm level, assets, technical know-how and labour availability can limit diversification into higher value crops. In agroclimatically less favoured areas, there are fewer opportunities to produce higher value products for modern chains. Extensive livestock production offers some potential, as does production of lower value, non-perishable raw materials for processing. Biofuels markets could provide high return opportunities in some places where other options are not available. Farmers in less favoured areas are more likely to be competitive in diversified and mixed-livestock systems (Cassman, 1999). Without specific R&D efforts targeting less favoured areas, however, prospects will remain limited. Major constraints include lack of irrigation, pests, poor soil structures and nutrient limitations. Interventions to alleviate these constraints may focus on breeding and variety development, improving best practices for field management and capacity building with technology transfer.

In many agricultural economies at the low end of the development process, agricultural inputs are expensive relative to global prices and, as a result, underutilized. Costliness of inputs arises partly from underdevelopment of infrastructure and underinvestment in institutions (Jayne, this volume). When input prices are too high relative to farm gate output prices, it simply does not make sense for farmers to purchase modern inputs. Furthermore, input providers are not well regulated, and many farmers bear the costs of dubious quality seeds, fertilizer and other agrochemicals (e.g. Crawford et al, 2003; Omiti, this volume; Tobgay and McCullough, this volume). Increasing input use is only profitable to the extent that productivity gains offset the costs of inputs. In many Asian and Latin American countries, input subsidy programmes played a historic role in raising crop yields (Falcon et al, 1983). Most of these programmes were phased out as economies were liberalized, with government agencies now participating less directly in input provision. Similarly, government programmes for agricultural credit, extension, marketing and germplasm development have been scaled back across the developing world as governments have come into compliance with international trade agreements and unsustainable budget imbalances (Jayne, this volume).

The void in agricultural support services has been at least partly filled by the private sector. Input manufacturers and retailers have long played a part in providing agricultural extension. But now buyers are playing a more prominent role in the provision of agricultural services. This includes fertilizer and chemicals, technical assistance and the provision of seeds. Because of their scale, modern buyers can leverage government programmes to subsidize extension or irrigation investments, for instance, receiving bulk payments in exchange for administering services and/or subsidies to farmers. By providing inputs and services free or at below retail prices, buyers can improve their control over production processes while producers improve their access to services.

Upstream from producers, there has been global consolidation in manufac-turing of and R&D for key agricultural inputs (Kimle and Hayenga, 1993). This reinforces the hourglass structure, in which a growing number of producers find themselves sandwiched between large, multinational firms who control input manufacturing on one side, and processing and retail on the other (Pingali et al, 2007). Consolidation in input manufacturing is a result of the considerable economies of scale involved on the R&D side. The example of consolidation that took place in the seed industry is telling. Crop by crop, as the industry has advanced from the pre-industrial to the mature stage, private firms replace state agencies in dominating key germplasm R&D activities. The private sector invests more and more in R&D where intellectual property laws are more secure. Even in mature seed sectors, though, the state's role remains important in regulating the sector and providing complementary public goods (see Morris et al, 1998). The same consolidation is taking place with respect to other agricultural inputs, and the state's role in regulating the input manufacturing sector is underscored. Another role of the state is to facilitate R&D for agriculture in less favoured areas, which can bring high returns but may nevertheless be ignored by the private sector (Fan and Chan-Kang, 2004).

Formalizing terms of sale

The ability of smallholders to sustain participation in organized chains depends on how the terms of sale and cost of participation for the modern chain compare with those for traditional alternatives. Expected returns are impacted by prices and their stability, cost of transporting goods, rates of rejection and timing of payment. Terms of sale relate to the price used for a transaction, but also when, where and how the transaction takes place. They dictate what product changes hands, what standards it must meet and how testing will be conducted.

Terms may depend entirely on the bargaining skills of the parties involved; they may be governed by the regulations of a marketplace; or they may be agreed upon in advance and specified in a written contract. As food systems transform from traditional to structured to modern, there is a shift from the former to the latter. Terms of sale matter because they determine how incentives, risk and marketing costs are distributed between the buyer and the seller. While price and quantity sold can be tracked rather easily, costs (particularly transaction costs) are more difficult to measure and differ greatly between farmers and contexts. Differences in negotiation skills, experience and affiliations can lead to differences in terms of sale (Pingali et al, 2007).

Modern procurement systems may offer participants higher prices, but they also introduce new risks and costs. With fewer and more powerful buyers, farmers have reduced power for negotiation (Gibbon, 2003; Timmer, this volume). Some farmers reported that modern chains offered lower prices but more stability. Others perceived them as offering higher prices but being more risky due to a lack of transparency in quality assessment or price setting. In many transactions, the party that bore more risk (i.e. through price variability) also garnered incentives for doing so (i.e. a higher share of marketing margins). In Bhutan, for example, citrus exports to India constitute one of the more modern chains. The model relies on intermediaries, who receive advance finance from exporters, to procure oranges from smallholders (Tobgay and McCullough, this volume). As soon as citrus trees blossom, collectors provide advance credit to their producers in exchange for assured access to their orange harvests at a fixed price, determined by the blossoms. The collector oversees the harvest, transport and marketing of the products and bears all associated risks. In the absence of such arrangements, smallholders would probably be deterred altogether from citrus marketing by the labour costs of harvest and the risk of product spoilage due to poor road and market infrastructure.

In general, perceptions of fairness regarding terms of sale have a lot to do with prevailing conditions in surrounding markets. True impacts can only be evaluated after multiple years of repeated participation in a chain, but judgements are often made much sooner. In general, modern chains stabilize inter-annual risk related to price and market instability while introducing new risks related to higher costs of participation and more exacting requirements. Problems arose when risks were delinked from rewards. Sellers, in particular, who bore more risk with less reward, felt they had received asymmetric terms of sale. The perception of unfairness in terms of sale most commonly arose from buyers' quality assessment, require-ments for chain-specific investments and misconceptions between buyers and sellers that led to side-selling.

For instance, when a farmer becomes party to a contract with a fixed price, he or she bears the risk of a price increase while the buyer bears the risk of a price decrease. With a floating market price, both parties share all price risk when infor-mation is symmetric. The specific way in which quality standards are enforced also affects the distribution of risks and rewards. An agreement may be designed to penalize a seller for failing to meet standards, either with a price cut or outright rejection. If quality assessment takes place at the point of sale, and the seller assumes transport costs, the seller bears a disproportionate risk from crop rejec-tion. In India, contracts drafted by McCain and Frito Lay for potato growers allowed buyers to reject produce for any reason, despite the fact that producers were obligated to pay for transportation costs to the drop-off facility (Singh, this volume). Producers felt this placed too much risk on them and complained that the quality inspection process was not fair or transparent. Similarly, in Kazakhstan, cotton farmers complained that the buyers, who also performed quality assessment, had incentives to underestimate quality so they could pay lower prices (Swinnen, 2005).

When suppliers provide inputs and a fixed price, they may then offer a price that is lower than the average market price. From their own perspective, in this model, buyers bear a price risk and a default risk. Sellers, particularly those without a good relationship with the buyer, may not understand the logic behind price setting, and, on seeing a better price elsewhere, may choose to side-sell into a different channel. In Kenya, many dairy farmers were bound to sell to their cooperatives in return for the technical assistance they received. They often sold at least a portion of their milk production outside the cooperative, though, to illegal hawkers, who offered higher prices (Omiti et al, this volume). Unfairness in terms, or perceptions of unfairness, arise from a lack of transparency in the process of formulating and enforcing terms of sale. Interventions should be targeted towards improving understanding while opening channels for conflict resolution. Collectivizing farmers' bargaining holds the promise of improving terms of sale from the smallholder perspective. Tools for doing this are explored below, along with their costs of implementation.

Contracts

Contract farming is a mechanism for vertical coordination that is growing in popularity in modern chains. Contracts usually involve advance agreement between producers and purchasers on some or all of four parameters: price, quality, quantity (or acreage) and time of delivery (Singh, 2002). Specific contract terms and arrangements determine how the parties involved share the benefits, costs and risks of coordination. These may deal with timing of payment; mechanisms for setting price; provision of services and inputs; documentation requirements; quality and quantity produced; arrangements for assessing quality; and mechanisms for settling disputes and enforcing agreements. When contracts fix output prices in advance, they may allow farmers to produce risky high-value, perishable crops that they otherwise would avoid because they are prone to a price glut. These arrangements can also help to ensure a reliable supply for companies that have made sub-sector specific investments (Simmons et al, 2005).

In labour markets, farm owners and wage labourers choose to enter fixed labour contracts because of shortcomings in labour markets. The shortcomings arise from seasonal risk in the demand and supply of labour (Bardhan, 1983) and from difficulties in monitoring casual labourers in tasks like irrigation and input application (Eswaran and Kotwal, 1985). Similarly, buyers and sellers may choose to enter fixed marketing contracts in order to overcome risk and uncertainty in spot markets. These risks of spot markets are similar to those of casual wage labour markets, arising from seasonal variability in supply and demand (resulting risk of shortage and surplus) and from the need to assure quality in the absence of perfect monitoring.

From the buyer's perspective, the cost of procuring via contracts includes transaction costs arising from the design and implementation of a contracting system (Pingali et al, 2007). Managerial costs, along with capital investments in facilities, are involved. Retailers and processors who procure through contracts must also plan for the costs of abiding by contract terms, which may involve providing inputs at fixed or below-market cost, providing technical assistance and providing credit. More costs result from carrying out transactions and enforcing contracts, including testing product quality and safety, and arbitration where necessary. Many of these costs have fixed, per farmer components, which buyers can cut by targeting larger producers.

As with terms of sale in a non-contract transaction, specific contract terms will determine the extent to which small farmers can share in the benefits from vertical coordination because they allocate risks between interested parties, such as price and market risk, crop failure risk and the risk that a contractual party defects. Important contract terms include timing of payment; mechanisms for setting price; provision of services and inputs to suppliers; demands on documentation, timing, quality and quantity; arrangements for assessing quality; and mechanisms for settling contract disputes and enforcing agreements. A favourable legal and institutional environment helps contracts to be fairer for small farmers. The Model APMC Act in India, for example, requires contracts to be registered with a local authority and includes provisions on contracts, liabilities, asset indemnity and dispute resolution (Singh, this volume). Direct contract relationships between producers and corporations proved to be more beneficial for small farmers in Punjab than state-sponsored contracts. They resulted in better delivery of extension services and more reliable purchase of commodities (Kumar, 2005).

Contracts can help smallholder farmers access key inputs and services that may otherwise constrain production. The contract itself gives buyers some assurance that they will capture the benefit stream from investing resources in producers. Buyers often provide inputs to farmers with whom they are contracting at below-market prices or at cost, or they may provide technical support and extension services, often of better quality than publicly provided extension services (e.g. Kumar, 2005). Contracts can also facilitate access to credit. In Kazakhstan, credit was the primary reason that smallholder cotton farmers entered contractual arrangements (Swinnen, 2005). In Lithuania, the only source of credit for small dairy farmers was through buyers procuring with contracts. Dairy purchasers in Poland offered credit along with extension services and inputs, and farmer participation was very high in return (Dries and Swinnen, this volume). Supermarkets have offered similar provisions to small farmers, via contracts, throughout eastern Europe and central America. Farm assistance programmes created for contract farmers have been replicated by other companies and by state agencies because of their success (Swinnen, 2005).

Farmers have probably benefited from contractual arrangements in a number of instances, but it is difficult to attribute benefits to participation in the contract itself as opposed to participation in the chain. Benefits arising from contract farming often spill over to participants' non-contract fields and to neighbouring farmers. In central and eastern Europe and the former Soviet Union, contract farmers enjoyed higher productivity with lower risk on their non-contract crops (Swinnen, 2005).

However, there is also abundant evidence that smallholder farmers are excluded from entering formal contracting arrangements. In India, the contract farming system favours larger farmers at the expense of small producers, very few of whom are participating in contract farming (Kumar, 2005; Singh, this volume). In central and eastern Europe, it is more common for farming corporations to enter contractual agreements than it is for small farmers (Swinnen, 2005). Although contract farming has risen to the point of including 9 per cent of farmers in Suphan Buri, Thailand, very small farmers are much less likely to enter contracts (Dawe, 2005). They are also less likely to receive favourable terms, such as a fixed output price, and therefore bear more risk.

Farmer organizations

One possible method for small farmers to overcome some of their size disadvantages is to form production and/or marketing groups. By joining together in the name of common production and marketing interests, small farmers can increase their effective size and bargain for more favourable terms. Cooperation can increase bargaining power, allow for economies of scale, and lower marketing and negotiation costs by pooling negotiation efforts. Cooperative marketing can ease supply constraints faced by individual farmers, allowing them to meet buyers' orders year-round, where production systems permit. Internal incentives can be provided for farmers who fill off-peak orders. When agricultural systems are dominated by smallholders, farmer organizations have been designed in order to supply large buyers who have no other options for procurement. In India, Mahagrapes successfully arose as an export-oriented umbrella marketing organization for several cooperatives of smallholder grape producers (Narrod et al, this volume).

When buyers require investments, farmer organizations may offer a cost-effective way of upgrading through pooling of investments. By organizing, smallholders can access information and share knowledge more easily, decreasing their search and information costs. There is a strong tradition of farm cooperatives in the Netherlands, which have served as a farmer safety net and helped to raise productivity. Now Dutch cooperatives are assuming many more roles, including innovation and direct involvement with consumers (Bijman and Hendrikse, 2003).

Farmer organizations are not a panacea, as they can be very costly to set up and maintain. Efforts to design and start an organization in one place are not necessarily replicable because management structures are so contextualized. Group decision-making can be costly, and, in some cases, the success of organizations is unduly dependent on the charisma, intelligence and altruism of one leader. An informal survey of supermarket procurement officers worldwide suggested that retailers have negative associations with procurement from farmer groups, stating that they can be difficult to work with, unreliable and inexperienced (Reardon and Hopkins, 2006).

Lowering marketing costs: other strategies

Beyond the widely discussed cooperative, there are other models for achieving economies of scale through coordination between farmers. Large farmers, for instance, can serve as intermediaries between smallholders and supermarkets by subcontracting for some of their production needs (e.g. in Honduras) (Lundy et al, 2006; Meijer et al, this volume). Different forms of tenant farming (e.g. exchange of labour for a portion of harvest) and reverse tenancy (e.g. leasing of land management to a larger operator in exchange for rent) have long been in practice to solve various inefficiencies in factor markets, particularly for land, labour and capital.

Geographic clustering by product has been put forward as a way to economize on sub-sector specific investments in production and post-harvest infrastructure. This strategy may offer some promise, but picking sub-sectors that will retain price stability is notoriously difficult. Mistakes have been made in the past, with farmers suffering the effects of price glut due to overproduction while struggling to repay debt on specific assets (Shepherd, 2007).

Costs of participation

Modern chains often dictate production methods and may or may not facilitate support for production systems via technical assistance and input provision. Production costs are likely to be higher in modern chains, which are more demanding than traditional chains. Evaluation of explicit costs and returns, and less explicit transaction costs associated with maintaining and enforcing agree-ments, will dictate smallholders' competitiveness in and preferences for different chains. Because the same characteristics that allow a farmer to supply a high-value market will also influence the farmer's income regardless of market, higher incomes observed in a chain can result from either the chain's characteristics or the farmer's, or some combination of the two (Sadoulet and De Janvry, 1995). Sustained participation over time is a good indication that a chain is profitable for participants compared to other options. If farmers are required to make specific investments, though, especially in specialized assets and equipment with low resale value and convertibility, ex post continued participation might reflect investment irreversibility and sunk costs rather than satisfaction. Farmers who make specific investments in order to participate in a chain must bear the risk of the buyer defaulting (Gow and Swinnen, 1998). It is important to have watchdog organizations or institutions accessible so that they can voice their complaints and pursue arbitration when they feel they are being exploited.

Apart from the ability to specialize in specific crops, farmers selling into modern chains must be able to meet their more exacting quality and safety requirements. Complying with private and public standards has implications for on-farm production systems. It may require investments in capital equipment, such as post-harvest storage facilities, or a system for preventing contamination of fields with household waste water (Narrod et al, this volume). In Kenya, small-holders who were supplying fresh green bean export chains switched to chains for processed beans once stringent quality and safety standards were introduced into the fresh green bean chain (Narrod et al, this volume). It is very difficult to meet high quality standards for horticultural crops without an irrigation system, which allows for efficient application of inputs (Rosegrant et al, 2002). In the heavily groundwater-dependent Indian state of Gujarat, McCain informally required its potato suppliers to use efficient irrigation systems, citing concern about sustain-ability of water use as the reason (Singh, this volume).

In order to encourage better quality, modern buyers urge their suppliers to adopt specific management practices regarding varieties used, planting, fertilizer and pest management, and harvest. This was observed in virtually all case studies. Retailers have been known to request their suppliers to adopt integrated pest management to reduce the prevalence of pesticide residues in final products. To encourage uniformity of produce, processing firms may dictate specific dimensions for seed bed height and width and planting date (e.g. Singh, this volume). In general, modern chains will be more closely linked with consumer demands (or processor requirements) since they will have in place mechanisms to transmit information and incentive systems upstream to reward compliance. In countries where quality requirements for traditional domestic systems differ greatly from those in developed countries, production practices can differ drastically between fields with crops produced for export and with the same crops produced for the domestic market (e.g. Narrod et al, this volume).

Smallholder participation is limited

Ultimately, not all farmers have the option of supplying all markets. From the options available to them, farmers will choose the ones that bring the most expected returns to the household. It is rather easy to observe whether or not smallholder farmers are participating in a given marketing chain. But non-participation is not the same as exclusion, since it can also arise from a farmer's decision not to participate because a different option is preferred. Distinguishing between these two types of non-participating farm households can be difficult without targeted surveys at the household level, but confusing them can lead one to erroneous conclusions. There is evidence from all areas of the world of smallholders participating in many different types of modern chains, both domestic and for export, with contracts or without, as part of producer organizations or independently. However, it is very difficult to assess the extent of participation because most studies adopt a case study approach, tracing a particular retailer or producer group, or targeting a location because participation is known to take place there.

This case-based approach is necessary for identifying and assessing emerging trends, but it is not good for estimating their extent. Evidence from central and eastern Europe suggests that smallholder inclusion is robust in areas where most landholdings are uniformly small (Swinnen, 2002). Where smallholders are part of a dualistic system with the presence of large landholders, modern buyers show a preference for procuring from large farmers. Evidence from Latin America and Africa supports this hypothesis (Berdegue et al, 2005; Reardon et al, this volume). Modern buyers have been known to develop mechanisms for procuring from smallholders because there is no one else to procure from (Narrod et al, this volume) or for public relations purposes. It is difficult to know the extent to which public relations incentives have motivated smallholder inclusion, but such incentives are likely to be limited in nature and short-lived.

Scale mismatch is perhaps the most common constraint to smallholder participation in modern chains. Individual smallholders have limited ability to negotiate and bargain for beneficial price and non-price terms from major retailers and processors on the output side and major multinational manufacturers on the input side (Vorley, 2003; Pingali et al, 2007). Smallholder farmers can be excluded from preferred supplier lists or contract-based marketing channels because buyers specify a minimum cut-off acreage or product volume that exceeds their capacity, given finite land holdings. It is much more likely, though, that smallholders will be excluded de facto because of fixed costs involved with participating in modern chains. Buyers may require specific on-farm investments in assets (e.g. irrigation systems) that are not profitable for small-scale producers. In Honduras, for example, Hortifruti's regional specialized wholesale arm required farmers to pay for their own costs of supervision. The costs started at US$1,000 per year in each farmer's first year but were reduced to $500 in subsequent years (Meijer et al, this volume). In the Shandong province of China, farm size and household assets had little effect on which marketing channel apple and grape farmers took part in, but strict quality and safety standards were not present (Huang et al, this volume).

Another key barrier to smallholder participation in modern, high-value marketing opportunities arises from business orientation. Identifying, solidifying and exploiting opportunities to sell to modern buyers requires a certain entrepreneurial quality. Some farmers have fewer opportunities to develop their managerial human capital (Bingen et al, 2003). Because transaction costs associated with joining modern chains are likely to be large at the start and decline with time and experience, policies directed at lowering initial barriers to entry for farmers who are otherwise competitive are likely to be effective at facilitating the inclusion of smallholder farmers. Interventions aimed at reducing uncertainty surrounding new outlets and improving advocacy tools available to small farmers are likely to reduce one-time transaction costs associated with entering modern chains. Negotiation costs can be reduced with capacity building and legal assistance with forming agreements. Search and information costs can be alleviated with the expansion of market information systems that make marketing outlets and their terms more explicitly known and allow farmers to compare different outlets (Pingali et al, 2007).

Empirically, it is difficult to distinguish between buyer exclusion and farmer self-exclusion because the observed outcome (non-participation) looks the same. If modern chains involve higher costs but bring higher returns, and smallholder farmers are resource constrained, buyer exclusion is probably a more common cause of non-participation than self-exclusion. Several examples uncovered in this research suggest instances where smallholders were capable of participating in modern chains but chose not to. In India, for instance, farmers who were selling potatoes under contract to modern processors chose only to sell about 50 per cent of their output to the processor. They were qualified to be preferred suppliers, but in order to hedge the risks of full participation, they only committed a portion of their land holdings to the contract (Singh, this volume). With time, the costs associated with introducing formal coordination into transactions should fall as transactions are repeated between the same parties, who acquire experience and build trust in the process (Rademakers, 2000).

It is important to note that even farmers who sell into modern chains also sell into traditional (or structured) wholesale markets at some point, even for the same crops that are being sold to modern buyers (McCullough and Pingali, this volume). Improving the performance of traditional markets benefits everyone, as alternative procurers must compete with the traditional system. The issue of smallholder participation in modern chains has limited poverty reduction implications for farmers who are not already participating in markets. It is important to note that, for many smallholders, participation in even traditional markets remains a more pressing concern. Household surveys conducted across eastern and southern Africa suggest that the majority of rural households do not sell any grain but buy it regularly (Jayne, this volume). For many of these households, the most important source of 'income' is household production that is consumed at home. By improving productivity and reducing marketing costs, households can divert more labour to cash-earning activities.

Interactions between the transformation of food systems and the rural non-farm economy

With income growth, increased opportunities are available for off-farm employment, and more pressure is placed on labour markets, resulting in rising wage rates which also affect seasonal agricultural labourers. The diversification of production systems out of staple crops and into higher value products is another characteristic associated with the transformation of food systems. Higher value crops, such as horticulture and livestock, often require more labour input. High-value exports from Senegal had a poverty reduction effect through labour markets rather than smallholder participation (Maertens and Swinnen, 2006). Households' willingness and ability to grow higher value crops is impacted by the availability of labour within the household and the predominant wage rates for hiring-in labour. In the Shandong province of China, greater household participation in off-farm income-earning activities was associated with lower participation in fruit production. Fruit production and off-farm employment were seen as competing demands for the time of household members. Those who were involved in off-farm employment faced higher opportunity costs on their time and were less likely to turn to apple and grape farming (Huang et al, this volume). Some evidence suggests that off-farm income is correlated with agricultural input use, which is consistent with the hypothesis that it eases credit constraints (Davis et al, 2007).

As food systems transform, so will the non-agricultural prospects of smallholder households. Households may choose to pursue off-farm work in agricultural processing, other manufacturing, agricultural labour markets or through migration to other places. Little is known about the impacts of changing food systems on the broader rural economy (Reardon et al, 2007). Impacts will arise from subsidiaries of supermarkets moving into small towns and rural areas to sell food and other consumer items, thus knocking out local small-scale retailers and businesses. Since smallholder agriculture constitutes the backbone of the rural economy, marginalization of smallholders will probably have net labour effects in rural areas (Anriquez and Stamoulis, 2007). It is natural for populations to move from farms to cities as an economy grows and the relative importance of the agricultural sector falls. But agriculture is important for supporting households until better opportunities emerge in other sectors, preventing premature exit. Many African countries have much higher urbanization rates than they would if agriculture was more productive (Jayne, this volume). Managing the 'push' out of agriculture would help alleviate social problems arising from growth rates of urban areas. For those without prospects for migrating or working in other sectors, agriculture is the only hope.

Way forward

Because of organizational changes in food systems, smallholders now face many new opportunities to benefit from rapidly growing market segments. Modern chains are capable of lowering the risks of participating in higher value markets while transmitting rewards for meeting quality and safety standards. Because of the high costs of participating in these marketing chains, smallholders risk being excluded from a lucrative market segment. In many transforming economies with modernizing food systems, modern chains account for a substantial share of food retail. In these countries, if retailers are unable to procure through traditional channels, they will form a separate, vertically coordinated procurement system that competes with the traditional system. This can be observed in many countries in Latin America. In this case, the risk to smallholders is that, unless they can link into the modern procurement system, they will be relegated to a low-value, shrinking market segment. Throughout Asia, traditional markets have continued to supply the modern retail sector, which itself has captured a limited share of food retail. While rising food safety concerns among Asian consumers could threaten ties between traditional wholesalers and modern retailers, for now Asia's smallholders appear to be well linked in with domestic urban markets. In most of Africa, however, modern retail is not expected to capture a substantial share of food retail over the next decade. Furthermore, lucrative opportunities to link with high-value export markets are quite limited in scope. The real danger is that smallholders in remote areas are excluded from agricultural marketing altogether due to high transportation and transaction costs and the widespread availability of cheap imports.

The transformation of food systems presents a set of problems that vary drastically between countries, based on characteristics of the food system, the place or the households involved. Different countries will prioritize problems differently depending on the context. There is no one policy response, but a common objective between all situations is to see smallholders through the transition, in recognition of their importance for rural poverty. Facilitating the transformation ultimately boils down to a three-pronged policy approach:

1   facilitating the inclusion of smallholders in modern chains by reducing costs of participation;
2   upgrading traditional marketing systems;
3   supporting those who cannot supply traditional markets with social safety nets.

Policy responses

We explore in greater depth what each initiative entails and outline a role for governments, the private sector and civil society to play in facilitating the transformation for smallholder farmers (Table 1.3). In general, identifying and pursuing appropriate policy responses to the transformation of food systems presents several challenges. The transformation of food systems is an unwieldy

Table 1.3 *Policy tools in traditional, modernizing and industrial food systems*

	Traditional	Modernizing	Industrialized
Consumption	• Targeting chronic hunger victims • Promoting diet diversification	• Promoting health and diet diversification • Preventing obesity through consumer education	• Minimizing health burden of aging and obese population • Internalizing public health costs of unhealthy foods
Retail	• FDI for retail and agribusiness • Basic hygiene in traditional markets	• Public safety standards and regulation • FDI for retail	• Post-supermarket retail • Certification for niche products
Processing	• Expanding value added through processing	• Expanding exports of processed goods	• Downscaling 'safe' processing facilities
Wholesale	• Upgrading traditional wholesalers • Improving safety • Reducing spoilage	• Upgrading traditional markets • Improved safety • Better traceability	• Improved ICT for bypassing wholesalers
Marketing	• Transport infrastructure • Enabling marketing institutions and information systems	• Targeted incentives to source from smallholders • Improve marketing capacity • Improve regulatory environment	• Improved farmers' tools for direct marketing
Production	• Increasing market orientation • Investing in productivity • Diversifying out of low-value staples • Regulate input providers	• Meeting standards • Improving productivity and input use efficiency • Sustaining natural resource support systems	• Phasing out unsustainable subsidy schemes • Sustaining natural resource support systems

phenomenon, often spilling out of the traditional policy space of Ministries of Agriculture. Responses at different phases of the food chain must be coordinated, and it is not always clear which institutions and ministries can and should take the lead role. Responding to the transformation of food systems does not require drastic reforms. Relatively minor adjustments, beginning with removing market distortions and maligned incentives, can be very effective. However, developing country institutions are rarely of the cross-cutting nature needed to face such problems. While specific policy interventions should be addressed at the right scale, political boundaries and political capital do not always correspond with the scales at which market interventions are needed (i.e. market-shed, watershed, etc.).

Most of the policy interventions described below are relevant for governments in developing countries that are going through the agricultural transformation process. While appropriate government policies are absolutely necessary for managing the transformation of food systems, there are nevertheless roles to be played by the private sector and civil society organizations. Multinational corporations who are building procurement programmes in developing countries should be discouraged from pursuing monopsonistic procurement conditions through anti-competitive behaviour.[3] When procurement practices are open and transparent, it is easier to monitor and regulate them. Private companies in retail and processing cannot be expected to save smallholder farmers while serving their business interests. Therefore, creative institutional innovations are welcome to align the interests of smallholders with those of the modern retailers and processors who are controlling a growing share of food retail.

Non-governmental organizations (NGOs) can play a key role in supporting smallholders through the transformation when government policies fall short. They can help link smallholders with modern chains by lowering the one-time, initial barriers to entry. NGOs can do this by building capacity, providing information and experience, and financing investments in assets. Furthermore, NGOs can monitor vulnerable groups who risk marginalization by the transformation process. They can flag problems and mobilize political capital for addressing problems. NGOs and socially oriented businesses have been involved in developing markets, through certification programmes and direct trade, in building niche markets for products whose supply chains are socially responsible, which have benefited the participants although the scope is still limited.

Governments in developed countries bear the responsibility of promoting a balanced system of global trade. In many developed countries, domestic support systems for agriculture have been widely criticized because they are linked with price distortion and commodity dumping. A new form of protectionism is arising in some developed countries, with retailers being urged to label the 'food miles', or physical distance travelled by all products on their shelves. Improving consumer access to information about the energy footprint of the products available to them is essential, but food miles labelling isolates only one stage in the supply chain, the transport stage, rather than the entire chain. Products that are produced by smallholders in developing countries are likely to travel a longer distance to get to retailers' shelves, but their carbon footprints may nevertheless be lower than those of locally produced alternatives due to differences in production technology.

Facilitating the inclusion of smallholders in modern chains

At the country level, opportunities for linking smallholders into modern chains are determined by the size of the domestic market, which is set by urbanization rates, the average income and the prevalence of a middle class. Potential for trade is set by macroeconomic conditions and trade policies. Overall governance influences the cost of doing business (which has a large impact on transaction costs), and the institutional setting (which affects the climate in which agricultural activities occur). In countries with a strong urban demand, good institutions supporting financial services and R&D, and good governance, it is less of a battle to link smallholders with consumers through organized chains.

Most modern chains involve higher costs of production along with fixed investments. Households with asset constraints may not be able to overcome initial hurdles associated with entering a chain. Off-farm sources of income and household ownership of fixed assets most probably improve the household's ability to access finance and invest in productive activities. Investments in rural education and improving rural public health systems can help alleviate constraints that commonly afflict smallholder farming households (Schultz, 1988). Capacity will influence a household's willingness to pursue and ability to meet the requirements posed by modern chains. It will also affect a household's ability to access credit and reduce the burden of many transaction costs specific to modern chains (Barrett et al, 2001). Capacity, in turn, is built through education and experience, among other factors.

Inclusion/exclusion happens at the farm–market interface. As long as there are entities or intermediaries that can buffer the scale-specific needs of buyers against the capabilities of the small-scale producer, and cover their costs by adding value, then there is no reason why smallholders should be excluded in a world where organized retail is expanding rapidly. However, because different strategies for bridging the scale mismatch are associated with different types of transaction costs, the appropriate model depends on the context.

Organization and cooperation seem to be natural responses to reducing transaction costs arising from the scale mismatch between individual farmers and those procuring from them. Local organizations are essential for the scaling up function, linking small-scale producers with larger scale buyers. Without some local initiative, it is highly improbable that individual households can tap into modern chains. A critical threshold must be crossed, either by local producers who band together and pursue market opportunities, or by a buyer coming to a place with the purpose of procuring a product. As governments across the world are diminishing their institutional support for agriculture, local organizations are stepping in to fill the void. Organizations have tackled the challenges of marketing produce, adding value through processing, input provision, financial services and market information, and vocalizing key elements of the policy agenda. There has been no magic formula for developing these organizations or ensuring their effectiveness. But local capacity gives rise to leadership and transparency seems to promote perceptions of fairness, thus keeping members and clients satisfied (Shepherd, 2007).

In evaluating different strategies to link smallholders with markets, it is important to consider the cost of implementing them against the benefits, along with the distribution of costs and benefits between households. It would be hard to justify, by any reasonable cost-effective criteria, many supply chain development projects that have been carried out to promote smallholder participation in modern chains (Shepherd, 2007; Meijer et al, this volume).

In general, interventions to facilitate smallholder participation in modern chains should not be heavy-handed. A top priority is creating an enabling environment through the provision of public goods that reduce transaction costs. There are many ways to lower the costs of doing business with smallholders. Governments can leverage incentives for including smallholders without being directly involved. In India, the state government of Punjab provided incentives for contracting with farmers that included reimbursement of extension costs. Such incentives could, instead, be specifically targeted towards those who contract with smallholders, in order to negate the higher per-farmer transaction costs that the procuring company incurs by contracting with smallholders. Information asymmetry costs can be reduced with improved marketing extension and capacity building and market information systems. Improving market and transportation infrastructure, as well as transportation services, will reduce the transaction costs associated with negotiation as marketing costs are lowered and more marketing channels become available. Finally, improving the legal and institutional environment surrounding contract formulation and arbitration will reduce smallholders' costs of entering into more formal agreements by making them more available.

Public investments in specific chains and projects should be carefully considered. Picking 'winners' is problematic. Public investments should be weighed against the benefits they generate and how those benefits are distributed. Well-placed public chain investments can be catalytic. However, chain-specific investments to link smallholders into modern chains are likely to be costly in terms of the number of farmers reached and the income effect on each farmer. Such targeted investments benefit participants, but there are almost always few participants relative to non-participants, and there is a threat of further alienating non-participants. Governments will do best by supporting a competitive, investment-friendly environment that is also well regulated and by allowing the market to pick the winners while leveraging maximum social benefit from private investments in modern chains.

Upgrading the traditional system

While benefits from investments in modern supply chains for specific sub-sectors are largely held by participants, investments in traditional wholesale markets are shared more equitably. Well functioning traditional markets facilitate procurement for modern retailers and processors who can avoid investing in alternate infrastructure to bypass the traditional system if it serves their needs. When retailer bypassing becomes widespread, incentives for upgrading traditional markets with public resources are reduced. Key advocates for upgrading the public system may be appeased if the private system meets their needs, leaving behind the traditional market and widening the gap between modern chains and traditional ones, leading to 'duality' in domestic food systems. Improvements in traditional markets also serve traditional processors and retailers, who do not have the option of bypassing traditional wholesale markets. Traditional market improvements even serve farmers who are participating in modern chains because modern buyers must compete with the traditional marketplaces.

Some simple improvements in market structure can improve traceability and public health standards while reducing spoilage rates. Improved flow of information and regulation of market transactions will reduce the transaction costs that arise from information asymmetry and trader corroboration. These interventions must be financed somehow, and they could have an impact on price margins. Traditional markets will never compete with vertically coordinated private chains in product differentiation and information exchange, but strategic investments in market structure could allow traditional markets to achieve a minimum standard that meets the needs of many retailers and processors.

In countries at the low end of the transformation process, the priority is in expanding traditional wholesale markets, improving their structure and forging upstream linkages with producers and downstream linkages with retailers and processors. In modernizing food systems, it is important to improve traceability and reduce spoilage rates in wholesale markets to reduce retailers' incentives for bypassing. The HACCP (Hazard Analysis and Critical Control Point) system offers some promise for implementing basic safety standards in traditional chains, but its implementation requires widespread education and cooperation throughout the chain (Unnevehr and Jensen, 1999). Opportunities for differentiating products based on quality attributes should be further explored within traditional wholesale markets, particularly in Asia where they still hold a large market share, so that traditional markets can continue to serve organized retailers, street vendors and everything in between. The wider the barriers separating traditional and modern chains, the more difficult and risky it is for a farmer to participate in modern chains relative to alternatives (Narrod et al, this volume). When there is a healthy and domestic retail and/or processing sector, and a wholesale system that accounts for product differentiation, farmers have more options between the opposite extremes of basic traditional commodity markets and high value exports of fresh produce. In China, the vibrant traditional wholesale sector accommodated the full spectrum of quality needs.

Poor infrastructure for transport raises the price of inputs while lowering the price of outputs. Where infrastructure is poor, the input to output price ratio is a key determinant of competitiveness in a given location (Heisey and Mwangi, 1998). Post-harvest infrastructure for storage will improve marketing flexibility while decreasing the burden of spoilage. When wholesale market infrastructure and collection points are present, farmers have the opportunity to earn higher marketing margins. On the whole, investments in transport and marketing infrastructure will expand the range of consumers that farmers can reach while increasing the prices they can earn, lowering marketing risk while raising incomes.

Safety nets for non-participants

For many smallholders throughout the world, and particularly in sub-Saharan Africa, opportunities to participate in modern, organized chains are eclipsed by the more fundamental challenge of participating in any market. Market linkages for smallholders can be improved by lowering transaction costs, investing in market and transport infrastructure, boosting smallholder productivity and improving access to inputs. Supporting smallholder productivity is essential and benefits both non-sellers and sellers. When markets are thin and prices are variable, livestock and cassava can be harvested flexibly, allowing smallholders to manage price risk more effectively (Jayne, this volume). In countries where very few farmers are participating meaningfully in markets, commodity price supports benefit a few 'elite' farmers disproportionately (Jayne, this volume).

Many places are simply unsuitable for high-value agriculture because of agroclimatic limitations. Only a narrow range of agroclimatic conditions is suitable for rainfed horticulture, for instance. To an extent, physical factors determine the set of crops that can be grown in any place. However, local investments, for example in water resource development, can expand the set of options available, and the potential for diversification. Targeted investments in R&D for production in less-favoured areas can also help overcome agroclimatic constraints, but in most cases technical expertise must be brought in from other places. Production technology for less favoured areas could become disruptive in the long term, but a lack of foreseeable pay-offs in the short term deters sufficient investment.

Improved infrastructure can possibly alleviate land constraints. In Zambia, for example, land holdings are clustered in higher potential areas, with lower potential and more remote areas being less inhabited (Jayne, this volume). Improving road infrastructure could effectively increase a country's productive land area. In some instances, smallholders in isolated areas and low input production systems may be competitive in local markets because poor infrastructure raises retail prices. While improving transport infrastructure may reduce some farmers' ability to market some crops profitability, the benefits of infrastructure expansion are likely to be shared more widely and outweigh the costs. In southern and eastern Africa, there are many more buyers of staple grains than sellers (Jayne, this volume). As needed, mechanisms can be devised to compensate those who are hurt by infrastructure expansion.

Even after improving productivity and market access, many smallholders will remain in production on a subsistence basis or will pursue off-farm income or migrate to towns and cities. Through the process of agricultural transformation, it is normal for the size of the population dependent on agriculture to decrease over time as agriculture's share in the economy falls and as per capita incomes rise. When migration out of rural areas occurs faster than growth in opportunities to earn income in rural areas, this migration results in a transfer of poverty rather than true poverty reduction associated with the agricultural transformation (Ravallion et al, 2007). Developing alternative incomes in rural areas is essential for seeing smallholders who have no future in farming through the transition. Social safety nets, such as targeted feeding programmes for chronic hunger victims, are essential for those who have no sources of income and limited prospects.

Notes

1   According to the World Bank's classifications in the World Development Report, modernizing economies fall into two categories: 'transforming' and 'urbanized' (World Bank, 2008). Relative to the urbanized economies, transforming ones are marked by a greater share of agriculture in the work force, a lower GDP per capita, lower urbanization rates, higher overall poverty and rural poverty rates. It is not necessarily implied, though, that agricultural economies must pass from agricultural to transforming to urbanized rather than directly from agricultural to urbanized.
2   Originally the European Retailer Produce Working Group Good Agricultural Practices.
3   Monopsony is a market condition characterized by one buyer and many sellers.

References

Anriquez, G. and Stamoulis, K. (2007) 'Rural development and poverty reduction: Is agriculture still the key?', ESA Working Paper no 07-02, Agricultural Development Economics Division, FAO, Rome

Ashley, C. and Maxwell, S. (2001) 'Rethinking rural development', *Development Policy Review*, vol 19, no 4, pp395–425

Balsevich, F., Berdegue, J., Flores, L., Mainville, D. and Reardon, T. (2003) 'Supermarkets and produce quality and safety standards in Latin America', *American Journal of Agricultural Economics*, vol 85, no 5, pp1147–1154

Barboza, D. (2007) '774 arrests in China over safety', *International Herald Tribune*, 29 October

Bardhan, P. K. (1983) 'Labor-tying in a poor agrarian economy: A theoretical and empirical analysis', *The Quarterly Journal of Economics*, vol 98, no 3, pp501–514

Barret, C., Reardon, T. and Webb, P. (2001) 'Non farm income diversification and household livelihood strategies in rural Africa: Concepts, dynamics and policy implications', *Food Policy*, vol 26, pp315–331

Barry, P. J., Sonka, S. T. and Lajili, K. (1992) 'Vertical coordination, financial structure, and the changing theory of the firm', *American Journal of Agricultural Economics*, vol 74, no 5 (Proceedings Issue), pp1219–1225

Bénassy-Quéré, A., Coupet, M. and Mayer, T. (2007) 'Institutional determinants of Foreign Direct Investment', *The World Economy*, vol 30, no 5, pp764–782

Beng-Huat, C. (2000) *Consumption in Asia: Lifestyles and Identities*, Routledge, London

Berdegue, J., Balsevich, F., Flores, L. and Reardon, T. (2005) 'Central American super-markets' private standards of quality and safety in procurement of fresh fruits and vegetables', *Food Policy*, vol 30, pp254–269

Berry, R. and Cline, W. (1979) *Agrarian Structure and Productivity in Developing Countries*, Johns Hopkins University Press, Baltimore, MD

Bijman, W. J. and Hendrikse, G. W. (2003) 'Cooperatives in chains: Institutional restruc-turing in the Dutch fruit and vegetables industry', *ERIM Report Series Research in Management*, no 089-ORG

Bingen, J., Serrano, A. and Howard, J. (2003) 'Linking farmers to markets: Different approaches to human capital development', *Food Policy*, vol 28, pp405–419

Boselie, D., Henson, S. and Weatherspoon, D. (2003) 'Supermarket procurement practices in developing countries: Redefining the roles of the public and private sectors', *American Journal of Agricultural Economics*, vol 85, no 5, pp1155–1161

Caldhilon, J. J., Moustier, P., Poole, N. D., Giac Tam, P. T. and Fearne, A. P. (2006) 'Traditional vs. modern food systems: Insights from vegetable supply chains to Ho Chi Minh City (Vietnam)', *Development Policy Review*, vol 24, no 1, pp31–49

Cassman, K. (1999) 'Ecological intensification of cereal production systems: Yield poten-tial, soil quality and precision agriculture', *Proceedings of the National Academy of Sciences USA*, vol 96, pp5952–5959

Chen, K. (2004) 'Retail revolution, entry barriers and emerging agri-food supply chains in selected Asian countries: Determinants, issues and policy choices', FAO/AGS, Rome

Chen, K., Shepherd, A. and da Silva, C. (2005) 'Changes in food retailing in Asia: Implications of supermarket practices for farmers and traditional marketing systems', Agricultural Management, Marketing and Finance Occasional Paper 8, FAO/AGS, Rome

Chen, K. and Stamoulis, K. (this volume) 'The changing nature and structure of agri-food systems in developing countries: Beyond the farm gate'

Coe, N. and Hess, M. (2005) 'The internationalization of retailing: Implications for suppy network restructuring in east Asia and eastern Europe', *Journal of Economic Geography*, vol 5, pp449–473

Crawford, E., Kelly, V., Jayne, T. S. and Howard, J. (2003) 'Input use and market develop-ment in Sub-Saharan Africa', *Food Policy*, vol 28, no 4, pp277–292

D'Andrea, G., Lopez-Aleman, B. and Stangel, A. (2006) 'The supermarket's revolution in developing countries: Policies to address emerging tensions among supermarkets, suppliers and traditional retailers', *The European Journal of Development Research*, vol 18, no 4, pp522–545

Davis, B., Winters, P., Carletto, G., Covarrubias, K., Quinones, E., Zezza, A., Stamoulis, K., Bonomi, G. and DiGiusseppe, S. (2007) 'Rural income generating activities: A cross country comparison', ESA Working Paper No. 07–16, FAO, May

Dawe, D. (2005) 'Economic growth and small farms in Suphan Buri, Thailand', Paper prepared for the symposium, *Agricultural Commercialization and the Small Farmer*, Agricultural and Development Economics Division (ESA), FAO, Rome

Digal, L. (2004) 'Quality grading in the supply chain: The case of vegetables in southern Philippines', *Journal of International Food and Agribusiness Marketing*, vol 17, no 1, pp71–93

Dirven, M. and Faiguenbaum, S. (this volume) 'The role of Santiago wholesale markets in supporting small farmers and poor consumers'

Dolan, C. and Humphrey, J. (2002) 'Changing governance patterns in trade in fresh vegetables between Africa and the United Kingdom', [online] www.hubrural.org/pdf/dolan_humphrey_2004.pdf

Dries, L. (2005) 'The impact of supermarket development on the rural economy.

Conceptual framework', draft 21 July

Dries, L., Reardon, T. and Swinnen, J. (2004) 'The rapid rise of supermarkets in central and eastern Europe: Implications for the agrifood sector and rural development', *Development Policy Review*, vol 22, no 5, pp525–556

Dries, L. and Swinnen, J. (this volume) 'The impact of globalization and vertical integration in agri-food processing on local suppliers: Evidence from the Polish dairy sector'

Eswaran, M. and Kotwal, A. (1985) 'A theory of contractual structure in agriculture', *The American Economic Review*, vol 75, no 3, pp352–367

Falcon, W., Timmer, C. and Pearson, S. (1983) *Food Policy Analysis*, Johns Hopkins University Press, Baltimore, MD

Fan, S. and Chan-Kang, C. (2004) 'Returns to investment in less favoured areas in developing countries: A synthesis of evidence and implications for Africa', *Food Policy*, vol 29, pp431–444

FAO (2004) 'The state of food insecurity in the world', FAO, Rome

FAO (2006) *World Agriculture: Towards 2030/2050*, Interim Report, FAO, Rome, June

FAOSTAT (2006) FAOSTAT, FAO, Rome

Filmer, D. and Pritchett, L. (1999) 'The effect of household wealth on education attainment: Evidence from 35 countries', *Population and Development Review*, vol 25, no 1, pp85–120, March

Foer, A. (2001) 'Small business and antitrust', *Small Business Economics*, vol 16, pp3–20

Fransoo, J. and Wouters, M. (2000) 'Measuring the bull whip effect in the supply chain', *Supply Chain Management*, vol 5, no 2, pp78–89

Gibbon, P. (2003) 'Value-chain governance, public regulation, and entry barriers in the global fresh fruit and vegetable chain into the EU', *Development Policy Review*, vol 21, nos 5–6, pp615–625

Globerman, S. and Shapiro, D. (2002) 'Global Foreign Direct Investment flows: The role of governance infrastructure', *World Development*, vol 30, no 11, pp1899–1919

Golan, E., Krissoff, B., Kuchler, F., Calvin, L., Nelson, K. and Price, G. (2004) 'Traceability in the U.S. food supply: Economic theory and industry studies', Agricultural Economic Report No 830, Economic Research Service, US Department of Agriculture, Washington, DC

Gow, H. and Swinnen, J. (1998) 'Up and downstream restructuring, Foreign Direct Investment and hold-up problems in agricultural transition', *European Review of Agricultural Economics*, vol 25, pp331–350

Hallam, D., Liu, P., Lavers, G., Pilkauskas, P., Rapsomanikis, G. and Claro, J. (2004) 'The market for non-traditional agricultural exports', FAO Commodities and Trade Technical Paper, FAO, Rome

Heisey, P. and Mwangi, W. (1998) 'Fertilizer use and maize production', in D. Byerlee and C. Eicher (eds) *Africa's Emerging Maize Revolution*, Lynne Reinner, Boulder, CO

Helfand, S. and Levine, E. (2004) 'Farm size and the determinants of productive efficiency in the Brazilian Center-West', *Agricultural Economics*, vol 31, nos 2–3, pp241–249

Heltberg, R. (1998) 'Rural market imperfections and the farm size – productivity relationship evidence from Pakistan', *World Development*, vol 26, no 10, pp1807–1826

Hu, D., Reardon, T., Rozelle, S., Timmer, C. and Wang, H. (2004) 'The emergence of supermarkets with Chinese characteristics: Challenges and opportunities for China's agricultural development', *Development Policy Review*, vol 22, no 4, pp557–586

Huang, J., Wu, Y. and Rozelle, S. (this volume) 'Marketing China's fruit: Are small, poor farmers being excluded from the supply chain?'

Jayne, T.S. (this volume) 'Forces of change affecting African food markets: Implications for public policy'

Kennedy, E. and Reardon, T. (1994) 'Shift to non-traditional grains in the diets of east and west Africa: Role of women's opportunity cost of time in prepared-food consumption', *Food Policy*, vol 19, no 1, pp45–56

Kimle, K. and Hayenga, M. (1993) 'Structural change among agricultural input industries', *Agribusiness*, vol 9, no 1, pp15–27

King, R. and Phumpiu, P. (1996) 'Reengineering the food supply chain: The ECR initiative in the grocery industry', *American Journal of Agricultural Economics*, vol 78, no 5, pp1181–1186

King, R. and Venturini, L. (2005) 'Demand for quality drives changes in food supply chains', New directions in global food markets, A1b–794, Economic Research Service USDA

Kinsey, J. and Senauer, B. (1996) 'Consumer trends and changing food retailing formats', *American Journal of Agricultural Economics,* vol 78, no 5, pp1187–1191

Kirsten, J. and Sartorius, K. (2002) 'Linking agribusiness and small-scale farmers in developing countries: Is there a new role for contract farming?', *Development Southern Africa*, vol 19, no 4

Kumar, K. (2001) 'Technology for supporting supply', *Communications of the Association for Computing Machinery (ACM)*, vol 44, no 6

Kumar, P. (2005) 'Commercialization of Indian agriculture and its implications for small and large farmers: A case study of Punjab', Paper prepared for the symposium *Agricultural Commercialization and the Small Farmer*, Agricultural and Development Economics Division (ESA), FAO, Rome

Lundy, M., Banegas, R., Centeno, L., Rodriguez, I., Alfaro, M., Hernandez, S. and Cruz, J. A. (2006) 'Assessing small-holder participation in value chains: The case of vegetables in Honduras and El Salvador', *FAO Commodities and Trade Proceedings*, FAO, Rome

Maertens, M. and Swinnen, J. F. M. (2006) 'Trade, standards and poverty: Evidence from Senegal', Licos discussion paper no177/2006, Catholic University of Leuven

Maruyama, M. and Viet Trung, L. (2007) 'Supermarkets in Vietnam: Opportunities and obstacles', *Asian Economic Journal 2007*, vol 21, no 1, pp19–46

McCluskey, J. (2007) 'Public and private food quality standards: Recent trends and strategic incentives', in J. Swinnen (ed.) *Global Supply Chains, Standards and the Poor*, CABI International, Wallingford, UK

McCullough, E. and Pingali, P. L. (this volume) 'Overview of case studies assessing impacts of food systems transformation on smallholder farmers'

McKean, J. D. (2001) 'The importance of traceability for public health and consumer protection', *Revue Scientifique et Technique de l'Office International des Epizooties*, vol 20, no 2, pp363–371

Meijer, M., Rodriguez, I., Lundy, M. and Hellin, J. (this volume) 'Supermarkets and small farmers: The case of fresh vegetables in Honduras'

Morris, M. L., Rusike, J. and Smale, M. (1998) 'Maize seed industries: A conceptual framework', in M. L. Morris (ed.) *Maize Seed Industries in Developing Countries*, Lynne Rienner Publishers, Boulder, CO

Narrod, C., Roy, D., Avendaño, B. and Okello, J. (this volume) 'Impact of international food safety standards on smallholders: Evidence from three cases'

Neven, D. and Reardon, T. (this volume) 'The rapid rise of Kenyan supermarkets: Impacts on the fruit and vegetable supply system'

OECD (2007) Stat database, [online] www.oecd.org/statsportal

Omiti, J., Otieno, D., Nyanamba, T. and McCullough, E. (this volume) 'The transition from maize production systems to high-value agriculture in Kenya'

Opara, L. (2003) 'Traceability in agriculture and food supply chain: A review of basic concepts, technological implications and future prospects', *Food Agriculture and*

Environment, vol 1, no 1, pp101–106

Pingali, P. (1997) 'From subsistence to commercial production systems: The transformation of Asian agriculture', *American Journal of Agricultural Economics*, vol 79, no 2, pp628–634

Pingali, P. (2006) 'Agricultural growth and economic development: A view through the globalisation lens', Presidential Address to the 26th International Conference of Agricultural Economists, Gold Coast, Australia, 12–18 August

Pingali, P. (2007) 'Westernization of Asian diets and the transformation of food systems: Implications for research and policy', *Food Policy*, vol 32, no 3, pp281–298

Pingali, P., Khwaja, Y. and Meijer, M. (2007) 'The role of the public and private sectors in commercializing small farms and reducing transaction costs', in J. F. M. Swinnen (ed.) *Global Supply Chains, Standards and the Poor*, CABI International, Wallingford, UK

Popkin, B. (1999) 'Urbanization, lifestyle changes and the nutrition transition', *World Development*, vol 27, no 11, pp1905–1916

Population Division of the Department of Economic and Social Affairs of the United Nations Secretariat (2006) *World Population Prospects: The 2006 Revision* and *World Urbanization Prospects: The 2005 Revision*, [online] <http://esa.un.org/unpp>

Rademakers, M. (2000) 'Agents of trust: Business associations in agri-food supply systems', *International Food and Agribusiness Management Review*, vol 3, pp139–153

Ravallion, M., Chen, S. and Sangraula, P. (2007) 'New evidence on the urbanization of global poverty', Background Paper for the WDR 2008

Reardon, T. and Berdegue, J. (2002) 'The rapid rise of supermarkets in Latin America: Challenges and opportunities for development', *Development Policy Review*, vol 20, no 4, pp371–388

Reardon, T. and Hopkins, R. (2006) 'The supermarket revolution in developing countries: Policies to address emerging tensions among supermarkets, suppliers and traditional retailers', *The European Journal of Development Research*, vol 18, no 4, pp522–545

Reardon, T., Stamoulis, K. and Pingali, P. (2007) 'Rural nonfarm employment in developing countries in an era of globalization', in K. Otsuka and K. Kalirajan (eds) *Contributions of Agricultural Economics to Critical Policy Issues: Proceedings of the Twenty-Sixth Conference of the International Association of Agricultural Economists*, Brisbane, Australia, 12–18 August, Blackwell Publishing, Malden

Reardon, T., Timmer, C. and Berdegue, J. (this volume) 'The rapid rise of supermarkets in developing countries: Induced organizational, institutional and technological change in agri-food systems'

Regmi, A. and Dyck, J. (2001) 'Effects of urbanization on global food demand', in A. Regmi (ed.) *Changing Structures of Global Food Consumption and Trade*, Economic Research Service, United States Department of Agriculture, Washington, DC

Rosegrant, M., Cai, X., Cline, S. and Nakagawa, N. (2002) 'The role of rainfed agriculture in the future of global food production', EPTD discussion paper no 90, International Food Policy Research Institute, Washington, DC

Sadoulet, E. and De Janvry, A. (1995) *Quantitative Development Policy Analysis*, Johns Hopkins University Press, Baltimore, MD

Schultz, T. (1988) 'Education investments and returns', in H. Chenery and T. N. Srinivasan (eds) *Handbook of Development Economics, Volume 1*, Elsevier Science Publishers, Amsterdam

Schwentesius, R. and Ángel Gómez, M. (2002) 'Supermarkets in Mexico: Impacts on horticulture systems', *Development Policy Review*, vol 20, no 4, pp487–502

Shepherd, A. (2007) 'Approaches to linking producers to markets', Agricultural Management, Marketing and Finance Occasional Paper 13, Rural Infrastructure and Agro-Industries Division, FAO, Rome

Simmons, P., Winters, P. and Patrick, I. (2005) 'An analysis of contract farming in east Java, Bali and Lombok, Indonesia', *Agricultural Economics*, vol 33, pp513–525

Singh, I., Squire, L. and Strauss, J. (1986) *Agricultural Household Models: Extensions, Applications and Policy*, Johns Hopkins University Press, Baltimore, MD

Singh, S. (2002) 'Contracting out solutions: Political economy of contract farming in the Indian Punjab', *World Development*, vol 30, no 9, pp1621–1638

Singh, S. (this volume) 'Marketing channels and their implications for smallholder farmers in India'

Solamino, A. (2006) 'Asset accumulation by the middle class and the poor in Latin America: political economy and governance dimensions', *Macroeconomics of Development*, no 55, Economic Commission for Latin American and the Caribbean (ECLAC)

Steinfeld, H. and Chilonda, P. (2006) 'Old players, new players: Livestock report 2006', Rome, FAO

Swinnen, J. (2002) 'Transaction and integration in Europe: Implications for agricultural and food markets, policy and trade agreements', *The World Economy*, vol 25, pp481–501

Swinnen, J. (2005) 'Small farms, transition and globalisation in Central and Eastern Europe and the former Soviet Union', Paper prepared for the symposium, *Agricultural Commercialization and the Small Farmer*, Agricultural and Development Economics Division (ESA), FAO, Rome.

Swinnen, J. (2007) *Global Supply Chains, Standards and the Poor: How Globalization of Food Systems and Standards Affects Rural Development and Poverty*, CABI International, Wallingford, UK

Timmer, C. P. (this volume) 'Food policy in the era of supermarkets: What's different?'

Tobgay, S. and McCullough, E. B. (this volume) 'Linking small farmers in Bhutan with markets: The importance of road access'

Traill, W. (2006) 'The rapid rise of supermarkets?', *Development Policy Review*, vol 24, no 2, pp163–174

Unnevehr, L. and Jensen, H. (1999) 'The economic implications of using HACCP as a food safety regulatory standard', *Food Policy*, vol 24, pp625–635

Unnevehr, L. and Roberts, T. (2002) 'Food safety incentives in a changing world food system', *Food Control*, vol 13, pp73–76

Vorley, B. (2003) 'Food, Inc. Corporate concentration from farm to consumer', UK Food Group, London

Weatherspoon, D. and Reardon, T. (2003) 'The rise of supermarkets in Africa: Implications for agrifood systems and the rural poor', *Development Policy Review*, vol 21, no 3, pp333–355

Welch, R. and Mitchell, P. (2000) 'Food processing: A century of change', *British Medical Bulletin*, vol 56, no 1, pp1–17

Wilkinson, J. (this volume) 'The food processing industry, globalization and developing countries'

World Bank (2006) *World Development Indicators*, World Bank, Washington, DC

World Bank (2008) *World Development Report 2008: Agriculture for Development*, World Bank, Washington, DC

Chapter 2

The Rapid Rise of Supermarkets in Developing Countries: Induced Organizational, Institutional and Technological Change in Agri-Food Systems

Thomas Reardon, C. Peter Timmer and Julio Berdegue

Supermarkets[1] are traditionally viewed by development economists, policy makers and practitioners as the rich world's place to shop. The three regions discussed here are where the great majority of the poor on the planet live. But supermarkets are no longer just niche players for rich consumers in the capital cities of the countries in these regions. The rapid rise of supermarkets in these regions in the past five to ten years has transformed agri-food markets, albeit at different rates and depths across regions and countries. Many of those transformations present great challenges – even exclusion – for small farms, processing and distribution firms, but also potentially great opportunities. Development models, policies and programmes need to adapt to this radical change.

This chapter describes this transformation of agri-food systems in Africa, Asia (excluding Japan) and Latin America. First, we describe the traditional retail and wholesale system in the midst of which emerged modern food retailing and its procurement system. Second, we discuss the determinants of and patterns in the diffusion of supermarkets in the three regions. Third, we discuss the evolution of procurement systems of those supermarkets and consequences for agri-food systems from the perspectives of organizational, institutional and technological change. In the conclusions we suggest emerging implications for farms and firms in the developing regions.

The spread of supermarkets in developing regions[2]

Determinants of diffusion of supermarkets

The determinants of the diffusion of supermarkets in developing regions can be conceptualized as a system of demand by consumers for supermarket services and supply of supermarket services, hence investments, by supermarket entrepreneurs.

On the demand side, several forces drive the observed increase in demand for supermarket services (and are similar to those observed in Europe and the US in the 20th century). The 'demand incentives' side forces include urbanization, with the consequent entry of women into the work force outside the home, which increased the opportunity cost of women's time and their incentive to seek convenience and processed foods to save cooking time; and supermarkets, often in combination with large-scale food manufacturers, which reduced the prices of processed products.

On the 'demand capacity' side, several variables were key. Real mean per capita income growth in many countries of the regions during the 1990s, along with the rapid rise of the middle class, increased demand for processed foods – the entry point for supermarkets, as they could offer lower cost and greater variety of these products than traditional retailers due to economies of scale in procurement. Rapid growth in ownership of refrigerators during the 1990s meant the ability to shift from daily shopping in traditional retail shops to weekly or monthly shopping. Growing access to cars and public transport reinforced this trend.

The supply of supermarket services was driven by several forces, only a subset of which overlap with the drivers of initial supermarket diffusion in Europe and the US. On the 'supply incentives' side, the development of supermarkets was very slow before (roughly) the early to mid-1990s, as only domestic/local capital was involved. In the 1990s and after, foreign direct investment (FDI) was crucial to the take-off of supermarkets. The incentive to undertake FDI by chains from Europe, the US and Japan and chains in richer countries in the regions under study (such as Hong Kong, South Africa and Costa Rica), was due to saturation and intense competition in home markets and much higher profit margins to be made by investing in developing markets. For example, Carrefour had three times higher margins on average in its Argentine compared to its French operations in the 1990s (Gutman, 2002). Moreover, initial competition in the receiving regions was weak, generally with little fight put up by traditional retailers and domestic-capital supermarkets. There are distinct advantages to early entry, especially occupation of key retail locations.

On the 'supply capacity' side, there was a deluge of FDI induced by the policy of full or partial liberalization of retail sector FDI undertaken in many countries in the three regions in the 1990s and after (e.g. partial liberalization of retail trade in China in 1992, with full liberalization of the sector in 2004; Brazil, Mexico and Argentina in 1994; various African countries via South African investment after apartheid ended in the mid-1990s; Indonesia in 1998; India in 2000). Overall FDI grew five- to ten-fold over the 1990s in these regions (UNCTAD, 2001) and growth of FDI in food retailing mirrored that overall growth. In addition, retail procurement logistics technology and inventory management (such as efficient consumer response (ECR), an inventory management practice that minimizes inventories-on-hand and uses internet and computers for inventory control and supplier–retailer coordination) were revolutionized in the 1990s. This was led by global chains and is diffusing now in developing regions through knowledge transfer and imitation and innovation by domestic supermarket chains.

These changes were in turn key to the ability to centralize procurement and consolidate distribution in order to 'drive costs out of the system', a phrase used widely in the retail industry. Substantial savings were thus possible through efficiency gains, economies of scale and coordination cost reductions. China Resources Enterprise (2002), for example, notes that it is saving 40 per cent in distribution costs by combining modern logistics with centralized distribution in its two large new distribution centres in southern China. These efficiency gains fuel profits for investment in new stores and, through intense competition, reduce prices to consumers of essential food products.

Patterns of diffusion

The incentive and capacity determinants of demand for and supply of supermarket services vary markedly over the three regions, within individual countries and within zones and between rural and urban areas at the country level. Several broad patterns may be observed.

One pattern is from earliest to latest adopter of supermarkets; the regions range from Latin America to Asia to Africa, roughly reflecting the ordering of income, urbanization and infrastructure and policies that favour supermarket growth. The first wave of supermarket diffusion hit major cities in the larger or richer countries of Latin America. The second wave hit in east/southeast Asia and central Europe; the third in small or poorer countries of Latin America and Asia (including, for example, central America) and southern, then eastern, Africa. By this time, secondary cities and towns in the areas of the 'first wave' were being hit. The fourth wave, beginning in the new millennium, is starting in southern Asia and western Africa.

Latin America has led the way among developing regions in the growth of the supermarket sector. While a small number of supermarkets existed in most countries during and before the 1980s, they were primarily domestic capital firms and tended to exist in major cities and wealthier neighbourhoods. That is, they were essentially a niche retail market comprising a maximum of 10–20 per cent of national food retail sales in 1990. However, by 2000 supermarkets had risen to occupy 50–60 per cent of national food retail among the Latin American countries, almost approaching the 70–80 per cent share in the US or France. Latin America had thus seen in a single decade the same development of supermarkets that the US experienced in five decades.

The supermarket share of food retail sales for the leading six Latin American countries averages 30–75 per cent: Brazil has the highest share, followed by Argentina, Chile, Costa Rica, Colombia and Mexico. Those six countries account for 85 per cent of the income and 75 per cent of the population in Latin America. Other countries in the region have also experienced rapid growth of their super-market sectors, but these started later and from a lower base. For example, supermarkets accounted for 15 per cent of national food retail in Guatemala in 1994 and by 2002 accounted for 35 per cent (Reardon and Berdegue, 2002).

The development of the supermarket sector in east and southeast Asia is gener-ally similar to that of Latin America. The 'take-off' stage of supermarkets in Asia started, on average, some five to seven years behind that of Latin America, but is registering even faster growth. The average processed/packaged food retail share over several southeast Asian countries – Indonesia, Malaysia and Thailand – is 33 per cent, but is 63 per cent for the east Asian countries of the Republic of Korea and Taiwan (ACNielsen, 2002). The supermarket sector in China is the fastest growing in the world: it started in 1991, by 2003 had 55 billion dollars of sales and 30 per cent of urban food retail and is growing by 30–40 per cent a year (Hu et al, 2004).

Supermarket diffusion is also occurring rapidly in central and eastern Europe (CEE). This is occurring in three waves, with the earliest (mid-1990s) take-off of the sector in northern CEE (Czech Republic, Hungary, Poland and Slovakia), where the share of supermarkets in food retail now stands at 40–50 per cent. The second wave is in southern CEE (such as Croatia, Bulgaria, Romania and Slovenia), where the share is on average 25–30 per cent but growing rapidly. The third wave is in eastern Europe, where income and urbanization conditions were present for a take-off but policy reforms lagged (so that the share in, for example, Russia is still only 10 per cent) – but it has been identified by international retail-ers as the number one retail FDI destination (Dries et al, 2004).

The most recent[3] venue for supermarket take-off is in Africa, especially eastern and southern Africa. South Africa is the front-runner, with roughly a 55 per cent share of supermarkets in overall food retail and 1700 supermarkets for 35 million people. The great majority of that spectacular rise has come since the end of apartheid in 1994. To put these figures in perspective, note that 1700 super-markets is roughly equivalent to 350,000 mom and pop stores, or *spazas*, in sales. Moreover, South African chains have recently invested in 13 other African countries and in India, Australia and the Philippines. Kenya is the other front-runner, with 300 supermarkets and a 20 per cent share of supermarkets in urban food retail (Neven and Reardon, 2004). Other African countries are starting to experience the same trends: for example, Zimbabwe and Zambia have 50–100 supermarkets (Weatherspoon and Reardon, 2003).

Second, within each of the four very broad regions there are large differences over sub-regions and countries. Usually, these can be ranked for supermarket growth according to the variables in the supply and demand model presented above. In Latin America, for example, Brazil with a 75 per cent share of super-markets in food retail store sales can be contrasted with Bolivia with at most 10 per cent; in developing Asia, Korea with 60 per cent can be contrasted with India with 5 per cent; and in Africa, South Africa with 55 per cent can be contrasted with Nigeria with 5 per cent; Hungary or Poland with shares of 40–50 per cent can be contrasted with Russia with 10 per cent.

Third, the take-over of food retailing in these regions has occurred much more rapidly in processed, dry and packaged foods such as noodles, milk products and grains, for which supermarkets have an advantage over mom and pop stores due to economies of scale. The supermarkets' progress in gaining control of fresh food markets has been slower and there is greater variation across countries because of local habits and responses by wetmarkets and local shops. Usually the first fresh food categories where the supermarkets gain a majority share include 'commodities' such as potatoes and sectors undergoing consolidation in first-stage processing and production: often chicken, beef, pork and fish.

A rough rule of thumb, applicable from Latin America, is that the share of supermarkets in fresh foods is roughly one half of the share in packaged foods. For example, in Brazil, where the overall food retail share of supermarkets is 75 per cent, the share in São Paulo of fresh fruits and vegetables is only 50 per cent; in Argentina, the shares are 60 and 25 per cent, respectively. This kind of rough '2 or 3 to 1' ratio appears to be typical in these regions. This difference is also common in developed countries: in France, supermarkets have 70 per cent of overall food retail, but only 50 per cent of fresh fruits and vegetables. The convenience and low prices of small shops and fairs, with fresh and varied produce for daily shopping, continues to be a competitive challenge to the supermarket sector, with usually steady but much slower progress for supermarkets requiring investments in procurement efficiency.

Despite the slower growth in the supermarket share of the domestic fresh produce market, it is very revealing to calculate the absolute market that supermarkets now represent, even in produce, and thus how much more in other products where supermarkets have penetrated faster and deeper. For example, Reardon and Berdegue (2002) calculate that supermarkets in Latin America buy *two and a half times* more fruits and vegetables from local producers than all the exports of produce from Latin America to the rest of the world.

Fourth, the supermarket sector in these regions is increasingly and overwhelmingly multinationalized (foreign-owned) and consolidated. The multinationalization of the sector is illustrated in Latin America where global multinationals constitute roughly 70–80 per cent of the top five chains in most countries. This element of 'FDI-driven' differentiates supermarket diffusion in these regions from that in the US and Europe. The tidal wave of FDI in retail was mainly due to the global retail multinationals Ahold, Carrefour and Wal-Mart, smaller global chains such as Casino, Metro and Makro and regional multinationals such as Dairy Farm International (Hong Kong) and Shoprite (South Africa). In some larger countries domestic chains, sometimes in joint ventures with global multinationals, have been at the fore. For example, the top chain in Brazil is Pão de Açúcar (in partnership with Casino, of France, since 1999) and the top chain in China is the giant national chain Lianhua (based in Shanghai), with some 2500 stores, in partial joint venture with Carrefour.

The rapid consolidation of the sector in those regions mirrors what is occurring in the US and Europe. For example, in Latin America the top five chains per country have 65 per cent of the supermarket sector (versus 40 per cent in the US and 72 per cent in France). The consolidation takes place mainly via foreign acquisition of local chains (and secondarily by larger domestic chains absorbing smaller chains and independents). This is done via large amounts of FDI: for example, in the first eight months of 2002, five global retailers (British Tesco, French Carrefour and Casino, Dutch Ahold and Makro and Belgian Food Lion) spent US$120 million in Thailand (Jitpleechep, 2002). Wal-Mart spent US$660 million in Mexico during 2002 to build new stores.

These trends of multinationalization and consolidation fit the supply function of our supermarket diffusion model. Global and retail multinationals have access to investment funds from their own liquidity and to international credit that is much cheaper than the credit accessible by their domestic rivals. The multinationals also have access to best practices in retail and logistics, some of which they developed as proprietary innovations. Global retailers adopt retailing and procurement technology generated by their own firms or, increasingly, via joint ventures with global logistics multinationals, such as Carrefour (France) does with Penske Logistics (US) in Brazil. Where domestic firms have competed, they have had to make similar investments; these firms either had to enter joint ventures with global multinationals, or get low-cost loans from their governments (e.g. the Shanghai-based national chain) or national bank loans.

Fifth, again as predictable from the diffusion model above, the interspatial and inter-socioeconomic group patterns of diffusion have differed over large and small cities and towns and over richer, middle and poor consumer segments. In general, there has been a trend from supermarkets occupying only a small niche in capital cities, serving only the rich and middle class, to supermarkets spreading well beyond the middle class in order to penetrate deeply into the food markets of the poor. They have also spread from big cities to intermediate towns and in some countries, already to small towns in rural areas. About 40 per cent of Chile's smaller towns now have supermarkets, as do many small-to-medium sized towns, even in low-income countries like Kenya. And supermarkets are now spreading rapidly beyond the top-60 cities of China in the coastal area and are moving to smaller cities and to the poorer and more remote northwest and southwest and interior.

Supermarkets' transforming procurement systems

We have found that supermarket chains have a dual objective – one qualitative (to increase quality and eventually safety of the product) and one quantitative (to reduce costs and increase volumes procured). Supermarket chains have a difficult time meeting those objectives by using the traditional wholesale sector to procure their products. Here is a statement from Javier Gallegos (2003), the head of marketing for Hortifruti (a specialized/dedicated wholesaler for the CARHCO chain in Central America), enumerating the deficiencies of the traditional market in the face of a supermarket's needs:

> *The realities and problems of our growers and markets are as follows. The market is fragmented, unformatted, unstandardized. The growers produce low-quality products, use bad harvest techniques, there is a lack of equipment and transportation, there is deficient post-harvest control and infrastructure, there is no market information. There are high import barriers and corruption. The informal market does not have: research, statistics, market information, standardized products, quality control, technical assistance, infrastructure.*

Driven to close the gap between their supplies and their needs, supermarket chains in developing regions have been shifting away from the old procurement model based on sourcing products from the traditional wholesalers and the wholesale markets, toward the use of four key pillars of a new kind of procurement system: (1) specialized procurement agents we call 'specialized/dedicated wholesalers'; (2) centralized procurement through distribution centres (DCs), along with regionalization of procurement; (3) assured and consistent supply through 'preferred suppliers'; and (4) high quality and increasingly safe products through private standards imposed on suppliers.

The first three pillars (organizational change in procurement) together make possible the fourth (institutional change in procurement – that is, the rise of private standards for quality and, increasingly, for safety of fresh fruits and vegetables). Below we lay out a conceptual framework for understanding that shift and then discuss the four pillars.

Determinants of change in supermarket procurement systems

Technology change in the procurement systems of supermarkets in developing regions is a key determinant of change in the markets facing farmers. The diffusion of technology (defined broadly as physical production practices as well as management techniques) in the supermarket sector in developing countries can also be conceptualized as a system of demand and supply for new technology. Here we focus on technology for retail product procurement systems as these choices most affect suppliers.

Demand for technology change in food retailer procurement practices is, in general, driven by the overall competitive strategy of the supermarket chain. However, specific choices are usually taken by procurement officers, for example in the produce procurement division. Hence it is crucial to understand the objective function of these officers in supermarkets in developing countries. We present a working hypothesis based on numerous interviews with these officers.

The decisions related to purchasing products for retail shelves rests with the procurement officers in supermarket chains. Whether in the US, Europe, Nicaragua, Chile or China, the officers are under several common pressures from supermarket managers, operating under intense competition and with low average profit margins. They are caught between the low-cost informal traditional retailers selling fresh local products on one side and efficient global chain competitors like Wal-Mart on the other. The procurement officers strive to respond to this pressure by reducing purchase and transaction costs and raising product quality. Reflecting the varied demand of consumers, procurement officers seek to maintain diversity, year-round availability and products with assured quality and safety levels.

Based on those objectives, we outline a rough model of change in procurement systems (technology, organization, institutions), looking at demand (by procurement officers in the produce division) and supply (by the supermarket chain to the produce division).

We begin with the demand function variables of incentives and capacity. Incentives include the ability of the traditional wholesale system to meet procurement officer objectives without the chain having to resort to costly investments in an alternative system. Usually procurement officers find this ability low, as Boselie (2002) shows in the case of Ahold for fresh produce in Thailand. Compared with the North American or the European market, produce marketing in these regions is characterized by poor institutional and public physical infrastructure support. Private infrastructure, such as packing houses, cold chains and shipping equipment among suppliers and distributors is usually inadequate. Risks and uncertainties, both in output and in suppliers' responsiveness to incentives, are high. The risks may arise due to various output and input market failures, such as inadequacies in credit, third-party certification and market information. A second incentive is the need to reduce costs of procurement by saving on inputs, in this case purchased product costs and transaction costs with suppliers. A final incentive is to increase procurement of products that can be sold at higher margins – that is, diversify the product line into 'products' rather than mere commodities (bulk items).

Demand capacity variables include the consumer segment served by the chain (crucial because higher value products cannot be marketed to poorer consumers where cost considerations are paramount) and the resources of the procurement office, including numbers of staff. The latter is important because it can determine the ability to make organizational and institutional changes in procurement systems such as operating a large distribution centre. A variable that reflects both incentive and capacity is the size of the chain and thus product throughput in the procurement system. Usually retailers have a 'step level' or threshold throughput where they move from per-store to centralized procurement as economies of scale permit and require.

The supply of procurement technology by the chain as an overarching enterprise to the specific product category procurement office(s), such as the fresh foods categories, is an investment and is a function of several variables. The incentive variables include the importance of the product category to the chain's profits and marketing strategy. For example, we observed a small chain in an intermediate city in China that invested in building a DC for processed/packaged foods but continues to buy fresh foods from the spot market (traditional wholesalers); while a national chain invested in a large DC for packaged/processed foods and has recently built a large DC for fresh foods because throughput has attained a critical mass and these products have attained a threshold importance in profits and chain marketing strategy. A second incentive variable is the need for assurance of various product attributes in order to meet customers' demands (expansion of product choice, attribute consistency over transactions, year-around availability, quality and safety); and a third is the costs of the technology, such as costs of transport, construction, logistics services, etc.

The capacity variables include the size of the chain and/or access to financial capital to make the investments; and the capacity of the chain to manage complex and centralized procurement systems.

The incentive and capacity determinants of demand for and supply of changes in procurement system technology vary markedly over the three regions and countries and within countries, over chains and zones. Several broad patterns are observed in the procurement technologies that result.

First pillar of change: Towards centralization and regionalization of procurement

There is a trend toward centralization of procurement (per chain). As the number of stores in a given supermarket chain grows, there is a tendency to shift from a per-store procurement system to a distribution centre serving several stores in a given zone, district, country or region (which may cover several countries). This is accompanied by fewer procurement officers and increased use of centralized warehouses. Additionally, increased levels of centralization may also occur in the procurement decision-making process and in the physical produce distribution processes. Centralization increases efficiency of procurement by reducing coordination and other transaction costs, although it may increase transport costs by extra movement of the actual products.

The top three global retailers have made or are making shifts toward more centralized procurement systems in all the regions in which they operate. Wal-Mart uses a centralized procurement system in most of its operating areas. Having centralized its procurement in France, Carrefour has been moving quickly to centralize its procurement system in other countries. For example, in 2003 and 2004 Tesco and Ahold established large distribution centres in Poland, Hungary and the Czech Republic. In 2001 Carrefour established a distribution centre in São Paulo to serve three Brazilian states (with 50 million consumers) with 50 hypermarkets (equivalent to about 500 supermarkets) in the southeast region. Similarly, Carrefour is building a national distribution system with several distribution centre nodes in China, while Ahold centralized its procurement systems in Thailand (Boselie, 2002). The list goes on.

Regional chains, such as China Resources Enterprises (CRE) of Hong Kong with Vanguard stores in southern China, are also centralizing their procurement systems. CRE is tenth in retail in China and has 17 large stores in the provinces of Shenzhen and Guangdong. In anticipation of growth following its planned US$680 million investment in China over the next five years, a shift from store-by-store procurement to a centralized system of procurement covering each province is under way. Two large distribution centres were completed in 2002. The distribution centre in Shenzhen is 65,000 square metres and will be able to handle 40 department stores and 400 superstores/discount centres.

Moreover, the regional (over several countries) chains are moving toward sourcing regionally. We hypothesize that this will be, over the next decade, a factor inducing greater intra-regional trade and economic integration in regions. For example, in January 2002, a regional chain called Central American Retail Holding Company (CARHCO) was formed, composed of a Costa Rican chain (CSU Supermarkets) that had expanded into Honduras and Nicaragua and a Guatemalan chain (La Fragua) that expanded into El Salvador and Ahold. The chain started with 253 stores in five countries and US$1.3 billion of sales, a large operation with about two-thirds of the supermarket sector in those countries. It started by sourcing only locally (the chain in each country mainly sourcing from local producers). With the takeover of the chain by Wal-Mart in 2006, the region-alization of the procurement system has continued to develop.

Second pillar of change: Shift towards use of specialized wholesalers and logistics firms

There is growing use of specialized/dedicated wholesalers. They are specialized in a product category and dedicated to the supermarket sector as their main clients. The changes in supplier logistics have moved supermarket chains toward new intermediaries, side-stepping or transforming the traditional wholesale system. The supermarkets are increasingly working with specialized wholesalers, dedicated to and capable of meeting their specific needs. These specialized whole-salers cut transaction and search costs and enforce private standards and contracts on behalf of the supermarkets. The emergence and operation of the specialized wholesalers has promoted convergence, in terms of players and product standards, between the export and the domestic food markets. Moreover, there is emerging evidence that when supermarket chains source imported produce they tend to do so mainly via specialized importers. For example, hyper-markets in China tend to work with specialized importers/wholesalers of fruit, who in turn sell nearly half of their imported products to supermarket chains (McClafferty, 2002). Similarly, Hortifruti functions as the buying arm of most stores of the main supermarket chain in Central America, as does Freshmark for Shoprite in Africa.

Moreover, there is a trend toward logistics improvements to accompany procurement consolidation. To defray some of the added transport costs that arise with centralization, supermarket chains have adopted (and required that suppliers adopt) best-practice logistical technology. This requires that supermarket suppliers adopt practices and make physical investments that allow almost frictionless logistical interface with the chain's warehouses. The 'Code of Good Commercial Practices' signed by supermarket chains and suppliers in Argentina illustrates the use of best-practice logistics by retail suppliers (Brom, 2002). Similar trends are noted in Asia. For example, Ahold instituted a supply improvement programme for vegetable suppliers in Thailand, specifying post-harvest and production practices to assure consistent supply and improve the efficiency of their operation (Boselie, 2002).

Retail chains in the three regions increasingly outsource (sometimes to a company in the same holding company as the supermarket chain) logistics and wholesale distribution functions, entering joint ventures with other firms. An example is the Carrefour distribution centre in Brazil, which is the product of a joint venture of Carrefour with Cotia Trading (a major Brazilian wholesaler distributor) and Penske Logistics (a US global multinational firm). Similarly, Wumart of China announced in March 2002 (CIES, 2001) that it will build a large distribution centre to be operated jointly with Tibbett and Britten Logistics (a British global multinational firm). Ahold's distribution centre for fruits and vegetables in Thailand is operated in partnership with TNT Logistics of the Netherlands (Boselie, 2002).

Third pillar: Towards preferred supplier systems

Many supermarket chains are undertaking institutional innovation by establishing contracts with their suppliers – in particular via their dedicated, specialized wholesalers managing a preferred supplier system for them. This trend is similar to that in agroprocessing during the past decade (Schejtman, 1996). The contract is established when the retailer (via its wholesaler or directly) 'lists' a supplier. That listing is an informal (usually) but effective contract[4] in which delisting carries some cost, tangible or intangible. We have observed such contracts in all the regions under study. Contracts serve as incentives to the suppliers to stay with the buyer and over time make investments in assets (such as learning and equipment) specific to the retailer specifications regarding the products. The retailers are assured of on-time delivery and the delivery of products with desired quality attributes.

These contracts sometimes include direct or indirect assistance for farmers to make investments in human capital, management, input quality and basic equipment. Evidence is emerging that for many small farms these assistance programmes are the only source of such much-valued inputs and assistance – in particular where public systems have been dismantled or coverage is inadequate. In some cases, the assistance is indirect, such as the case of the German chain Metro intervening with the bank in Croatia, noting that would-be strawberry suppliers would be given contracts that served as a 'collateral substitute', so that suppliers could make needed greenhouse investments (Reardon et al, 2003b).

This constitutes resolution by retailers or their wholesaler agents of idiosyncratic factor market failures facing small producers – such as credit, information and technical assistance. There is evidence of this in the processing sector also, for example in the CEE (Gow and Swinnen, 2001; Dries and Swinnen, 2004). Some cases of this are remarkable in their extent and nature. Codron et al (2004) note a case of the Turkish retailer MIGROS, which contracts with a whole village near its Antalya market to grow 1000 tons of tomatoes during the summer. Hu et al (2004) describe the case of Xincheng Foods in Shanghai acting as a specialized wholesaler for the top two chains in China. Xincheng leases long-term (from townships) 1000 hectares of prime vegetable land, hires migrant labour, installs greenhouses and uses tractors and drip irrigation (thus changing production technology) and produces in-house large quantities of high-quality vegetables for the supermarket chains and for export. It also has contracts with 4500 small farmers to add to its own production. This kind of operation can be described as a major 'agent of change' in the Chinese agri-food economy.

While the contracting is quite recent for produce, it has been a practice for years among chains sourcing from processed product suppliers. Manufacturers of private label processed fruit and vegetable and meat and cereals products typically operate under formal contract with the supermarkets. Supermarket chains have contracts with processing firms, who in turn may sign contracts with producers. For example, the processing firm IANSAFRUT supplies processed vegetables to supermarkets in Chile under such an arrangement (Milicevic et al, 1998). Similarly, processed fruits and vegetables are sold under the label SABEMAS for the supermarket CSU in Costa Rica and various firms produce under contract the products for the private label. As retail sales of private label products continue to grow, such contract arrangements are expected to increase in Latin America and Asia.

Fourth pillar: The rise of private standards

While food retailing in these regions previously operated in the informal market, with little use of certifications and standards, the emerging trend indicates a rapid rise in the implementation of private standards in the supermarket sector (and other modern food industry sectors such as medium-/large-scale food manufactures and food service chains). The rise of private standards for quality and safety of food products and the increasing importance of the enforcement of (otherwise virtually not enforced) public standards are crucial aspects of the imposition of product requirements in the procurement systems. In general, these standards function as instruments of coordination of supply chains by standardizing product requirements over suppliers, who may cover many regions or countries. Standards specify and harmonize the product and delivery attributes, thereby enhancing efficiency and lowering transaction costs. In turn, the implementation of these standards depends crucially on the establishment of the new procurement system organization noted in the three pillars above.

The general adoption framework can be applied to 'institutional adoption' such as the adoption of private standards by supermarket chains' procurement arms or agents in developing regions. The incentives include the following.

First, the chain has an incentive to implement private standards where there are missing or inadequate public standards; private standards act as a substitute for the missing institution. As the large chains (and processing firms) competed in national and regional markets and attempted to differentiate their products to protect and gain market share, they found that the public standards needed for that differentiation did not exist (common in developing regions – see Stephenson, 1997); or relatively undifferentiated public standards existed, inherited from the protected, homogeneous commodity markets that were common before market liberalization and structural adjustment. The latter were inadequate either to meet consumer demand for product differentiation and quality differences, or to reward producers for their investments in quality and safety (Reardon et al, 1999; Reardon and Farina, 2001). As noted above, governments in these regions tend to have the incentive and capacity to implement public standards mainly for the export market interface and much less so for domestic markets. Moreover, public standards tend to be applied where they are 'public goods' such as for plant and animal health. At the opposite extreme are quality standards that are typically private goods – and private standards used to differentiate products and create a competitive advantage for the company implementing the standards.

Lying between the two are food safety standards. In principle, these should be considered public goods, set and enforced by governments. The issue here is not conceptual but rather practical – governments might occasionally establish regulations but usually do not have the capacity to monitor and enforce them (for the case of Guatemala, see Flores, 2003). Yet supermarket chains have incentives to set private safety standards, at least for 'at-risk' products such as leafy greens, berries and other products where pesticide residuals and bacteria can produce short–medium-run health problems among their clientele. In some countries there are liability laws that make this a legal issue. Yet even where there are not laws, there are two other reasons to have such standards. On the one hand, as noted above, most of the chains are global or regional and a health crisis caused by an unsafe product in one country can hurt sales and stock prices in the region or globally. On the other hand, safety standards – and the belief on the part of the consumer that chains are able to actually monitor and enforce them – gives a big advantage to supermarkets over traditional retailers and thus is a major competitive instrument.

Of course, where there are public standards for safety, private standards can meet or exceed the stringency of public standards thus affording 'domain defence', limiting exposure to penalties from public regulations (Caswell and Johnson, 1991). Communicating to the urban or developed country consumer that the private standards exceed the stringency and enforcement of public standards encourages consumers to buy products from countries that they may see otherwise as having lax quality and safety regulations.

Second, private standards are used to increase profits through facilitating product differentiation – and thus provide incentives to suppliers to make asset-specific investments and to consumers to satisfy their desire for product diversity by shopping at the chain. Supermarkets (as well as large-scale processors and fast-food chains) use private standards to differentiate their product lines (adding stock keeping units and thus product diversity) and differentiate their products from each other and from traditional actors. Private standards make product differentiation easier and more flexible, allowing companies to take advantage of new market opportunities ('domain offence', Caswell and Johnson, 1991). Consistent implementation of private standards, plus certification, labelling and branding systems that link high quality and safety standards to the product and the company in the consumer's mind, produces reputation and competitive advantage. One sees this in the application of the Carrefour Quality Certification programme and labels for meat and produce in Mexico, China, Brazil and elsewhere.

Third, chains use private standards to reduce cost and risk in their supply chains. The main cost reduction comes from using process standards to coordinate chains. Farina (2002) and Gutman (2002) illustrate these cost savings in the case of supermarkets and dairy products in Brazil and Argentina. Chains complement private standards with other elements of a 'metasystem of quality control' (Caswell et al, 1998), adding elements such as branding to the system governance structure. Building trust and reputation around the visible symbol of a brand name and label make standards systems credible to consumers (Northen and Henson, 1999). To build consumer confidence (and thus build market volume and reduce market risk) by consistency in standards implementation, tight vertical coordination is needed, especially for process standards – hence the use of the organizational structure of procurement, plus contracts, noted above.

An important element of this is the reduction of coordination costs in procurement systems that become progressively broader in geographic scope, as the discussion of the first pillar above establishes as a trend. Regional and global chains want to cut costs by standardizing over countries and suppliers as this occurs – which induces a convergence with the standards of the toughest market in the set, including with European or US standards. One sees this in Wal-Mart between Mexico and the US, in the Quality Assurance Certification used by Carrefour over its global operations that include developing countries and in the regional chains such as CARHCO discussed above. In some cases this has meant that global chains actually apply public standards from their developed country markets as private standards to suppliers to their local developing country markets, such as the use of FDA standards for some products by US chains. The chains might also use private standards from the developed country portions of their markets, such as European chains using Euro-Retailer Produce Working Group on Good Agricultural Practices (EurepGAP[5]) standards for some produce and meat items applied to suppliers in developing country markets.

The capacity variables involved in the diffusion of private standards are as follows. First, the chains, or their specialized/dedicated wholesalers, must have the requisite degree of buying power to impose private standards on suppliers – either because the chain has some oligopsonistic power, or because it offers higher producer prices, or it offers other assistance to producers. The size of the front-runner chains (the same ones that are the main implementers of private standards) relative to the urban market certainly gives them the buying power (for example, Carrefour has about 25 per cent of all food retail in Argentina).

Large chain size is necessary but not sufficient. Chains need the procurement organization changes noted above, in particular distribution centres that allow the product procurement to be centralized, making possible efficient standards monitoring and implicit contracts (via the preferred supplier systems) which in turn allow traceability and a delivery vehicle for the standards.

Sometimes chains also offer prices higher than the wholesale market prices to producers who meet their standards; little systematic information exists about this point, but in general we have found that the premium is around 10–15 per cent, just enough to meet additional costs implied by meeting the standards. But sometimes no price premium is offered: what then is the incentive for the producer to meet the (usually more stringent) private standards? The answer is related to the discussion of the preferred supplier systems above: chains (or their specialized/dedicated wholesalers) sometimes offer technical assistance, input credit or collateral substitutes in the form of a contract and transport to their suppliers. An example is Hortifruti's technical assistance and credit to vegetable suppliers in Costa Rica. The technical assistance and credit resolve idiosyncratic factor market failures that often plague producers after public systems for these items were dismantled during the structural adjustment period – and one can hypothesize that public systems were never nor are now adequate to meet the kinds of upgrading needs that face suppliers to supermarkets.

Second, all of the above is necessary but not sufficient to implement private standards; the final ingredient is the capacity of producers to meet the standards. A poignant illustration of this was the limitation felt by the La Fragua chain in Guatemala to implement broadly its new 'Paiz Seal' quality and safety certification system in the past two years. They found the following: (1) for key bulk items such as Roma tomatoes, there were simply not enough producers with the capacity to supply over the full year or sufficient volume to meet the chain's needs and so the chain has to rely on traditional wholesalers to bulk the product from many small producers – obviating traceability and imposition of safety standards and quality consistency; (2) for key 'at-risk' items such as leafy greens and berries, the chain has been forced to take a gradual approach of approving suppliers, at a rate much slower than it wanted, simply because few producers can make the needed investments and those producers have export market alternatives. Because of these limitations on finding enough suppliers that can meet the private standards, some chains take an intermediate position between no application of standards and full, rigorous application. For example, CSU Supermarkets/Hortifruti in Costa Rica monitors standards compliance, but then is loathe to 'delist' suppliers who violate standards, even safety standards. Instead, when a problem is identified, they increase technical assistance combined with warnings, with some eventual delisting – a combination carrot and stick approach, but not so stern as to find themselves with inadequate supply (Berdegue et al, 2004).

Implications for producers and agricultural development

Meeting transaction requirements implied by the organizational change in super-market procurement systems, and the product requirements implied by institutional change in the form of private standards, can present clear opportunities for producers. Adopting the new practices can open the door to suppliers of selling through supermarket chains that are expanding the market in terms of volume, value added and diversity. A supplier can move from being a local supplier to a national, regional or global supplier. Moreover, private process standards can increase efficiency of firm operations and raise profitability. The market scope could also increase, compensating for per-unit profit decreases arising from costs incurred to meet the standards.

However, meeting these non-traditional market requirements implies changes in production practices and investments, such as coordinating to aggregate volumes, reducing pesticide use or investing in 'electric eyes' in packing sheds and cooling tanks in dairies. Some of these investments are quite costly and are simply unaffordable by many small firms and farms. It is thus not surprising that the evidence is mounting that the changes in standards and the implied investments have driven many small firms and farms out of business in developing countries over the past 5–10 years and accelerated industry concentration.

The supermarket chains, locked in a struggle with other chains in a highly competitive industry with low margins, seek constantly to lower product and transaction costs and risk, which points toward selecting only the most capable farmers – and in many developing countries that means mainly the medium and large farmers. Moreover, as supermarkets compete with each other and with the informal sector, they will not allow consumer prices to increase in order to 'pay for' the farm-level investments needed. Who will pay for wells with safe water? Latrines and hand-washing facilities in the fields? Record-keeping systems? Clean and proper packing houses with cement floors? The supplier does and will bear the financial burden. As small farmers lack access to credit and large fixed costs are a burden for a small operation, this will be a huge challenge for small operators. It is thus inevitable that standards demanded by consumers are increasingly a major driver of concentration in the farm sector in developing regions. Retail concentration will cascade, sooner or later, into supplier concentration.

To help many small farmers grasp the opportunities these changes imply in the short to medium run and those that cannot to transition into other employment in the medium to longer run, development programmes will have a challenge and a mandate to assist small farmers to make the transition.

Notes

1   For simplicity, we use the term 'supermarkets' to indicate all large-format modern retail (supermarkets, hypermarkets, discount and club stores, which typically constitute about 95 per cent of the sales of modern retail in developing countries, the rest being chain convenience stores), distinguishing formats only where necessary.
2   This section and the next draw on several publications, in particular on Reardon and Timmer (2007) and Reardon et al (2003a) for overall trends; as well as: for Latin America, Reardon and Berdegue (2002), Balsevich et al (2003) and Berdegue et al (2004); for Central and Eastern Europe, Dries et al (2004); for China, Hu et al (2004); and for Africa, Weatherspoon and Reardon (2003) and Neven and Reardon (2004).
3   South Asia is poised at the edge of a take-off, with the share of supermarkets in India at 5 per cent, but identified as number 2 in the top 10 destinations for retail FDI today (Burt, 2004).
4   'Contracts' is used in the broad sense of Hueth et al (1999), which includes informal and implicit relationships.
5   EurepGAP, the Euro-Retailer Produce Working Group on Good Agricultural Practices, is now GLOBALGAP.

References

ACNielsen (2002) *China Dynamics: FMCG Sales Grow 8 percent in 2001* [online] <www.asiapacific.acnielsen.com.au> September
Balsevich, F., Berdegue, J. A., Flores, L., Mainville, D. and Reardon, T. (2003) 'Supermarkets and produce quality and safety standards in Latin America', *American Journal of Agricultural Economics*, vol 85, no 5, pp1147–1154
Berdegue, J. A., Balsevich, F., Flores, L. and Reardon, T. (2004) 'Central American supermarkets' private standards of quality and safety in procurement of fresh fruits and vegetables', *Food Policy*, vol 30, no 3, pp254–269
Boselie, D. (2002) *Business Case Description: TOPS Supply Chain Project, Thailand,* Agrichain Competence Centre, Den Bosch, KLICT International Agri Supply Chain Development Program [online] <www.kc-acc.org/pdf/thailand.pdf>
Brom, F. (2002) *Experiencia Argentina: Relación entre los proveedores y los supermercados,* Speech at the 7th Biennial Congress of the Costa Rican Food Industry Chamber of Commerce, Costa Rica, June
Burt, T. (2004) 'Global retailers expand markets', *Financial Times*, 22 June, p15
Caswell, J. A. and Johnson, G. V. (1991) 'Firm strategic response to food safety and nutrition regulation', in J. A. Caswell (ed.) *Economics of Food Safety*, Elsevier, New York
Caswell, J. A., Bredahl, M. and Hooker, N. (1998) 'How quality management metasystems are affecting the food industry', *Review of Agricultural Economics*, vol 20, no 2, pp547–557
China Resources Enterprise (2002) *Retailing Strategies and Execution Plan, July 2002* [online] <www.cre.com.hk/index.asp>
CIES (2001) Wu-mart, *Food Business Forum: News of the Day*, no paging
Codron, J. M., Bouhsina, Z., Fort, F., Coudel, E. and Puech, A. (2004) 'Supermarkets in low-income Mediterranean countries: Impacts on horticulture systems', *Development Policy Review*, vol 22, no 5, pp587–602

Dries, L. and Swinnen, J. (2004) 'Foreign Direct Investment, vertical integration and local suppliers: Evidence from the Polish dairy sector', *World Development*, vol 32, no 9, pp1525–1544

Dries, L., Reardon, T. and Swinnen, J. (2004) 'The rapid rise of supermarkets in Central and Eastern Europe: Implications for the agrifood sector and rural development', *Development Policy Review*, vol 22, no 9, pp525–556

Farina, E. (2002) 'Consolidation, multinationalization and competition in Brazil: Impacts on horticulture and dairy product systems', *Development Policy Review*, vol 20, no 4, pp441–457

Flores, L. (2003) Private Standards for Food Safety and Supermarkets in Guatemala, Working Paper, Michigan State University, East Lansing, MI

Gallegos, J. (2003) *CSU (Corporación Supermercados Unidos): Excelencia sin Barrera*, San Jose, Costa Rica, Hortifruti (Powerpoint presentation)

Gow, H. and Swinnen, J. (2001) 'Private enforcement capital and contract enforcement in transition countries', *American Journal of Agricultural Economics*, vol 83, no 3, pp686–690

Gutman, G. (2002) 'Impacts of the rapid rise of supermarkets on dairy products systems in Argentina', *Development Policy Review*, vol 20, no 4, pp409–427

Hu, D., Reardon, T., Rozelle, S., Timmer, P. and Honglin, W. (2004) 'The emergence of supermarkets with Chinese characteristics: Challenges and opportunities for China's agricultural development', *Development Policy Review*, vol 22, no 5, pp557–586

Hueth, B. M., Ligon, E., Wolf, S. and Wu, S. (1999) 'Incentive instruments in agricultural contracts: Input control, monitoring, quality measurement and price risk', *Review of Agricultural Economics*, vol 21, no 2, pp374–389

Jitpleechep, S. (2002) 'Who is who', *Bangkok Post* (posted on www.siamfuture.com, 28 August)

McClafferty, C. (2002) *China: Produce Industry Market Research Study*, Delaware Produce Marketing Association Final Report to USDA/FAS, Emerging Markets Program, December

Milicevic, X., Berdegue, J. and Reardon, T. (1998) *Impacts on Rural Farm and Non-farm Incomes of Contractual Links Between Agroindustrial Firms and Farms: The case of tomatoes in Chile*, Proceedings of the meetings of the Association of Farming Systems Research and Extension (AFSRE), Pretoria, South Africa, 30 November–4 December

Neven, D. and Reardon, T. (2004) 'The rise of Kenyan supermarkets and evolution of their horticulture product procurement systems: Implications for agricultural diversification and smallholder market access programs', *Development Policy Review*, vol 32, no 9, pp1525–1544

Northen, J. and Henson, S. (1999) Communicating credence attributes in the supply chain: The role of trust and effects on firms' transactions costs', Paper presented at the IAMA World Food and Agribusiness Forum, Florence, Italy, 13–14 June

Reardon, T. and Berdegue, J.A. (2002) 'The rapid rise of supermarkets in Latin America: Challenges and opportunities for development', *Development Policy Review*, vol 20, no 4, pp317–334

Reardon, T. and Farina, E. (2001) 'The rise of private food quality and safety standards: illustrations from Brazil', *International Food and Agricultural Management Review*, vol 4, no 4, pp413–421

Reardon, T. and Timmer, C. P. (2007) 'Transformation of markets for agricultural output in developing countries since 1950: How has thinking changed?' in R. Evenson and P. Pingali (eds) *Handbook of Agricultural Economics*, vol 3, Elsevier, Holland

Reardon, T., Codron, J.-M., Busch, L., Bingen, J. and Harris, C. (1999) 'Global change in agrifood grades and standards: Agribusiness strategic responses in developing countries', *International Food and Agribusiness Management Review*, vol 2, no 3, pp195–205

Reardon, T., Timmer, C. P., Barrett, C. B. and Berdegue, J. (2003a) 'The rise of supermarkets in Africa, Asia and Latin America', *American Journal of Agricultural Economics*, vol 85, no 5, pp1140–1146

Reardon, T., Vrabec, G., Karakas, D. and Fritsch, C. (2003b) *The Rapid Rise of Supermarkets in Croatia: Implications for Farm Sector Development and Agribusiness Competitiveness Programs*, Report for USAID under the project RAISE/ACE, DAI and MSU, September

Schejtman, A. (1996) *Agroindustry and small-scale agriculture: Conceptual guidelines for a policy to encourage linkage between them*, Report LC/R.1660, Economic Commission for Latin America and the Caribbean (ECLAC), Santiago, Chile

Stephenson, S. M. (1997) *GandS and Conformity Assessment as Non-tariff Barriers to Trade*, Policy Research Working Paper No. 1826, Development Research Group, World Bank, Washington, DC

UNCTAD (2001) *World Investment Report 2001: Trends and Determinants*, Geneva

Weatherspoon, D. and Reardon, T. (2003) 'The rise of supermarkets in Africa: Implications for agrifood systems and the rural poor', *Devolpment Policy Review*, vol 21, no 3, pp333–355

Chapter 3

Food Policy in the Era of Supermarkets: What's Different?

C. Peter Timmer

The purpose of the central analytical vision of food policy, articulated two decades ago, was to integrate farmer, trader and consumer decision-making into the open-economy, macro framework needed for rapid economic growth (Timmer et al, 1983). The explicit goal was a sharp reduction in hunger and poverty, which would be possible if market incentives stimulated productivity and income gains in agriculture while poor consumers were protected by stable food prices and rising real wages. The marketing sector was the key to connecting these two ends of the food system. Supermarkets were not mentioned because they were a feature of developed countries' economies and the 'food policy paradigm' focused on hunger and poverty in developing countries, where supermarkets were virtually non-existent in the early 1980s.

The analytical story, policy design and programme implementation were complicated, requiring analysts to integrate models of micro and macro decision-making in a domestic economy open to world trade and commodity markets. At its best, the food policy paradigm sharply improved the development profession's understanding of the underlying structure and dynamics of poverty and the role of the food system in reducing it (Eicher and Staatz, 1998). As part of this understanding, food security came to be seen as involving two separate analytical arenas. The first, at the 'micro household' level, required analysis of food access and entitlements. The second, at the 'macro market' level, required analysis of food price stability, market supplies and inventory behaviour. Again, supermarkets did not seem relevant to either level of analysis.

The 1983 book *Food Policy Analysis* provided policy makers with a comprehensive, but intuitively tractable, vision of how to connect these two arenas and improve food security for the consumers in their societies. This vision was always consumer-driven. Farmers (as food producers) and middlemen in the marketing sector (who transformed farm output in time, place and form) were seen as 'intermediate' actors in the efficient production of consumer welfare. Thus the food policy paradigm fits squarely within the standard framework of neoclassical economic analysis.

Over the years, there have been a wide range of challenges to this paradigm, quite independently of the recent emergence of supermarkets in poor countries. In response, in 2008 Simon Maxwell and Rachel Slater edited a special issue of *Development Policy Review* under the theme 'food policy old and new'. Their introduction includes the following observations on the evolution of food policy.

- *The very term 'food policy' induces nostalgia for the 1970s and 1980s; the first meetings of the World Food Council, the establishment of the International Food Policy Research Institute, the establishment of the journal* Food Policy.
- *The world food crisis of 1972–1974 had triggered new interest in the interdependence between supply- and demand-side issues and the value of applying especially economic analysis to the links, but the key question was where the food system was headed (see Timmer et al, 1983).*
- *It was not long before developing countries began to answer that question, and pilot food strategy programmes were launched in Kenya, Zambia, Rwanda and Mali.*
- *Amartya Sen is usually credited with shifting the discourse from food strategies towards entitlement, vulnerability and risk, with 'food security' dominating the debate from the early 1980s. National food security planning served in part as a proxy for poverty planning during the darkest years of structural adjustment. The International Conference on Nutrition, the World Food Summit and WFS-five years later, and the Millennium Development Goals cemented the consensus.*
- *New issues receiving attention mainly in developed countries included a concern for the commercialization and industrialization of food systems, a stronger focus on the institutional actors in food trade (including supermarkets), warnings about the environmental consequences of new technologies and issues to do with health, including problems of food safety and the growth of nutrition-related illnesses. To those concerned primarily with famine and severe undernutrition in the very poorest countries, such issues might have seemed superfluous.*
- *Not so. The pace of change of the world food system is accelerating, with immediate and daunting challenges that need to be on the agenda of policy makers. A preoccupation with food security is no longer sufficient. It is necessary to rediscover food policy.* (Paraphrased from Maxwell and Slater, 2003)

The 'new' food policy agenda is very broad and many of its core topics are treated in this volume. This chapter tries to set the context for these discussions, focusing especially on what kind of analysis can best help us understand the impact of supermarkets on the food systems of developing countries. Even this narrower focus intersects most of the topics now incorporated in the 'new' food policy. There are many questions to address.

How does the rapid emergence of supermarkets as the dominant intermediary between farmers and consumers, even in poor countries, change the analytical task and the nature of the food policy vision? How does policy design change? What new programmes need to be implemented to keep the food system focused on reducing poverty?

There are four parts to the chapter. The first addresses specifically what is different between the old and the new food policy paradigms, and where supermarkets influence that difference. The second part puts the entire food policy debate in historical perspective as a reminder to focus our attention on the long-term process of economic development as the basic driver of the phenomena we are observing. The new role of supermarkets is addressed in this context. The third part of the chapter addresses sectoral and macro dimensions of the supermarket revolution. The fourth part offers some generic policy recommendations, in the form of a list of 'dos and don'ts', and proposes an integration of the old and new food policy paradigms as a framework for the research needed to make the policy recommendations more concrete.

Food policy: What's different?

It is useful to characterize the 'old' and 'new' food policy paradigms in relatively simple two-by-two figures that capture the key concerns of each paradigm. Both focus analytical attention on issues at the country and household levels, and this provides one dimension of the comparison. The original food policy paradigm focused analysis on the links between poverty and food security. This provides the other dimension for discussion in Table 3.1, which fills in the four cells of the original food policy paradigm.

Table 3.1 *The 'old' food policy*

	Food security	Poverty
Country focus	Market prices: level and stability	Economic growth and rising real wages
Household focus	Access to food – incomes – prices – knowledge (especially for micro-nutrients)	Jobs, especially through a dynamic rural economy, migration, and labour-intensive manufacturing

Table 3.2 *The 'new' food policy*

	The 'double burden' of hunger and obesity	Exclusion
Country focus	Government costs of health care and pensions	'Non-globalizers' (governance issue?)
Household focus	Lifestyle and health knowledge (are we 'hard-wired' for scarcity?)	Small farmers Unskilled workers Low education

Alternatively, the new food policy stresses the 'double burden' on societies facing substantial degrees of hunger at the same time that they face rising levels of the nutritional problems of affluence such as obesity, heart disease and diabetes. The 'development' or poverty dimension is more sharply focused on the problem of exclusion at both the national and household levels. Table 3.2 fills in the cells for this paradigm.

The food and health dimension

A comparison of Tables 3.1 and 3.2 shows how starkly the two paradigms are different (although it is notable that supermarkets per se do not appear in any of the cells of either paradigm). At the country level, the earlier concern for keeping food prices at a level that balanced producer and consumer interests, with price stabilization around this level an important policy objective, gives way to equally important concerns for the budgetary consequences for governments (at national and local levels) of the health outcomes for entire societies of dietary choices.

At the household level, the traditional focus on access to foods (including intra-household access and distribution) stressed income and price variables, with a very limited role for household education and knowledge (except possibly in the derived demand for micro-nutrients). Much of the quantitative research in food policy over the past three decades has involved a search for the behavioural regularities that linked households to these market-determined variables (Timmer, 1981; Chaudhri and Timmer, 1985; Bhargava, 2008).

Again, the contrast with the new concerns is sharp. Health professionals are either pessimistic about the political reality of using economic variables to influence dietary choices (one debate was over the efficiency of taxing fats in foods, taxing fat people or taxing the health consequences of being fat), or are doubtful whether economic incentives will actually change dietary behaviour where affluence permits a wide array of choices. Consequently, there is a much sharper focus on trying to change lifestyle through improved health knowledge and nutrition education.

A pointed debate is under way concerning the impact of approaches to changing lifestyles through education. In particular, if the dietary patterns of affluence have a significant genetic component – that is, humans are 'hard-wired' for an environment of food scarcity and have few internal control mechanisms over dietary intake in an environment of permanent affluence and abundance – much more coercive efforts may be needed to change dietary behaviour (and activity levels) than is implied by the education approach. On the other hand, such coercion directly contradicts consumer sovereignty and the basic principles of a democratic society.

Supermarkets are both the purveyors of food abundance (and much of the 'junk' food sold) and a possible vehicle for bringing about dietary change, either through improved nutrition education within stores, health warnings on particular foods that cause nutritional damage or even regulations on what kinds of foods are available for purchase. The rapid spread of private standards of food safety and aspects of production technologies shows that public policy is not necessarily the fastest or most effective way to bring about changes in food marketing. These standards could easily incorporate health dimensions, especially if lawsuits over 'fast food' contributions to obesity begin to be won by litigants.

The poverty and development dimension

One of the key messages for developing countries in *Food Policy Analysis* was the link between poverty and food security, at both the national and household levels. In turn, poverty was considered primarily an economic problem that could only be addressed in a sustainable fashion by linking the poor, mostly in rural areas, into the process of economic growth. A dynamic agriculture as a stimulus to forward and backward linkages within the rural economy served as the 'prime mover' in this process. Through improved agricultural technology, public investments in rural infrastructure, and the end of 'urban bias' that distorted incentives for farmers, policy makers could have a simple and clear approach to reducing poverty and improving food security.

With success in the rural economy, migration to urban areas would be more of a 'pull' rather than a 'push' process, especially if favourable macroeconomic and trade policies were stimulating rapid growth in a labour-intensive manufacturing (and construction) industry. In combination, these activities pulled up real wages and, when sustained, led to rapid reductions in poverty (Timmer, 2002, 2005). In many ways, this paradigm could be described as an 'inclusion model' because of its focus on including the poor in the rural economy, including the rural economy in the national economy and including the national economy in the global economy. Its greatest success was in east and southeast Asia from 1960 to 1997, but the model has been under attack since then as the benefits of globalization have not been as widely shared as had been hoped earlier.

The failures of globalization provide the analytical theme for the new food policy paradigm. Table 3.2 characterizes this theme around the analytics of 'exclusion'. At the national level, the question is why so many countries have been 'non-globalizers'. The essence of the debate is whether the global economy, in the form of rich countries and transnational corporations, has excluded these countries from participating in trade and technology flows, or whether the countries themselves have been unsuccessful in the process because of domestic shortcomings in policies and governance (including corruption).

The debate has a local focus as well. Within an otherwise well-functioning and growing economy, many groups can be excluded from the benefits of this growth. Unskilled workers unable to graduate to higher technologies and uneducated youth unable to compete in a modern economy are a sizeable proportion of the work force in countries with poor policies and limited resources for developing the work force. Globalization makes it more difficult for these countries to compete for trade and investment flows that would provide the first steps up the ladder of higher productivity.

The 'exclusion' lens focuses especially on small farmers. Their fate has been a source of policy concern well before the supermarket revolution gained speed in the early 1990s in Latin America, but there is no question that the issue is now squarely on the policy agenda. Indeed, this is the agenda for much of this volume. It was precisely over this topic that the debate between the relevance of the old and new food policy paradigms took shape: which approach offers the most useful insights and policy/programme guidance for assisting small farmers in their efforts to remain as viable suppliers to supermarket procurement officers? The answer, it was argued, depended on the time horizon of analysis. In the short run, finding income opportunities for small farmers is essential, but in the longer run they have other options, including migration to urban jobs.

Food policy and supermarkets in historical perspective

The 'big' question in social science is whether to study diversity or central tendencies. In the context of economic development, this question translates into whether to analyse the process from the perspective of changing welfare of entire societies over long periods of time, or whether to study inequality in its many dimensions during a particular epoch. The two perspectives obviously relate to each other, possibly even in causal ways, as is illustrated by the modern debate over the contribution of income inequality to economic growth, and vice versa (Easterly, 2003).

From an economics perspective, the ultimate impact of supermarkets in developing countries will be on the level and distribution of improved welfare for consumers. What happens to small farmers, traditional traders and family-run retail shops will be factors in both the size of welfare gains and their distribution, but many other factors will also come into play. A full judgement on the impact of the supermarket revolution must incorporate all of those factors. A political process, informed (we hope) by good economic analysis, will then determine the nature of compensatory actions needed so that losers in this revolution do not end up in poverty or mobilize enough political resources to stop the technological transformation itself.

This view of economic progress as a process of 'creative destruction' dates to Joseph Schumpeter and Adam Smith, but it finds continuing relevance as powerful new technologies boost productivity in rich and poor countries alike

(McCraw, 2007). From this perspective, supermarkets are simply a vehicle for the transmission into developing countries of new technologies, (the potential for) scale economies and new tastes, and are thus the latest manifestation of a long-run process of globalization and structural transformation (Goldberg and Pavcnik, 2007).

Figure 3.1 provides a framework for thinking about these issues in the context of the rapid emergence of supermarkets as the dominant retail supplier of food, even in developing countries. The horizontal axis depicts the long-run process of economic growth, or the transformation of societies from 'poor' to 'rich'. This is the dominant transformation that humanity has undergone in the past ten millennia and is 'the natural course of things', to quote Adam Smith's observation in the 18th century.[1] To see the dominance of this transformation requires a very long time horizon, more the purview of economic historians than of development specialists.

The various dimensions of this process have been summarized as the 'structural transformation', wherein entire societies undergo the wrenching changes associated with agricultural modernization, migration of labour from rural to urban areas and the emergence of urban industrial centres. As part of this process, as both effect and cause, the demographic transition moves a society from an equilibrium of high birth and death rates to a 'modern' equilibrium of low birth and death rates. The structural transformation has taken as long as three centuries in the UK and the US (and is still continuing) and as little as a century in Japan and its east Asian followers. The lengthy process provides a cautionary message to those in a rush to transform their societies (Timmer, 2007).

At the same time that this structural transformation is unfolding, there is enormous diversity across societies in how they organize themselves politically, define themselves culturally and reward themselves economically. This is the vertical dimension that Figure 3.1 illustrates in a crude and simple fashion. During any historical epoch, there will be a set of identifiable 'drivers' that are pushing the economy from poor to rich, while at the same time structuring the diversity within societies and among them.

In the current era (post-Second World War) these drivers are globalization, urbanization and technology. It is no accident that these three forces provide the general theme for this volume, and the question is how have they influenced the rapid emergence of supermarkets? There is now widespread agreement that the supermarket revolution itself has been driven by precisely these three drivers of overall economic change, but a dilemma remains in using this as an answer to the speed of change in the food retail sector. After all, globalization, urbanization and technology were equally cited for the rapid economic advances in the 19th century. What is different now?

The answer is given by changes in the relative scarcity of important economic resources, changes that are themselves driven by the new industrial organization of the global food supply chain. Transnational corporations (TNCs), using supermarkets as their instruments, are increasingly dominant in this global food supply chain – indeed, arguments are heard that the TNCs are using this dominance to extract monopoly profits from consumers worldwide. The dominant role of the TNCs is not in question; there is plenty of evidence from Reardon and his colleagues on the role of foreign direct investment in the consolidation of food retailers in all countries they have studied (Reardon and Berdegue, 2002; Reardon and Timmer, 2007).

But despite the straight line often drawn in traditional industrial organization literature from structure to conduct to performance, the new focus is on performance itself, in the form of profit rates above a competitive norm. Not surprisingly, these profits tend to accrue to the relatively scarce resource in the system under analysis, and to whomever controls those resources. In the global food retail system, there are three basic possibilities for what resource is scarce, although these extend outside the traditional 'land, labour and capital' trio.

First, in a world of global competition, the scarce resource might be physical and marketing access to food consumers, especially food consumers in affluent countries and relatively affluent consumers in poorer countries. If supermarkets come to control this access because of scale economies and modern shopping habits, excessive profits might be earned exploiting consumers who are forced to shop in these supermarkets.

A second possible scarce resource is access to or control of (through intellectual property rights) the technology that lowers transaction costs throughout the entire food supply chain. Increasingly, this is information technology that permits supermarket managers extensive control over procurement, inventory levels and knowledge of consumer checkout profiles. One of the world's largest supercomputers is in Bentonville, Arkansas, the headquarters of Wal-Mart. Every product on every shelf in every Wal-Mart store is in that computer, and the supplier of the product does not get paid until a customer has it scanned at the checkout counter. Then, instantly, the supplier is paid and notified that the item needs to be restocked. Such technology provides a powerful competitive advantage in cost control, quality maintenance and product tracking in case of defects or safety problems. When this technology is applied globally to the food supply chain of a transnational supermarket, transaction costs will be 'pushed out of the system' all the way from the food aisle, through global marketing functions, to individual farmers.[2]

The third possibility for the scarce resource in this system is the food product itself – the rice, potato, Belgian endive, bell peppers, fresh fish or chuck steak. Because supermarket quality and safety standards are so high and rigid, the ability to supply the raw commodities that meet these standards might command a price premium and additional profits for the farmers. Beneath commodity supply, of course, is the land and labour (and knowledge and technology) required to grow the commodities. Thus, ultimately, if commodities themselves are the scarce resource, capable of earning excess profits, these profits will accrue to land, labour or both (or to the management function that harnesses the knowledge, technology and finance, although for small farmers this tends to be in the same hands as the land and labour).

Basic competitive forces will lead most 'monopoly' profits or rents to end up in the hands of the owners of the scarcest resource. The evidence so far is that access to affluent consumers and powerful information technology is scarcer than the ability to produce high-quality commodities, especially when individual producers are forced to compete on a global playing field. But this does not mean that TNC supermarket chains are earning monopoly profits because they have access to, or even control of, these scarce resources. The cost of information technology is dropping with Moore's Law, and access to affluent consumers has turned out to be highly contestable, thus generating competitive results despite the industry structure. Surprisingly, the picture so far is one of intense competition and low profits. Ahold, once the world's largest food retailer, lost over \$5 billion in 2003 and did not return to profitability until divesting itself of many foreign operations.

In summary, what does a long-run perspective have to say about the supermarket revolution? First, it is understandable within the context of the structural transformation and the long-run evolution of agriculture within that process. Second, basic economics, with its stress on returns to scarce factors of production, is surprisingly helpful in understanding the inner dynamics of the process.

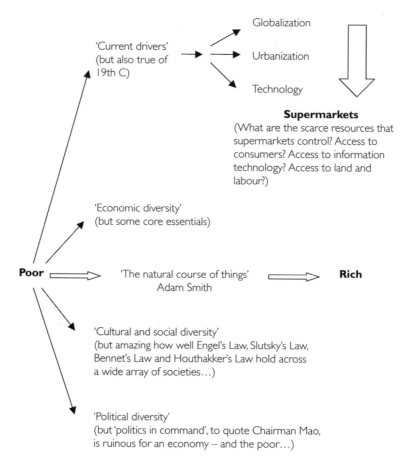

Figure 3.1 *The long-run perspective*

But third, this perspective provides little guidance on how to assist small farmers as they compete for contracts from supermarket procurement officers. For that, the diversity of the global food system, rather than its common themes and forces, needs to be understood. Still, there are some important lessons that come from combining the food policy perspective and the historical, analytical perspective. These lessons tend to play out at the sectoral (marketing) level – and at the macro-level in terms of how the overall economy is performing.

The sectoral and macro perspective

This part of the chapter outlines the basic issues for development presented by the supermarket revolution. These issues cut across the entire economy, from agricultural technology and farmer responsiveness, to concentration in processing and retailing channels, to standards for food quality and safety, to food security at both micro- and macro-levels. Thus understanding the impact of supermarkets presents serious analytical and policy challenges.

These challenges transcend the issues dealt with by the 'old' and 'new' food policy paradigms. In particular, the key issues remain of how to achieve and sustain rapid reductions in poverty and hunger through interventions (or ending interventions) in the food system. The supermarket revolution cuts both ways in this, offering greater consumer choice and lower prices for the retail services provided, but with a track record of consolidating supply chains to a handful of reliable producers able to meet quality, safety and cost standards, and thus excluding many small farmers from access to supermarket customers. The key issue is whether policy makers have an opportunity – in the face of very serious challenges – to leverage the impact of supermarkets on consumers in ways that do not increase rural poverty. To answer that, a deeper understanding of the impact of supermarkets on the marketing sector and the macro economy is needed.

Supermarkets and the marketing sector: Complements or substitutes?

The marketing sector serves two primary functions in a market economy: it generates signals between consumers' desires and farmers' costs through price formation, and it performs the physical functions of marketing – transforming raw commodities at the farm in time, space and form, and delivering them to consumers' tables. These are inherently 'coordination' tasks, and they require an adroit combination of public and private investments if they are to be carried out efficiently. Historically, these investments have been made very gradually as farmers evolved from subsistence activities toward a more commercial orientation. Now that commercial activities are the norm, even in economies where efficient marketing networks have not had time to emerge, policy makers are seeking new models and approaches to speed the creation of these networks. Supermarkets may get there first.

The growing importance of market interactions for farmers stems from at least three separate forces. First, the collapse of socialism has stimulated a rapid, if often painful, transition to a market economy. Second, increasing incomes have stimulated increased commercialization and diversification as part of an agricultural transformation.[3] Third, this commercialization and diversification is increasingly taking place with supermarkets as the main buyer of agricultural output.

The agricultural sector as a whole is likely to become much more diversified over the course of the agricultural transformation, when compared with a representative individual farm, but significantly less diversified than food consumption patterns. Unless agro-ecological endowments are nearly identical throughout the country, farmers with different resources are likely to specialize in different crops. This increasing specialization of farms (*decreasing* diversification) is consistent with *greater* diversity at more aggregate levels because of the commercialization of agriculture. As summarized by Pingali and Rosegrant:

> *Commercialization of agricultural systems leads to greater market orientation of farm production; progressive substitution out of non-traded inputs in favour of purchased inputs; and the gradual decline of integrated farming systems and their replacement by specialized enterprises for crop, livestock, poultry and aquaculture products.* (Pingali and Rosegrant, 1995, pp171–172)

Likewise, patterns of food consumption become more diversified than patterns of domestic agricultural production because of the rising significance of international trade, that is globalization. Bennett's Law suggests that there is an inherent desire for diversity in dietary patterns among most populations of the world. Low-cost transportation systems and falling trade barriers have generally opened to consumers a market basket that draws from the entire world's bounty and diversity.[4] Supermarkets are increasingly the vehicle for providing this diversity and consumers clearly support the trend with their buying power.

The growing roles of commercialization and globalization in connecting diversity of production at the farm level with diversity of consumption at the household level spawn new problems, however. In particular, increased commercialization requires that farmers learn how to cope with a type of risk that is of little concern to subsistence farmers: the risk of fluctuating prices. At the same time, specialization in crop production increases their risk from yield fluctuations. Mechanisms for coping with risk, including contractual arrangements with supermarkets, thus play a crucial role in understanding the commercialization of agriculture and the government's role in it. The interplay among price fluctuations, increasing reliance on international trade, specialization of farmers in production for the market in response to profitable new technology and continued failure of market-based mechanisms for risk management in rural areas accounts for much of the policy interest of governments in the process of rural diversification. A key task of a new food policy paradigm will be to improve the policy choices governments make as they respond to this interplay of forces with interventions into the diversification process, especially efforts to regulate the emergence and behaviour of supermarkets.

One intervention in nearly all countries is to make public investments that stimulate market development and efficiency. Efficient development of entire commodity systems, from input production and marketing through to downstream processing and consumption of the final product, requires the formation of extensive backward and forward linkages from the producer level. These linkages can be both technological (depending on engineering relationships and quality requirements, for example) and financial (depending on investment patterns from profits generated by commodity production and consumption patterns from the incomes earned in the sector). Many of these linkages exhibit economies of scale and can be developed to efficient levels only if the commodity is produced in a relatively cohesive spatial pattern. This process of market deepening is a natural result of regional specialization and one of the major forces that gradually but persistently produce such specialization.

Most countries want to speed up this gradual process, but have found that government investments alone are inadequate. Well-developed, low-cost marketing systems require sufficient supplies of the specific commodities being marketed to justify the full investments needed to capture any economies of scale to the system. Achieving this balance is a simultaneous process, which historically has meant the gradual evolution of both the supply and demand side of the market. The interesting question now is whether supermarkets are internalizing this coordination process and speeding the rate of specialization. If so, as specialized production grows in a region, the marketing system will expand to serve it in a coordinated (but closed to outside parties) way. The lower costs generated by specialization can confer very significant competitive advantages on regions that are both low-cost producers of a commodity and have an efficient marketing system with adequate volume to capture the economies of scale implicit in the forward and backward linkages.[5]

Regional specialization in a range of agricultural products would thus seem to be the answer to the problem of too much diversification at the farm level. Such specialization permits the cost economies of scale (and learning) to be captured, while still diversifying the country's agricultural output. A problem remains, however. Although the country may be well diversified, individual farmers and regions are not. Significant price instability, whether generated strictly in domestic markets or transmitted from international markets, would have substantial income-distribution consequences for the farmers and regions concerned – unless their output is sufficiently negatively correlated with prices that net revenue is stabilized by unstable prices. When large regions depend heavily on a single crop for their economic base, the vulnerability from specialization is similar to that at the national level when cultivation of a staple food crop is widespread. When rubber producers, coffee growers or maize farmers specialize in production, each can face problems of income stabilization in the face of unstable prices or yields.

The consequences for income distribution of crop specialization at the farm or regional level are straightforward. With domestic price stability, small farmers can specialize in single crops, and regional diversification can keep surpluses from developing. But this strategy depends on price stabilization. Otherwise individual farmers must diversify to spread risks from price fluctuations. Such diversification is likely to incur high costs because of forgone effects of 'learning by doing' and the scale economies inherent in marketing systems. Compared with national specialization in a single commodity, the macroeconomic consequences of regional vulnerability are not as great – unless all prices and yields move together. But the individual and regional problems should also receive the attention of policy makers. Especially in countries with diverse regional interests, appearing to ignore the economic plight of distressed regions can have devastating consequences for the political stability of the country as a whole.

How will the increasing dominance of supermarkets influence performance of the marketing system in coping with these issues? First, there will be concern for both the efficiency and equity of price formation, as more and more transactions are internalized by supermarket procurement officers. Such transactions are not open and transparent, and hence concern will grow over the shift in market power toward a few, large buyers and over the likely exclusion of suppliers from these arrangements. Second, however, and partially offsetting the first concern, supermarkets can also internalize consumers' desires for price stability and hence can manage procurement contracts with stability in mind. Finally, if supermarkets in developing countries are as competitive as in rich countries, fears about monopoly control and market power will turn out to be ill-founded. The market for the food consumer's dollar seems to be highly contestable, even when only a small handful of players are able to survive the cost competition.

Macroeconomic and growth issues

Most effects of supermarkets in developing countries are likely to play out at the firm and sector level, and macroeconomic effects will be modest. But they will not be trivial, especially as lower food costs translate into greater real purchasing power for consumers. The impact will then be felt through differential Engel elasticities – greater stimulus to manufactured goods and modern services; gradual retardation for staple foods, traditional clothing and basic housing. Managers of supermarkets themselves are fully aware of these trends, as a stroll down any aisle will demonstrate. By passing on lower costs, or improving food quality and convenience, supermarkets can actually speed up the structural transformation and the agricultural transformation that is part of it (Timmer, 1988).

There will also be significant efficiency effects. The mantra of supermarket procurement officers is to 'drive costs out of the food marketing system'. Although these 'costs' are also someone's income, especially farmers and traders in the traditional agricultural marketing chain, lowering food marketing costs not only allows lower consumer costs, with the effects noted above, but they also free up productive resources that can be used in more profitable activities. This is the process by which total factor productivity improves. This improvement, including in the food system, is the basic long-run source of economic growth (Timmer, 2002).

A final growth effect may be the most important in the long run: the technology spillover effects that result from the use by supermarket managers of imported information technology and modern management techniques honed in the fierce competition of Organisation for Economic Co-operation and Development (OECD) food markets. Most of this technology arrives as part of foreign direct investment (FDI), which has been the main vehicle of rapid penetration of supermarkets into developing countries (Reardon et al, 2003; Reardon and Timmer, 2007). It is often proprietary, and supermarket owners go to great lengths to keep it internal to the company. But like most technologies, the knowledge that these tools and techniques exist is the key to rapid emulation, as local managers trained by the first wave of foreign supermarkets leave to establish their own companies and consulting firms. Thus the spillovers from introducing modern information technologies and management techniques can occur fairly rapidly and have widespread effects across the entire economy, not just in food retailing.

Supermarkets will affect not only the efficiency of the food marketing chain, but also the distribution of benefits from the value added in the process. In general, it is very difficult to say whether these distributional changes will be positive or negative – that is, whether income distribution will improve or not.

There are two important offsetting effects. On the negative side, the evidence is clear that rapid supermarket penetration into traditional food marketing systems can quickly displace 'mom and pop' retail shops, traders in wet markets and small-scale wholesalers. In most of these cases, the people displaced earn relatively low incomes and will have to make significant adjustments to find new livelihoods. The distributional effect is likely to be negative and can be substantial if these small-scale food marketing firms are numerous and widely visible. Their imminent demise can also generate significant political resistance to the spread of supermarkets, an effect already being seen throughout Asia, but with historical antecedents in the US, Europe and Japan.

The impact of supermarket penetration on the farm sector is, of course, the big question. The Latin American experience suggests that small farmers rapidly lose access to supermarket supply chains and are thus cut off from the rapidly growing 'value added' component of the retail food basket. The suggestion is that these farmers risk falling further into poverty (Reardon and Berdegue, 2002). The African and Asian experience is not so clear, and research is well under way to understand the nature of the problem and any potential governmental responses. Keeping a significant number of small farmers in the supply chain of supermarkets is likely to be essential for poor countries to reap widespread social benefits from the rapid domination by supermarkets. The impact on the traditional food marketing sector will be small relative to this impact on small farmers.

What are these potential widespread social benefits that could have positive distributional effects? The extraordinary spread and speed of supermarket penetration suggests that consumers love them. It is hard to argue that low-income consumers benefit differentially, at least initially (see Asfaw, 2007), but lower real food costs across the board (corrected for quality, safety and convenience, all of which consumers value) clearly have an impact of greatest importance to the poor. Efforts to slow the penetration of supermarkets on behalf of small farmers and traditional agents in the food marketing chain need to keep this widespread consumer benefit in the calculus.

Lessons: Or, can the supermarket revolution be influenced?

There is great interest among policy makers in how to influence the behaviour of supermarkets in ways that serve the interests of important groups in society, especially small farmers and the owners of traditional, small-scale food wholesale and retail facilities. This volume presents many objectives and approaches, and several broader issues can also be put on the table. Two are especially important: (1) finding a way for food prices to 'internalize' the full environmental costs of production and marketing; and (2) finding a way for supermarkets to be part of the solution, rather than part of the problem, to the health problems generated by an 'affluent' diet and lifestyle. There are also concerns over the growing concentration in global food retailing and the potential market power that concentration implies. The evidence of fierce competition at the retail level, however, and the high contestability for consumer spending on food, has kept this issue in the background.

A number of generic policy recommendations on how to approach these issues are offered below. As with most policy advice, the most important start with the word 'don't'. But there are positive steps as well, although all the recommendations lack specificity to local situations. To address these, further research within a clear and policy-oriented framework will be needed. A first cut for this framework is presented at the end of the chapter.

Three things not to do

1   *Do no harm.* Especially with respect to the broader policy agenda, many of the suggestions can only be described as 'social engineering'. It is important to remember that the great political and economic experiments of the past two centuries, most of them done in the name of improving the welfare of the poor, have turned out to be catastrophic for the citizenry.
2   *Don't miss the forest for the trees.* It is important to keep our eye on the real objective of economic policy, which is to improve the welfare of as many people as possible, with special attention to the absolute poor. The objective is not to improve the lives of small farmers, unless that is a means to our end. In many circumstances, agriculture can be the engine of pro-poor growth, and small farmers can participate in that growth directly. But they might also participate indirectly – perhaps more effectively – by getting jobs in rural non-farm activities or by migrating to urban jobs.

3   *Don't throw out the baby with the bathwater.* The debate between the 'old' food policy and the 'new' food policy, especially over how to analyse and intervene to offset the damaging health consequences of the 'double burden of malnutrition', is sharper than it needs to be. The basic question is whether economic analysis of the food system remains useful in the context of the broader, interdisciplinary problems now manifested in that food system. Just as *Food Policy Analysis* (Timmer et al, 1983) pushed economists to extend the range of interests considered relevant to economic methodologies, so does the new food policy call for incorporating health and environmental dimensions, for example, into this analysis. Economics is not unique in having methodologies for addressing these broader dimensions of decisions by food producers, marketers and consumers. But no interventions to solve these problems will be sustainable unless the economics make sense.

Three things to do

1   *Do incorporate the 'new' food policy issues into the analysis.* It is much better to solve real and relevant problems than 'pretend' problems that have neat analytical solutions (despite the intellectual appeal of the latter kind of problem, especially to academics). But incorporating these issues into the analysis requires getting the facts straight. Emotions, prejudices and anecdotes run rampant in this arena, and development studies as a field is particularly prone to follow fads. There are immediate implications for how we do research and how we train scholars and policy analysts to work in this field. The research will require long-term panel data to carry out the sophisticated analyses that can disentangle subtle health and environmental effects from other, often more powerful, trends driven by short-run economic, ecological or weather phenomena. Training will require a breadth of interdisciplinary perspectives on top of deep disciplinary skills.

2   *Do design, lobby for and implement social safety nets.* In doing so, however, it is important to realize that social safety nets are most efficient in helping families cope with transition problems and short-run crises, not with chronic poverty. To solve the problem of chronic poverty, especially as experienced by small farmers, there is no alternative to economic growth, sustained over decades. There are opportunities to make this growth more 'pro-poor' than it might be if left to market forces, but getting the growth process going in the first place will be critical to reducing poverty.[6]

3   *Do try to make corporations more socially responsive.* But be careful what you wish for. R. J. Reynolds now advertises itself as a 'health company', with information on its website on how to keep children from smoking and how to help adults quit. According to Wal-Mart's advertising campaign, its 'associates' (workers, in any other company) believe in community action and actively volunteer their time for local causes. The multinational banks (including the World Bank) can afford to 'love us to death' with non-governmental organization (NGO) advisory panels and local participation in their development projects.

As an economist, I put a lot more of my trust in competition and market forces to bring about higher standards of living than I do in unregulated corporate efforts to do good works. In particular, individual corporate efforts to 'internalize' environmental, health and social (distributional) costs that are currently external to market prices bring no guarantee that they will actually improve overall social welfare. If societies genuinely want these costs internalized, the democratic process and consumer sovereignty offer mechanisms to do so.

Finally, it is useful to think through what an integrated food policy framework would look like, even roughly, in an effort to move the research agenda forward. Figure 3.2 illustrates the likely components. It is organized around the familiar vertical structure of the food system, with farmers at the bottom, passing their produce up through the marketing system – now divided into traditional markets and supermarkets – with consumers at the top of the chain.

The four major policy issues confronting the food system are arrayed in a diamond around this vertical structure: health and poverty concerns on the 'welfare' side and food security and environmental concerns on the 'efficiency' side of the diamond. From below, the basic forces affecting small farmers are the structural transformation and the role of agriculture in that process. From above, the basic forces affecting food consumers are behavioural changes in the context of increasing affluence and choices available.

Within this framework, it is possible to identify the key linkages from supermarkets through the rest of the food system that policy makers will want to understand if they are concerned about food security. At the micro- (or household) level, the issue is impact of supermarkets on poor consumers, especially the role of supermarkets in distribution of starchy staples. There has been remarkably little research on this aspect of the impact of supermarkets on food security (Asfaw, 2007).

At the macro-level, the issue will be the impact of supermarkets on staple food supplies, price stability and links to global grain markets. What role are supermarkets playing in these markets at the moment? Is there any way to use supermarkets (instead of parastatals, for example) to manage 'macro' food security by being the intermediary between a country's consumers and the world grain markets?

The last issue asks whether supermarkets are a major factor in the health epidemic seen in affluent countries and among the affluent in poor countries. Are processed foods, snack foods and fatty foods the cause of obesity, heart disease and diabetes? Are supermarkets to blame for our rapidly rising consumption of these foods?

Taken together, these questions form the core of a research agenda that is complementary to the current attention focusing on the impact of supermarkets on small farmers and research directed at finding policy and/or programme mechanisms to help them compete successfully within the global supply chain. In combination, consumer-oriented and producer-oriented research, linked as they are by the rapid emergence of supermarkets as the dominant players in the food marketing arena, fit comfortably within the expanded food policy paradigm discussed in this volume.

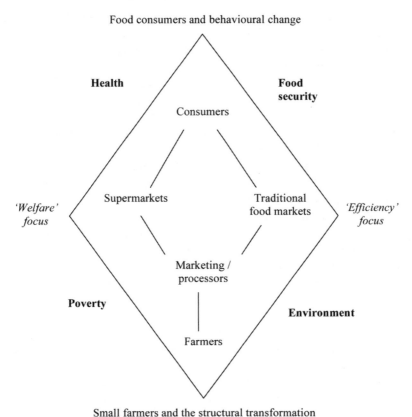

Figure 3.2 *An integration of the food policy paradigms*

Notes

1   The full citation is: 'Little else is requisite to carry a state to the highest degree of opulence from the lowest barbarism than peace, easy taxes, and tolerable administration of justice; all the rest being brought about by the natural course of things.' Lecture by Adam Smith in 1775, cited in Jones, 1981, p235. The perspective here also draws heavily on Jones' *Growth Recurring* (1988).

2   The phrase is used constantly by supermarket procurement officers as their primary objective in setting up relationships with suppliers. Obviously, not all transaction costs can be eliminated, but squeezing margins is an ongoing goal.

3   Three processes of agricultural change are closely related and often confused: the agricultural transformation, agricultural commercialization and agricultural diversification. See Timmer (1997) for a fuller explanation of how these three topics are connected. The discussion in this section draws on that paper.

4   See chapter 2 of *Food Policy Analysis* for further discussion of Bennett's Law (Timmer et al, 1983) and Chaudhri and Timmer (1985) for the greater diversity of diets as affluence permits.

5   This perspective on regional specialization has been generalized and formalized in Krugman's work on economic geography. See Krugman (1993).

6   See Besley and Cord (2006).

References

Asfaw, A. (2007) 'Supermarket purchases and the dietary patterns of households in Guatemala', IFPRI Discussion Paper 696, Washington, DC

Besley, T. and Cord, L. (2006) 'Delivering on the promise of pro-poor growth: Insights and lessons from country experiences', World Bank Publications, Washington, DC

Bhargava, A. (2008) 'Demand for food and nutrients in developing countries', in A. Bhargava (ed.) *Food, Economics and Health*, Oxford University Press, Oxford

Chaudhri, R. and Timmer, C. (1985) 'The impact of changing affluence on diets and demand patterns for agricultural commodities', Staff Working Paper no 785, World Bank, Washington, DC

Easterly, W. (2003) 'Inequality does cause underdevelopment?', Center for Global Development Working Paper no 1, Washington, DC

Eicher, C. and Staatz, J. (eds) (1998) *International Agricultural Development*, 3rd edn, Johns Hopkins University Press, Baltimore, MD

Goldberg, P. and Pavcnik, N. (2007) 'Distributional effects of globalization in developing countries', *Journal of Economic Literature*, vol XLV, no 1, pp39–82

Jones, E. (1981) *The European Miracle: Environments, Economics and Geopolitics in the History of Europe and Asia*, Cambridge University Press, Cambridge

Jones, E. (1988) *Growth Recurring: Economic Change in World History*, Clarendon Press, Oxford

Krugman, P. (1993) 'On the number and location of cities', *European Economic Review*, vol 37, nos 2–3, pp293–298

Maxwell, S. and Slater, R. (eds) (2003) 'Food policy old and new', Special double issue of *Development Policy Review*, vol 21, nos 5–6

McCraw, T. (2007) *Prophet of Innovation: Joseph Schumpeter and Creative Destruction*, Harvard Business School Press, Boston, MA

Pingali, P. and Rosegrant, M. (1995) 'Agricultural commercialization and diversification: Processes and policies', *Food Policy*, vol 20, no 3, pp171–185

Reardon, T. and Berdegue, J. (eds) (2002) 'Supermarkets and agrifood systems: Latin American challenges', Theme Issue of *Development Policy Review*, vol 20, no 4

Reardon, T. and Timmer, C. (2007) 'Transformation of markets for agricultural output in developing countries since 1950: How has thinking changed?', in R. E. Evenson and P. Pingali (eds), *Handbook of Agricultural Economics, 3: Agricultural Development: Farmers, Farm Production and Farm Markets*, Elsevier Press, Amsterdam, pp2808–2855

Reardon, T., Timmer, C., Barrett, C. and Berdegue, J. (2003) 'The rise of supermarkets in Africa, Asia, and Latin America', *American Journal of Agricultural Economics*, vol 85, no 5, pp1140–1146

Timmer, C. (1981) 'Is there "curvature" in the Slutsky matrix?', *Review of Economics and Statistics*, vol 62, no 3, pp395–402

Timmer, C. (1988) 'The agricultural transformation', in H. Chenery and T. Srinivasan (eds) *Handbook of Development Economics*, vol 1, North-Holland, Amsterdam, pp275–331

Timmer, C. (1997) 'Farmers and markets: the political economy of new paradigms', *American Journal of Agricultural Economics*, vol 79, no 2, pp621–627

Timmer, C. (2002) 'Agriculture and economic growth', in B. Gardner and G. Rausser (eds) *The Handbook of Agricultural Economics*, vol 2, North-Holland, Amsterdam, pp1487–1546

Timmer, C. (2005) 'Agriculture and pro-poor growth: An Asian perspective', Working Paper No. 63, Center for Global Development, Washington, DC

Timmer, C. (2007) 'A world without agriculture: The structural transformation in historical perspective', The Wendt Lecture, American Enterprise Institute, Washington, DC

Timmer, C., Falcon, W. and Pearson, S. (1983) *Food Policy Analysis*, Johns Hopkins University Press for the World Bank, Baltimore, MD

Chapter 4

The Food Processing Industry, Globalization and Developing Countries

John Wilkinson[1]

Introduction

The widespread adoption by developing countries of export-led growth strategies has drawn attention to the economic potential of their food processing sectors, especially in the light of the crisis facing many traditional primary commodity export markets. Food processing can be understood as post-harvest activities adding value to the agricultural product prior to marketing. In addition to the primary processing of food raw materials, it includes final food production and the preparation and packaging of fresh products, chiefly horticulture and fish. Non-traditional exports, particularly of these latter two categories of products, have become the focus of considerable debate. For some, they represent a strategic opportunity for developing countries not only for new sources of revenue but also for employment generation and the internalization of new knowledge and technology. Others would argue that they are the reflection of the outsourcing tendencies of global value chains dominated by transnationals taking advantage of low wages and less stringent environmental regulation, with little potential for internal upgrading.

At the same time, processed food exports from the developed countries have been accompanied and greatly superseded in the 1990s by foreign direct investment (FDI) into the food processing sectors of developed and developing countries alike. Here again, evaluation in the literature varies widely with regard to the impact of these investments. On the one hand, they are seen as a driving force behind the surge of non-traditional food exports from developing countries. Other analysts would focus on the negative and/or positive impacts of FDI on the recipients' domestic markets in relation to productivity, innovation and industry concentration. These discussions have been complemented by recent attention to the dietary implications for developing countries. FDI is seen as accelerating the adoption of a food regime based on animal protein and highly processed food, leading to new forms of malnutrition where poverty is now combined with obesity.

Transformations in the food processing sectors of developing countries, therefore, are increasingly seen as strategic whether analysed from the point of view of export earnings, domestic and global industry restructuring or dietary issues. In this chapter, we review a selection of the literature and secondary data sources on these themes. Our analysis begins with a brief discussion of trends in the food processing industries of the three regional blocs of the developed world (the North American Free Trade Area (NAFTA), the European Union (EU) and Japan) forming what has become known as the Triad. At the same time we show how, with rapid sustained economic growth in the large developing countries, globalization is now imposing itself on the Triad dynamic. This is followed by a discussion of the importance of non-traditional food processing exports by developing countries and the interpretations to which it has given rise. The internal transformations of the food processing sector of developing countries under the combined impact of imports and FDI are then considered. We conclude with a discussion of the heterogeneous dynamic of food processing in developing countries and the different possibilities for strengthening the participation of small and medium enterprises (SMEs).

Major trends in the food processing sector of the developed world Triad

The US

The US processing industry has traditionally had a strong international presence, with such firms as Heinz, Kellogg's and Campbell Soup becoming household names from the first half of the 20th century. Forty out of the world's top 50 food processors are from the US, although this is largely due to the size of its domestic market. The globalization of its leading firms and products accelerated, however, towards the end of the last century in response to the maturity of its domestic market, the liberalization of regulatory regimes in most countries and the potential for exploiting global brands. As an individual country, the US is by far the world's leading trader of processed foods and drinks, although it comes second now to the EU, viewed as a single market. Exports, which were at US$30 billion in 2000 and had stagnated and fallen off since the second half of the 1990s, had only increased to US$32.4 billion by 2005. Imports, on the other hand, which were already at US$37 billion in 2000, have increased considerably, reaching US$53.1 billion by 2005. Between 1997 and 2005 the US share of total food and drinks exports declined from 15 to 10 per cent.

Principal US exports are meat products, miscellaneous foods, grains, oils, fruit and vegetables. The strength of the dollar at the turn of the millennium had a negative impact on price-sensitive commodity exports but did not affect exports of branded products. Nor has the subsequent weakening of the dollar impeded the rapid growth of imports or the continued stagnation of exports. By order of importance the principal importers of US processed food and drinks in 2000 were Japan, Canada, Mexico, Thailand, South Korea and Hong Kong. By 2005, the effects of NAFTA were making themselves felt and Japan fell behind both Canada and Mexico; these are now followed in order of importance by the EU and China. Imports in 2000 came primarily from Canada, Mexico, Thailand, France and Italy. Here again China now occupies a leading position behind the NAFTA countries, followed by Indonesia and Brazil. Various tendencies with regard to trade in processed foods can be noted here: the importance of regional blocs, including the growing importance of the regional bloc formed by the southern cone countries of Latin America (Mercosur); the competitiveness of high-quality European products; the westernization of diets in the developed Asian economies, China and southeast Asia.

Since the mid-1990s, FDI by US food and drinks firms has become more important than exports, reaching US$33.9 billion in 1998, with sales by foreign affiliates totalling US$133.1 billion. By 2004, food and drinks manufacturing FDI had risen to US$53 billion, with a further US$14 billion in retail and services. Beverages, however, counted for half of FDI in 2003/04 and food FDI alone had tended to stagnate. In 1995, 75 per cent of FDI was located in three major trading zones – the EU, NAFTA and Mercosur. Ten years later, in 2004, this figure was over 80 per cent.

The relationship between exports and FDI has been the object of many studies, as has the impact of FDI on the host country in terms of rates of growth of gross domestic product (GDP), possible crowding effects vis-à-vis domestic investment, re-exports and the repatriation of capital (Gopinath, 2000). The importance of the Mercosur for US FDI attests to the latter's relevance to the analysis of food processing in developing countries, although here it is clear we are dealing with a regional dynamic that in strategic terms includes the Free Trade Area of the Americas (FTAA). In addition, 60 per cent of this FDI is concentrated in this region's leading country, Brazil, although new investments in any of the Mercosur countries must be considered in terms of their regional implications (Wilkinson, 1999). During the years 2001–2004, Asia and the Pacific increased its share of FDI more than Latin America, with the main beneficiaries being Japan, South Korea, China and the Philippines. Africa also increased its participation, although less notably and from a much lower baseline. FDI, therefore, would appear to be playing an important role in the food industries of developing countries, whether in term of processed food exports or the modernization of their domestic food industries.

The EU

In contrast with the US, the EU has a trade surplus in the food and drinks sector, exporting €59.2 billion as against imports of €52.7 billion in 2004. The US is by far the leading destination country (€10.4 billion), followed by Russia (€3.9 billion), Japan (€3.4 billion) and Switzerland (€2.6 billion). Exports to the top 12 developing countries in 2005 reached €4.8 billion, led by South Korea, China and Mexico. Imports into the EU are dominated by the Mercosur countries: Brazil with €7 billion and Argentina with €3.7 billion. The US is in third place, followed by China whose exports increased by 42 per cent in the years 2000–2005, with Turkey in fifth position. Indonesia and Thailand were in eighth and tenth positions respectively. The 2006 report of the Confederation of the Food and Drink Industries in the EU (CIAA) highlights the growth of Association of South-East Asian Nations (ASEAN) country exports to the EU, increasing by 66 per cent between 2000 and 2005, and notes also that the Andean countries registered the highest increase in exports in 2005. Andean exports to the US are also expected to increase significantly as a result of the bilateral agreements.

In spite of an overall positive trade balance in the EU, when broken down by sector there are three product categories with large deficits. Fish products are way ahead, with a deficit of nearly €10 billion in 2005, followed by animal and vegetable oils to the value of €6 billion and processed fruits and vegetables with a deficit of over €2.5 billion. Meat products and animal feed are in equilibrium. The existence of intrasectoral trade, however, means that there are imports in this and other categories. Nevertheless, the first three categories are the crucial ones since they coincide with the identified opportunities for developing country growth strategies, based on non-traditional food products. Fish products, as we will see, are particularly important here because in addition to the EU, Japan and increasingly the US are also heavily dependent on imports. China, for its part, is both a major exporter and importer of fish products. The EU food and drinks trade surplus has tended to shrink since 2000, with its share in global trade declining from 24 per cent to 20 per cent between 1997 and 2005.

Only four European firms were among the world's top 15 agri-food companies by value of sales in 2005 – Nestlé (2), Unilever (4), Diageo (13) and Danone (14) – as against 11 US firms. Nevertheless these four had combined sales outside Europe of €77 billion, with 410,000 employees. Nestlé claims to have operations in almost every country in the world and Unilever and Diageo are each present in 100 countries. Numerous other firms in the sectors of 'other food products' (Cadbury Schweppes, Associated British Foods, Tate & Lyle), drinks (Heineken, Interbrew, Allied Domecq, Carlsberg, Pernod Ricard) and dairy (Parmalat, Bongrain) have a strong international presence. FDI became very important in the 1980s when the weak dollar attracted a large volume of European food industry investment to the US market. With the formation of the single market in the early 1990s, intra-EU FDI became substantially more important. In the most recent period, it is the new members and candidate members and the countries of the former Soviet Union that have become a privileged focus of FDI strategies.

According to the 2006 CIAA report,[2] the food and drinks industry in Europe is the leading manufacturing sector in terms of production (13.6 per cent), employment (13 per cent) and value added (11.6 per cent). Small and medium enterprises represent 99.1 per cent of firms in the food and drinks industry, responsible for 47.8 per cent of the sector's turnover and 61.3 per cent of its employment. Large companies (250 employees and above), therefore, represented only 0.9 per cent of firms in the sector in 2005 but generated 52.2 per cent of the turnover, 53.8 per cent of value added and 38.7 per cent of employment. The food and drinks processing sector remains a key component of production and employment even in the most developed economies, with important employment and business opportunities in the SME sector. Nevertheless employment has shown a consistent downward trend in recent years, as a result more of productivity gains than of offshoring.

Japan

Although Japan has only one company in the world's top 15, it is, as we have seen above, a major trading partner of both the US and the EU.[3] Processed foods now account for two-thirds of Japan's food consumption, which is heavily dependent on imported final products from Japanese subsidiaries in neighbouring countries, in addition to a rapidly increasing percentage of western products. Imports now amount to 60 per cent of Japan's food consumption. Exports, on the other hand, are limited to a few specialities and are insignificant as a proportion of total exports (less than 1 per cent). The government aims to reduce import dependence to 45 per cent by 2010 but this has been increasing as consumers become more accustomed to western foods. In 2006, total food imports were US$48.4 billion, whereas exports were only US$2.3 billion. Japanese subsidiaries overseas have only 22 per cent of their total sales in the host market, as against 45 per cent in the case of European subsidiaries and 33 per cent for US firms overseas. The dominant strategy of Japanese food multinationals, therefore, is that of developmental imports: offshore production for the Japanese market.

The five leading exporter countries of processed food to Japan in 2006 were: the US (21.9 per cent), China (17 per cent), Australia (8.5 per cent), Canada (5.6 per cent) and Thailand (5.3 per cent). In 1970, Australia was the principal exporter with 17.6 per cent and China was responsible for only 2.9 per cent, positions that have now been substantially reversed. Seafood represents 28.2 per cent of imports, followed by meat 17.6 per cent, grains 12.6 per cent, vegetables 7.3 per cent and fruits 5.8 per cent – pointing to the strong influence of western dietary patterns.

Japanese FDI has fluctuated substantially since the 1970s, with Australia and east Asia declining relative to the US and the EU. In 2000, east Asia's share was 12.4 per cent, the US accounted for 28 per cent and the EU for 45.2 per cent. In part, this is to be explained by the severe restrictions on equity participation in east Asia. By contrast, this latter region has by far the largest number of Japanese affiliates (212), followed by North America with 86 and the EU with 65. In the east Asian region China has 85 affiliates, Hong Kong 31, Thailand 23 and Singapore 21. Although there is still very little incoming FDI, both exports and imports are positively correlated with FDI flows, although in recent years, the proportion of sales inside the host countries has increased significantly. The resource advantages of developing countries tend to be offset by stringent non-tariff measures in the case of imports of processed food, particularly relating to sanitary conditions. Japanese trade in processed food, as in other sectors, has a strong intrafirm profile and independent access to the Japanese market is notoriously difficult.

Processed food exports and developing countries

The food processing sector has recently received attention within the framework of export-led industrialization in developing countries. According to Athukorala and Sen (1998), the share of manufacturing exports in total world trade increased from 66 per cent to 81 per cent from 1970 to 1994, and the developing country share in manufacturing exports leapt from 6 per cent to 24 per cent. At the same time, the value of processed food in comparison with primary product exports (agriculture plus mining) increased from 26 per cent to 37 per cent. With notable exceptions (Bangladesh), middle- and high-income developing countries have performed better than low-income countries in this respect. Four developing countries – Argentina, Brazil, Malaysia and Thailand – and Taiwan were responsible for 40 per cent of total processed food exports by developing countries, but the evidence points to a continuous increase in the number of developing countries participating in such exports. Countries with a superior overall export record – Chile, Indonesia, Turkey, Tunisia, Guatemala, El Salvador and Sri Lanka – have also been most notable in the increase of processed food in their share of total non-manufactured exports.

Athukorala and Sen also note what they see as a remarkable shift in the commodity composition of processed food exports since the 1970s, with current export growth coming from products of less importance in the initial period. Processed fish, whose share in total processed food exports from developing countries in 1970 was 8.8 per cent, occupied 30.7 per cent of total exports in 1994. Preserved fruit has also continued to increase its share over time, although less spectacularly. For most developing countries these two products account for some 40 per cent of total processed food exports; for as many as 17 countries, processed fish alone has accounted for 40 per cent of total exports. On the other hand, traditional products, such as meat, sugar, animal feeds and vegetable oils, have either fluctuated wildly or declined in importance.

The authors go on to point out that there is no clear relation between income levels and export growth and that, furthermore, the final stages of food processing tend to be labour intensive, particularly canning and fish processing. The authors conclude, provisionally, that trade implications are positive when compared to primary products because processed foods have greater income and price elasticity demand trends. Spillover effects would seem to be superior to traditional manufacturing since food processing is less dependent on imports, involves a greater degree of learning through interaction with exporters, and has to respond to more demanding quality specifications.

A similarly optimistic assessment can be found in the UNCTAD report 'Opportunities for vertical diversification in the food processing sector in developing countries' (1997), which analyses the prospects for four groups of food products: horticulture, fish, meat and tropical beverages. Trade opportunities are identified in three major country blocs: higher-income developing countries such as southeast Asia as a result of market expansion; the economies of eastern Europe and the Russian Federation as a consequence of the transition effect; and developed and high-income developing countries through the impact of changing lifestyles. The principal problems of market access are identified as sanitary and quality demands, the control of marketing channels by the established transnationals and the reliability of supplies, which places great demands on logistics. Factors favourable to the development of a food processing export sector include geographical and cultural proximity and the existence of a large domestic market that allows for economies of scale and scope. Three areas for further analysis were identified for developing countries seeking to promote processed food exports in these four sectors: the new conditions for market access as a result of the World Trade Organization (WTO) regulatory framework; the types of corporate strategies appropriate for seizing market opportunities; and the ways to use the domestic market as a platform together with the promotion of adequate supporting structures.

These studies converge with the literature discussed earlier on the key role of new non-traditional products in the export dynamic of processed food products from developing countries. In line with the positive interpretation of the significance and opportunities for developing countries of processed food exports adopted by Athukorala and Sen (1998), much research has focused on the obstacles to access posed by considerably higher tariffs for processed products when compared to raw material exports (Rae and Josling, 2003), and more importantly by technical barriers consequent on greater rigour with regard to quality and food safety. Following on the decisions of the Uruguay Round, in the future protectionist measures will tend to be based increasingly on those barriers, which can be justified within the terms of the Sanitary and Phytosanitary (SPS) and Technical Barriers to Trade (TBT) agreements (Valdimarsson et al, 2003; TAFT-Iceland, 2003). An important workshop on food safety management in developing countries, organized in 2000 by the Food and Agriculture Organization of the United Nations (FAO) and the *Centre de cooperation internationale en recherche agronomique pour le développement* (CIRAD), explored these issues in detail, with examples from country experiences in Asia, Africa and Latin America (Hanak et al, 2000). The ability to negotiate the dispute settlement mechanisms of the WTO, therefore, becomes a key component of competitiveness in these non-traditional export markets (Athukorala et al, 2002).

In their conclusions to a recent contribution on this theme, Athukorala and Jayasuriya (2003) argue:

> *Unlike conventional trade policy reforms, SPS regulations cannot be implemented simply through legislative declaration. Their effective implementation in developing countries requires that binding commitments are made to provide adequate financial and technical assistance. In particular, there is a need for a global framework to support national capacity-building and improve the design of international standards.* (Athukorala and Jayasuriya, 2003, p17)

A less sanguine interpretation of the increasing importance of processed food exports from developing countries has been developed by environmentally oriented research, which would see this tendency as part of a broader movement either to export 'dirty' industries to, or deplete the resources of, countries with less rigorous legislative and regulatory controls. The fishing industry in particular has come under attack in this regard. A 2001 report of the United Nations Environment Programme (UNEP) has warned of the dangers of selling rights to fishing stocks under pressure for short-term export cash, particularly when the developed countries are subsidizing the fishing vessels.

Another critical line of research has been developed by the global commodity or value chain approaches, which would see this surge in processed exports as part of a broader outsourcing strategy of production chains dominated by transnational firms that are taking advantage of trade liberalization and regulatory flexibility to harness the cheaper labour and abundant resources of developing countries. The strategy is no longer limited to raw materials but includes basic processing activities, to the extent that value added is increasingly concentrated closer to the activities directly related to final demand in the consuming countries (Gereffi, 1995; Fitter and Kaplinsky, 2002).

The United Nations Conference on Trade and Development (UNCTAD) *Trade and Development Report* (2002) gives strong support to such an interpretation when it notes that, with the exception of a small number of newly industrializing east Asian economies, 'high technology' manufactured exports from developing countries often represent 'the low-skill assembly stages of international production chains organized by transnational corporations (TNCs)' – with the technology and skills embodied in imported parts and components (UNCTAD, 2002, pv). It further adds that while developed countries now 'have a lower share in world manufacturing exports, they have actually increased their share in world manufacturing value added over this period' (UNCTAD, 2002). In line also with the global value chain analysis, the report argues that 'perhaps a more decisive influence on product dynamism has been the strategy of TNCs' and that 'trade based on specialization within such networks is estimated to account for up to 30 per cent of world exports' (UNCTAD, 2002, pvi).

Particularly interesting examples of this line of analysis are the studies being carried out by the Institute of Development Studies (IDS) of the horticulture commodity chain, which, after fish products, is the most dynamic food processing export sector for developing countries. Building on Gereffi's distinction between supply- and demand-driven commodity or value chains, these studies analyse the outsourcing strategies of British retail, particularly in relation to African supply bases (Kenya and Zimbabwe), and note the increasing tendency to locate the preparation and packaging stages in the supplier countries. The quality and logistical demands of this pattern of outsourcing provoke greater concentration within the agricultural sector of the producer countries, marginalizing small farmers and consolidating large farms based on casual, predominantly female labour (Barrientos et al, 2003). In addition, the competitive advantage of producer countries is constantly undermined as production bases can be quickly mobilized in other countries with similar material and human resources (Dolan et al, 1999). The impact of the global change in agri-food grades and standards on developing country (and particularly small producer) access to domestic and export markets has also been extensively studied by Reardon and colleagues, who focus on the differential strategies of transnationals, medium to large domestic farms and small firms and farms in relation to grades and standards (Reardon et al, 1999).

FDI, imports and food processing in developing countries

Studies on the transnationalization of the British food industry are notable for their focus on the way retail is constructing new global value chains (Marsden, 2000; Humphrey and Schmitz, 2001). Studies on European food FDI initially focused on US-to-EU flows (Green, 1989) and more recently intra-European investments related to the consolidation of the single market. As we have seen, studies of Japanese FDI focus on its role in creating first regional, and now global, supply bases for its own domestic market. Research on US FDI, on the other hand (probably reflecting its leading role in global food industry FDI), has tended to focus on the impact of the transnationalization of food processing firms on the host countries in terms of a series of variables such as domestic capital formation, growth rates, efficiency, repatriation of profits, exports and imports, employment, changes in diet and consumption patterns (Gopinath, 2000). At the same time, important research has been carried out on the impact of food processing FDI on the innovation dynamic of developing countries (Christensen et al, 1996).

In their overview of US FDI, Bolling et al (1999) note that in earlier decades investments were mainly directed at primary processing facilities for both export and the domestic market, particularly in the grains and oils sectors. In the 1990s, on the other hand, these declined relative to investments directed to final food demand in the domestic markets of the host countries, most notably in beverages, where FDI more than tripled, and 'other processed foods', where investments more than doubled.

Given the importance of NAFTA, which accelerated the creation of a regional North American food industry, US investments in the Mexican food industry are of particular note, increasing from US$210 million in 1987 to US$6.1 billion between 2000 and 2004 and generating US$6.1 billion in sales in 2003. Investments were stimulated by changes in FDI law, which permitted a majority foreign capital share for firms in Mexico. (Similar laws have been enacted in many other countries to attract FDI, Brazil being a notable case in Latin America's Southern Cone). According to Bolling et al (1999) these investments have been fundamentally directed to the Mexican domestic market and are heavily concentrated on convenience and highly processed foods, especially snacks, beverages, instant coffee, mayonnaise and breakfast cereals. In many cases the ingredients for these products (vegetable oils, dried milk, flavourings) are imported from the US on the basis of intrafirm transactions. These investments therefore accelerate trends toward the adoption of highly industrialized global diets, which have come under considerable attack in recent years for their negative impact on health (indices of obesity and juvenile diabetes), and may be leading to a substitution of domestic raw materials and ingredients through imports. Sustained economic growth, higher incomes and population trends are seen to be the principal stimulus for these FDI flows. It should be noted that Mexican firms are also beginning to establish affiliates in the US market, with investment increasing from zero in 1990 to US$1 billion in 2000, largely stimulated by the demand for Hispanic foods.

Bolling et al (1998) identify important US FDI flows into Brazil and Argentina in the 1990s. In the cases of these Mercosur countries, however, investments to control key exporting sectors (oils, grains, coffee, fruit juice) are considerably more important. Canada, Mexico, Argentina and Brazil make up 90 per cent of all US FDI in the Americas. The authors see FDI as complementary to US exports and argue that 'FDI seems to have beneficial effects on the economy of the host country', pointing to improvements in food production infrastructure, lower costs of domestic production vis-à-vis imports, job creation, gains in efficiency by local firms faced with competition from the multinationals, products and process innovations, contribution to GDP and foreign currency earnings. Studies conducted within the Mercosur countries have given greater importance to the increase in industry concentration, which has occurred in the wake of the acceleration of FDI (Belik and Rocha dos Santos, 2002; Guezan, 1999; Gutman, 1999), together with the regional character of recent investments, which have led to a greater number of greenfield initiatives (Wilkinson, 1999). Other authors have emphasized the importance of the new institutional environment (deregulation, liberalization), which tends to make greater transnationalization compatible with increased competition, price stability and an acceleration of new product, process and logistical innovations (Farina and Viegas, 2003).

In his review of the FDI literature, Gopinath (2000) identifies three schools of thought. The first, based on Bhagwati's 'immiserizing growth' thesis, would stress the lock-in consequences of tariff-induced FDI in small countries where cheap labour becomes combined with the increasing import of capital-intensive components and equipment. In these cases, Athukorala and Sen (1998) have argued that food processing would be one of the lesser affected sectors to the extent that it has a lower dependence on imports. This, however, may only be the case for processed food exports. We have seen above the combination of exports and FDI in the case of Mexico, and this tendency is well documented in the literature and in line with the complementarity thesis identified by much econometric analysis of trade and FDI flows (Marchant et al, 1999). The second approach, associated with Markusen, identifies a trade-off between increased technical efficiency and increased monopoly power, where the existence of competition between transnationals would be sufficient for the establishment of welfare benefits in terms of prices. Here the size of the domestic market and/or the nature of the institutional framework would seem to be crucial. And finally, the third approach, that of new growth theory, would give pride of place to the institutional framework, seeing positive benefits to the extent that export promotion policies, deregulation and liberalization characterize the domestic policy regime. As Farina and Viegas (2003) point out, however, it is impossible to know whether, in a changed institutional climate, domestic firms would not have developed the same competitive strategies. In this case, the entry of FDI, especially in the form of acquisitions, may have had the effect of 'crowding out' potential domestic investment.

Be that as it may, there has been a virtual universal adjustment of domestic regimes in developing countries to create an attractive environment for FDI. As we noticed earlier, US food processing FDI was responsible for four times more than its food processing exports. FDI is heavily concentrated in the EU, NAFTA and the Mercosur regions. In 2004, however, some US$5 billion in food FDI was invested in developing countries. In the case of small countries, low levels of investment may have a decisive impact and to the extent that it is accompanied by imports, it will also involve a displacement of domestic raw material supplies.

Most discussion of FDI and trade flows focuses on generic variables (growth rates, technical efficiency, concentration, etc.), but our earlier discussion of the major developed blocs made it clear that the bulk of investments were related to highly processed food and drinks, especially snacks, convenience foods and soft drinks. This second generation of FDI, therefore, is no longer focused so much on primary processing, which involved a shift from local grains and oils to wheat-, corn- and soy-based products, but on final foods for the domestic market, deepening the pressures for substantial changes in diet. In developing countries, where these investments are more solidly implanted, in addition to the emergence of new diet-associated diseases, where malnutrition predominates, the perverse combination of malnutrition and obesity is now in evidence. Whether this should be associated with the 'westernization' of dietary practices or the structural consequences of urbanization and changes in family and work practices (especially the opportunity cost of female domestic labour) is an area of debate – particularly as this process begins to affect Asian countries where convenience foods would seem to be adapting to local tastes (Pingali, 2007).

European and US exports to developing countries, however, are not restricted to the 'highly processed products' category but involve also the heavily subsidized commodities of the post-war urban industrial diet, involving a shift from a vegetable-based to an animal protein-based diet which is, at the same time, subject to more rapid and more individualized methods of food preparation and consumption. Milk powder and white meats, particularly poultry, are the two anchor products of this diet – both heavily subsidized exports from the two major trading blocs. World trade in the case of poultry has been based largely on developing country demand and is a sector that can be put into place rapidly in developing country economies. Nevertheless, 75 per cent of this trade remains controlled by the EU and the US, with only Brazil, Thailand and China able to compete with EU and US subsidies. With a more level playing field, a number of developing countries would have greater opportunities for the development of a domestic poultry industry. Similar considerations could be made in the case of the world trade in dried milk. However, as we have seen above, both the US and the EU have been losing global market share in agri-food since the mid-1990s.

The food processing sector and the domestic markets of developing countries

Since the 1980 UNCTAD study 'The food processing sector in developing countries: Some recent trends in the transfer and development of technology', the macroeconomic and regulatory climate has undergone dramatic changes. Import substitution has given way everywhere to export-oriented growth strategies and most developing countries have now adjusted to the post-Uruguay Round WTO framework. Increased participation of developing countries in the share of global manufactured exports is seen to vindicate and point the way for future development (UNIDO, 1995). The dominant orthodox view focuses primarily on the need for macroeconomic and regulatory adjustment, which is seen to be the basic strategy for integrating developing countries into global economic growth under the coordination of transnationals in the form of FDI or external subcontracting. According to this scenario, sectoral measures would be focused on policies to promote SMEs, combined with initiatives directed at poverty alleviation. Other analysts have pointed to the selective character of FDI, particularly in the case of the least developed countries where de-industrialization (Africa) or a de-intensification of industrialization (Latin America) have been identified in this period; they have stressed the need for more pro-active industrial strategies at the domestic level. On the one hand, the case of South Korea and other Asian countries, where FDI was less important, and on the other, the inspiration of the 'third Italy' for the development of cluster strategies would provide the principal support for this approach.

A further fundamental change has been the shift to the formation of regional blocs that has accompanied globalization and that has also become a feature of the developing world. In Latin America, Mexico became integrated into NAFTA, while the Southern Cone developed the Mercosur, complementing earlier blocs such as the Andean Pact, with similar initiatives in Central America and the Caribbean. In Asia, Japan had long been the focus of regional integration, but more recently the ASEAN countries have established a free trade area with China, principally as a strategy for benefiting from FDI flows. After many setbacks in Africa, a new regional dynamic is emerging in the Southern African Development Community (SADC), with South Africa as its hub. These tendencies to regionalization are now reinforced by the global strategies of the TNCs, which, as we have seen in the case of the Mercosur, increasingly adopt regional considerations when defining their investment options.

At the same time, the heterogeneity of the developing world has increased markedly in this period. Alongside newly industrializing Asian countries, this category also includes the 49 least developed countries (LDCs), which have 10 per cent of the world's population but contribute only 0.4 per cent to global manufacturing value added (MVA). On the other hand, the impact of liberalization and deregulation on the giant but low-income economies of China and India has radically transformed trade and investment flows in the developing world.

In increasingly open economies, where an export orientation is combined with rapid rates of transnationalization, it is more difficult to distinguish specifically domestic tendencies. On the one hand, exports have less of an enclave character and, on the other, the domestic dynamic is being radically transformed by the presence of transnational firms. Nevertheless, for the food processing industry of developing countries, trends in population growth, rural–urban migration and income levels and their distribution (particularly the size of the middle class) are seen to be crucial differentiating variables.

As much as 97 per cent of the increase in world population from 2000 to 2050 will occur in today's developing countries with the developed countries' share falling from 20 per cent of the total in 2000 to only 13 per cent in 2050.[4] Africa will undergo the most rapid growth, increasing from 784 million in 2000 to nearly 1.8 billion in 2050. India will overtake China as the most populous country, rising from just over 1 billion to more than 1.5 billion between 2000 and 2050. Although rural–rural migration continues in certain countries of Latin America and Africa, rural–urban migration is the most significant and relevant trend from the point of view of the food processing industry. On a world scale, half of urban growth is still based on rural–urban migration. Globally, urban areas are currently growing at a rate of 2.2 per cent as against 0.4 per cent for rural areas, and rates of urbanization in developing countries are much higher than in developed countries. Generational differences between developed and developing countries also have an important bearing on food consumption, both in terms of niche markets (baby foods) and broader changes in the composition of food demand. A study in Japan has shown that the younger generation there consumes more beef and beer whereas older people eat more rice, vegetables and fruits. In general, developing country populations are marked by a higher percentage of youth than developed countries, which are older on average. This has clear consequences for food consumption in developing countries.

As an indication of the impact of urbanization on food consumption and the processing industry in the context of rapid and sustained economic growth, we can take the example of China.[5] A Chinese household survey showed that urban per capita consumption of meat was 40 per cent higher than in rural areas, fish consumption three times higher, and egg and poultry production two and a half times higher. On the other hand, urban grain consumption was three times lower than in rural areas. Higher-income urban residents in the same survey were seen to consume more of most foods on a per capita basis than low-income urban residents, but particularly so in the case of milk, fruits, beer, poultry, meat, fish, eggs and vegetables. Food processing output value in China, increasingly of final food products, is said to have grown 14 per cent per year during the 1980s and 1990s, while 15 per cent of urban food spending is now done away from home. As a reflection of these tendencies, since 2004 China has become a net importer of agri-food products.

If we contrast this scenario with that of the LDCs, we find that the food processing sector is, if anything, more strategic for economic development, but here we are dealing fundamentally with primary processing, combined in certain countries with processed food exports (Bangladesh in fisheries, and some African countries in fruit and vegetables and also fisheries), while the final foods sector is still heavily dominated by artisan cooking and street sales.[6] These countries recall the PL480[7] 'aid-to-trade' analyses showing a heavy reliance on imports of rice and grains, which undercut local production and break down dynamic relations between urban consumption and agricultural production. The LDCs receive only 2.2 per cent of FDI flows to developing countries (concentrated in mining and energy) and rely more on aid, international loans and the actions of non-governmental organizations. Their manufacturing sectors represent less than 10 per cent of GDP, but the food and drinks industries make up some 35 per cent of total MVA, rising to 50 per cent in many of these countries and over 80 per cent in 17 of the 37 African LDCs. In Asian LDCs, on the other hand, while the share of food manufacturing in MVA was lower, the import content of food manufacturing industries was near to zero.

Even in the highly polarized cases presented briefly above, it is clear that behind the growing heterogeneity of the developing world a number of similar patterns, challenges and opportunities emerge. In varying degrees, internal deregulation and external liberalization of markets, together with legislative reform favourable to foreign investments, is now a general feature of all developing countries, including the LDCs. This has led to an intensification of foreign trade and investment, with priority being given to the development of processed food exporting capacity based on intensive use of human and labour resources, which is combined with efforts to attract FDI as a substitute for domestic capital and know-how. This has led to an intensification of the transnationalization of the food processing sector, either directly in the domestic market or as part of a global value chain. Even in LDCs, where transnationalization is much less in evidence, the latter remains a key strategic objective of local governments and regional blocs. While this overall strategy has brought important results in food manufacturing growth rates, to the extent that more and more countries become involved, there is a greater risk of producing the 'fallacy of composition'[8] to which the UNIDO *Trade and Development Report* (UNCTAD, 2002) draws attention.

This combination of liberalization and transnationalization has a range of implications, which vary from country to country but apply to the developing world as a whole. There tends to be a weakening/elimination of the dualism between the domestic market for urban consumption and export/import sectors, which accelerates with the consolidation of an urban middle class. Brazil is a world leader in poultry exports, but 70 per cent of total production is consumed domestically and per capita consumption has increased from 2kg per capita in 1970 to 36kg per capita in 2007. Similarly 30 per cent of soy meal and 70 per cent of soy oil are consumed domestically. The same tendencies are now at work in other products, including fruit juices and coffee. While, however, the dualism of domestic market versus exports is becoming attenuated, a dualism based on income differentiation persists in the prevalence of the informal sector, which even in a country such as Brazil registers levels of 30–50 per cent in meats, milk and soft drinks, and which now comes under heavy attack in the efforts to implement new minimum standards of quality.

Liberalization and transnationalization has increased the competitive structure of the food industry, leading to more rapid product and process innovations, and has accelerated the homogenization of food consumption patterns. At the same time, it has been accompanied by a significant de-nationalization of leading domestic food firms, increasing concentration and the elimination of many medium-sized firms, as market segments become dominated by at most three leading brands. While there is a clear trend towards a protein diet based on fish, meat and dairy products, together with a sharp increase in prepared fruits and vegetables, the integration of local products would seem to depend on their adaptability to the pressures for convenience foods.

As we mentioned at the beginning of this review, the food and drinks industry is no longer the hegemonic player in the overall food system, which has now been assumed by large-scale retail (Wilkinson, 2002). In addition, large-scale retail is as heavily involved in FDI as the food processing sector itself, and depending on the level of development of the food system in each country, it tends to reproduce the strategies that it has developed in the industrialized countries. The rise in supermarket brands is particularly notable in some Latin American countries.

A common characteristic of the global food system is the adoption of ever-more-stringent quality criteria to which developing countries are increasingly being forced to adhere. To the extent that developing country governments do not impose international-level standards, private standards are being implemented by the leading players in retail and food processing (Reardon and Farina, 2000). Hazard analysis critical control point (HACCP), international quality standards such as ISOs, traceability systems and private quality labels are becoming entry tickets to international markets and increasingly the reference for quality in the domestic market of developing countries. This has led to an acceleration of obligational contract relations with raw material suppliers, involving detailed specification of production and delivery conditions. There is much evidence to suggest that this is leading to a considerable degree of exclusion of small farms and firms, an issue to which we will now turn in our final section.

Opportunities for the participation of small firms

There is a sharp contrast between the literature that focuses on the combined exclusionary effects of scale and quality for SMEs, and that which sees SMEs as the main opportunity for employment creation given that strategies of 'downsizing' in large firms have produced the phenomenon of growth without employment. In addition to studies demonstrating the numerical importance of SMEs in the economies of the industrialized world (OECD, 2000), research has focused on the role of SMEs in innovation (Lundvall and Borrás, 1997; Cooke and Willis, 1999), in local development and the promotion of industrial districts on the cluster model (UNIDO, 2001b) and as components of global value chains (UNIDO, 2001c). Inspired by the work of Piore and Sabel (1984), the most emphatic view sees SMEs as the basis for a new model of economic development.

Small and medium enterprises continue to be an important component of the food processing sectors in developed countries, both numerically and in terms of MVA, particularly in the case of Europe and Japan. At the same time, the trends to concentration are evident as, increasingly, different product segments on the retail shelves are reduced to three or four leading brands. The reduction in farm numbers and the successive increase in minimum viable cultivation sizes are also evident in the industrialized countries, and in this case we are faced with an absolute reduction of the agricultural economically active population (EAP) to levels of 5 per cent and under, which poses an enormous challenge to developing countries, where the EAP in agriculture can range from 20 per cent to as much as 50 per cent of the total EAP.

A detailed consideration of the dynamic of SMEs in the food processing sector of developing countries would have to take into account sharp differences according to the agri-food product involved, as regards both processing and raw material supplies. In this sense, the rice-based activities of many Asian countries have a totally different dynamic than the agriculture that can be readily mechanized in much of Latin America, parts of Africa and indeed other parts of Asia. Many traditional processing activities, especially in grains, oil and sugar, have reached levels of scale and automation that offer virtually no space for SMEs. Recent developments in the dairy sector, so critical to the small-scale farming sector of many developing countries, would seem to be advancing in this same direction (Dirven, 1999). On the other hand, the surge in demand for prepared fruits and vegetables, affecting developing countries in all continents, is based on labour-intensive on- and off-farm activities, where the possibilities for participation by SMEs would appear to be significantly higher.

The opportunities and challenges facing SMEs in food processing and related activities derive, therefore, from the impact of the new competitive environment on scale, minimum quality and the perspectives for non-traditional products. At the same time a distinction should be made between traditional SME activities/actors and what we might call 'new entrants', which may be SMEs in new activities or new actors in traditional activities. This relates to a point made earlier when discussing the LDCs, that size as such is not necessarily the barrier to competitiveness, which is increasingly located in the greater learning intensity of all activities in a demand-driven market environment. From a strategic point of view, where possible policies should be directed at increasing the capacity of traditional actors through retraining and the provision of services, rather than focusing on new, often 'urban' entrants with professional experience. Six areas can be identified as potential spaces for strengthening the presence of SMEs, each of which should therefore be the subject of appropriate policy initiatives.

1   *Traditional activities, which still escape the effects of scale and new quality demands.* We have seen that the leading food processing firms involved in FDI tend to concentrate their activities on highly processed products and convenience foods. Lack of adequate physical infrastructure ('weatherproof' roads, transport, cold storage, household refrigerators), especially in the case of highly perishable products, can favour local supplies, where short distance and time between production and consumption can make traditional supplies compatible with basic criteria of hygiene and sanitation. Low-density communities can also make villages and small towns less attractive for modern distribution systems. Extreme income inequalities and the prevalence of high levels of absolute poverty ensure the persistence of informal food processing activities, which demand appropriate quality control support measures that are neither punitive nor unrealistic in their requirements. This may point to opportunities for SMEs and local firms in less sophisticated food processing activities or in earlier phases of the production chain, either for the leading food firms or for retail.

2   *Innovative firms supplying niche markets, services and technologies.* These may be urban, often emerging from university or local government 'incubator' policies that specifically promote SMEs. Artisan bakeries and confectioneries are also emerging to compensate in part the marginalization of traditional SMEs in this sector (Scarlatto, 1999). They may also emerge in rural areas through the introduction of new crops and livestock. Very often these are individual initiatives and have become the object of generic policies to promote 'entrepreneurialism'.

3   *SMEs as suppliers for large firms.* Outsourcing by food processing firms and large-scale retail are opening opportunities for small firms. As in manufacturing more generally, there is a tendency for the food processing industry to externalize many activities: design, market studies, transport, distribution and even manufacturing, as the leading firms concentrate on brand promotion and competitive strategy. Opportunities are therefore opened up for the emergence of SMEs, often in a long-term relationship with the leading firm, although there are also pressures for concentration within these activities. It remains to be seen to what extent this sector is also suffering the effects of scale economies.

4   *Obligational subcontracting between SMEs and large firms.* New quality demands, preoccupations with health hazards, supply management and

efficient consumer response techniques are all leading to a marked increase in formal contracts with raw material suppliers, based on a clear specification of production and delivery conditions. In many cases, this has been seen to be associated with a shift from small farms to medium or large farms run along business lines. However, adequate resource support (information technology, credit, technical assistance, market information services), combined with organizational initiatives for the promotion of associativism and cooperatives, have shown themselves to be effective in integrating small farmers into these more demanding coordination networks.

5   *SMEs organized in autonomous networks.* These have been traditionally associated with the industrial districts of Italy and the notion of clusters. Most examples in developing countries seem to be associated with light industries based on local raw materials but for non-food markets such as footwear, clothing and woodwork. In Latin America, the notion is being associated with the development of territorial strategies for local and regional development based on SMEs. In Brazil, the notion of clusters of small rural agroindustries is currently being promoted as a solution to the problems of scale for SMEs, which are located primarily in the areas of management practices, market access and technical support.

6   *The promotion of traditional SMEs associated with special quality or artisan products.* In many cases the most realistic short-term strategy for small farms has been to engage in organizational innovations (new forms of associativism) and technological modernization to accompany the more stringent conditions of agroindustry. Medium- and long-term prospects, however, would seem to be on firmer ground to the extent that they are based on strategies for establishing the market value of process and product characteristics typical to family farming and its traditions. The model here would be the European strategy of products with denominated origins, which has now received some support in the framework of the WTO; in the case of developing countries this would include features such as indigenous products, products associated with sustainability (particularly non-wood forest products), products based on social criteria (fair trade, products from agrarian reform areas), together with products that represent the preservation of biodiversity and traditional cultures. There are indications that the modern retail sector may prove to be an important catalyst for these markets.

Conclusions

This chapter's critical review of the literature on current transformations in the food processing industry has highlighted the industry's strategic role for developing countries in the context of globalization. The increasing importance of processed food exports when compared with primary commodities confirms this sector as a key component of export growth strategies for developing countries. At the same time, it was noted that these opportunities are currently heavily concentrated on a limited number of product categories, notably fish and seafood, fruit and vegetables. Researchers are divided on the 'upgrading' potential of these export sectors, with some authors emphasizing the positive effects of creating employment and knowledge, and others identifying the trend with the 'spurious' advantages of cheap labour and lax environmental legislation. The phenomenon of FDI in the food processing sectors of developing countries, while partially identified with the promotion of these non-traditional exports, is seen as transforming the competitive environment of the food industry in developing countries. The focus here has been on the trade-off between increased productivity and innovation on the one hand and a sharp rise in concentration ratios on the other.

In addition to the impact of FDI on industry structure, attention has been drawn increasingly to the role of the food processing sector in the transition to animal protein and highly processed food diets in developing countries. Of particular concern here has been the growing combination in developing countries of poverty, malnutrition and obesity. On the other hand, the food processing industry has become a key source of employment opportunities and the evidence from Europe and Japan suggests that this will continue to be the case along the course of development. Ten years ago, discussions on food processing in developing countries were largely restricted to the employment benefits agroindustry could provide in the rural areas. This continues to be a key concern. Today, however, the food processing sector is seen, in addition, to be playing a strategic role in the overall growth strategies of developing countries and within which SMEs occupy a privileged position.

Notes

1   This chapter is based on a paper prepared for the FAO Scientific Workshop 'Globalization, urbanization and the food systems of developing countries: Assessing the impacts on poverty, food and nutrition security', 8–10 October 2003, FAO, Rome.
2   www.ciaa.be/uk/library/statistics, last accessed September 2004.
3   This section draws on Rural Industries Research and Development Corporation (2003), chapters 2, 3 and 4.
4   The data in this section are taken from ILO (2002).
5   This paragraph draws on Gale (2002).
6   This paragraph draws on UNIDO (2001a).
7   Public Law 480 was enacted in the US in 1954 and is still in force. Its provisions cover long-term credit for commodity imports, donations for humanitarian reasons and grants for the promotion of economic development in developing countries. It has been widely criticized as leading to food import dependence, the adoption of US-style food consumption patterns and the undermining of local agriculture.
8   This expression refers to the danger of generalizing specific solutions. In the case of non-traditional food exports as a solution for developing countries this may be the case for individual countries, but to the extent that it becomes generalized it may lead to overproduction and a collapse in prices, to the detriment of all.

References

Athukorala, P.-C. and Jayasuriya, S. (2003) 'Food safety issues. Trade and WTO rules: A developing country perspective', *The World Economy*, vol 26, no 9, pp1395–1416

Athukorala, P.-C. and Sen, K. (1998) 'Processed food exports from developing countries: Patterns and determinants', mimeo

Athukorala, P.-C., Jayasurita, S., Mehta, R. and Nidhiprabha, B. (2002) 'International food safety regulation and processed food exports from developing countries', paper presented at the conference on International Food Safety Regulation and Processed Food Exports from Developing Countries, October 2002, Bangkok, Thailand

Barrientos, S., Dolan, C. and Tallontire, A. (2003) 'A gendered value chain approach to codes of conduct in African horticulture', *World Development*, vol 31, no 9, pp1511–1526

Belik, W. and Rocha dos Santos, R. (2002) 'Regional market strategies of supermarkets and food processors in the extended Mercosur', *Development Policy Review*, vol 20, issue 4, pp515–528

Bolling, C., Elizalde, J. C. and Handy, C. (1999) 'US firms invest in Mexico's processed food industry', *Food Review*, vol 22, no 2

Bolling, C., Neff, S. and Handy, C. (1998) *US Foreign Direct Investment in the Western Hemisphere Processed Food Industry*, ERS/USDA, Washington, DC

Christensen, J. L., Rama, R. and von Tunzelman, N. (1996) *Study on Innovation in the European Food Products and Beverages Industry*, European Commission Report, Brussels

Cooke, P. and Willis, D. (1999) 'Small firms, social capital and the enhancement of business performance through innovation programmes', *Small Business Economics*, vol 13, no 3, pp219–234

Dirven, M. (1999) *Local Industry Survival Difficulties in a Globalising World – Illustrated Examples from the Chilean Milk Industry*, ECLAC, Santiago

Dolan, C., Humphrey, J. and Harris-Pascal, C. (1999) 'Horticulture commodity chains: The impact of the UK market on the African fresh vegetable industry', Working Paper 96, IDS, Sussex

Farina, E. M. M. Q. and dos Santos Viegas, C. A. (2003) 'Multinational firms in the Brazilian food industry', in Rana, R. (ed) *Multinational Agribusinesses*, Haworth Press, Binghampton, New York, pp283–322

Fitter, R. and Kaplinsky, R. (2001) 'Can agricultural "commodity" be de-commodified, and if so who is to gain?', Institute of Development Studies Discussion Paper 380, IDS, Sussex

Gale, F. (ed) (2002) 'China's food and agriculture: issues for the 21st century', Agricultural Information Bulletin No. 775, ERS/USDA, Washington, DC

Gereffi, G. (1995) 'Global production systems and third world development' in B. Stallings (ed.) *Global Change, Regional Response*, Cambridge University Press, Cambridge

Gopinath, M. (2000) 'Foreign Direct Investment in food and agricultural sectors', Department of Agricultural and Resource Economics, Oregan State University, 9pp

Green R. (1989) 'Les déterminants de la restructuration des grands groupes agro-alimentaires', *Economie et Societé*, no 7

Guezan, G. (1999) *Trajetorias y Demandas Tecnológicas de las Cadenas Agroindustriales en el Mercosur Ampliado – Hortalizas: Tomate Fresco y Procesado*, Proyecto Global, PROCISUR, Montevideo

Gutman, G. (1999) *Trayectorias y Demandas Tecnológicas de las Cadenas Agroindustriales en el Mercsur Ampliado – Oleaginosas: Soja y Girasol*, Proyecto Global, PROCISUR, Montevideo

Hanak, E., Boutrif, E., Fabre, P. and Pineiro, M. (2000) 'Food safety management in developing countries', Centre de coopération internationale en Recherche Agronomique pour le Développement (CIRAD), Montpellier, France

Humphrey, J. and Schmitz, H. (2001) 'Governance in global value chains', *Institute of Development Studies Bulletin*, vol 32, no 3, pp19–23

International Labour Organization (ILO) (2002) 'An inclusive society for an ageing population: the employment and social protection challenge', Second World Assembly on Ageing, Madrid, available online at www.ilo.org/public/english/employment/ skills/older last accessed June 2004

Lundvall, B-Å and Borrás, S. (1997) *The Learning Economy – Implications for Innovation Policy*, TSER/EU, DG XII, European Commission, Brussels

Marchant, M., Saghaian, S. and Vickner, S. (1999) 'Trade and foreign direct investment management strategies for US processing firms', *The International Food and Agribusiness Management Review*, vol 2, no 2, pp131–143

Marsden, T., Flynn, A. and Harrison, M. (2000), *Consuming Interests: The Social Provision of Food*, UCL Press, London

OECD (2000) *The OECD Small and Medium Enterprise Outlook*, Organisation for Economic Co-operation and Development, Paris

Pingali, P. (2007) 'Westernization of Asian diets and the transformation of food systems: Implications for research and policy', *Food Policy*, vol 32, no 3, pp281–298

Piore, M. and Sabel, C. (1984) *The Second Divide*, Basic Books, New York

Rae, A. and Josling, T. (2003) 'Processed food trade and developing countries: Protection and trade liberalisation', *Food Policy*, no 28, pp147–166

Reardon, T. and Farina, E. M. M. Q. (2000) 'The rise of private food, quality and safety standards: Illustrations from Brazil', Paper presented at the International Food and Agribusiness Association's 2001 Food and Agribusiness Symposium, Sydney

Reardon, T., Codron, J.-M., Busch, L., Bingen, J. and Harris, C. (1999) 'Global change in agrifood grades and standards: Agribusiness strategic responses in developing countries, *International Food and Agribusiness Management Review*, vol 2, no 3, pp421–435

Rural Industries Research and Development Corporation (2003) *Japan Food Market Study*, chapters 2, 3 and 4, available online at www.rirdc.gov.au/reports/GLC/02-icu.pdf, last accessed September 2004

Scarlatto, G. (1999) *Trayectoria y demandas tecnológicas de las cadenas agroindustriales en el Mercosur ampliado – cereales: trigo, maiz y arroz*, serie, Documentos No. 2, Proyecto Global, PROCISUR, Montevideo

UNCTAD (1980) *The Food Processing Sector in Developing Countries. Some Recent Trends in the Transfer and Development of Technology*, UNCTAD, Geneva

UNCTAD (1997) *Opportunities for Vertical Diversification in the Food Processing Sector in Developing Countries*, UNCTAD, Geneva

UNCTAD (2002) *Trade and Development Report*, UNCTAD, Geneva

United Nations Industrial Development Organization (UNIDO) (2001a) *Building Productive Capacity for Poverty Alleviation in Least Developed Countries (LDCs)*, UNIDO, Vienna

UNIDO (1995) 'Report of the global forum on industry: Perspectives for 2000 and beyond', 16–18 October, New Delhi, India

UNIDO (2001b) *The Development of Clusters and Networks of SMEs*, UNIDO, Vienna

UNIDO (2001c) *Integrating SMEs in Global Value Chains*, UNIDO, Vienna

Valdimarsson, G., Comier, R. and Ababouch, L. (2003) 'Fish safety and quality in times of globalization', *Proceedings of the Trans Atlantic Fisheries Technology Conference*, 11–14 June 2003, Reykjavik, Iceland

Wilkinson, J. (1999) *Demandas tecnológicas, competitividad e innovación en el sistema agroalimentario del Mercosur ampliado*, Proyecto Global, PROCISUR, Montevideo

Wilkinson, J. (2002) 'The final foods industry and the changing face of the global agrofood system: Up against a new technology paradigm and a new demand profile', *Sociologia Ruralis*, vol 42, pp329–347

Chapter 5

Forces of Change Affecting African Food Markets: Implications for Public Policy

Thomas. S. Jayne[1]

Introduction

Global agricultural conditions are changing rapidly. World trade protocols appear to be breaking down. Investments by huge agribusiness and food retail chains in developing countries have raised fears that smallholder farmers are becoming increasingly marginalized. Local and international political economy problems are changing the nature of access to markets and technology. One might easily conclude that farmers in developing countries face an inevitable onslaught which neither they nor the governments representing them can influence, let alone use to their advantage. However, the risk of conceiving global food systems as irreversible exogenous shocks on developing countries is to neglect the role of public policy in moderating and shaping the way international forces affect local agricultural sectors.

The premise of this paper is that, far from being an irreversible tsunami, global supply chains and supermarkets are one of many forces affecting the evolution of food systems in developing countries. The evolution of food systems and their distributional effects are also being fundamentally driven by local demographic, institutional and technical change, as well as by history. These local forces, along with domestic policy and investment decisions, determine the scope for international agribusiness investment. The implication of viewing food system modernization in this framework is that there is no deterministic 'future of smallholder farms' or food systems. The future of food systems, and smallholder farmers' roles in them, will be influenced greatly by the local enabling environment, which is fundamentally determined by the nature of government policies and investments. This chapter illustrates these points based on the case of eastern and southern Africa.

We identify seven locally driven issues fundamentally affecting outcomes and distributional effects within food systems in the eastern and southern Africa region:

1   how historical and political factors impede the pace of transformation of the food grain systems of the region;
2   why historical underinvestment in public goods has created political pressure for state interventions, which reinforce a continued underprovision of market-facilitating public goods investments;
3   how land allocation and demographic change is affecting the feasibility of a broad-based agricultural growth strategy based on staple food grains;
4   shifts over time in crop production patterns toward higher-valued activities;
5   the implications of both eastern and southern Africa's transition toward structural grain deficits;
6   why the performance of traditional food marketing systems will, for the foreseeable future, remain a much more important determinant of rural and urban welfare in the region than global retail chains; and
7   how public policy and investment decisions will crucially affect the ability of smallholder farmers to meaningfully engage in agricultural markets and grow their way out of poverty.

Understanding these local dynamics will allow governments in the region to better anticipate the forces of change affecting their food systems, the future challenges that they raise and the scope for policy and public investments to achieve national development and poverty reduction objectives.

Historical and political factors shaping food marketing and trade policy options

There is a certain degree of path dependence in the evolution of food systems.[2] Understanding the likely evolution of food systems in eastern and southern Africa requires an understanding of the historical role of food policy in the post-independence 'social contract' between states and their constituents, and the increasing politicization of food policy.

The 'social contract'

White maize is the strategic political crop in eastern and southern Africa. Maize became the cornerstone of an implicit and sometimes explicit 'social contract' that the post-independence governments made with the African majority to redress the neglect of smallholder agriculture during the former colonial period (Jayne and Jones, 1997). The controlled marketing systems inherited by the new governments at independence were viewed as the ideal vehicle to implement these objectives. The benefits of market controls designed to produce rents for European farmers during the colonial period instilled the belief after independence that the same system could simply be scaled-up to promote the welfare of millions of smallholders.[3] The social contract also incorporated the belief that governments were responsible for ensuring cheap food for the urban population, a view that remains widely held even today. While this approach achieved varying levels of success in promoting smallholder and consumer welfare, a common result in all cases was an unsustainable drain on the treasury. The cost of supporting smallholder production – through input subsidies, credit programmes with low repayment rates, commodity pricing policies that subsidized transport costs for smallholders in remote areas and the export of surpluses at a loss – contributed to fiscal crises and in some cases, macroeconomic instability. Under increasing budget pressure, international lenders gained leverage over domestic agricultural policy starting in the 1980s, which culminated in structural adjustment programmes in each country (Jayne and Jones, 1997). While structural adjustment is commonly understood to have been exogenously imposed on African governments, some sort of adjustment was unavoidable due to the fiscal crises that the social contract policies imposed on governments.[4] Continuation of the status quo policies was not an option in countries such as Malawi, Tanzania, Zambia, Zimbabwe and Kenya, and in some of these countries, controlled marketing systems had already broken down prior to 'market liberalization' as governments could no longer offer supplies to buyers at controlled prices, and parallel markets swiftly became the preferred channel for most farmers and consumers.

However, the rise of multiparty electoral processes in the 1990s (which largely coincided with structural adjustment) has made it difficult for governments in these countries to withdraw from the 'social contract' policies. Elections can be won or lost through policy tools to reward some farmers with higher prices and reward others with lower prices and this is hardly unique to developing countries (Bates, 1981; Bates and Krueger, 1993; van de Walle, 2001; Bratton and Mattes, 2003; Sahley et al, 2005). Because maize purchasing and fertilizer and seed distribution programmes are obvious demonstrations of support for millions of smallholders, a retreat from the social contract policies exposes leaders to attack from opposition candidates (Sahley et al, 2005).[5] For this reason, it remains difficult for leaders to publicly embrace food market and trade liberalization, even as they accepted structural adjustment loans under conditionality agreements from international donors to open their markets to private investment and unhindered external trade. Such a stance becomes even more politically difficult when relatively rich nations heavily subsidize their own farmers and institute various programmes designed to penetrate local food markets (Jayne et al, 2002).[6]

The resurrection of social contract policies and their impact on the evolution of grain trading systems

Starting in the early 2000s, two factors have relieved governments' budget constraints and made it easier for them to reinstate some elements of the social contract policies: the transition of the World Bank and other donors from conditionality agreements to direct budget support and debt forgiveness under the HIPC programme. Both of these recent developments have provided additional discretionary funds to scale up the former social contract policies. Not coincidentally, by the early 2000s, grain marketing boards have once again become the dominant players in the market in Kenya, Malawi, Zambia and Zimbabwe (Jayne et al, 2002).[7] Large-scale input subsidy programmes have been reinstated in Malawi, Tanzania, Zambia and Ethiopia and have been recently advocated by the governments of Kenya and Mozambique.

Regardless of policy makers' views about how these state-led grain marketing and input subsidy policies affect their national development objectives, micro-level evidence across all countries in the region (for which data is available) indicates that benefits are highly concentrated, being captured primarily by relatively large farms that produce most of the marketed grain surplus (Jayne et al, 2006). In most countries of the region, the political elite are often engaged in large-scale farming and/or commodity trading (Toye, 1992). For this group, the profitability of large-scale grain production is ensured by income transfers implemented through government marketing board price supports and input subsidy programmes.

The historical roots of current beliefs about the role of government in food markets, and the market institutions that have evolved to reinforce them have clear implications for the possibility of robust modernization of food systems in the region. Because foreign direct investment in food value chains is generally impeded where government retains a high degree of discretionary power over price levels and trade flows, the transition to more open grain trading systems, hospitable to investment by global agribusiness firms, is likely to continue to be slow in most of eastern and southern Africa. Global retail chains enjoy only a very small share of consumer food expenditure even in western areas of Africa. The large international grain trading firms have made relatively few inroads into the strategic grain sector and retain a negligible market share in assembly, wholesaling and storage operations in the region.[8] While this appears to be a deliberate outcome of government operations in the region and represents an example of how states can and do use their power to limit the influence of international forces in the evolution of food systems, we will argue later that in this particular case governments have so far missed opportunities to promote smallholder farmers' and consumers' interests by constructively involving foreign investors in carefully circumscribed ways in their grain systems.

Historical underinvestment in public goods, leading to high marketing costs and price instability

Research has shown that high transaction costs and risks in developing countries inhibit the development of markets. However, the level of transaction costs and risks in any marketing system are a function of lagged public policy and investment choices.

A considerable part of the food price instability problem in the region is due to the high cost of transportation, which widens the price wedge between import and export parity prices throughout the region. During the 2005/06 food crisis in Zambia, the cost of importing grain from Johannesburg to Lusaka was US$135 per ton, which added about 35 per cent to the landed cost of grain in Lusaka. Public investments in transportation and communication infrastructure could significantly shrink the amplitude of price fluctuation between import and export parity.

Policy choices also affect transaction costs and risks. A common practice at border crossings is that trucks carrying maize are unloaded on one side of the border, carried across in bicycles one bag at a time and re-loaded onto trucks on the other side of the border – all to evade import duties. While contributing to the 0.5km cross-border bicycle trade, these duties raise transaction costs for long-distance traders, which are ultimately borne by farmers and/or consumers. Chapoto and Jayne (2007) show that the unconditional and conditional variances of maize wholesale prices in the region are greatest in countries that maintain discretionary tariffs, frequently ban imports and exports, and use other policy tools to restrict trade.

Other public goods investments that can promote the performance of domestic and regional trade are those that raise smallholder productivity, such as improved seed generation and other types of crop science, innovative extension programmes to improve farmers' management practices and the generation and dissemination of accurate crop production forecasts and price information. Unfortunately, in many countries, crop forecasts are notoriously unreliable. Zambia, for example, has lost its ability to estimate maize production from the large-scale farming sector. This injects a great deal of guesswork into the food balance sheets that the government uses to estimate import requirements and/or export potential, which in turn increases the probability of undershooting or overshooting and the price unpredictability associated with it.

These points illustrate that while transaction costs and risks are a ubiquitous feature of food systems, their magnitude is neither fixed nor exogenous. Both the costs and risks faced by actors in the food systems and the rate of investment in food value chains are affected by the nature of public investments and policy choices.

If public goods investments are so important in improving the performance of strategically important food markets, then why have relatively small portions of government budgets been devoted to these investments? For example, during the past five years, 10 per cent or less of the Government of Zambia's budget allocation to the agricultural sector has been devoted to crop science, extension services, irrigation and other activities with clear public goods characteristics. Over 60 per cent of the Government's agricultural budget has consistently been spent on fertilizer subsidies and maize price stabilization operations (Govereh et al, 2006). In a recent article entitled 'Under-investing in public goods: Evidence, causes and consequences for agricultural development, equity and the environment', Lopez (2003) uses a political economy framework to show that unequal competition in the political lobby market causes the allocation of public expenditures to be biased in favour of private goods (such as input subsidies) that can be captured by politically influential groups and against the provision of public goods that would improve the overall performance of markets and thus have broad-based benefits for the poor. Other scholars describe the political landscape in much of Africa as being dominated by neo-patrimonial relationships, in which government commodity distribution is an important tool by which leaders maintain loyalty and patronage among rural leaders and their constituents (van de Walle, 2001; Bird et al, 2003; Pletcher, 2000). Even without resorting to neo-patrimonial arguments, it is clear that the next election provides incentives for policy makers' budget allocation decisions to be influenced by what can be achieved in the short run. Unfortunately, the pay-offs from many public goods investments accumulate over the long run. The high food marketing costs and risks currently observed in most of eastern and southern Africa reflect low investment in market-facilitating public goods in prior decades. The challenge is how to provide incentives to influence the public budget allocation process in favour of greater expenditures on public goods that can generate a stream of large social benefits over time but which might not begin to manifest until after the next election.

Demographic change, farm structure and the concentration of agricultural surpluses

Relative to other areas of the developing world, Africa has been seen as a continent of abundant land and scarce labour. While this was true decades ago, access to land has now become a critical problem in much of southern and eastern Africa. One of the most important but underemphasized trends in African agriculture is a steady decline in land-to-person ratios. Between 1960 and 2000, according to FAO data, the amount of arable land under cultivation (including permanent crops) has risen marginally, but the population of households engaged in agriculture has tripled. This has caused a steady decline in the ratio of arable land to agricultural population (Table 5.1). In Kenya, Ethiopia and Zambia, for example, this ratio is about half as large as it was in the 1960s.

Moreover, the distribution of available land is highly inequitable. It is well known that the colonial legacy has left much of Africa with severe land inequalities between smallholder, large-scale and state farms. Redressing inequalities between these sectors is likely to be an important element of an effective rural poverty

Table 5.1 *Ratio of cultivated land to agricultural population (10-year means)*

	1960–1969	1970–1979	1980–1989	1990–1999
Ethiopia	0.508	0.450	0.363	0.252
Kenya	0.459	0.350	0.280	0.229
Mozambique	0.389	0.367	0.298	0.249
Rwanda	0.215	0.211	0.197	0.161
Zambia	1.367	1.073	0.896	0.779
Zimbabwe	0.726	0.664	0.583	0.525

Note: Land to person ratio = (land cultivated to annual and permanent crops) / (population in agriculture).
Source: FAOSTAT (2007)

reduction strategy in countries such as Zimbabwe and Kenya. Perhaps less well acknowledged is that there are major disparities in land distribution within the small farm sector itself. Landholdings within the smallholder farm sector in eastern and southern Africa are often characterized as small but relatively 'unimodal', equitably distributed and situated within a 'bimodal' distribution of land between large-scale and small-scale farming sectors. By contrast, Jayne et al (2003) found consistently large disparities in land distribution within the small farm sector using national household survey data in Ethiopia, Kenya, Malawi, Mozambique, Rwanda and Zambia (Table 5.2). While average landholdings in the small farm sector range from between 2.5 and 3.0 hectares in Kenya and Zambia to around 1 hectare in Rwanda, Malawi and Ethiopia, these mean farm size values mask great variation.

After ranking all farms by per capita land size and dividing them into four equal quartiles, households in the highest per capita land quartile controlled between 5 to 15 times more land than households in the lowest quartile (Table 5.2). In Kenya, for example, mean farm sizes for the top and bottom land quartiles were 5.91 and 0.58 hectares, respectively, including rented land. The range of computed Gini coefficients of rural household land per capita (0.50–0.56) from these surveys show land disparities within the smallholder sectors of these countries that are comparable to or higher than those estimated for much of Asia during the 1960s and 1970s (Haggblade and Hazell, 1988). If the large-scale and/or state farming sectors in our case countries were included, the inequality of landholdings would rise even further.

As a result of rising land pressures and inequitable distribution, semi-landlessness is becoming a major problem. In each country, at least 25 per cent of the small-scale farm households in these nationwide surveys in every country are approaching landlessness, controlling less than 0.11 hectares per capita. In Ethiopia and Rwanda, the bottom land quartile controlled less than 0.02 and 0.03 hectares per capita (Jayne et al, 2003). In Malawi, where land pressures are particularly severe, 70 per cent of all smallholder households possess less than 1 hectare of land and only 9 per cent of smallholders in a nationally representative survey in 1997/98 sold maize (Chirwa, 2006). While many farms in Asia were similarly very small at the time of their green revolutions, many of them enjoyed irrigation, higher returns to fertilizer that could be achieved with water control and more than one cropping season. These factors substantially improved Asian land productivity and partially relieved the severity of the land constraint among small farms. By contrast, the vast majority of African farms are dependent on rain and one crop season per year.

The data in Table 5.2 show a strong relationship between access to land, agricultural commercialization and household income in southern and eastern Africa. Revenues from crop sales among households in the top land quartile are 4–8 times higher than households in the bottom land quartile. Total per capita incomes of households in the top land quartile are generally double those in the bottom quartile. With the exception of Kenya, for households in the bottom landholding quartile, even a doubling of crop income – resulting for example from the use of new technology or additional purchased inputs – would have little impact on households' absolute level of income or absolute poverty rates. These results are especially troublesome in light of evidence that 'pro-poor' agricultural growth is strongly associated with equitable asset distribution (Ravallion and Datt, 2002). To date, surprisingly little attention has been devoted to considering the implications of African land inequality for poverty reduction strategies.

There are alternative explanations, none mutually exclusive, for the observed variation in farm size, especially in countries that are apparently land-abundant. Some of these are related to differences in entrepreneurialism and effort between households, colonial policies, social capital and kinship relationships and the time in which the household or its clan settled in the area. Jayne et al (2007) tested all of these factors in smallholder landholding size models for Zambia. Their results indicate that each of these explanations has some explanatory power and contributes to the explained variation in landholding size. Landholding size is positively related to variables signifying productive farming potential and wealth, which is most likely correlated with initiative and effort. However, they also find that blood/kinship relations between the male and female head-of-household's family and the local chief at time of the family's settlement are positively and significantly associated with current landholding size. In many areas, respondents stated that unallocated land is unavailable, particularly in areas close to urban areas and district towns and along major highways. These findings reinforce the view that over time rural populations tend to cluster in areas where agro-ecological conditions and access to markets and services are best, leading to a highly nucleated pattern of settlement. Land shortages in favourable areas are exacerbated by the apparent rise in patronage-based land allocations to political elites (Munshifwa, 2002; Stambulis, 2002; the *Standard*, 2004). At the same time, there are still large tracts of unallocated land in the more remote parts of the region, but the economic value of this land is limited because of a lack of access to markets and services. Thus, in densely settled areas where population growth and subdivisions have created land constraints, rural poverty has become closely associated with inadequate access to land.

Agricultural productivity growth is centrally important for improving welfare levels in both rural and urban areas. Currently, land pressures and low productivity are combining to generate a 'push' form of rural-to-urban labour migration

Table 5.2 *Mean farm household characteristics by farm landholding size per capita, based on nationwide smallholder household surveys*

Country (survey year)	Household attribute	Total sample mean	Means for household quartiles ranked by per capita farm size			
			1	2	3	4
Kenya 2003/04	Landholding size (ha)	2.46	0.58	1.25	2.12	5.91
	Gross value of crop sales (2000 US$)	653.2	199.8	514.2	749.1	1151.8
	Total household income/capita (2000 US$)	540.6	239.1	394.3	561.8	967.2
	Off-farm income share (%)	34.7	42.1	36.3	30.9	29.5
Ethiopia 1996	Landholding size (ha)	1.17	0.20	0.67	1.15	2.58
	Gross value of crop sales (1996 US$)	145.8	33.7	82.3	120.6	265.2
	Total household income/capita (1996 US$)	71.6	53.1	52.1	88.3	91.0
	Off-farm income share (%)	8.1	13.7	9.0	5.4	4.6
Rwanda 2001	Landholding size (ha)	0.94	0.32	0.63	1.00	1.82
	Gross value of crop sales (1991 US$)	68.0	34.1	45.1	72.4	169.3
	Total household income/capita (1991 US$)	78.7	54.5	59.4	79.3	139.7
	Off-farm income share (%)	24.8	34.5	24.4	22.2	18.2
Mozam-bique 2002	Landholding size (ha)	1.66	0.53	1.20	1.76	3.14
	Gross value of crop sales (2002 US$)	26.7	9.4	20.9	27.3	49.1
	Total household income/capita (2002 US$)	59.5	45.7	46.4	55.4	90.6
	Off-farm income share (%)	27.3	34.3	26.6	24.9	23.5
Zambia 2000	Landholding size (ha)	2.72	0.71	1.60	2.75	5.81
	Gross value of crop sales (2000 US$)	68.6	32.7	59.2	83.6	113.4
	Total household income/capita (2000 US$)	113.9	87.5	107.0	115.6	159.2
	Off-farm income share (%)	31.2	31.4	39.7	27.0	25.0

Notes: Samples include only 'agricultural households' defined as households growing some crops or raising animals during the survey year. Total household income includes income from crop production (including value of retained food crops), sales of livestock and livestock products, income from wage employment, income from own-business activities and remittance income. All numbers are weighted except Kenya. Income figures include gross income derived from crop production on rented land. For Rwanda: data are not available for land loaned out; only data on rented land are included.

Source: compiled from data in Jayne et al, 2003 and collected by the authors

(rather than the 'pull' effect that would occur if rising demand for labour in cities and towns attracted people out of rural areas). The pushing of labour from rural to urban areas associated with land constraints and low farm productivity have contributed to the swelling of Africa's cities, the rise of huge slums and their social problems. The view that many rural areas have effectively reached the limits of their carrying capacity is consistent with Tiffen's (2003) observation that rural population growth is less than 1 per cent per year in most of Africa while urban population continues to grow rapidly.

A relatively small share of African incomes is in the form of cash, which is required to fuel demand for off-farm activities and generate growth linkages. Even considering that food for home consumption accounts for the majority of agricultural income in the region, many households are still net buyers of major staple crops such as maize (Table 5.3). Widespread productivity increases in food crops would therefore release labour and capital from food crop produc-tion – for large numbers of households, especially the poorest – making them available for the production of higher value crops and non-farm activities such as manufacturing and services. This is likely to not only increase the food consumption of poor households but, as incomes grow, should also eventually increase the portion of household disposable cash income that is spent on non-staple foods and consumer goods, as per Engel's law. Finally, history suggests the necessity of productivity increases in agriculture to achieve broad-based improvements in living standards. Except in the cases of a handful of city-states, there are virtually no examples of mass poverty reduction since 1700 that did not start with sharp rises in employment and self-employment income due to higher productivity in small family farms (Johnston and Kilby, 1975; Mellor, 1976; Lipton, 2005).

Concentration of marketed agricultural surplus

Following from the wide disparities found in farm size and assets across small-holder farms (as well as other factors), the pattern of production and marketing output is similarly highly concentrated (Table 5.3). In each of the countries for which survey data were available, small-scale farm households fall into one of the following four categories with respect to grain markets:

1   *Sellers of staple grains.* Roughly 20–35 per cent of the smallholder farms sell grain in a given year. Of course this figure will rise in good harvest years and fall in a drought year. However, there are two sub-groups within this category: (1) a very small group of relatively large and well-equipped smallholder farmers with 5–10 hectares of land, usually in the most favourable agro-ecological areas (about 1–4 per cent of the total rural farm population); and (2) a much larger group of smallholder farms (20–30 per cent of the total rural farm population) selling much smaller quantities of grain, between 0.1 and 1 tons per farm. These households, especially the largest farmers, clearly benefit from higher grain prices and have tended to be the main advocates of continued state intervention by marketing boards to support food prices.

2   *Buyers of staple grains.* These rural households generally make up 50–70 per cent of the rural population, higher in drought years and lower in good production years. These households are generally poorer and have smaller farm sizes and asset holdings than the median rural household. They are directly hurt by higher mean grain prices.

3   *Households buying and selling grain within the same year.* In all of the nationwide surveys, relatively few households both buy and sell maize.[9] Only about 5–15 per cent of the rural population buys and sells the main staple commodity in the same year. They comprise both relatively large farms that sell grain and buy back small quantities of processed meal, as well as relatively poor households that make distress sales of grain after harvest only to buy back larger later in the season. However, this latter subgroup typically comprises less than 10 per cent of the rural farm population.

4   *Households neither buying nor selling maize.* These households make up a small proportion of the rural population. However, in parts of northern Zambia and Mozambique, cassava is the main staple. Because of this, a sizeable fraction of the rural population at the national level is autarkic with respect to grain.

Staple grain sales can be highly concentrated among a relatively small number of large and commercialized farmers in the smallholder sector. Table 5.4 disaggregates smallholder households included in the nationwide surveys into three groups: (1) the largest smallholder sellers of maize, who accounted for 50 per cent

Table 5.3 *Distribution of small-scale farm population according to their position in the staple grain market, selected countries*

Household category with respect to main staple grain	Zambia (maize)	Mozambique (maize)	Kenya (maize)	Malawi (maize)	Ethiopia (maize and teff)
	% of rural farm population				
Sellers only:	19	13	18	5	13
top 50% of total sales*	2	2	2	1	2
bottom 50% of total sales**	17	11	16	4	11
Buyers only	33	51	55	na	60
Buy and sell (net buyers)	3	12***	7	na	13
Buy and sell (net sellers)	6		12	na	12
Neither buy nor sell	39	24	8	na	2
	100%	100%	100%	100%	100%

Notes: * After ranking all households by quantity sold, this row shows the percentage of households in the smallholder sector accounting for the first 50 per cent of total maize sale;

** Percentage of households accounting for the other 50 per cent of total maize sales.

*** The survey in Mozambique was not able to ascertain quantities of maize purchased and therefore whether these households are net buyers or net sellers is unknown.

Source: Reproduced from Jayne et al, 2006

of the marketed maize output; (2) the remaining households that sold maize during the year, who accounted for the other 50 per cent of the marketed output; and (3) those households that sold no maize during the 12-month marketing season.

As shown in Table 5.4, 1 or 2 per cent of the farms account for 50 per cent of the overall marketed maize surplus from the smallholder sector. These farm households appear to enjoy substantially higher welfare levels, in terms of asset holdings, crop income and non-farm income, than the rest of the rural population. The relatively 'elite' smallholder farmers had roughly 2–6 times as much land and productive assets as the non-selling households, 6–9 times more gross revenue from the sale of all crops and 5–7 times as much total household income.

When a broader set of staples are aggregated together (maize, cassava, sweet potato, millet and sorghum) more than 55 per cent of the sales of staples are still accounted for by 10 per cent of the farmers with the largest sales. This concentration of surplus production and marketing by a relatively few farmers is one of the most important points to be borne in mind when thinking about the effects of policy instruments designed to alter the mean level of food prices.

These findings hold several important policy implications. First, cereal producer price supports or stabilization policies that involve altering mean price levels over time (as they usually do) can have unanticipated income distributional effects that run counter to stated poverty alleviation goals. To the extent that the poor are net purchasers of staples such as maize, wheat and rice, they are directly hurt by policies that raise prices of these commodities.[10] Forms of price stabilization that do not raise the average price of food would most likely avoid these adverse distributional effects and would also help to promote diversification toward higher-valued crops by maize purchasing households (Fafchamps, 1992; Jayne, 1994).

A second implication of the substantial differentiation within the smallholder farm sector is that the benefits of food price stabilization policies that raise mean prices are likely to be extremely concentrated. This was a major outcome of the price support and stabilization policies pursued during the pre-liberalization period, which contributed to peasant differentiation and the subsequent differences in smallholders' abilities to participate in markets during the post-liberalization era. For example, using data on maize purchases by Zimbabwe's Grain Marketing Board (GMB) between 1985/86 and 1991/92, Jayne and Rukuni (1993) found that 1 per cent of the nation's smallholder households accounted for 44 per cent of all the maize delivered to the Board by smallholder farmers. These 9,000 households sold an average of 28.2 tons per year to the Board. Another 80,000 households (the next 9 per cent of smallholder households in terms of maize sales) sold an average of 3.4 tons, accounting for 26 per cent of the smallholder sector's maize deliveries to the GMB. Of the remaining 800,000 smallholder households in the country, only 24,000 sold any maize and those that did so accounted for 4 per cent of the total maize delivered to the GMB by the smallholder sector. Of course, the total smallholder sector of 900,000 households received only 54 per cent of the government

Table 5.4 *Characteristics of smallholder farmers in Zambia (2000/01),*
Mozambique (2002/03), Kenya (1999/00), and Malawi (2003/04),
classified by participation in the maize market

| | Maize sellers | | |
| | Farms accounting for top 50% of total maize sales | Rest of maize sellers | Households not selling maize |
	(1)	(2)	(3)
Number of households			
Zambia (weighted)	23,680 (2.2%)	234,988 (23%)	762,526 (75%)
Mozambique (weighted)	4,654 (1.0%)	654,771 (15%)	2,466,572 (83%)
Kenya (unweighted)	25 (1.7%)	535 (37%)	897 (61%)
Malawi (unweighted)	13 (0.5%)	136 (11%)	2,301 (88%)
		Mean values	
Land holding size (hectares)			
Zambia	6.00	3.91	2.79
Mozambique	3.46	1.70	1.60
Kenya	8.09	2.77	1.56
Malawi	3.78	1.27	0.98
*Value of farm assets (US$)**			
Zambia	1,558	541	373
Mozambique	205	47	62
Kenya	4,081	1,107	617
Malawi	1,336	186	154
Total household income (US$)			
Zambia	2,282	629	291
Mozambique	2,159	315	328
Kenya	8,849	2,357	1,565
Malawi	2,601	458	308
Total crop income (US$)			
Zambia	1,348	483	233
Mozambique	1,247	176	114
Kenya	5,479	1,147	628
Malawi	1,445	144	71

Notes: * Livestock plus farm equipment except for Mozambique, which is livestock assets only.

Sources: Zambia: Supplemental Post Harvest Survey, Central Statistical Office, Lusaka, 2003/04. Kenya: Tegemeo/Egerton Rural Survey, 2003/04. Mozambique: TIA, 2002/03, Ministry of Agriculture, Maputo. Malawi: Integrated Household Survey-2, 2003/04 and 2002/03 seasons, National Statistical Office, Lilongwe

outlays on maize purchases over this 7 year period, as 4,000 large-scale farmers received the rest.

A final implication of the data in Tables 5.2, 5.3 and 5.4 is that strategies attempting to link African farmers to markets must take account of how low crop productivity and inequality in productive assets constrain most smallholders' ability to participate in markets. There appears to be a vicious cycle in which low surplus production constrains the development of markets, which in turn constrains smallholders' ability to use productive farm technologies in a sustainable manner, reinforcing semi-subsistence agriculture. Crop production expansion is difficult to sustain in the face of highly inelastic product demand, which causes precipitous price plunges when local markets are unable to absorb surplus output. Such price drops are a major cause of subsequent farm disadoption of improved technology. This was the experience of the Sasakawa-Global 2000 programmes implemented in many African countries in the 1990s (Putterman, 1995; Howard et al, 1999). However, the shape of the demand function is not exogenous from the standpoint of governments. The demand function for staple grain crops can be made more elastic and shifted outward, through market-facilitating public investments and policy choices and by nurturing important marketing institutions. On this list are the crucially important investments in physical infrastructure to increase the size of the market, regional trade to take advantage of covariant production fluctuations within the region, streamlining the numerous regulations and barriers which inhibit trade and the development of rural financial markets to finance agricultural trade and inputs. These investments and policies would enable supply expansion due to the uptake of new technology to be better absorbed by the market without a dramatic effect on prices. We will return to these points later.

Shifts in crop production patterns away from cereal crops

In the 1980s, maize in Eastern and Southern Africa was largely equated with smallholder agriculture. Maize dominated crop income shares in the region, largely due to the maize self-sufficiency policies adopted by governments in the region during this time (Byerlee and Eicher, 1997). However, in the post-liberalization period, the various subsidies in support of maize production were partially withdrawn, which has slowed maize production growth and led to more diversified crop production and marketing patterns (Table 5.5). Crops such as cotton, fruits and vegetables, roots and tubers and animal products have experienced significant growth in most of the region and are now accounting for a large share of smallholders' revenue from crop sales. In Kenya, Zambia and Mozambique, more smallholders sell animal products than maize. The value of animal product sales and horticultural product sales both rival that of maize. Urbanization and the rising demand for marketed food have also stimulated smallholders' participation in some of these activities. Even though cereal crop production has been slow,

Table 5.5 *Crop production and marketing patterns, small-scale farm sector,*
Kenya (2003/04), Zambia (2003/04) and Mozambique (2004/05)

Crop	% of households cultivating	Share of total value of farm output	% of households selling	Share of total value of farm sales revenue
Maize and other cereals:				
Kenya	99.0	24.1	39.9	23.1
Zambia	87.9	34.6	28.4	23.9
Mozambique	87.0	31.8	20.0	14.4
Roots and tubers:				
Kenya	82.4	4.5	33.3	3.4
Zambia	52.3	13.7	14.8	2.5
Mozambique	78.0	32.2	14.9	8.0
Beans and oilseeds:				
Kenya	94.9	4.9	38.1	2.9
Zambia	46.5	16.1	40.3	25.2
Mozambique	78.0	13.8	22.4	15.9
Industrial cash crops:				
Kenya	39.2	16.2	38.8	27.7
Zambia	1.4	2.9	1.4	6.7
Mozambique	8.6	3.6	8.6	9.6
Fruits and vegetables				
Kenya	98.6	17.8	81.3	16.7
Zambia	na	16.8*	16.3	21.4
Mozambique	84.9	12.3**	35.5	31.9
Animal products:				
Kenya	84.0	29.1	83.5	24.9
Zambia	na	15.9*	44.5	20.2
Mozambique	26.0	4.5	26.0	20.2
Other crops:				
Kenya	47.5	3.4	8.9	1.3
Zambia	22.1	na	na	na
Mozambique	na	na	na	na
Total:		100		100

Notes: * Only sales information was available, hence production is estimated as twice the value of gross sales revenue for the particular crop. ** No value of production was available for fruits and vegetables retained by the household, with the exception of cashew and coconut (which are the primary tree crops); we impute FV retained production for FV sellers as 0.5 × (the household's FV sales value), while ensuring that this imputed value does not rise above the provincial median sales value for FV. For Mozambique: industrial cash crops include cotton, tobacco, tea (cotton and tobacco are 95% of this category); Fruits & Vegetables includes cashew, coconut and sugar cane; Animal products = sales of live animals, meat and dairy products.

Sources: Zambia: Supplemental Post Harvest Survey, Central Statistical Office, Lusaka, 2003/04. Kenya: Tegemeo/Egerton Rural Survey, 2003/04. Mozambique: TIA, 2002/03, Ministry of Agriculture, Maputo. Malawi: Integrated Household Survey-2, 2003/04 and 2002/03 seasons, National Statistical Office, Lilongwe

partially due to the removal of market board price subsidies and input subsidies to promote maize self-sufficiency, overall per capita agricultural growth rates appear to be positive (World Bank, 2008).

Implications of the region's transition to structural cereal deficit

Both the eastern and southern Africa regions are moving towards structural maize deficit.[11] This conclusion is based on trend analysis of net export data (the difference between total exports and imports) of maize grain and meal. Although FAO trade data do not capture unrecorded trade flows between countries, the net impact on regional net exports is virtually zero, since each bag of unrecorded cross-border exports from one country in the region is imported by another country in the region. For the purposes of this paper, the southern Africa region consists of Zambia, Zimbabwe, Mozambique, South Africa, Botswana, Namibia, Lesotho, Swaziland and Malawi. Eastern Africa includes Kenya, Uganda, Tanzania, Rwanda, Democratic Republic of Congo and Ethiopia.

We regressed regional and country-specific net export data on linear time trends and on models allowing for shifts in the slope of the trend between the 1960–1981 and 1982–2005 periods. Net exports regressed on a linear time trend in both regions show statistically significant downward slopes. Net maize (grain plus meal) exports in the southern Africa region declined at a rate of –72,201 metric tons per year for the period 1960–2005. Net maize exports over the same period in eastern Africa declined at the rate of –9,798 metric tons per year (Figure 5.1). There is no significant difference in the trend in net exports in eastern Africa between 1960–1981 and 1982–2005. Net exports in southern Africa increased by 85,544 metric tons per year for the period 1960–1981 and then declined by 94,586 metric tons per year during the period 1982–2005 (Figure 5.2).

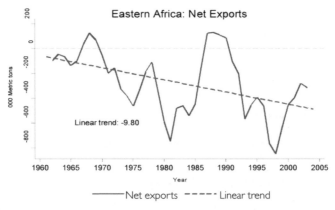

Source: FAOSTAT, 2006

Figure 5.1 *Net exports of maize grain and maize meal in eastern Africa*

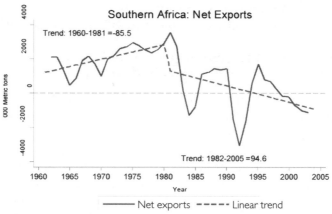

Source: FAOSTAT, 2006

Figure 5.2 *Net exports of maize grain and maize meal in southern Africa*

At the country-level, there was a downward trend in net maize exports in all countries of southern Africa, with all of these being statistically significant at the 5 per cent level. In eastern Africa, there was a significant downward trend in net maize exports for two of the six eastern African countries (Kenya and Rwanda), while for Ethiopia the trend is positive and significant. The trend is weakly negative in Tanzania and weakly positive in the Democratic Republic of the Congo (DRC). Kenya, Malawi and Zimbabwe, all net exporters of maize in the 1970s and 1980s, are now chronic importers. The reduction of maize production subsidies in South Africa has also reduced the exportable surplus in that country, although it remains a reliable exporter.

In recent years and especially after the inception of political turmoil in Zimbabwe in the late 1990s, South Africa has become the only reliable exporter of white maize in the region. Areas of Mozambique, Zambia and Malawi typically produce maize surpluses, but these surpluses are usually depleted halfway through the marketing year. Informal trade flows from Zambia to the DRC and from northern Mozambique into Malawi, appear to be substantial in some years, despite frequent official efforts to suppress these flows or tax them heavily.

One major implication about the region becoming structurally grain deficient is that the investments of global grain trading firms will be primarily aimed at the milling and retailing stage – supplying mostly urban markets with internationally sourced grain, for milling by large-scale mills and subsequent distribution through various retail channels, including small kiosks, local shops, open markets and supermarkets. Global private investment in grain assembly, storage and wholesaling is likely to be impeded by political economy reasons discussed earlier. A greater alignment of interests will converge to develop supply chains that can reliably meet the residual grain requirements of urban populations from international sources after local supplies are exhausted. However, as we will discuss later, the stagnation of maize production is related to the rise of cassava in the region and these trends will provide a comparative advantage to informal marketing actors in linking surplus food production areas with deficit rural and urban areas.

Demand for food is growing rapidly but African smallholders are not filling this demand

A recent study by the FAO (2006) determined that of the US$3.7 billion of cereals imported annually by African countries, only 5 per cent is produced by African farmers. Between 1990–92 and 2002–04, cereal imports by sub-Saharan Africa have been rising at 3.6 per cent per year. Almost all of the growing demand in the region is due to rising urban populations, which are growing at over 4 per cent per year compared to less than 1 per cent per year for rural populations. This highlights the importance of developing more effective systems for linking small-holder farmers to urban demand centres, so that consumers are relying on their rural counterparts for food rather than international sources. This brings us back to the importance of public goods investments to raise smallholder farm produc-tivity and to reduce the costs of domestic food marketing.

There are also important trends toward more diversified food consumption patterns in both urban and rural areas. Recent urban consumption surveys in Nairobi, Maputo and the Umtata area of eastern Cape, South Africa attest to the rising importance of wheat and rice products in food consumption patterns (Muyanga et al 2005; Traub and Jayne, 2005; Tschirley et al, 2005). In all three surveys, wheat and/or rice was the main staple expenditure item of urban consumers. Maize appears to be an 'inferior good' in the sense that the poor spend a greater share of their income on maize than the wealthy. The rising importance of other staples that are widely traded on world markets and consis-tently available at import parity levels will increasingly contribute to more stable food expenditure patterns over time. Moreover, increased diversification in food consumption patterns has likely diluted the 'wage-good' effects of maize price fluctuations on the overall economy.

In rural areas, maize is still the dominant food crop, but cassava production has risen dramatically in the post-liberalization period in many parts of the region (Figure 5.3).[12] The rise of cassava is not unrelated to maize policy. The elimina-tion of pan-territorial maize pricing policies in early 1990s has reduced the profitability of surplus maize production in remote areas. Cassava production has risen substantially in many of these areas.

These shifts in production have apparently nurtured several highly produc-tive, regularly surplus food production zones in the region. Even more flexible and equally reliable as exporters of staple foods are those ecosystems that combine the production of multiple staples, particularly cereals in combination with perennial food crops such as banana, cassava or root crops. These areas are generally characterized by favourable rainfall, areas that do not get too cold in the winter (cassava and banana do not grow well in cold conditions) and in water-sheds where small-scale irrigation appears to be economical.

Examples of these 'stable food basket zones' include: northern Mozambique, where cassava and potatoes provide local food security, enabling regular maize

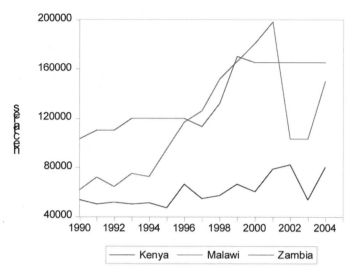

Source: FAOSTAT, December 2005

Figure 5.3 *Trends in area to cassava in Kenya, Malawi and Zambia, 1985–2004*

exports; most of Tanzania, where a blend of rice, cassava, banana and maize enable regular cereal exports both north into Kenya and south into Malawi; northern Zambia, where cassava ensures local food security, even in drought years, enabling the region to export maize to DRC, Malawi and elsewhere in Zambia; and Uganda, where banana and cassava ensure food security, thereby enabling maize exports to chronically deficient Kenya (Haggblade, 2006).[13]

Because farmers can harvest perennial foodcrops such as banana and cassava any time of the year and over multiple seasons and years, they are able to respond very flexibly to crises as well as chronic shortfalls in neighbouring regions. In drought years, when most maize-dominated zones face shortfalls, farmers from neighbouring cassava/banana zones are able to harvest more of their perennial reserve crops and in turn free up more of their cereals (primarily maize) for export to deficit zones (Haggblade, 2006).

It appears that these built-in shock absorbers serve a valuable role in moderating regional food shortages. Future analysis by Michigan State University, COMESA and local collaborators is under way to test this hypothesis empirically. Another hypothesis is that in order to maintain and sustain producer incentives, farmers in the 'stable food basket zones' need access to growing markets, both internally and across national boundaries. Successful expansion of regional trade has long been understood as a means to improve prices for farmers in surplus areas, dampen price spikes in deficit zones and diminish hunger (e.g. Koester, 1986). Failure to allow regional trade in food staples risks stalling production growth and investment in agriculture.

To conclude, therefore, while preferences appear to be shifting somewhat away from maize to imported grains in urban areas, it is difficult to determine the future demand for maize in these countries a priori, because they are importantly a function of government trade policies on imported rice and wheat and on how active governments are in improving the competitiveness of smallholder agriculture. If governments and donor agencies actively support crop science, adaptive research and extension programmes, invest in road and rail infrastructure, support improved processing technologies for cassava and make other important public goods investments, then urban food demand may increasingly be met through locally produced food, which would then provide advantages to the development of informal marketing systems, allowing them to become integrated and coordinated with the activities of formal sector processing and retailing firms. By contrast, a continued underprovision of public goods investments in support of smallholder agriculture is likely to further erode the competitiveness of smallholder agriculture, exacerbate the region's growing dependence on imported staple foods and increase the role of international firms in supplying domestic processing and retailing networks.

The continued dominance of traditional food distribution channels

The 'rapid rise' of supermarkets in Africa has received great attention in recent years.[14] Several recurring themes in this literature concern the difficulties of traditional food distribution channels to compete with supermarket-driven supply chains and fears over the marginalization of smallholders with respect to participation. If supermarkets are able to capture a significant portion of consumers' food expenditures in sub-Saharan Africa and develop procurement channels back to the wholesale or farm level requiring exacting crop quality standards, then this would indeed raise major challenges for the viability of smallholder agriculture.[15]

However, the empirical evidence of supermarket penetration in Africa shows, so far, very negligible influence. There is now a relative consensus that earlier warnings were probably overstated. Humphrey concludes that 'the extent of transformation of retailing ... as a consequence of (supermarket expansion) is overestimated' (2007). In Kenya, where supermarkets had penetrated more than in any sub-Saharan African country outside South Africa, Tschirley et al (2004a) and Tschirley et al (2004b) show that supermarket chains held less than 2 per cent of the national urban fresh produce market in late 2003, and that nearly all fresh produce purchases in these supermarkets were made by consumers in the top 20 per cent of the income distribution. They calculate that, to reach a 10 per cent market share in 10 years, supermarket sales of fresh produce would have to grow 22 per cent per year in real terms. In a cross-country econometric analysis, Traill (2006) estimates that Kenyan supermarkets will hold at most a 16 per cent share of total food sales by 2013; this would correspond to a 4–5 per cent share of fresh produce. Reardon and Timmer (2006) also indicate that there is 'considerable uncertainty about the rate at which the supermarket sector will grow' even in

Kenya. In most of the rest of SSA, they deemed it 'unlikely that ... we will see supermarket growth for several decades'.

A certain fear over export horticultural channels being captured by firms preferring to deal with larger farms (to the exclusion of smallholders) is also put into context by considering the fact that less than 10 per cent of total horticultural production goes into export markets (even in relatively commercialized Kenya). Domestic demand constitutes by far the largest share of horticultural production and sales, and the domestic market accounted for over 90 per cent of the total growth in Kenya's horticultural production between 1995 and 2004 (Tschirley et al, 2004a). As shown earlier, fresh fruits and vegetables now account for a larger share of smallholder revenue from crop sales than maize. Most of this growth in horticultural sales is due to expansion of the domestic market, not export demand. Clearly, the horticultural success story in Kenya is driven by rapid growth in local demand and the ability of smallholders to supply this market.

The situation is largely the same regarding the major food staples. Again even in the relatively modernized capital of Kenya, Nairobi, small kiosks, informal shops and small independent stores accounted for 71 per cent of consumers' expenditures on food staples (Muyanga et al, 2005).[16] Local open markets and small millers account for another 13 per cent. The big supermarket chains accounted for 17 per cent. Throughout the country, across all retail consumer food expenditures, the share of supermarkets is estimated to be roughly 3 per cent.

There are several important reasons why supermarkets' share of African consumer food expenditures will not grow much for the foreseeable future. Although urban Africa is growing rapidly, it is fuelled by land constraints and low labour productivity in rural areas, leading to poverty-driven urbanization. The rapid rise of huge slums in many African cities attests to this. Given that at least half of the urban populations are below the poverty line, and another 40 per cent are not far above it, the vast majority of urban African households will, for the foreseeable future, have relatively low disposable incomes. Shopping patterns of the poor follow distinct patterns all over the developing world (Shaffer et al, 1985; Goldman et al, 1999). They buy low value-added goods, in small units, with minimal processing and packaging. They lack easy access to transportation and hence tend to make most of their food expenditures within walking distance of their homes and work. An unrecognized large share of the urban poor's food expenditures is in the form of street food eaten at small kiosks and purchased from street vendors. For these reasons, informal corner stores in high-density neighbourhoods, open markets, street kiosks other traditional retail outlets – and the marketing chains that supply them – will remain the dominant food supply systems in almost all of sub-Saharan Africa for the foreseeable future.

These findings put into context the fears over smallholder exclusion from supermarket supply channels. While warnings have been issued that medium- and large-scale farmers supply the overwhelming majority of produce moving through 'preferred supplier' programmes in Africa, these programmes account for an infinitesimal fraction of the food trade in African countries. In Kenya, this share was less than two-tenths of 1 per cent of all food purchased in urban areas (Tschirley, 2007, based on information in Neven and Reardon, 2004). Thus, as stated by Tschirley, 'while smallholder exclusion from large supermarket supply chains is a reality, it cannot now be considered among the top tier of rural policy concerns in this area of the world; nor is it likely to become a top tier concern over the next 10–20 years, given projected market shares of supermarkets over this time' (Tschirley 2007, p3).

In light of this situation, a much greater priority should be focused on upgrading the performance of urban wholesale and retail marketing systems and facilities on which the vast majority of smallholder farmers and consumers are likely to depend for the foreseeable future. Currently, traditional wholesale markets are congested, unsanitary, sometimes unsafe, and difficult for trucks to move in and out of smoothly. Squalid conditions add transaction costs and reduce consumer demand for products sold in these markets. More sanitary conditions with a modicum of amenities like clean water and toilets would help to solidify their position in the future development of the value chain, and with it, a greater chance that strong multiplier effects would benefit local farmers, traders and associated local commerce. Public policy and investments in upgrading traditional wholesale markets will be a major determinant of how the sector evolves, and whether it promotes smallholder interests.

For these reasons, the more salient issues of wholesale and retail food modernization revolve around whether the growing food demands of an increasingly urbanized continent will be met by local production or by imports, not whether they will be met by supermarkets or traditional channels. If smallholders are made more competitive by public goods investments (R&D, extension, farmer organization, physical infrastructure for regional trade, etc.), then many more smallholders will remain commercially viable in grain staples and other food crops, and will provide growth linkage effects that support overall economic development and poverty reduction. But if governments continue to underinvest in these productivity-enhancing public goods, then international imports are likely to continue to penetrate local urban markets.

Conclusions

Many global forces are affecting the evolution of food systems in developing countries. Yet the evolution of food systems is also fundamentally driven by local changes in demographics, institutions and technology, and by history. The resulting impacts on smallholder farmers and consumers are determined by public policy and investment choices. The implication of viewing food system modernization in this framework is that there is no deterministic 'future of smallholder farms' or food systems. The future of food systems, and smallholder farmers' roles in them, will be influenced greatly by the local enabling environment, which is fundamentally determined by the nature of government policies and investments.

Increasing public goods investments in order to raise agricultural productivity and reduce poverty

Many African governments' spending on agriculture has fallen in real terms between 1990 and 2006, having peaked in the late 1980s and declined substantially thereafter. Although the conventional wisdom is that the fiscal resources available to African governments have been slashed under the burden of structural adjustment, this picture does not square with actual figures. In a cross-country study, Jayarajah and Branson (1995) find that state revenues as a proportion of GDP declined at most one percentage point during the course of World Bank adjustment programmes. Nashashibi et al (1992) conclude that, after implementing macro reform policies, real government revenues went up in nine African cases and down in nine, relative to a base year. According to published World Bank data across Africa (excluding South Africa and Nigeria), government revenues have declined from an average of 16.3 per cent of GDP during 1975–1984 to 15.8 per cent for 1990–1996. Thus, while there is abundant evidence that government investment in physical infrastructure, agricultural research and other key public goods has declined, this trend cannot be explained by severely reduced government revenues in most African countries, especially in the era of direct donor budget support and debt forgiveness.

There are signs that African states and some leading donor agencies are trying to stop or reverse the trend in declining support to African agriculture. Through the Comprehensive African Agriculture Development Programme (CAADP), all African governments have committed themselves to devoting at least 10 per cent of their budgets to agriculture by 2008. However, a recent assessment by Mwape (2007) indicates that, as of 2006, only about a third of these countries are moving in the direction of meeting this commitment. For about 25 per cent of the countries reported by Mwape, shares of public expenditures to agriculture are trending downward. Mwape's computations also include as 'agricultural expenditures' the expenditures by state marketing boards on food imports as well as expenditures targeted for agriculture provided by donor budget support through the treasury. Moreover, increased attention has been focused on how African governments allocate their expenditures to agriculture. This has given rise to recent emphasis on public expenditure reviews. Govereh et al (2006), for example, found that in 2005 the Government of Zambia devoted 6 per cent of its budget to agriculture and that of this amount, 65 per cent was in the form of fertilizer subsidies and maize marketing board purchase and sales. Meanwhile, the genetic advances that were a major factor in maize productivity growth in earlier decades have waned as funding by both donors and government has declined. The Government of Zambia devoted less than 4 per cent of its agricultural budget to agricultural research and extension. Of this 4 per cent, 75 per cent is for salaries and wages. Effectively, public sector agricultural research and extension has come to a standstill in Zambia, as in much of Africa. Rural poverty alleviation will require renewed commitment to public investments in these key areas.

As stated previously, there are virtually no examples of mass poverty reduction since 1700 that did not start with sharp rises in employment and self-employment income due to higher productivity in small family farms (Lipton, 2005). Research evidence from Africa as well as around the world indicates that the greatest contribution that public sector resources can make to sustained agricultural growth and poverty reduction is from sustained investment in crop science, effective extension programmes, physical infrastructure and a stable and supportive marketing policy environment for a range of crops that provide income growth opportunities for smallholders in a range of different agro-ecological environments. This evidence, and that presented and cited in this paper on smallholder income, land access and crop productivity from various African countries, suggests that investment in improving food crop productivity is critical to poverty alleviation efforts, but also for providing African households with lower priced food and increased effective demand for services, which in turn will foster agricultural and demographic transformations supportive of broad-based economic growth.

Addressing land and resource constraints on smallholders' ability to participate in markets

Given the existing distribution of landholding sizes within the small farm sectors of eastern and southern Africa, strategies to improve rural households' access to land may need to be on the agenda. Farmer organization can help to some extent to overcome diseconomies of scale associated with small farmers' attempts to acquire inputs and marketing output. However, the evidence suggests that as the land frontier closes in many parts of the region, mean smallholder farm size continues to gradually decline even with very low rural population growth (Jayne et al, 2003). The bottom 25 per cent of rural agricultural households are virtually landless, having access to 0.50 hectares per capita or less in each country examined. Even farmers in the second land quartile have under 1.2 hectares. Without major productivity growth or shifts to higher-return activities, at least 50 per cent of the smallholder households in the region are unlikely to produce any significant food surplus or escape from poverty directly through agriculture. In this context, to frame the issue as how to ensure that smallholders do not become excluded from evolving supermarket supply chains is largely mislaid. The more fundamental questions involve how most smallholder farmers can improve the productivity of their scarce resources, how to acquire additional resources to become able to produce a surplus and the role of public goods investments and input and output marketing policies in promoting these objectives. International agribusiness can become an ally of smallholder agriculture if its farmers can be made more productive and produce reliable food surpluses through appropriate policies and public investments.

The commercialization of smallholder agriculture (i.e. their ability to produce a surplus and utilize markets for raising incomes from participation in agricultural markets) is completely compatible with the modernization of the food system. Food systems are indeed undergoing new investment and modernization in sub-Saharan Africa. Whether this modernization benefits smallholder farmers or not depends on the nature of public policies and investments. While it has sometimes been contended that retail food modernization spells the marginalization of smallholder agriculture, this is based on the assumption that supermarkets are (or will soon be) reaching backward to develop procurement systems from farmers or wholesalers and that these systems are gaining a dominant share of marketed production. This situation is not even close to occurring for the vast majority of crops produced by smallholders in Africa. By contrast, there is great potential for smallholder farmers to benefit from participation in outgrower companies (with its many organizational variants), as has already occurred in the cases of cotton in many African countries (Poulton et al, 2003; Govereh and Jayne, 2003), sugarcane in Kenya (von Braun and Kennedy, 1994; Jayne et al, 2004). The fact that smallholders in many parts of Africa have been the main farmer participants in many cash crop outgrower or contract farming arrangements points to the great potential for further commercialization of smallholder agriculture if the enabling environment is conducive.

Policies and programmes to open up unexploited land for settlement

In many parts of the region, governments may be able to promote equitable access to land through a coordinated strategy of public goods and services investments to raise the economic value of customary land that is currently remote and unutilized. This would involve investments in infrastructure and service provision designed to link currently isolated areas with existing road and rail infrastructure and through allied investment in schools, health care facilities, electrification and water supply and other public goods required to induce migration, settlement and investment in these currently underutilized areas. Such investments would also help to reduce population pressures in areas of relatively good access and soils, many of which are being degraded due to declining fallows associated with population pressure. The approach of raising the economic value of land through public investments in physical and marketing infrastructure and service provision was pursued successfully by Southern Rhodesia and Zimbabwe starting in the 1960s with its 'growth point' strategy in the Gokwe area, once cleared of tsetse fly. Key public investments in this once desolate but agro-ecologically productive area induced rapid migration into Gokwe from heavily populated rural areas, leading to the 'white gold rush' of smallholder cotton production in the 1970s and 1980s (Govereh, 1999). A second and complementary approach would be to institute more transparent and orderly procedures for the allocation of state and customary land (Munshifwa, 2002; Stambulis, 2002). Such an approach would be of limited feasibility in countries such as Rwanda, but could have much potential in parts of Zambia, Mozambique and even Malawi.

Concluding comments

In the longer run, the brightest prospect for many smallholders' escape from poverty (which is by no means a sure thing) is likely to involve being 'pulled' off the farm into productive non-farm sectors. But allowing the most marginal farmers to escape from poverty agriculture will require agricultural growth, in order to generate the demand for non-farm employment. Abundant evidence of the transformation process elsewhere indicates that growth in non-farm sectors typically starts from a robust stimulus to agriculture, which generates rural purchasing power for goods and services. For many African countries, this implies increased crop productivity in order to increase household disposable income for non-staple crops and consumer goods. During this process, there will be high pay-offs to education, as the most highly skilled households have the best access to the well-paying non-farm jobs. Therefore, while greater equity in land allocation and increased food crop productivity are both critical to rural poverty reduction in the short run, an important long-run goal may be to enable the rural poor to access skilled off-farm jobs through investments and policies that support the processes of structural transformation. Education, which played an important role in Asia by allowing households to exit agriculture into more lucrative off-farm jobs, is relatively low in most areas of rural Africa by world standards. Investments in rural education and communications are likely to become increasingly important to facilitate structural transformation. Yet the pay-offs to education will depend on non-farm job opportunities, which is ultimately dependent on broad-based agricultural growth. This brings us back to the centrality of basic public goods investments and supportive policies. The future evolution of food systems and smallholder farmers' roles in them will be fundamentally influenced by governments' commitment to smallholder farmers and poverty reduction, manifested through its policy choices and the composition and extent of its public goods investments to agriculture.

Can a local constituency be formed that can stake a claim on public resources in support of agricultural research, infrastructure, marketing institutions and other kinds of growth-promoting public goods? There is an obvious connection between agricultural development and governance. The early success of the maize industry in Zimbabwe and Kenya can be largely attributed to the strength of the institutions built by settler farmers, which mobilized a constituency to support public and private investments. Today, farm lobbies in the region are largely captured by the interests of relatively large and commercialized farmers. Representation has always been weak for the majority of small-scale farmers with inadequate resources to produce a surplus but for whom equity-promoting investments in agricultural research, infrastructure and market institutions are important. From where will the domestic political pressure for these public investments originate?

Notes

1   Much of the data used in this paper was collected under the Food Security III Cooperative Agreement and the Tegemeo Agricultural Monitoring and Policy Analysis Project, both funded by USAID. Additional support for the research underlying this study was funded by the World Bank's Agriculture and Rural Development

Division and by the Rockefeller Foundation. Parts of this paper draw heavily from Jayne et al (2007) and Tschirley (2007).

2   Pioneering work on path dependence and its impact on economic systems is laid out in Arthur (1994). A historical treatment of path dependence in the evolution of the maize sectors of southern Africa is laid out in Jayne et al (1995).

3   For an analysis of how maize marketing and trade controls in the colonial period were used to support colonial settler farmers, often at the expense of African farmers, see Mosley (1975) for the case of Kenya; Keyter (1975) for Southern Rhodesia/Zimbabwe and Jansen (1977) for Northern Rhodesia/Zambia.

4   For example, in the early 1990s, the deficits of Zimbabwe's Grain Marketing Board were 5 per cent of GDP (Jenkins, 1997). By the late 1980s, Zambia's subsidies to the maize sector reached 17 per cent of the national budget (Howard and Mungoma, 1997) and the country was experiencing hyperinflation.

5   In Zambia, President Frederick Chiluba adopted food and input market reform programmes in the early 1990s, but after a groundswell of charges that he deserted the small farmer, reintroduced major input subsidy programmes by 1994 and created a new food marketing parastatal, the Food Reserve Agency, in 1996.

6   Consider, for example, the editorial in the *Zambia Post*, stating, 'The MMD's overzealous pursuance of capitalist policies under the directives of the IMF and World Bank have registered no success – they have been a disaster for the nation. We believe that neoliberalism is not simply an economic doctrine, it is a political project that seeks to perpetuate the present unfair, exploitative world economic order' (*Zambia Post*, 2000).

7   Using data provided by the national marketing boards between 1995 and 2004, the boards' annual purchases have fluctuated from an estimated 15–57 per cent of the domestic marketed maize output in Kenya, 3–32 per cent in Malawi and 12–53 per cent in Zambia (Jayne et al, 2006). These figures understate the boards' full impact on markets because they do not count their often sizeable maize imports and subsequent release onto domestic markets.

8   The exception being South Africa, which has a fundamentally different history and political economy of agriculture.

9   This empirical regularity contrasts with the common notion that, because of a lack of credit, farmers typically sell at harvest at low prices and buy back later at higher prices.

10   Of course, a general equilibrium approach, taking into account indirect effects on welfare through labour market effects, would need to be undertaken before the welfare effects of mean-altering price policies could be fully understood.

11   This section draws heavily on Jayne and Chapoto (2006).

12   OLS time trends showed annual increases of 1.9, 7.1 and 5.2 thousand hectares of cassava in Kenya, Malawi and Zambia, respectively, with t-statistics of 3.74, 3.66 and 7.68.

13   Policy-induced shifts in cropping patterns from maize to cassava and other food crops are apparent in Northern Zambia and parts of Tanzania. However, Uganda and most of Tanzania have historically had highly diversified food production patterns.

14   This section draws from the work of David Tschirley of Michigan State University and colleagues working on retail food modernization.

15   The following quote encapsulates this view: 'Our premise is that supermarkets will continue to spread over the (African) region ... and thus their requirements will either gradually or rapidly, depending on the country, become those faced by the majority of farmers... Understanding those procurement systems ... is thus a way of

predicting what will be the challenges and opportunities facing farmers ... *in the next 5–10 years.*' (Weatherspoon and Reardon, 2003; parentheses and emphasis added)

16   The data used in this study come from a survey of 542 households in Nairobi's urban areas and environs. The Tegemeo Institute in collaboration with the Central Bureau of Statistics (CBS) using the CBS's NASSEP IV frame implemented the survey in November/December 2003 to ensure statistical representativeness.

References

Arthur, W. B. (1994) *Increasing Returns and Path Dependence in the Economy*, University of Michigan Press, Ann Arbor

Bates, R. (1981) *Markets and States in Tropical Africa: The Political Basis of Agricultural Policies*, University of California Press, Berkeley, CA

Bates, R. and Krueger, A. (eds) (1993) *Political and Economic Interactions in Economic Policy Reform: Evidence from Eight Countries*, Basil Blackwell, Oxford

Bird, K., Booth, D. and Pratt, N. (2003) 'Food security crisis in Southern Africa: the political background to policy failure', Forum for Food Security in Southern Africa, Theme paper No. 1, Overseas Development Institute, London

Bratton, M. and Mattes, R. (2003) 'Support for economic reform? Popular attitudes in Southern Africa', *World Development*, vol 31, no 2, pp303–323

Byerlee, D. and Eicher, C. K. (eds) (1997) *The Emerging Maize-based Revolution in Africa: The Role of Technologies, Institutions and Policies*, Lynne Rienner, Boulder, CO.

Chapoto, A. and Jayne, T. S. (2006) 'Emerging structural maize deficits in eastern and southern Africa: Implications for national agricultural strategies', Policy Synthesis 16, Food Security Research Project, Lusaka Zambia, available online at www.aec.msu.edu/agecon/fs2/zambia/ps16.pdf, last accessed April 2008

Chirwa, E. (2006) 'Commercialization of food crops in Malawi: Insights from the household survey', Working Paper 2006/04, Department of Economics, University of Malawi, Chancellors College, Zomba, Malawi, available online at www.economics.chanco.mw/papers/wp2006_04.pdf, last accessed April 2008

Fafchamps, M. (1992) 'Solidarity networks in pre-industrial societies: Rational peasants with a moral economy', *Economic Development and Cultural Change*, vol 41, no 1, pp147–174.

FAO (2006) 'Enhancing intra-African trade in food and agriculture', Background paper for the African Union/FAO Meeting of Agricultural Experts and Ministers, Libreville, Gabon, 27 November–December, ESTD Division, FAO, Rome

FAOSTAT (2007) FAOStat Website, maintained at FAO Headquarters, Rome, online at http://faostat.fao.org/

Goldman, A., Krider, R. and Ramaswami, S. (1999) 'The persistent competitive advantage of traditional food retailers in Asia: Wet markets' continued dominance in Hong Kong', *Journal of Macromarketing*, vol 19

Govereh, J. (1999) 'Impacts of tsetse control on immigration and household accumulation of capital', Zambezi Valley, Zimbabwe, Ph.D. Diss., Michigan State University, East Lansing, MI

Govereh, J. and Jayne, T. (2003) 'Cash cropping and food crop productivity: Synergies or trade-offs?' *Agricultural Economics*, vol 28, no 1, pp39–50

Govereh, J., Shawa, J., Malawo, E. and Jayne, T. (2006) 'Raising the productivity of public investments in Zambia's agricultural sector', Working Paper 20, Food Security Research Project, Lusaka, Zambia, available online at www.aec.msu.edu/agecon/fs2/zambia/wp_20.pdf, last accessed April 2008

Haggblade, S. (2006) 'Improving African food security through expanded regional trade in food staples: A concept note', Michigan State University in collaboration with Regional Partners, East Lansing, MI

Haggblade, S. and Hazell, P. (1988) 'Prospects for equitable growth in rural sub-Saharan Africa', AGRAP Economic Discussion Paper 3, World Bank, Washington, DC

Howard, J. and Mungoma, C. (1997) 'Zambia's stop-and-go maize revolution', in D. Byerlee and C. Eicher (eds), *Africa's Emerging Maize Revolution*, Lynn Rienner, Boulder, CO

Humphrey, J. (2007) 'The supermarket revolution in developing countries: Tidal wave or tough competitive struggle?' *Journal of Economic Geography*, vol 7, no 4, pp433–450

Jansen, D. (1977) *Agricultural Policy and Performance in Zambia: History, Prospects and Proposals for Change*, University of California, Institute of International Studies, Berkeley, CA

Jayarajah, C. and Branson, W. (1995) *Structural and Sectoral Adjustment: The World Bank Experience, 1980–1992*, A World Bank Operations Evaluation Study, World Bank, Washington, DC

Jayne, T. S. (1994) 'Do high food marketing costs constrain cash crop production?' *Economic Development and Cultural Change*, vol 42, no 2, pp387–402

Jayne, T. S. and Chapoto, A. (2006) 'Emerging structural grain deficits in eastern and southern Africa: Implications for national agricultural strategies', Policy Synthesis 16, Food Security Research Project, Lusaka, Zambia, online at www.aec.msu.edu/agecon/fs2/zambia/policy.htm, last accessed April 2008

Jayne, T. S. and Jones, S. (1997) 'Food marketing and pricing policy in eastern and southern Africa: A survey', *World Development*, vol 25, no 9, pp1505–1527

Jayne, T. S. and Rukuni, M. (1993) 'The costs of food self-sufficiency: Maize pricing and trade policy in Zimbabwe', *Agricultural Economics Analysis and Rural Development*, vol 3, pp7–31

Jayne, T. S., Mather, D. and Mgheneji, E. (2007) 'Principle challenges facing smallholder agriculture in Africa', draft mimeo, Michigan State University, East Lansing, MI

Jayne, T.S., Rubey, L., Tschirley, D., Mukumbu, M., Chisvo, M., Santos, A., Weber, M. and Diskin, P. (1995) 'Effects of market reform on access to food by low-income households', International Development Paper 19, Michigan State University, East Lansing, online at www.aec.msu.edu/agecon/fs2/papers/idp.htm, last accessed April 2008

Jayne, T. S., Yamano, T., Weber, M., Tschirley, D., Benfica, R., Chapoto, A. and Zulu, B. (2003) 'Smallholder income and land distribution in Africa: Implications for poverty reduction strategies', *Food Policy*, vol 28, no 3, pp253–275.

Jayne, T. S., Govereh, J., Mwanaumo, A., Nyoro, J. and Chapoto, A. (2002) 'False promise or false premise: The experience of food and input market reform in eastern and southern Africa', *World Development*, vol 30, no 11, pp1967–1986

Jayne, T. S., Yamano, T. and Nyoro, J. (2004) 'Interlinked credit and farm intensification evidence from Kenya', *Agricultural Economics*, vol 31, no 6, pp209–218

Jayne, T. S., Zulu, B. and Nijhoff, J. J. (2006) 'Stabilizing food markets in eastern and southern Africa', *Food Policy*, vol 31, no 4, pp328–341

Jenkins, C. (1997) 'The politics of economic policy-making in Zimbabwe', *Journal of Modern African Economies*, pp575–602

Johnston, B. F. and Kilby, P. (1975) *Agriculture and Structural Transformation: Economic Strategies in Late Developing Countries*, Oxford University Press, New York

Keyter, C. (1975) *Maize Control in Southern Rhodesia: 1931–1941: The African Contribution Toward White Survival*, Local Series 34, Harare, Central African Historical Association

Koester, U. (1986) *Regional Cooperation to Improve Food Security in Southern and Eastern African Countries*, Research Report 53, Intl. Food Policy Research Institute, Washington, DC

Lipton, M. (2005) 'Crop science, poverty and the family farm in a globalizing world', Discussion paper 40, International Food Policy Research Institute, Washington, DC

Lopez, R. (2003) 'Under-investing in public goods: Evidence, causes, and consequences for agricultural development, equity, and the environment', *Agricultural Economics*, vol 32, pp211–224

Mellor, J. (1976) *The New Economics of Growth: A Strategy for India and the Developing World*, Cornell University Press, Ithaca

Mosley, P. (1975) *Maize Control in Kenya 1920–1970*, Centre for Development Studies, University of Bath, Bath

Munshifwa, E. (2002) 'Rural land management and productivity in rural Zambia: The need for institutional and land tenure reforms', paper presented at the Surveyor's Institute of Zambia Seminar, July, Oxfam, available online at www.eldis.org/go/display/?id=10914&type=Document, last accessed April 2008

Muyanga, M., Jayne, T., Kodhek and Ariga, J. (2005) 'Staple food consumption patterns in urban Kenya: Trends and policy implications', Working Paper 19, Tegemeo Institute, Egerton University, available online at www.tegemeo.org/documents/work/tegemeo_workingpaper_19.pdf, last accessed April 2008

Mwape, F. (2007) 'Trends in African states' public expenditures to the agricultural sector', Presentation at the Re-SAKSS Workshop on Public Expenditures to Agriculture, 29–30 May, Lusaka

Nashashibi, K., Gupta, S., Liuksila, C., Lorie, H. and Mahler, W. (1992) 'The fiscal dimensions of adjustment in low-income countries', IMF Occasional Paper No. 95, International Monetary Fund, Washington, DC

Neven, D. and Reardon, T. (2004) 'The rise of Kenyan supermarkets and the evolution of their horticulture product procurement systems', *Development Policy Review*, vol 22, no 6, pp669–699

Pletcher, J. (2000) 'The politics of liberalizing Zambia's maize markets', *World Development*, vol 28, no 1, pp129–142

Poulton, C., Gibbon, P., Hanyani-Mlambo, B., Kydd, J., Maro, W., Larsen, M., Osorio, A., Tschirley, D. and Zulu, B. (2003) 'Competition and coordination in liberalized African cotton market systems', *World Development*, vol 32, no3, pp519–536

Putterman, L. (1995) 'Economic reform and smallholder agriculture in Tanzania: A discussion of recent market liberalization, road rehabilitation, and technology dissemination efforts', *World Development*, vol 23, no 26, pp311–326

Ravallion, M. and Datt, G. (2002) 'Why has economic growth been more pro-poor in some states of India than others?', *Journal of Development Economics*, vol 68, pp381–400

Reardon, T. and Timmer, C. (2006) 'Transformation of markets for agricultural output in developing countries since 1950: How has thinking changed?", in R. Evenson and P. Pingali (eds), *Handbook of Agricultural Economics*, vol 3, Elsevier, London

Sahley, C., Groelsema, B., Marchione, T. and Nelson, D. (2005) 'The governance dimensions of food security in Malawi', USAID Bureau of Democracy, Conflict, and Humanitarian Assistance, Washington, DC

Shaffer, J., Weber, M., Riley, H. and Staaz, J. (1985) 'Influencing the design of marketing systems to promote development in third world countries', in *Agricultural Markets in the Semi-Arid Tropics: Proceedings of the International Workshop*, October

Stambulis, K. (2002) 'Elitist food and agricultural policies and the food problem in Malawi', *Journal of Malawi Society – Historical & Scientific*, vol 55, no 2

The *Standard* (2004) 'Who owns Kenya?', *The East Africa Standard Newspaper*, 1
   October, available online at //www.eastandard.net/archives/cl/hm_news/
   news.php?articleid=1916, last accessed April 2006
Tiffen, M. (2003) 'Transition in sub-Saharan Africa: Agriculture, urbanization, and
   income growth', *World Development*, vol 31, no 8, pp1343–1366
Toye, J. (1992) 'Interest group politics and the implementation of adjustment in sub-
   Saharan Africa', *Journal of International Development*, vol 4, no 2, pp183–198
Traill, B. (2006) 'The rapid rise of supermarkets?', *Development Policy Review*, vol 24, no
   2, pp163–174
Traub, L. and Jayne, T. (2005) 'Opportunities to improve household food security
   through promoting informal maize marketing channels: Experience from eastern Cape
   province', South Africa International Development Working Paper 85, Michigan State
   University, East Lansing, available online at
   www.aec.msu.edu/agecon/fs2/papers/IDWP85.pdf, last accessed April 2008
Tschirley, D. (2007) 'Supermarkets and beyond: Literature review on farmer to market
   linkages in sub-Saharan Africa and Asia', Paper prepared for the AgInfo Project funded
   by the Bill and Melinda Gates foundation
Tschirley, D., Abdula, D. and Weber, M. (2005) 'Toward improved marketing and trade
   policies to promote household food security in central and southern Mozambique',
   Paper prepared for the Conference on 'Toward improved maize marketing and trade
   policies in the southern Africa region', Sponsored by the Food, Agriculture, and
   Natural Resources Policy Analysis Network (FANRPAN). 21–22 June, Centurion Park
   Hotel, Centurion, South Africa, available online at www.aec.msu.edu/agecon/
   maizemarket/South_Central_Mozambique_David_Tschirley_Paper.pdf, last accessed
   April 2008
Tschirley, D., Ayieko, M., Mathenge, M. and Weber, M. (2004b) 'Where do consumers in
   Nairobi purchase their food and why does this matter?', The Need for Investment to
   Improve Kenya's 'Traditional' Food Marketing System, Tegemeo Institute Of
   Agricultural Policy and Development, Policy Brief #2, Egerton University
Tschirley, D., Nijhoff, J., Arlindo, P., Mwinga, B., Weber, M. and Jayne, T. (2006)
   'Anticipating and responding to drought emergencies in southern Africa: Lessons from
   the 2002–2003 experience', Prepared for the New Partnership for Africa's
   Development (NEPAD) Conference on Successes in African Agriculture, 22–25
   November 2004, Nairobi, Kenya, also published as International Development
   Working Paper 89, Michigan State University, East Lansing, available online at
   www.aec.msu.edu/agecon/maizemarket/index.htm, last accessed April 2008
Tschirley, D., Kavoi, M. and Weber, M. (2004a) 'Improving Kenya's domestic horticul-
   tural production and marketing system: Current competitiveness, forces of change, and
   challenges for the future (Volume II: Horticultural Marketing), Tegemeo Institute of
   Agricultural Policy and Development, Working Paper 8B, Egerton University
van de Walle, N. (2001) *African Economies and the Politics of Permanent Crisis, 1979–1999*,
   Cambridge University Press, Cambridge
von Braun, J. and Kennedy, E. (eds) (1994) *Agricultural Commercialization, Economic
   Development, and Nutrition*, Johns Hopkins University Press, Baltimore, MD
Weatherspoon, D. and Reardon, T. (2003) 'The rise of supermarkets in Africa:
   Implications for agrifood systems and the rural poor', *Development Policy Review*, vol
   21, no 3, pp333–355
World Bank (2008) *World Development Report 2008*, Washington, DC

Part Two

The Changing Structure of Food Systems

Chapter 6

The Changing Nature and Structure of Agri-Food Systems in Developing Countries: Beyond the Farm Gate

Kevin Z. Chen and Kostas Stamoulis

Introduction

During the 1980s and 1990s, there was rapid industrialization of agriculture in the developed economies (Boehlje 1995, 1996). The trend toward greater concentration in agricultural input and food distribution, the increasing role of information and logistic technologies and the growing importance of food safety, quality and other technical requirements resulted in dramatic changes in food systems. Food systems became highly organized and linked from producer through consumer with an increasingly dominant role played by highly concentrated agro-industrial firms and retailers. With rapid economic growth, increasing urbanization and accelerated integration into the world market, many developing countries of Africa, Latin America and Asia have also seen a surge in the number of supermarkets and large agro-food firms operating within their borders, and trends similar to those that reshaped food systems in developed economies have been reported in developing countries (see for example Cook et al, 2001).

Many authors have already characterized the changes in agri-food systems and discussed implications for small farmers (i.e. Reardon et al, 2001; Chen, 2004; Stamoulis et al, 2004; Chen et al, 2005a; Reardon and Berdegue, 2006). This chapter reviews four country studies from the point of view of changes in agri-food systems.[1] The analysis is carried out in light of the literature available on such changes and their implications, and involves examples from other countries (especially China) with which the authors are familiar. It highlights major trends and presents new evidence, noting the rapid spread of supermarkets in the developing world, the new generation of wholesalers that has arisen, and the dominant role played by food processing firms. As a consequence of these changes, new business practices have developed for the procurement of agricultural raw materials, with implications for small suppliers and farmers. Alternative farmers' organizations and institutions are emerging in developing countries to overcome these market access barriers. At the same time, it is evident from the country studies and the literature that, while the traditional food system has been shaken by the arrival of new players, the traditional food systems are very much alive. The pace and scope of change differs depending on each country's stage of economic development and the sector concerned. An important conclusion of the paper is that policy makers need to be fully aware of changes in food systems and put in place appropriate policies which reflect the particular conditions in each country.

The rapid spread of supermarkets

Three of the country studies included here deal with the potential importance of supermarket expansion on horticultural producers in Chile, Kenya and Zambia. The Chile study reports that supermarkets' share of sales in the food retail market grew from 49 per cent in 1994 to 61 per cent in 2001 (Dirven and Faiguenbaum, this volume). The Kenya study shows that the supermarket sales share in the country had grown at a rate of 20–30 per cent each year during the 1990s, and that by 2002 Kenya had more than 220 supermarkets (Neven and Reardon, this volume). The Zambia study presents a case of supermarket business expansion by Shoprite, a South African retail outlet that expanded into other countries in Africa. Shoprite expansion in Zambia started with the purchase of eight buildings in 1995 following successful negotiations with the Zambia Privatization Agency (ZPA); currently it operates 18 outlets and runs Freshmark, a distributor of fresh vegetables and fruits (Haantuba and de Graaf, this volume).

This level of supermarket growth is certainly not unique to Kenya, Zambia and Chile. The 'supermarket revolution' (Reardon and Hopkins, 2006) began in most developing countries in the early 1990s and the speed with which they spread took many farmers, food companies and policy makers, among others, by surprise. While the rate has varied over regions, it can be characterized as occurring in four 'waves'.[2]

In the first-wave countries, the average share of supermarkets in food retail went from only 10–20 per cent in 1990 to 50–60 per cent on average by the early 2000s (Reardon and Berdegue, 2002; Reardon et al, 2003); these include many countries in South America, east Asian countries (outside China), north central Europe and the Baltic countries, and South Africa. Country-specific examples include Brazil, with a 76 per cent share of supermarkets in food retail (Farina, 2002); Argentina, with 60 per cent (Gutman, 2000); Taiwan with 55 per cent (Chang, 2005); and the Czech Republic with 55 per cent (Dries et al, 2004).

Compare that to the 75–80 per cent share of food retail that supermarkets in North America and Europe had in 2005 and a process of convergence becomes evident; these first-wave countries saw supermarket diffusion in a single decade that took some five decades to occur in the US and the UK. A slightly later group includes Costa Rica and Chile, with circa 50 per cent (Reardon and Berdegue, 2002; Berdegue et al, 2005); South Korea with 30 per cent (Lee and Reardon, 2005); Thailand and Malaysia with 40 per cent (Chen, 2004); the Philippines with 50 per cent (Manalili, 2005); and South Africa with 55 per cent (Weatherspoon and Reardon, 2003).

The second-wave countries, where supermarket take-off occurred later in the 1990s, include Mexico and much of southeast Asia, Central America and south central Europe, where the supermarket share grew from circa 5 or 10 per cent in 1990 to 30–50 per cent by the early 2000s. Examples include Mexico (56 per cent share), Guatemala (36 per cent), Indonesia (30 per cent) and Bulgaria (25 per cent) (Reardon and Berdegue, 2006; Orellana and Vasquez, 2004; Rangkuti, 2003; Dries et al, 2004).

The third-wave countries are those where the supermarket take-off started closer to 2000, generally reaching about 10–20 per cent of national food retail by around 2003; included in this group are Kenya (20 per cent share), Nicaragua (20 per cent) and China (with exceptional growth reaching 53 per cent) (Neven and Reardon, 2004; Balsevich et al, 2006; Chen, 2004). Recent rapid growth has been observed in Zambia, Vietnam, India and Russia, but no statistics on supermarket share there have been reported. There are indications that other countries are also seeing supermarkets take hold, including several in south Asia (outside India) and sub-Saharan Africa, and the poorer countries in southeast Asia (such as Cambodia) and South America (such as Bolivia). In Africa Mozambique, Tanzania, Uganda and Angola will probably be the next to see supermarket expansion, while many other countries are unlikely to see supermarket growth for several decades. The rate of expansion will be determined by levels of technology and demand. It is evident that supermarket growth depends largely on a country's stage of economic development.

Several aspects regarding the diffusion of supermarkets in developing countries are worth noting (Reardon and Berdegue, 2006; Chen, 2004). First, whereas previously supermarkets often occupied only a small niche in capital cities, serving primarily the rich and upper-middle class, they are now penetrating into mass food markets and have spread from big cities to smaller cities and even to towns. AC Nielsen's recent studies (2003) show the staggering development of modern trade in China's key cities in 2002, with increased penetration of chain store operation and supermarkets into non-metropolitan areas. In Thailand, the presence of more than 100 hypermarkets in Bangkok has meant there is limited room for expansion there, and chains such as BigC and Tesco have opened more stores in the provinces than they have in Bangkok. It is just a matter of time before supermarkets will eventually spread into the food market of the poor in Asia. (At the moment, however, in the poor states or provinces and in most rural areas of Thailand, Malaysia and China, supermarkets are still rare.)

The second aspect to note is that many consumers still prefer to buy fresh food at traditional markets. Though Kenya had more than 220 supermarkets in 2002,[3] supermarkets accounted for only 5 per cent of the total sales of fresh vegetables and fruits produced domestically. Similar observations have been made about Asia, where consumers prefer traditional outlets for fresh food (Chen, 2004; Chen et al, 2005). AC Nielsen (2003) reports that in most Asian countries, 80–90 per cent of urban shoppers use the wet market regularly. In Malaysia, 77 per cent of consumers still use traditional stores regularly for purchasing meat, 73 per cent for vegetables and 57 per cent for fruits. In Thailand, 85 per cent of consumers still use traditional stores regularly for purchasing meat, 86 per cent for vegetables and 87 per cent for fruits. A survey by the author of meat consumers in Shanghai indicated that more than 83 per cent of the respondents purchased their fresh meat from wet markets (Chen and Miao, 2000). Chinese Statistics on Chain Operation (2002) revealed that the proportion of consumers that purchased in modern self-service stores in seven major cities in China were in the ranges 1.9–9 per cent for fresh vegetables, 0.6–8.2 per cent for fruits and 1–3 per cent for ready-to-eat fish.

Another trend reported in the literature is toward regional, centralized distribution centres. So far, few supermarket chains outside of Latin America have such centralized distribution centres for fresh produce, which means that wholesalers and small retailers still have a role in those countries. With the recent rapid expansion of supermarket chains, it is anticipated that centralized distribution centres will eventually be in place, which would have a profound impact on how fresh produce is produced and marketed. Because it is impossible to know how fast such a shift could take place, it is difficult to advise farmers and other suppliers on the adjustments they need to make, but the trends have to be closely followed.

Characteristics of the new processing industries

Processors of food – that is, those companies (or individuals) that perform post-harvest activities that add value to agricultural raw materials – have played leading roles in the economic development of both developed and developing economies. The drive to achieve economies of scale has led to consolidation into larger plants and firms in order to cut costs. Consumers now expect a steady supply of foods tailored to their tastes, so processors need to assure such a supply and thus seek farm products with well defined characteristics. In many segments of agriculture, processors contract with producers for access to specific raw material.

Another factor to consider is that a growing, significant portion of the new generation of agricultural technology is both specific and proprietary. Companies that invest heavily to develop new technologies expect to make returns on their investments. Capturing those returns means, in many cases, controlling the production, processing and marketing of the resulting products. The Poland study looked at vertical coordination of the dairy processing sector (Dries and Swinnen, this volume).

Among the world's top 15 agri-industrial companies by value of sales, ten are from the US, four from Europe and one from Japan (Wilkinson, this volume). With the maturity of their domestic food markets, these large firms have looked increasingly at opportunities aboard. International food trade and foreign direct investment (FDI) have come to play important roles in re-shaping the food processing and input supply sectors in developing countries. Large retail relies on as large a share in FDI as other agro-industrial sectors; depending on the level of development of the food system in each country, it tends to reproduce the strategies developed in the industrialized countries. For example, FDI in Mexican food processing grew rapidly after the 1988 change in laws governing foreign investment, which allowed majority foreign ownership for the first time. US FDI in Mexican food processing grew from US$210 million in 1987 to US$5 billion in 1997 (Runsten, 2003).

A common characteristic of the global food system is the adoption of increasingly stringent quality criteria to which developing countries are expected to adhere. In Mexico, Runsten found that most small and medium packers and processors of vegetables were unprepared for supermarket requirements concerning quality control and certification (as well as such aspects as contracting, accreditation, electronic data interchange, volume, leasing of shelf space, finances, reporting and delayed payment practices) (Runsten, 2003). This presents a challenge for small and medium enterprises (SMEs) in food processing and is one explanation for the emergence of integrated chains that achieve economies of scale.

Processors in general complained that the powerful chain stores charged them high entry fees to place their products in mass-market stores. At the same time, chain stores have broadened the range of their house-brand products to further pressure brand-name suppliers. Some processors had found the losses too great to bear and had exited the business. To survive, processors have to invest in computerized systems to better track production and control costs and staff have to be better trained in handling orders from modern traders. The shake-out of local processors continues, but stronger ones (including some that have amalgamated) have adapted and are capturing a growing share of sales to supermarkets. However, the meat and vegetable industry shake-out is especially severe: half of the remaining firms are expected to merge or go bankrupt in Asia.

The impact on processors of this shake-out varies according to sector. Chen (2004) shows that chicken processors in Thailand, China and Malaysia were able to adapt to the changing organization of retail in Asia but that the shift had a significantly greater impact on packers and processors of vegetables. Chicken processing industries in these countries were transformed long ago by stringent export requirements and are highly concentrated. (In Thailand and Malaysia, independent processors account for less than 20 per cent of the total, while in China they account for less than 35 per cent.) The large companies were accustomed to stringent requirements in the export markets and so had little difficulty adapting to the supply requirements of the supermarket chains. Chen et al (2007) found that a handful of dairy processing companies in China played a dominant role in determining the price and standard of raw milk purchased, although Nestlé investment in dairy in Heilongjiang led to improved market access and quality improvements by small dairy farmers. The Poland study showed that foreign investment in dairy processing in Poland and its spill-over effects led to small local suppliers' having improved access to finance, which allowed them to increase investments and make quality improvements (Dries and Swinnen, this volume).

The Chile study found that in fruit and vegetable chains, it was not uncommon for supermarkets to have direct contact with farmers, while in dairy and meat chains, the supermarkets had direct contact only with a few cheese producers, where agro-industrial firms set the producer standards (Dirven and Faiguenbaum, this volume). Not only changes in food retail, but changes in processing could have a significant impact on the suppliers of raw agricultural products. It is important to assess carefully the perception that the role of agro-industrial companies has now been fully assumed by large retailers, particularly in the dairy and meat sectors. Focusing explicitly on the coordination of globally dispersed, but linked, production systems, Gereffi (1994) has shown that many chains are characterized by a dominant party which determines the overall character of the chain, a lead firm, which is responsible for coordinating interaction between the links and upgrading activities as necessary. This is a role of governance, and here a distinction is made between two types of governance: those cases where the coordination is undertaken by buyers such as supermarkets (buyer-driven commodity chains) and those in which suppliers such as processors play the key role (producer-driven commodity chains). Though a successful chain often has an effective 'channel manager', a role of the channel manager can frequently be taken by either supermarkets or processors in developing countries.

The changing role of wholesalers

Historically, wholesale markets have been important outlets for small producers around the world. However in the US, for example, the wholesale market is no longer a significant outlet for fresh produce: more than two-thirds of the fresh produce sold at supermarkets is now shipped directly to the retailer from production regions either by grower/shippers or by field brokers. The US and other industrialized countries (except Japan) shifted gradually to supermarket retail concentration between the 1920s and the 1960s. That process resulted in a food distribution system characterized by:

1   increased regional concentration of agricultural production;
2   increased assembly and packaging of products at the shipping point rather than at destination markets;
3   widespread development of private chain distribution centres capable of receiving truckloads of agricultural products directly from shipping points; and

4   a reduction in the importance of urban wholesale markets as a retail distribution mechanism.

Japanese wholesale markets have changed more slowly than in the US. Starting in 2000 vegetable wholesalers have been under tremendous pressure as supermarkets have worked hard to bypass them and source vegetables directly from farmers or farmer cooperatives (Chen, 2004). A general manager of a leading fruit and vegetable wholesaler estimated that the share of vegetables in Japan that passes through the wholesale markets will fall from 80 per cent in 2002 to less than 40 per cent in the next ten years.

Has a similar evolution started in developing countries? Significant development in wholesale markets took place during the 1970s and 1980s in most developing countries in Asia, the Middle East, South America and Africa (Seidler, 2001). In China, the most rapid development in the wholesale markets happened in the 1990s. Wholesale markets have been established in every major town and city in China, and the rapid spread of supermarkets that began during the 1990s has started to affect how they function. Supermarket chains aim to increase food safety and quality to meet the needs of modern consumers and to reduce costs by increasing volumes procured. It can be difficult for them to meet those objectives using the traditional wholesale sector.

Some shortcomings of the traditional wholesalers include sporadic and inadequate use of refrigerated storage such as temperature-controlled chambers (very few in the wholesale market can – or want to – invest in cold storage facilities); wide use of packaging materials that can undermine product quality; heavy reliance on manual labour, which prolongs merchandise exposure to ambient temperatures; and poor wholesale handling, which contributes to heavy losses. In China, for example, nearly 60 per cent of the total volume of perishables is lost between harvest and the time products reach the consumers. The Chile study showed that the country's largest wholesale market for fruits and vegetables is not seen as a reliable outlet for small farmers; vendors prefer to trade with middle to larger-scale farmers to reduce transaction costs, although forms of backward linkages were observed that ensured produce quality (Dirven and Faiguenbaum, this volume).

Chain stores in developing countries are increasingly attempting to purchase produce directly from agricultural regions, and vegetable and fruit wholesalers in particular are facing by-passing pressure from modern retail and service outlets (Chen, 2004).[4] 'New generation wholesalers' are emerging in order to assure the quality and consistency of delivery of products year-round and to provide a one-stop shop for several types of produce at once (Chen 2004; Balsevich et al, 2006; Reardon et al, 2007).

Producers with small-scale farm operations are individually unable to fulfil volume requirements, quality standards and packaging specifications imposed by new-generation wholesalers and will need to adjust to new retailing conditions.

The modern trade system requires very efficient information technology to manage inventory, logistics and administration in order to lower costs. At several fresh produce wholesale markets visited in Asia, most administrators and merchants appeared unconcerned about the proliferation of chain stores possibly undermining their businesses. Why don't they pursue chain store accounts more aggressively? In part it is because the wholesale markets consist of many stall operators who purchase small quantities for almost immediate resale to retailers at tight margins. While wholesalers are accustomed to receiving prompt payment from their clients, supermarkets often delay payments.

Though there is little doubt that the supermarket revolution has affected the functioning and viability of wholesale markets, wholesalers are still a dominant component of food systems in developing countries. Seidler (2001) points out that the high rates of urban growth in African and Asian developing countries will create the need for both expanded and new wholesale markets, especially in rapidly expanding 'secondary' cities. Some observers anticipate that fresh produce wholesalers will continue to play a key role in vegetable distribution in China, Thailand and Malaysia during the next 20 years (Chen, 2004), largely because of the absence of a well-developed marketing infrastructure in many of the fresh produce production areas. (This is especially true in those areas that have not been involved in export-oriented commerce.)

In addition, relatively little domestic fresh produce destined for the internal market is adequately prepared for retail sale at the farm gate. Only the largest growers routinely sort and classify produce by size and maturity at their packing sheds; items that do receive this treatment are primarily commodities for export. Sorting and classification of fresh produce for the internal market is usually conducted at central wholesale markets in major population centres. The inconsistent or nonexistent application of quality product standards at many rural packing facilities obliges retailers to depend heavily on wholesalers and other intermediaries for fresh produce that more closely meets their specifications for size, quality, appearance and maturity.

These dynamics can be expected to change quickly in the future. The first factor will be how soon supermarket chains attain the economy of scale needed to justify building independent distribution centres in certain developing countries. The second is how quickly cooperatives, farm groupings and other alliances can be developed in order to link farmers with large-scale distribution centres. The development of appropriate cooperatives and other farm groupings to handle such tasks has been limited in most developing countries. With the emerging large distribution centres associated with supermarkets, it can be expected that new generation wholesalers will become more popular in the future.

The traditional wholesale market has been recognized as an important outlet for smallholders in many developing countries. With the changes that have occurred in recent years, will it continue to be an outlet for small farmers? It is an important question pro-poor policy makers need to be able to answer, but few studies have attempted to do so. The Chile study observed that vendors at the wholesale market Lo Valledor preferred to trade with middle to larger-scale farmers, but it was based on a limited number of interviews at that market (and noted that efforts were being made to modernize the wholesale market and its downstream linkages with street markets) (Dirven and Faiguenbaum, this volume). If the findings turn out to be representative, an effort should be made to better understand the impediments that smallholders face in selling through the wholesale markets and to provide support for addressing the impediments.

New procurement practices

The country studies brought to light a number of significant changes that are commonly observed in developing countries, including the arrival of supermarkets, the new generation wholesalers and the emergence of large food processing firms. One direct consequence of these changes is that new business practices in procurement have also been adopted that are very different from the traditional ones (see Reardon et al, 2007; Chen, 2004). One characteristic of the new procurement practices is the increasing use of a variety of supply contracts (see da Silva, 2005). Supplier contracts allow buyers to control safety and quality, ensure desired supply volumes and reduce price uncertainty. There has been increased coordination between buyers and suppliers through more demanding contracts that typically last one to three years. Prices are usually open for negotiation, with the prevailing market price at the time and place of delivery as a minimum protected price.

A typical supplier/supermarket trading agreement for fresh vegetables usually includes (Chen, 2004):

1 prices that are negotiated weekly;
2 a 30- or 60-day delay in payment;
3 quality control procedures based on government standards, good agricultural practices (GAPs, including EurepGAP), Hazard Analysis and Critical Control Points (HACCP), traceability, phyto-certificates and Maximum Residue Limits (MRL) testing;
4 stringent delivery terms such as minimum volume and delivery times;
5 various types of listing fees such as supply listing fee and line listing fee (for introducing a new product category);
6 fees for promotional display and advertising;
7 requirements for other discounts such as new store opening discounts and volume rebates; and
8 occasionally, a probation period for the evaluation of initial sale performance.

Another significant change is in the numerous and costly criteria for supplier accreditation. There is increased demand for technical certification such as international quality standards (e.g. ISO 9000) and HACCP-based farm quality assurance. Requirements might include access to adequate facilities for sorting, grading, packing, storage and transport. (The Zambia study described how the government provided technical assistance for smallholders to adopt GAPs to help smallholders sell to the Shoprite supermarket chain) (Haantuba and De Graaf, this volume). Particularly in Japan, many supermarkets demand traceability of products back to producers, using bar codes. Suppliers are increasingly expected to have: (1) electronic systems such as electronic data interchange and continuous replenishment system; (2) adequate working capital and general financial strength; and (3) adequate management and personnel resources (such as a value-added tax (VAT) system compatible with company accounting). There is often a very wide gap between retail expectations and the services actually being delivered by suppliers (Chen, 2004). Only a small percentage of suppliers has responded to emerging retailers' needs and opportunities.

As the number of stores grows, there has been increasing consolidation of the procurement systems by store, distribution centre, zone, country and region. The bargaining power of buyers for supermarkets derives from their access to regional and global networks of suppliers and their huge volumes. Supermarket companies prefer to deal with large traders with regional and global supply networks, and retailers rely on them to produce large volumes at required times. Movement by retailers towards more regional and global sourcing is happening very fast for packaged products. However, the move towards centralized, regional distribution centres is much slower for the fresh food segment. Many small supermarket chains still use individual store purchasing systems, while most chains use central-ized purchasing. A handful of centralized distribution centres were observed, while larger centralized regional/global distribution centres have yet to be observed in Asia. Supermarkets source centralized chicken purchases from a few large vertically integrated processors in several Asian countries. In Thailand and China, each supermarket chain typically chooses one or two large integrated suppliers; in Malaysia, each supermarket chain typically chooses four or five large integrated suppliers to assure supply reliability.

Most supermarket chains have a centralized distribution centre for dried and canned foods but not for fresh foods. Virtually all supermarket chains interviewed in China, Thailand and Malaysia are considering establishing them; however, with the current volumes of fresh produce that supermarket chains handle, the extra costs of building distribution centres are likely to be greater than the benefits they bring in. While the number of chain-affiliated retail outlets is expanding rapidly, many supermarkets and chain stores do not yet operate a sufficient number of retail stores to justify building and operating their own proprietary distribution centres in every locality they serve. Several representatives of supermarket chains in Shanghai and Thailand indicated that it is economically feasible to build a centralized distribution centre only if a chain has at least 20 hypermarkets in a given region. Obviously the radius for shipping fresh vegetables is much narrower than for packaged foods. Once it does become feasible to build distribution centres this will, of course, usher in significant changes in how vegetables are produced and marketed. The Chile study noted that the presence of a distribution centre eliminated many small vegetable suppliers in Santiago (Dirven and Faiguenbaum, this volume).

The emerging intermediaries in the food system

While the new food system creates new markets for farming sectors, it is often claimed that its specifications are too demanding to be profitable for small suppliers, including small farmers. Because many small-scale producers are not accustomed to delivering products in a format that can be easily received by buyers and may be reluctant or unable to conduct long-distance sales transactions without advance payment, it comes as little surprise that chain stores or other buyers have frequently established direct shipment contracts with a relatively small group of larger producers or well-organized associations. Some evidence suggests that many small farmers that have a hard time meeting the demands of the new market can earn higher incomes selling to traditional markets.

The changing food system also changes the way some farmers work in developing countries. To keep pace with the demands, farms have to adjust by specializing in a particular commodity, consolidating fragmented land holdings to achieve scale economies and forging stronger links with processors and retailers. Closer relationships between firms at different stages of production and marketing are emerging as larger commercialized farm operations grow produce and animals under contract for processors, retailers or exporters. For example, there has been a huge increase in the number of privately and publicly owned vegetable and fruit distribution centres or companies that link small farmers to supply to modern retail and service outlets. There is growing use of specialized wholesalers and distributors specialized in a product category and dedicated to the supermarket sector as the main client. For example, in Thailand's largest vegetable wholesale market, six specialized wholesalers deliver to supermarket chains.

Many small farmers organize themselves in companies or organizations referred to as 'carriers' in order to be more competitive with larger suppliers. Many forms of these carriers have emerged in developing countries; they include private companies, franchisers, quasi-government companies, NGOs, farmers' markets, farmers' associations, farmer cooperatives, leading farmers and brokers. Chen et al (2005a) presents a case in Shandong, China on how vegetable growers formed various carriers to meet the increasing requirements for vegetable exports to Japan.

While there have been clear efficiency gains in some industries due to increased vertical coordination, the possibility remains that large processors will use their power to depress the prices paid for the inputs and to make other contract conditions that are disadvantageous for producers. This has motivated some producers to form associations or cooperatives to bargain collectively with processors in a manner similar to labour unions. This is a role frequently assumed by producer organizations in Europe, while in the US the Agricultural Fair Practices Act (AFPA) of 1967 offers some protection to farmers and ranchers who form associations in order to bargain with handlers and processors for better prices and terms. In Canada, producers' rights to organize are protected by provincial legislation. Commodity groups can also play a key role in the development of fair contract terms by bringing together large and small producers, processors, integrators, attorneys and others to jointly address the development of contracts that will serve the needs of all parties in the commodity group. Another option is for producers to work under contract for specific processors, thus creating a closely coordinated supply chain that reduces processors' transaction costs involved in locating and negotiating with suitable suppliers. Yet another possibility would be to lower transaction costs with cooperatives that focus on product differentiation.

Looking forward

More open markets, increasing per capita income, growing urbanization and facilitation of foreign investment have created the conditions for significant changes in food systems in developing countries. The expansion of supermarket chains is altering the traditional structure of marketing channels and creating new challenges and opportunities for participating agents. While modern retailers in developing countries source most of their produce, meat and other raw materials in the countries where they operate, they have had difficulty obtaining reliable supplies of standardized quality products from the traditional system of smallholders geared toward producing food for their own consumption. To keep pace with the demands of buyers, farmers will have to adjust by specializing in particular commodities, consolidating fragmented land holdings to achieve scale economies and forging stronger links with processors, retailers and other buyers. Closer relationships between firms at different stages of production and marketing are emerging as larger commercialized farm operations grow produce and animals under contract for processors, retailers or exporters. This trend is beginning to profoundly alter the way food is produced in these countries.

Just as there are significant market access issues for agri-food exports from developing countries, there are significant entry barriers for small farmers and other suppliers trying to access supermarkets and other modern retail outlets. This new market is often much more significant for small farmers than the export markets, yet there are few studies available on the identification of and response to these barriers in developing countries. There is evidence that smallholders are relying on carriers to link with modern supply chains. These can take many forms; there is little evidence on which forms produce the best outcomes in terms of providing higher income for the poor. Farmer organizations appear to have had some success in linking small farmers with supermarkets or intermediaries, yet their development in this regard is slow. Those that have been most successful at linking up small farmers have generally enjoyed technical assistances from industries, NGOs or governments (Shepherd, 2007).

Although traditional food systems are being shaken up by the arrival of new players, those in developing countries are still very much alive. The speed and scope of changes in the structures of food systems differ according to sector and to the stage of economic development in a country. It is important for policy makers to realize that the opportunities associated with the changing food systems are not all created equal; public policies should not create false incentives that push producers blindly into new markets.

Notes

1   The four country studies, presented as chapters in this book, include Poland (Dries and Swinnen); Chile (Dirven and Faiguenbaum); Kenya (Neven and Reardon); and Zambia (Haantuba and de Graaf). Any unattributed references to those countries in this chapter can be assumed to derive from the studies. Earlier versions of the studies were presented at the FAO technical workshop on 'Globalization of food systems: Impacts on food security and nutrition', 8–10 October 2003, Rome.
2   The characterization presented here draws heavily from Reardon and Berdegue (2006).
3   This number raises questions about the definition of 'supermarket' used here.
4   Some traditional wholesalers of other products have faced even more pressure. In Thailand, 50 per cent of local wholesale trading companies in the dried and canned food category amalgamated or went out of business as the supermarkets' share of retail sales increased.

References

AC Nielsen (2003) 'Asia retail and shopper trends', available online at www.acnielsen.com, last accessed September 2003

Balsevich, F., Berdegue, J. and Reardon, T. (2006) 'Supermarkets, new-generation whole-salers, tomato farmers and NGOs in Nicaragua', Staff paper 2006-03, Dept of Agricultural Economics, Michigan State University, East Lansing, MI

Berdegue, J. A., Balsevich, F., Flores, L. and Readon, T. (2005) 'Central American super-markets' private standards of quality and safety in procurement of fresh fruit and vegetables', *Food Policy*, vol 30, no 3, pp254–269

Boehlje, M. (1995) 'The "new" agriculture', *Choices*, Fourth Quarter, pp34–35

Boehlje, M. (1996) 'Industrialization of agriculture: what are the implications?', *Choices*, Fourth Quarter, pp34–35

Chang, C. C. (2005) 'The role of the retail sector in agri-food systems', Chinese Taipei, Presentation at the Pacific Economic Co-operation Council's Pacific Food System Outlook, 2005–06 Annual Meeting in Kun Ming, China, 11–13 May

Chen, K. (2004) 'Retail revolution, entry barriers and emerging agri-food supply chains in selected Asian countries: Determinants, issues and policy choices', FAO/AGS, Rome

Chen, K. and Miao, L. (2000) 'Consumer preference for fresh meat attributes and retail outlet choices in China', Final Report submitted to Alberta Agricultural Research Institute, Department of Rural Economy, University of Alberta, Alberta

Chen, K., Chen, Y. and Shi, M. (2005a) 'Globalization, pesticide regulation and supply chain development: A case of Chinese vegetable export to Japan', in Z. Huang, K. Chen and M. Shi (eds) *Food Safety: Consumer, Trade and Regulation Issues*, Zhejiang University Press, Hangzhou

Chen, K., Shepherd, A. and da Silva, C. (2005b) 'Changes in food retailing in Asia: Implications of supermarket practices for farmers and traditional marketing systems', Agricultural Management, Marketing and Finance Occasional Paper 8, FAO/AGS, Rome

Chen, K., Hu, D. and Hu, S. (2007) 'Linking markets to smallholder dairy farmers in China: Quality as a driver', A report to China Canada Small Farmer Adapting to Global Markets Project, July

Chinese Statistics on Chain Operation (2002) China Chain Store & Franchise Association

Cook, M. L., Reardon, T., Barrett, C. and Cacho, J. (2001) 'Agro industrialization in emerging markets: Overview and strategic context', *International Food and Agribusiness Management Review*, vol 2, no 3/4, pp277–288

da Silva, C. A. B. (2005) 'The growing role of contract farming in agri-food systems development: Drivers, theory, and practices', Occasional Paper, Rural Infrastructure and Agro-Industries Division, Department of Agriculture and Consumer Protection, FAO, Rome

Dirven, M. and Faiguenbaum, S. (this volume) 'The role of Santiago wholesale markets in supporting small farmers and poor consumers'

Dries, L. and Swinnen, J. (this volume) 'The impact of globalization and vertical integration in agri-food processing on local suppliers: Evidence from the Polish dairy sector'

Dries, L., Reardon, T. and Swinnen, J. (2004) 'The rapid rise of supermarkets in central and eastern Europe: Implications for the agri-food sector and rural development', *Development Policy Review*, vol 22, no 5, pp525–556

Farina, E. (2002) 'Consolidation, multinationalization, and competition in Brazil: Impacts on horticulture and dairy product systems', *Development Policy Review*, vol 20, no 4, pp441–457

Gereffi, G. (1994) 'The organization of buyer-driven global commodity chains: How U.S. retailers shape overseas production networks', in G. Gereffi and R. Korzeniewicz (eds), *Commodity Chains and Global Capitalism*, Praeger, London

Gutman, G. E. (2002) 'Impact of the rapid rise of supermarkets on dairy products systems in Argentina', *Development Policy Review*, vol 20, no 4, pp409–427

Haantuba, H. and de Graaf, J. (this volume) 'Linkages between smallholder farmers and supermarkets: Lessons from Zambia'

Lee, J. H. and Reardon, T. (2005) 'Forward integration of an agricultural cooperative into the supermarket sector: The case of Hanaro Club in Korea', Department of Industrial Economics, Chung-Ang University, Seoul, Korea, and Department of Agricultural Economics, Michigan State University, East Lansing, MI

Manalili, N. M. (2005) 'The changing map of the Philippine retail food sector: The impact on trade and the structure of agriculture and the policy response', Presentation at the Pacific Economic Cooperation Council's Pacific Food System Outlook 2005–6 Annual Meeting in Kun Ming, China, 11–13 May

Neven, D. and Reardon, T. (2004) 'The rise of Kenyan supermarkets and evolution of their horticultural product procurement systems', *Development Policy Review*, vol 22, no 6, pp 669–699

Neven, D. and Reardon, T. (this volume) 'The rapid rise of Kenyan supermarkets: Impacts on the fruits and vegetables supply system'

Orellana, D. and Vasquez, E. (2004) 'Guatemala retail food sector annual 2004', GAIN Report Number GT4018, USDA Foreign Agricultural Service, Washington, DC

Rangkuti, F. (2003) 'Indonesia food retail sector report 2003', USDA GAIN Report, ID3028, USDA, Washington, DC

Reardon, T. and Berdegue, J. (2001) 'Globalization, changing market institutions and agri-food systems in Latin America: Implications for the poor's livelihoods', Paper presented at 74th EAAE Seminar, Livelihood and Rural Poverty: Technology, Policy and Institutions, 12–15 September, Imperial College at Wye, UK

Reardon, T. and Berdegue, J. (2002) 'The rapid rise of supermarkets in Latin America: Challenges and opportunities for development', *Development Policy Review*, vol 20, no 4, pp317–334

Reardon, T. and Berdegue, J. (2006) 'The retail-led transformation of agri-food systems and its implications for development policies', RIMISP, Santiago, Chile

Reardon, T. and Hopkins, R. (2006) 'The supermarket revolution in developing countries: Policies to address emerging tensions among supermarkets, suppliers and traditional retailers', *European Journal of Development Research*, vol 18, no 4

Reardon, T., Cordon, J. M., Busch, L., Bingen, J. and Harris, C. (2001) 'Global change in agrifood grades and standards: Agribusiness strategic responses in developing countries', *International Food and Agribusiness Management Review*, vol 293, pp195–205

Reardon, T., Henson, S. and Berdegue, J. (2007) 'Proactive fast-tracking diffusion of supermarkets in developing countries: Implications for market institutions and trade', *Journal of Economic Geography*, vol 7, no 4, pp399–431

Reardon, T., Timmer, C., Barret, C. and Berdegue, J. (2003) 'The rise of supermarkets in Africa, Asia, and Latin America', *American Journal of Agricultural Economics*, vol 85, no 5, pp1140–1146

Reardon, T., Timmer, P. and Berdegue, J. (this volume) 'The rapid rise of supermarkets in developing countries: Induced organizational, institutional and technological change in agri-food systems'

Runsten, D. (2003) 'Globalization, NAFTA and the restructuring of Mexican food processing', paper presented to the FAO conference on Globalization of Food Systems: Impacts on Food Security and Nutrition, 8–10 October, Rome, Italy

Seilder, E. (2001) 'Wholesale market development – FAO's experience', paper prepared for the 22nd Congress of the World Union of Wholesale Markets, September, Durban, South Africa

Shepherd, A. W. (2007) 'Approaches linking producers to markets', Agricultural Management, Marketing and Finance Occasional Paper 13, FAO/AGS, Rome

Stamoulis, K., Pingali, P. and Shetty, P. (2004) 'Emerging challenges for food and nutritrion policy in developing countries', *eJADE*, vol 1, no 2, pp154–167

Weatherspoon, D. D. and Reardon, T. (2003) 'The rise of supermarkets in Africa: Implications for agri-food systems and the rural poor', *Development Policy Review*, vol 21, no 3, pp333–355

Wilkinson, J. (this volume) 'The food processing industry, globalization and developing countries'

Chapter 7

The Impact of Globalization and Vertical Integration in Agri-Food Processing on Local Suppliers: Evidence from the Polish Dairy Sector

Liesbeth Dries and Johan F. M. Swinnen

Introduction

There is growing concern about the negative effects of globalization on sustainable development, poor people and welfare in developing countries and on the weaker groups in society. Yet some analysts point out that the forces behind globalization are powerful factors that could contribute to stimulating growth in developing countries, reducing poverty and making development sustainable. This paper aims to contribute to this debate by demonstrating some impacts of globalization on agriculture and rural areas in transition countries. It presents new empirical evidence on how specific aspects of 'globalization', in particular the inflow of foreign capital and the integration in international commodity markets, have affected Polish agriculture – and more specifically the small-scale dairy sector. Given the characteristics of the sector (many poor small farmers, low-quality output, in need of investment and restructuring, etc.), the study yields insights that have wider implications.

We selected the Polish dairy sector for several reasons. First, Poland is the largest of the European Union (EU) new member states, yet a small economy in the world market. Poland accounted for around 2.5 per cent of total milk production in the world (12 million metric tons) in 2000, and the accession of Poland in 2004 increased total milk output in the EU by 10 per cent (FAO, 2003). Yet milk

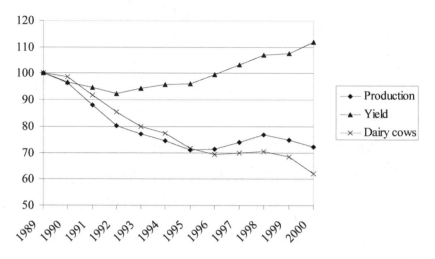

Source: ARR and IERiGZ (2001)

Figure 7.1 *Change in milk production, number of dairy cows and milk yields, 1989–1998*

production and the dairy sector were severely affected by the economic and institutional reforms of the transition. Milk production and the number of dairy cows fell by almost 30 per cent between 1989 and 1996 (Figure 7.1).[1] Productivity began to turn around in 1992 and since 1997 yields are above their pre-reform levels.

Second, agriculture is a very important sector in the Polish economy, with weak structures and low incomes. Almost 20 per cent of the population is employed in agriculture, mostly on small farms. Poland's agricultural sector is unique among the transition countries in that it had a mixed institutional structure under the communist regime. Small private family farms survived the communist collectivization and occupied 76 per cent of total agricultural land.[2] The remaining land was used by large-scale state farms; Poland had very few collective farms. Hence, in contrast to other communist countries where small farms resulted from the fragmentation and decollectivization of the former collective farms, both small and large farms have a strong historical and institutional basis in Poland.

Third, dairy plays an important role in Polish rural areas since many of the small farms have at least some milk production. At the time of our survey in 2001, more than 60 per cent of all dairy cows in Poland were kept in farms with fewer than four cows (see Table 7.1). (By 2000, 85 per cent of Polish dairy farms still had fewer than 5 cows (GUS, 2001).) Farms with fewer than ten cows produced 75 per cent of Poland's milk. Less than 60 per cent of total milk production was delivered to dairies; the rest was used for self-consumption or sold directly on the local market.

Fourth, the dairy sector – both the processing companies and the farms – were (and still are) in need of substantial restructuring in order to be competitive

Table 7.1 *Share of cows by herd size categories, 1996–2002*

Herd size (cows per farm)	1996 (%)	2002 (%)	Change 1996–2002 (%)
1–2	37.7	27.3	−10.4
3–4	24.9	15.5	−9.4
5–9	23.1	21.0	−2.1
10–29	7.5	26.1	+18.6
30–49	0.5	2.7	+2.2
50–99	1.3	1.7	+0.4
> 100	5.5	5.6	+0.1

Source: GUS and IERiGZ (2005)

on the international market. In the early 1990s Polish milk production was generally characterized by low productivity and low quality. While the situation has improved since the mid-1990s, even in 1999 only 20 per cent of the 450,000 producers delivering milk to dairies delivered exclusively milk of the highest quality (Swedish Board of Agriculture, 2001). The small scale of the family farms creates specific investment problems for upgrading milk quality, as well as problems for investors in the dairy processing companies, because of transaction costs of milk collection.

Fifth, Poland has attracted significant foreign direct investment (FDI) in the dairy sector,[3] but local companies continue to have a large share of the market. The liberalization of the Polish trade system and the privatization of the processing industry in the 1990s opened the Polish dairy sector to increased competition from abroad, allowed Polish exporters to search for new markets and allowed foreign companies to invest in the Polish dairy sector.[4] By 1999 there had been a total foreign investment inflow of US$4.6 billion into the Polish agri-food sector, 5 per cent of which had gone to dairy processing and dairy equipment companies.

The combined impact of privatization and FDI on the structure of the dairy sector has been modest: the total number of dairy processing companies with more than 50 employees decreased by 22 per cent between 1993 and 1999. The decrease was mainly in the number of cooperatives, as the number of (non-cooperatively owned) private companies doubled. Yet, cooperatives still controlled 70 per cent of the dairy market by 1999. Twenty of the privately owned dairies had majority foreign investor ownership (Majewski and Dalton, 2000).

The combination of these characteristics means that the Polish dairy sector is a very interesting one and a potentially rich source of insights for the study of the impacts of globalization, in particular regarding vertical spillover effects and the impact on small suppliers. Moreover, continued FDI in the Polish dairy sector could have very significant repercussions for the sector, the many small supplying farms and obviously for rural welfare and development more generally. Therefore, understanding the impacts is useful both for Poland itself and more widely.

Foreign investment, vertical integration and the impact on local suppliers

In this section we analyse how foreign investment, in combination with trade integration, has contributed to sustainable growth. Although FDI has been flowing into Poland since the transition, the strong internationalization of marketing chains is relatively new, especially in transition countries. Therefore the process and its impact deserve more attention.

Our insights are based on microeconomic evidence. More specifically, the analysis looks at how the opening of the Polish economy, especially to inflows of foreign capital, know-how and technology, is affecting the Polish dairy sector. The literature identifies several ways that foreign direct investors in the food industry can affect upstream suppliers: (1) by facilitating the adoption of new technologies, providing working capital and solving contract enforcement problems (Gow and Swinnen, 2001; Key and Runsten, 1999); (2) by imposing higher grades and standards for the supplied product (Reardon et al, 1999; Farina and Reardon, 2000; Henson et al, 2000; Dolan and Humphrey, 2000); and (3) by demonstrating a preference for large suppliers to minimize transaction costs (Runsten and Key, 1996; Key and Runsten, 1999; Winters, 2000; Dolan and Humphrey, 2000; Holloway et al, 2000).

Data and methodology

Our analysis is based on a 2001 survey of both dairy-producing rural households and dairy companies in the Warminsko-Mazurskie region in northeast Poland and statistical data from the region.

We surveyed 290 rural households involved in dairy production, selected randomly within municipalities. Because one of the objectives of the analysis was to study the impact of foreign investment and because there are relatively few foreign-owned processors in the region, we over-represented municipalities in the vicinity of the region's three foreign-owned dairies.

To complement the information from the household surveys we performed a series of in-depth interviews with one of the largest dairy equipment suppliers and with 6 of the 24 dairy companies to which the farmers deliver. Four of the six companies we interviewed were medium-size companies (50–70 million litres of milk), one large (420 million litres) and one small (2.5 million litres). Three were cooperatives, two private and one a joint venture of a cooperative and private company. In terms of foreign investment, two were majority foreign-owned and two had important links to foreign companies.

On-farm investments and quality upgrading

All the interviewed dairies had programmes that assisted their supplying farms. All had an input (especially feed) supply programme. The companies provided access to inputs such as feed, seed or fertilizer for on-farm feed production. Farmers purchased the inputs through company shops and the inputs were deducted from future payments for milk deliveries. Five out of six companies assisted farms in investing through credit programmes. Investment assistance took the form of leasing of equipment and cows, also with payments deducted from milk payments, and of loans for buying new or second-hand cooling and milking equipment. The only dairy that did not provide credit assistance programmes or agricultural extension services to its suppliers was the small dairy, probably because it did not have sufficient means. Most of the companies provided extension services to their suppliers. Five of the dairies also provided guarantees for bank loans to farmers. Almost all bank loans for farm investments were with preferential interest rates (subsidized interest rates around 5 per cent compared to commercial loans with interest rates often above 20 per cent). In order to obtain such a loan, the farmers needed collateral, but in many cases land or buildings were not accepted as guarantee; 45 per cent of the households who could not obtain preferential bank loans identified lack of sufficient collateral as the main reason. The dairies' co-signature facilitated its farmers' access to bank credits and was an important additional service to their suppliers.

The results from the farm survey indicated that by 2001, more than 70 per cent of the farms delivered to companies with input supply and credit programmes and there was no significant difference between foreign and local companies (Table 7.2). The only difference was in access to bank loan guarantees, which was significantly higher for those delivering to foreign companies (46 per cent) than for those delivering to local dairies (30 per cent).

These assistance programmes had a significant positive impact on on-farm investments in the region. More than three-quarters (76 per cent) of all households in the survey had made investments in the previous ten years (Table 7.3). Of those who invested, 58 per cent used loans. Loans came from dairies or from banks because of the type of investment rather than a farm's characteristics. Dairy loans were used almost exclusively for investments in enlarging and upgrading the livestock herd (30 per cent) and cooling tanks (56 per cent): together these accounted for 86 per cent of all dairy loans. In contrast, only 29 per cent of all bank loans were used for such investments.

Furthermore, the programmes that assisted farms in accessing inputs (mainly feed) enhanced investment indirectly by lowering input costs or reducing transaction costs in accessing inputs, thus improving profitability.

Table 7.2 *Foreign ownership and financial assistance programmes (% of farms delivering)*

	Total	Foreign-owned	Domestic
Credit programme, on-farm investment	71.5	71.6	71.4
Credit programme, cows	72.1	73.9	70.7
Input supply programme	78.1	78.9	77.5
Loan guarantee programme	37.2	46.2	29.8
Average	71.5	71.6	71.4

Source: Dries and Swinnen (2004)

Table 7.3 *Investments and loans of farm households*

Size (# of cows) (% of total)	Invests	Uses loan to invest (% of A)	Uses dairy loan (% of B)	Uses bank loan (% of B)	Uses dairy loan (% of A)	Uses bank loan (% of A)
	A	B	C	D	E	F
1–5	52	54	41	50	21	26
6–10	78	51	43	70	22	36
>10	92	74	43	75	31	54
ALL	76	58	43	69	25	40

Source: Dries and Swinnen (2004)

Evidence suggests that foreign investment played a more important role early in the transition, as an initiator of change and institutional innovation. By 2001 we found no significant difference between assistance programmes provided by foreign-owned companies and those provided by domestic dairies, except for the loan guarantee programmes, which were more extensively provided by the foreign dairies. The survey also showed that in 1995 the share of farms delivering top-quality milk (according to EU standards) was significantly larger among farmers delivering to foreign-owned dairies (58 per cent versus 38 per cent among farmers delivering to domestic dairies). However, by 2000 this gap had almost disappeared: 83 per cent versus 79 per cent (see Figure 7.2).

This is in line with qualitative evidence that foreign companies have played a role in providing an example of quality-improvement strategies. When one foreign dairy company invested in the region in 1994, the milk quality of its supplying farms – as everywhere in the region – was poor. From the start, the foreign investor set out a clear strategy to increase the quality of delivered milk. One

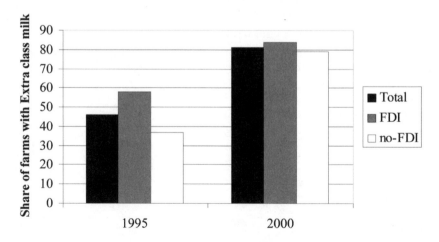

Figure 7.2 *Change in share of highest quality milk (EU standard) in the farm survey*

requirement was that the cooperative from which it leased collection stations install cooling tanks at those stations. It invested in agricultural extension to raise farmers' awareness of the importance of milk quality and to improve quality through basic hygienic rules for farmers handling the milk. From the beginning, the foreign investor also required germ count and cell count tests (in accordance with EU standard tests for milk quality classification). Farmers were allowed to have their milk tested for antibiotic residues free of charge in the dairy's laboratory. This was especially helpful for farmers who had had cow disease on their farms and needed to make sure that no antibiotic residue was left in the milk.

Local dairy companies quickly learned about the change in company policies implemented by foreign owners and began to copy quality improvement programmes. This led to important spillover effects, as shown by the dramatic improvement in milk quality throughout the region in the last five years.

Farm restructuring, survival and growth

A key issue is how the opening of the dairy sector to foreign competition and increased quality requirements affected the survival and growth of dairy farms. It is often argued that such forces can drive local companies, especially the smallest ones, out of business, either because of their inability to compete in a liberalized market or because restructuring induces processing companies to drop small suppliers to reduce transaction costs.

Our survey provides mixed evidence of these arguments. Of the 290 households in our sample, 283 delivered milk to dairy processing companies in 1995. Of these, 36 (13 per cent) stopped delivering milk between 1995 and 2000, ten of them (4 per cent) stopping milk production altogether, with the rest keeping some cows for home consumption. Hence, 87 per cent continued delivering to dairies despite radical dairy restructuring and tightened quality demands. Moreover, some of those who stopped delivering might have stopped in any case: the average age of those who stopped producing was 56, compared to 45 for the entire sample.

The size distribution changed gradually (see Figure 7.3). More than three-quarters of the households (232) had between 5 and 20 cows in 1995. The share of farms in the 5–20 cow category reduced significantly, with about the same number upgrading to a larger size as falling back to smaller (presumably subsistence) farms. Farmers with increased farm size were significantly younger (average age of 42) than those whose farm size declined (average age of 51).

These numbers – and the detailed evolution of farm sizes as illustrated in Figure 7.3 – suggest that the globalization and restructuring process contributed to a bimodal distribution of farms, but that it is not the only factor in these developments. (In order to separate out the different factors below we use an econometric model.)

It is clear from Figure 7.3 that the farm size distribution is now much flatter than before. However, if one considers the change in distribution based on numbers of cows by farm size, the dynamics look somewhat different. There is an

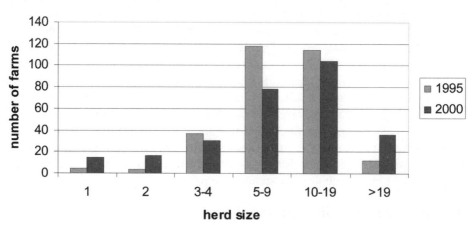

Figure 7.3 *Size distribution of dairy farms in total survey sample*

important increase in the number of cows kept by farms with at least 15 cows, while there is only a small increase in the number of cows kept on the smallest farms. Hence from this perspective there is a much stronger shift towards larger farms (which are still small by EU or US standards). It is not clear to what extent this redistribution process will continue. Some studies suggest that market economies are increasingly characterized by a bimodal farm distribution with a 'disappearing middle' in farm structures (Edwards et al, 1985; Garcia et al, 1987; Weiss, 1999). However, a recent study by Wolf and Sumner (2001) finds that farm size distributions for US dairy farms are not bimodal.

To complement our qualitative insights, we estimated econometrically the effects of FDI, assistance programmes and other factors (such as age and human capital of the farmers) on the survival and growth of the farms. The regression specifications and results are in Dries and Swinnen (2004). The regression analysis confirms the main arguments here. More specifically, assistance programmes provided by dairy companies had a significantly positive impact on the likelihood of farm survival. Dairy companies that provided more assistance programmes to their farmers had fewer farmers who left the sector. Moreover, farms delivering to dairy companies with more assistance grew faster. Interestingly, after domestic companies integrated the organizational innovations introduced by foreign companies, foreign ownership of the dairy company had no significant influence on the survival or growth of supplying farms.

In combination, these results lead to an important conclusion on the impact of foreign investment in Poland. Foreign investment has played an important positive role on the survival and growth of farms *indirectly*, by initializing farm assistance programmes and institutional innovations and providing an example of how such innovations could work. We did not find evidence that foreign-owned companies were more likely to cut off small farmers from their supply base.

Concluding comments

Globalization forces have played an important role in transition countries' agricultural development and rural livelihoods. There are multiple effects and interactions. Global integration was only one of several key reforms that affected agricultural development and rural incomes in transition countries and it has reinforced both positive and negative changes induced by other reforms. Despite the important disruptive effects of the international reorganization of the production activities process, there have been several important positive impacts of trade liberalization and integration in the regional and global economy. For example, labour migration has contributed to growth in several transition countries. Capital inflows from the west, in combination with integration into World Trade Organization (WTO) and regional trade agreements, have contributed to macroeconomic stability and policy credibility in those countries where basic reforms were implemented. Finally, since 1993 FDI has played a key role in stimulating strong and sustainable productivity growth in the central and eastern European agri-food economies.

Several studies conclude that foreign investment leads to a rapid consolidation of the local supplier base, with negative implications for those suppliers who cannot comply with higher standards and grading requirements, or who are cut out by the company in order to reduce transaction costs. Studies argue that this effect can be especially dramatic for small suppliers in developing countries. The conclusions of our study on Poland are different. We did not find that foreign investment led to either a rapid consolidation of the local supplier base or to small suppliers being cut out. On the contrary, our analysis shows that foreign investment and its spillover effects can lead to improved access to finance, increased investments and (dramatic) quality improvements by small local suppliers.

This occurs through a two-step mechanism. First, foreign investment leads processing companies to move toward vertical integration through contracting with local suppliers, interlinking input and output markets. The contracting is associated with enhanced standards requirements for supplies, while the companies provide assistance programmes to improve supplier management and enhance access to technology, credit and other inputs. The contracts and assistance programmes are designed to overcome market imperfections, a process that leads to important positive vertical spillovers for the suppliers.

The second step is that of horizontal spillovers. When domestic companies observe successful vertical integration strategies, they copy them. Our analysis shows that these horizontal spillover effects are strong and rapid. For several of the effects, after five years there was no longer a significant difference between foreign-owned and domestic companies and their suppliers. Only in some aspects, such as medium-term investments, had convergence not yet occurred.

In combination, these effects led to significant improvements in the investments, productivity and product quality of small suppliers over the five-year period studied. More than 85 per cent of all suppliers continued supplying despite restructuring of the dairy companies and strong tightening of quality requirements. The reduction in suppliers over the period was less than the average reduction in agricultural employment in Poland, and most of those who stopped supplying were older farmers who were very likely to have stopped delivering milk in any case. Younger and better-educated managers were associated with stronger supplier growth. The average size of the farms increased, but relatively little, and the vast majority of suppliers remained small.

In summary, our study found that foreign investment through a process of vertical integration had a significant positive effect on small suppliers, but that the most important effect over the period analysed was indirect, through vertical and horizontal spillover effects. There is growing evidence that such effects are increasingly important and that they are more widespread than is generally assumed.

Notes

1   Important causes of the decline in output were declining relative prices and subsidy cuts following liberalization; terms of trade for milk producers declined by almost 90 per cent between 1989 and 1992. Both output and productivity were negatively affected by disruptions from privatization and restructuring, contracting problems in the absence of enforcement mechanisms and the disruption of traditional exchange relationships between farms and upstream and downstream companies (Macours and Swinnen, 2000; Dries and Swinnen, 2002).

2   In the European formerly communist countries, only in the former Yugoslavia has private farming also survived to a large extent.

3   FDI has resulted from strategies such as serving the local market when trade constraints limit imports and to using the advantages of the Polish economy to export to home markets or third-country markets. Poland performed well in FDI inflows because of its stable political and institutional system, advanced reform strategy and cheap but relatively well-educated labour force. The EU accession process further stimulated FDI by reinforcing institutional and economic stability, providing the prospect of a large single market, leading to a growth in Polish incomes and food demand and – in some cases – giving rise to expectations of EU subsidies (Walkenhorst, 2001).

4   Poland is a net exporter of dairy products, mostly to countries of the former Soviet Union. The products it exports to the EU are mostly lower value. It imports mostly higher value cheese and other products from the EU, and although the total value of imports fell by half between 1992 and 1998, the share of imports from the EU increased. (In 1999, 59 per cent of all dairy imports were yoghurts, almost all from Germany.) Only licensed dairies are allowed to export their products to the EU. In 2000, only 19 of 400 dairy processing companies (5 per cent) had obtained an export licence, but that 5 per cent accounted for 25 per cent of total milk procurement (Kaspersson et al, 2002).

References

ARR and IERiGZ (2001) *Rynek Mleka. Stan I Perspektywy* [The Polish dairy market: Performance and developments], Warsaw

Dolan, C. and Humphrey, J. (2000) 'Governance and trade in fresh vegetables: The impact of UK supermarkets on the African horticulture industry', *Journal of Development Studies*, vol 37, no 2, pp147–176

Dries, L. and Swinnen, J. (2002) 'Institutional reform and labor reallocation during transition: Evidence from Polish agriculture', *World Development*, vol 30, no 3, pp457–474

Dries, L. and Swinnen, J. (2004) 'Foreign direct investment, vertical integration and local suppliers: Evidence from the Polish dairy sector', *World Development*, vol 32, no 9, pp525–1544

Edwards, C., Smith, M. and Peterson, R. (1985) 'The changing distribution of farms by size: A Markov analysis', *Agricultural Economics Research*, vol 37, no 4, pp1–16

FAO, 2003, FAOSTAT Agriculture Data available online. FAO (available at www.fao.org)

Farina, E. M. M. Q. and Reardon, T. (2000) 'Agrifood grades and standards in the extended Mercosur: Their role in the changing agrifood system', *American Journal of Agricultural Economics*, vol 82, no 5, pp1170–1176

Garcia, P., Offutt, S. and Sonka, S. (1987) 'Size distribution and growth in a sample of Illinois cash grain farms', *American Journal of Agricultural Economics*, vol 69, no 2, pp471–476

Gow, H. and Swinnen, J. F. M. (2001) 'Private Enforcement Capital and Contract Enforcement in Transition Countries', *American Journal of Agricultural Economics*, vol 83, no 3, pp686–690

GUS *Statistical Yearbooks* (different editions) Central Statistical Office, Warsaw

Henson, S., Loader, R. and Brouder, A. (2000) 'Food safety standards and exports of perishable products from developing countries: Fish exports from East Africa to the European Union', *American Journal of Agricultural Economics*, vol 82, no 5, p1159–1169.

Holloway, G., Nicholson, C., Delgado, C., Staal, S. and Ehui, S. (2000) 'Agroindustrialisation through institutional innovation. Transaction costs, cooperatives and milk-market development in the East-African Highlands', *Agricultural Economics*, vol 23, pp279–288

IERiGZ (2005) *Rozwój rynku mleczarskiego i zmiany jego funkcjonowania w latach 1990–2005* [Development of the dairy market and changes in its functioning during the period 1990–2005], IERiGZ, Warsaw 21/2005

Kaspersson, E., Rabinowicz, E. and Schwaag Serger, S. (2002) *EU Milk Policy after Enlargement – Competitiveness and Politics in Four Candidate Countries*, Swedish Institute for Food and Agricultural Economics, Lund

Key, N. and Runsten, D. (1999) 'Contract farming, smallholders and rural development in Latin America: The organization of agroprocessing firms and the scale of outgrower production', *World Development*, vol 27, no 2, pp381–401

Macours, K. and Swinnen, J. (2000 'Causes of output decline during transition: The case of central and eastern European Agriculture', *Journal of Comparative Economics*, vol 28, no 1, pp172–206

Majewski, E. and Dalton, G. (2000) *The Strategic Options for the Polish Agro-Food Sector in the Light of Economic Analyses*, FAPA, Warsaw

Reardon, T., Codron, J.-M., Busch, L., Bingen, J. and Harris, C. (1999) 'Global change in agrifood grades and standards: Agribusiness strategic responses in developing countries', *International Food & Agribusiness Management Review*, vol 2, no 3, pp421–435

Runsten, D. and Key, N., (1996) *Contract Farming in Developing Countries:Theoretical Issues and Analysis of some Mexican Cases*, Report LC/L.989, UN-ECLAC, Santiago, Chile

Swedish Board of Agriculture (2001) *A Study of the Milk Sector in Poland, Hungary, the Czech Republic and Estonia*, Market Regulations Division

Walkenhorst, P. (2001) 'The geography of foreign direct investment in Poland's food industry', *Journal of Agricultural Economics*, vol 52, no 3, pp71–86

Weiss, C. (1999) 'Farm growth and survival: Econometric evidence for individual farms in Upper Austria', *American Journal of Agricultural Economics*, vol 81, pp103–116

Winters, A. (2000) 'Trade liberalisation and poverty', www.worldbank.org/poverty/wdrpoverty/winters.htm, last accessed 2003

Wolf, C. and Sumner, D. (2001) 'Are farm size distributions bimodal? Evidence from Kernel density estimates of dairy farm size distributions', *American Journal of Agricultural Economics*, vol 83, no 1, pp77–88

Chapter 8

The Role of Santiago Wholesale Markets in Supporting Small Farmers and Poor Consumers

Martine Dirven and Sergio Faiguenbaum[1]

It is generally assumed that the wholesale markets in Chile provide an outlet for all kinds of farmers, including small-scale farmers (either directly or through an intermediary). In addition, it is often claimed that both directly and through the street markets for which they are the suppliers, wholesale markets offer real benefits to poor consumers. Fruits and vegetables are an important agriculture crop for small farmers and most fruit and vegetable transactions in Chile take place in the traditional (small farmer–wholesale market–street market) marketing chain; in turn, fruits and vegetables are by far the most important commodity in that chain. But supermarkets are entering in force in both the upper-middle class and lower-income neighbourhoods, and not only in Santiago. The rapid increase of supermarket numbers and sales all over Chile in all types of neighbourhoods has a large and increasing impact on the entire food chain, from farmers through to consumers.

The agents participating along the traditional chain are perceiving these changes (to varying degrees) and devising strategies to face them. They advocate policy support to the traditional system based on the claim that it plays two important social and economic roles: that it can provide an outlet for small farmers, and that the wholesale markets enable their own small-scale vendors and downstream street market vendors to remain competitive with supermarkets, providing a wider range of quality and variety to the consumer at a lower price than at supermarkets, while providing employment and adding the value of personal relationships between vendors and customers.

The potential impacts on small farmers and lower-income consumers are important issues for Chile in view of its extremely polarized structures of production and income. Nevertheless, researchers and policy makers have devoted little attention to the traditional value chain. While figures on the growth and characteristics of supermarkets are relatively easy to find, information on street markets, wholesale markets and trade flows with farmers are much harder to come by. This chapter tries to help fill that gap using both the available (though limited) quantitative data and original qualitative research. It tries to answer two questions: (1) Is the wholesale market indeed an outlet for small-scale farmers? and (2) Does the producer–wholesale market–street market chain provide benefits to consumers that the supermarket chains do not provide?

The chapter first provides basic information on Chile's population, economic development and fruit and vegetable production and consumption habits. It describes the organization and linkages of the two major marketing chains (supermarkets and traditional), focusing on fruits and vegetables. It then goes on to present the results of our research in relation to how the traditional system compares with the supermarket system; we argue that while the traditional system probably does offer advantages to workers and consumers downstream, it does not appear to support small farmers. Finally, the chapter describes initiatives taken to strengthen (mostly downstream) linkages and suggests public investments that could be made in the traditional chain, urging improved links between small farmers, fruit and vegetable markets and poor consumers.

Context

Population and economic development

According to the latest (2002) population census, the urban population of the Metropolitan Region surrounding Santiago is 5.8 million inhabitants (an increase of 800,000 since 1992), which is about 40 per cent of Chile's total population of 15.1 million.

A period of vigorous 7 per cent annual growth in gross domestic product (GDP) from the mid-1980s to the mid-1990s was followed by much slower economic growth, and from 1990 to 2001, GDP grew at an annual rate of 4.1 per cent (at 1995 prices). In 2001, GDP stood at US$5884 per capita (at 1995 prices), while the Gini income distribution coefficient was 0.55, showing, as in most of Latin America, strongly uneven income distribution. Over the course of the 1990s, Chile was able to bring poverty levels down and it now has one of the lowest poverty levels in Latin America. In 2000, extreme poverty was 5.6 per cent (down from 12.9 per cent in 1990) and poverty was 20.6 per cent (down from 38.6 per cent in 1990) (Economic Commission for Latin America and the Caribbean (ECLAC), 2002). The rural population, now 15 per cent of the total population, has decreased in both relative and absolute terms. Chile's agricultural GDP (including forestry, fisheries and animal husbandry) represents 6 per cent

Table 8.1 *Land with fruit or vegetables per farm type (in hectares)*

	Subsistence	Small-scale	Medium-scale	Large-scale	Total*	Subsistence + small-scale (%)ᵃ
Fruit	8,097	61,555	48,780	118,533	237,363	29.3
Vegetables	5,914	51,123	26,009	43,642	127,305	44.8

Notes *The totals in column 5 include hectares not classified and are based on the 1997 Agricultural Census figures. ᵃThe averages in column 6 fail to take into account that small-scale farmers tend to have lower yields per hectare than larger-scale farmers, a tendency more pronounced for fruits than vegetables; thus the authors' estimate is that closer to 20 per cent of total fruit and 35–40 per cent of total vegetable production was in the hands of small-scale and subsistence farmers.

Source: ODEPA (2000).

of total GDP; when direct linkages to other sectors are included the percentage triples to 18.

Fruit and vegetable production and sales

Because of the lack of reliable information on traded volume and value of fruits and vegetables at various retail outlets, we attempted to complement the quantitative information with educated guesstimates made by a group composed of representatives from government, NGO, peasant and international organizations.[2] This section presents both quantitative data and conclusions from the group's discussions.

Table 8.1 shows the classification of fruit and vegetable producers according to Chile's 1997 agricultural census. The classifications depended on size of landholdings, investments and use of technology.[3]

Table 8.2 is an illustration of the differences in regional fruit production. Major species are apples, pears, oranges, prunes, peaches, avocados, kiwi and grapes (for consumption); minor species are berries, nuts and fruit species that do not weigh heavily in total production. Table 8.3 shows the destination of fruit

Table 8.2 *Fruit production in Chile, major and minor species, per region (ha), based on a survey of commercial farms*

		Region, survey year								
	Total	III 1999	IV 1999	V 2002	R.M. 1998	VI 2003	VII 2001	VIII 2000	IX 2000	X 2000
Major species	193,033	8,270	12,339	37,519	38,831	59,145	32,493	2,719	1,339	378
%	100	4.3	6.4	19.4	20.1	30.6	16.8	1.4	0.7	0.2
Minor species	13,283	146	1,868	1,445	1,606	822	3,965	1,435	683	1,314
%	100	1.1	14.1	10.9	12.1	6.2	29.8	10.8	5.1	9.9

Source: ODEPA/CIREN (2003)

Table 8.3 *Destination to the domestic market of fruit production in Regions V and VI*

	Production (000 mt)		% of production destined for domestic market	
	Major species	Minor species	Major species	Minor species
V Region	325.0	19.6	30.5	61.8
VI Region	1609.1	11.2	21.5	47.5
Total, both regions	1934.1	30.8	22.6	56.5

Sources: ODEPA/CIREN (2003) and ODEPA/CIREN (2002)

production from two regions; major species are more oriented toward agro-indus-try and the export market, while minor species are oriented toward the domestic market. (Similar information was not available for vegetables.)

Consumption of fresh fruits and vegetables in Chile

Consumer spending on fruits and vegetables varies by income group but makes up about 12 per cent of the average Chilean's food budget. According to the National Statistics Institute (INE), in 1997 Chileans spent on average 27 per cent of their total expenditures on food and 3.2 per cent on fruits and vegetables (Table 8.4, column 1), of which 77 per cent are consumed fresh. The lowest quintile spends the equivalent of US$22 per month on fresh fruits and vegetables (6.6 per cent of their income) while the highest quintile spends US$38 per month (2 per cent of their income). Of total expenditures on food, 11.9 per cent corre-sponds to fresh fruit and vegetables (Table 8.4, column 2). The dominant fresh fruit purchases are oranges, apples and bananas and the dominant vegetable and tuber purchases are potatoes, tomatoes, lettuce, pumpkin and corn (ODEPA/University of Chile/RIMISP (OUR), 2002, pp25–26).

The marketing information company ACNielsen (2004) estimates that of Chileans' total retail expenditures, 70 per cent are spent in supermarkets, 20 per cent in small neighbourhood shops, 5 per cent in pharmacies and only 2 per cent in street markets. Because its estimates (like INE's consumption habits survey[4])

Table 8.4 *Fresh fruit and vegetable (F&V) sales through supermarkets and other channels (in %)*

	1 Proportion of total consumer expenditures	2 Proportion of total food expenditures	3 Proportion of total consumer expenditures spent at supermarkets	4 Proportion of fruits and vegetables in total supermarket food sales	5 Proportion of total consumer spending at non-supermarket retail
Food items	27	–	13.5	–	13.5
F&V	3.2	11.9	0.9	6.7	2.3

Source: Author compilations based on figures from INE and ASACH. Reported in OUR, 2002, p82

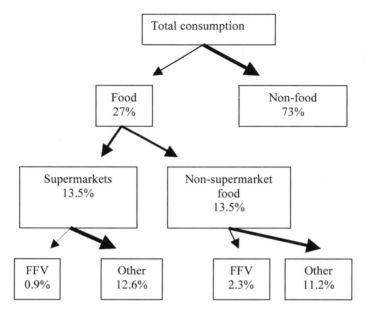

Note: FFV = fresh fruit and vegetables.

Figure 8.1 *Consumer spending in Chile*

are based on the greater Santiago area, our group's guesstimate was that close to 50 per cent of Chileans' expenditures on food are spent in supermarkets and this is the figure we will use for our next calculation. Supermarket figures indicate that fresh fruits and vegetables represented 4.6 per cent of their total sales in 2000, while food items overall represented 69 per cent of total sales. Thus, estimates on the penetration of supermarkets in food retail sales show that Chileans spend 13.5 per cent of their total budget at supermarkets (OUR, 2002, p82) (Table 8.4, column 3). The figures of the Chilean supermarket association *Asociación Gremial de Supermercados Chilenos* (ASACH) show fruits and vegetables representing 4.6 per cent of supermarket total sales and 6.7 per cent of supermarket food sales (Table 8.4, column 4). Fresh fruit and vegetables sold through supermarkets represent 0.9 per cent of total consumer spending, while those sold through non-supermarket retail represent 2.3 per cent of total consumer spending (Figure 8.1).

Of the total fresh fruits and vegetables available in the country (after deducting exports, sales to agro-industry and losses, and adding imports) 4 per cent of corn, 3 per cent of tomatoes, 5 per cent of potatoes and 9 per cent of apples are bought in supermarkets (Faiguenbaum et al, 2002). There is clearly a correlation between income levels and buying habits in supermarkets. ACNielsen estimates that in the higher-income neighbourhoods of Santiago, 94 per cent of food purchases are done in the supermarket. This percentage drops to 56 per cent in the low-income sectors, where 32 per cent of food purchases are through corner shops (OUR, 2002, p29).

Marketing chains

There are two marketing chains for fresh fruit and vegetables in Chile:

1   *the traditional channel:* producers to intermediaries to wholesale markets to street markets, local food stores or small supermarkets;
2   *the large-supermarket channel:* growers to supermarkets, or growers to traders to supermarkets. Whether the supermarket uses traders has to do with volume: early and out-of-season produce is bought largely from individual growers, while full-season produce is bought through traders. Some products (such as apples) are mostly rejects from export (OUR, 2002, p26). Many traders are also producers and some producers do joint sales.

The traditional channel: Wholesale markets

The oldest wholesale market in Santiago, La Vega Central, has been at its present location since 1912 and is within walking distance of the city centre. It has 800 stands inside and has expanded into the neighbourhood through related businesses (such as wholesalers and distributors). Market stands sell as little as one kilo or one crate, often to individual consumers, small shopkeepers, restaurant and hotel keepers in an area that is mostly working class (although upper-middle class customers also come from an area 5km away). Sellers buy from producers who come to the inside parking area to distribute out of the backs of trucks or other vehicles (including horse carts) or from wholesale distributors in the vicinity (who specialize in, for example, citrus, apples or pickles), in which case transport to the market stands is by hand-pulled cart. Buyers leave on foot, by taxi or with their own cars or trucks.

Representatives of La Vega Central say that wholesalers, distributors, retailers and the general public continue to buy there because of the large array of products and qualities, lower prices and the human contact during transactions, which does not exist in the large supermarkets. Low prices are possible because the market does no advertising and saves on costs such as showcases, cleaning, refrigerators and personnel.[5]

Lo Valledor wholesale market was established in 1968 by vendors from an overcrowded market who set up on an empty site in southern Santiago near the Pan-American Highway. The Municipality of Santiago was responsible for Lo Valledor until it was privatized in 1985, when spaces were sold to vendors at relatively modest prices and with easy payment conditions. According to its president it is the largest private market in South America and by far the largest in Chile. It has grown from 40 co-owners to 600, with 2000 sales points and 5000 people working in it. It is governed by a six-member Board of Administrators elected by the co-owners.

Lo Valledor is organized into an open space, where vegetables are sold, especially in summer, and a covered market where fruit is the main commodity throughout the year. Suppliers are charged through an arbitrary formula at prices that change frequently depending on the number of axles or whether the truck appears heavily loaded. Buyers pay a set fee for entering the market parking lot with trucks, no matter what amount they buy. It is open six days a week, with 1000 vehicles a day entering to sell and 7000 to buy, with total traffic of 2.5 million vehicles per year. The Ministry publishes a Bulletin for Family Farmers with minimum and maximum prices for the fruits and vegetables traded in Lo Valledor, with an explanation of the prices (product origins, quality, condition, supply fluctuations, etc.). *El Mercurio*, Chile's main daily newspaper, publishes a weekly summary of transactions at Lo Valledor and La Vega.[6] Tax inspectors frequently tour the market to make spot checks. Thus the markets combine elements of the formal, semi-formal and informal economy.

In 1997 the *Sociedad Mercado Mayorista de Santiago* (Mersan) inaugurated a model terminal for the distribution of food products on a 50-hectare site on the outskirts of Santiago in order to apply the principles of concentration and polyvalence to the direct sale of fruit, vegetables, meat and groceries. It invested US$70 million, mainly for the construction of offices, storage rooms, sales corridors and unloading platforms, with modern mechanized systems and an uninterrupted cold chain. By 2001, 280 businesses had bought or reserved offices at Mersan. Because it has been difficult to convince buyers and sellers to move from other markets (in part because of high rents), Mersan functions more as a warehouse than as a wholesale market.[7] In spite of Mersan's slow start, its administration has not cut the price of its services and envisages investing a further US$70 million to add office space for traders and exporters, bank offices, a cargo train and passenger terminal. Negotiations are underway to sell it to a French consortium specialized in the construction and operation of wholesale markets.

There are several other wholesale markets relatively close to Santiago, including at the port of San Antonio and in Calera (80km north of Santiago). Many transporters prefer to drive the extra distance into Santiago to avoid the risk of selling only a partial load on the smaller markets.

Market shares

The Ministry of Agriculture figures show that annually 1.3 million metric tonnes of fresh fruit and vegetables (equivalent to US$192 million) are traded in Lo Valledor. Some estimates[8] are that this represents 60 per cent of the total traded volume of fruit and vegetables through Santiago's wholesale markets, with another 20 per cent being traded through La Vega and 15 per cent through Mersan.[9] However, Lo Valledor's development manager claims that Lo Valledor is responsible for 90 per cent of the fresh fruits and vegetables traded through wholesale markets in greater Santiago (65 per cent of all the fresh fruits and vegetables traded through wholesale markets in Chile). In any case, Lo Valledor is clearly the major player in the wholesale market and was therefore the focus of our research for this chapter.

According to the INE, whose figures are based only on official tax figures (the formal economy), between 1991 and 1999, the number of traditional retail oulets for fruit and vegetables (specialized or multi-product corner shops, street markets, etc.) had dropped from 7572 to 5739, and the sales margin had dropped from 11 per cent to 7.5 per cent. Participants in a 2003 meeting of the *Asociación Chilena de Organizaciones de Ferias Libres* (ASOF) had a very different impression concerning their sector. Although they had faced a drop in sales and margins in the previous five years (following solid growth in the early 1990s during the country's economic boom), their feeling was that vendors had a 50 per cent mark-up rate and that the number of retail outfits was several times that indicated by INE. (Presumably the discrepancy between INE figures and ASOF estimates is due in part to the informality of the small-scale retail sector, which does not get registered through official statistics.) Some vendors that had tried selling other goods had gone back to selling fruit and vegetables, leading to increased competition among them and a drop in average sales per vendor. Reduced average sales had led vendors to feel that street market sales had declined overall more than they had in reality. ASOF pointed out that the number of retail licences extended tended to increase as mayoral elections approached[10] or when the country faced an economic crisis and a rise in unemployment.[11]

One emerging trend is that outside the metropolitan area small farmers of fruits and vegetables have organized to negotiate with local authorities to set up market space. This demand is the result of small farmers diversifying their production toward higher value products (such as fruits and vegetables as opposed to cereals or pulses) and of small town and rural populations diversifying their consumption habits toward diets containing more fruits and vegetables. Such consumption, however, probably amounts to only a tiny part of total production.

The large-supermarket channel[12]

> *Starting 28 August, all of our prices will be low, always, 365 days a year. Only we can keep all prices low forever, because there is only one Líder. The prices on 15,832 products have been cut.* (Supermarket leaflet distributed in Santiago)

Chile's first supermarket (defined as having more than three cash registers) was inaugurated in 1957. ALMAC (now D&S) pioneered three innovations: an increased assortment of goods, cash registers at the store's exit and parking space for its customers. Since then, the sector has grown quickly, especially since the early 1990s (Table 8.5), with its yearly growth double that of annual growth in

Table 8.5 *Annual supermarket sales growth (in real terms)*

Year	1992	1993	1994	1995	1996	1997	1998	1999	2000	2001	2002
% annual growth	11.7	19.0	10.8	9.9	9.5	8.1	6.3	12.6	8.0	9.0	7.1

Source: INE webpage, accessed 27 August 2003

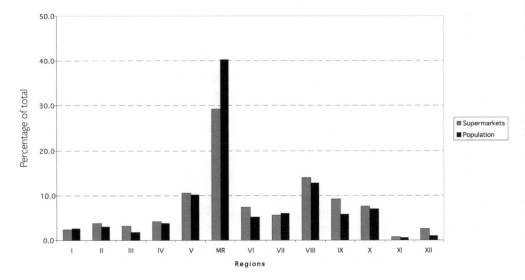

Source: INE web page, accessed 22 August 2003

Figure 8.2 *Chile 2003: Supermarkets and population*

GDP. Its participation grew from 49 per cent of the retail market in 1994 to 60–70 per cent in 2001,[13] while the specialized retail shop share decreased significantly over the same period. This is part of a worldwide trend.[14] In Chile, the trend was accompanied by a rapid increase in: per capita income; female participation in the labour force; and number of households having a refrigerator and private car.[15]

The supermarkets' competition strategy involves: high investments in infrastructure and logistics; increase in areas of sales; rationalization of operations and cost reductions; computerization of key areas such as stock management; and management by categories. They use efficient consumer response (ECR) technology, first used in the US, which aims at optimization of space and product mix, effective promotions, efficient new product introduction and rapid product replacement on supermarket shelves. In Chile 90 per cent of supermarkets have bar code reading systems and the larger ones have bought strategically located large plots of land for potential future expansion (OUR, 2002, pp17, 21).

A mega market (or hypermarket) is defined as having more than 10,000 square metres of sales space and 25,000 different products, with at least 40 cash registers. It also offers space for services such as pharmacies, shoe repair shops, photocopy and fax centres, flower shops, coffee shops and restaurants. In January 2002, there were 17 mega markets in the Metropolitan Region and six in other regions.[16] Together they represented 24.7 per cent of total supermarket area and 28.6 per cent of total supermarket sales (OUR, 2002, pp15, 73).

In June 2003, there were 678 retailers that could be defined as supermarkets, 56 more than a year earlier. Of these, 198 were in the Metropolitan Region and the rest in other regions. Their numbers generally follow the regional population distribution, but in the Metropolitan Region they make up a relatively smaller share (Figure 8.1). In 2001, the four largest supermarkets (three of them national) accounted for 52 per cent of total supermarket sales.[17] Since then, the concentration of nationally owned chains increased further with Jumbo/Cencosud purchasing Santa Isabel from Ahold and D&S purchasing the Carrefour operations in Chile. D&S opened a range of supermarkets in smaller cities and conducted a large publicity campaign claiming lower prices (see *El Mercurio*, 18 August 2003).

The introduction of a supermarket in a neighbourhood changes the buying habits of the surrounding population and also has a profound impact on local commerce, including corner shops, small self-service shops and street markets, which end up disappearing or relocating to more peripheral zones (OUR, 2002, p54). The large supermarkets sell clean, relatively homogeneous fruits and vegetables, but because they are usually picked and sold before optimal maturation point and then refrigerated to increase potential storage time, they are inferior in quality when compared with produce found in street markets and corner stores. The fresh fruit and vegetable section attracts buyers in any case and, in the consumer's mind, its quality reflects the quality of other products in the supermarket. Therefore, supermarkets make an effort to present their fruits and vegetables in an attractive way, although the standards used for vegetables are highly subjective and the categories imprecise: 'first', 'second', 'extra' or 'export' quality, 'late' or 'early' varieties, 'new' or 'stored' potatoes. (This is less true for fruit.) Internationally accepted standards such as colour or acidity are not used (OUR, 2002, p32).

Most larger supermarket chains in Santiago use centralized purchase and distribution channels for their fresh fruit and vegetables. (Supermarkets in other regions usually buy directly from suppliers.) The difficulties small-scale suppliers have selling directly to supermarkets have been detailed elsewhere;[18] the introduction of distribution centres in Santiago has eliminated many small vegetable suppliers. Fruit suppliers were generally large to begin with and therefore were better able to adapt or could supply the new increased volume requirements. For fruit labelled 'export' the situation is different: they are mostly rejected late in the process of export quality control and are supplied mostly by export firms (OUR, 2002, pp30, 56, 58). However, the amount of fruit and vegetables sold in supermarkets corresponds to a limited total area sown (roughly 389ha maize, 200ha tomatoes, 1866ha potatoes and 730ha apples) and a limited number of suppliers (10–12 for maize, 7 or 8 for tomatoes, 7 or 8 for potatoes and 10 for apples; some suppliers sell to more than one supermarket chain). Supermarkets buy most of their apples from export firms (OUR, pp28–29).

Fruit and vegetables for supermarkets are usually delivered in bulk or in simple packaging (mesh, styrofoam trays, etc.). The quality standards for them are not particularly high, varieties are generally the common ones and technology processes required for cleaning, grading, etc. are relatively simple. The entry barriers for smaller farmers are, instead, the supermarket demands for: large volumes with abrupt changes depending on stock needs; quality that is homogeneous and pre-established; frequent supply (once or twice a week); willingness to take back rejected produce if its quality does not meet standards; and the capacity to offer discounts when the supermarket launches a special promotion. Competition is stiff, profit margins thin and payment schedules long.

For other products (such as dairy) the supermarkets have little direct contact with the producers and it is the agro-industry that sets the producer standards (for example milk quality) and price. As for meat, new government quality standards have had a negative impact on butcher shops, while larger slaughterhouses have found it less difficult to adapt. The cattle farmers upstream have also had few difficulties meeting the new standards (OUR, 2002, pp59–60).

Backward and forward linkages of wholesale fruit and vegetable markets[19]

Not a spot market

The agricultural wholesale market is sometimes assumed to be the paradigm 'spot market', with many buyers and sellers concurring simultaneously, prices that respond precisely to the moment's supply and demand and with no dependency between sellers and buyers. In fact, in the literature on contracts, the agricultural wholesale markets are treated as the antithesis of vertical coordination (between different economic agents) and integration (of different economic activities under the same ownership).

In practice, however, many farmers in Chile sell highly perishable products and face high transportation costs (as in the case of fruits and vegetables), which confines them to local markets; most vegetable and fruit farmers do not sell directly at distances greater than 50km. This confines them to selling in a buyers' market, reducing their bargaining power. In addition, farmers specialize in some products by making investments (capital and know-how) that create important exit barriers and a relatively inelastic supply in the short term. Evidence shows that only a minority of agricultural products in Chile (cereals, vegetables for domestic consumption and cattle) are traded directly by the farmer on the spot market (Vargas and Foster, 2000). Most are traded through intermediaries, sold to agro-industries or sold through vertical (verbal or written) pre-established contractual arrangements.

Even at Lo Valledor, which is widely perceived to house spot market transactions, we observed very different interactions. Most sellers have a particular place in the market that they own or rent, while most buyers come twice or more each week to purchase fresh produce. Over time, buyers develop preferences, usually accompanied by preferential treatment from the seller on price, quality and service (such as help loading and faster attendance). Trust may arise that extends the possibility of paying by cheque, a privilege reserved for those with sufficient 'social capital/credibility', and very exceptionally, credit is extended.[20]

Upstream linkages: farmers

Relations between suppliers and trader/vendors in Lo Valledor go much further than the habit of regular trading and the trust and special treatment that may ensue. In fact, some 30–60 per cent of traders in Lo Valledor are farmers themselves or have family ties to farmers. Some left farming to dedicate themselves to trading; some of these return to farming part-time, partially integrating upstream in order to assure quality and quantity at the required moment for at least a portion of their sales. Another strategy is to extend the season of their specialized products (such as celery, tomatoes, potatoes or lettuce) by establishing pre-harvest arrangements with farmers along a route from northern to southern Chile. Arrangements might include financing, buying a part in the field and harvesting it, or buying on the spot. Most of these arrangements appear to be made with middle- to large-scale farmers (more than 20ha) rather than with small-scale farmers. Intermediaries that buy produce at the farm gate also appear to prefer trading with middle- to large-scale farmers, with a few exceptions (such as potatoes). Small-scale farmers around Santiago often take their own produce to Lo Valledor or La Vega.

Small-scale farmers produce an estimated 35–40 per cent of Chile's vegetable production and 20 per cent of its fruit (excluding grapes). How *do* small farmers sell their produce, given that even intermediaries and the wholesale markets in Santiago do not seem to prefer them? We were unable to document where small-scale farmers sell their produce, but it appears that small-scale farmers throughout Chile bring their produce directly to a market nearby and many sell produce from small wooden stalls along the road, and it also appears that Lo Valledor is not an outlet for small-scale farmers from all over Chile, as its promoters claim.

Downstream linkages: Street markets

> *We discovered that we had to support the street markets. Without street markets, Chile would have to forget about small- and medium-scale farmers and about folks being able to eat cheaply. Victor Cornejo, President of Lo Valledor market organization* (Cornejo, 2000)

Lo Valledor's main clients are street market vendors, who represent 80 per cent of its clientele and 50 per cent of its sales. Reardon and Berdegue (2002, p372) define the traditional street markets as

> *varying from 'plaza markets' in the centre of towns or neighbourhoods, with rows of small retailers or a mix of retailers and wholesalers, to 'street fairs'. The latter come under a variety of names depending on the country, roughly translating into public access, open-air street fairs and mobile markets... Street markets are essentially smaller versions of plaza markets, but focused on perishables, that move from neighbourhood to neighbourhood or village to village on a regular schedule.*

In Chile, 700 street markets house a total of 100,000 stands. Of these, 300 markets and 40,000 stands are in Santiago. At two to three persons per stand, they provide direct employment to 100,000 people in Santiago and 250,000 across the country. Street markets were traditionally geared exclusively to the sale of fresh fruits and vegetables, but they have slowly expanded to other products and have become a kind of open-air supermarket. The street market vendor organization ASOF estimates that normally street markets sell about 80 per cent fruits and vegetables and 10 per cent fresh fish and seafood, with the rest made up of an array of food and non-food products, some of which are disappearing because consumers prefer to buy them in supermarkets (for example beverages, household supplies, soap, perfumes and deodorants).

To participate in a street market, vendors need a permit issued by the municipality where the market takes place. There is a limited number of permits and they are rarely tradeable.[21] Vendors with non-registered stands surround most legal vendors. While the street markets in the higher-income neighbourhoods are mostly small (up to 30 stands) and organized in places provided especially for the purpose or in public parks, in Santiago's poorer areas they tend to be much larger, often extending through adjacent streets. The largest street market (in La Pintana Municipality) has 1500 stands. Street market customers usually come from nearby to avoid transportation costs.

The street market economy is semi-formal because many (perhaps most) vendors with a permit either under-declare their sales or are not registered with the tax service at all, and they do not generally provide receipts. Many market vendors are, however, organized into unions. There is a completely informal sector at the margin of the markets (the *coleros*), a significant number of whom are related to the registered vendors and are considered to be in training or waiting to become official vendors. It is difficult to ascertain whether vendors suffer more from aggressive internal competition or from the competition of supermarkets.

Consumers: Prices and other factors

In order to try to corroborate how well the supermarket chain and the traditional chain were serving consumers, we collected prices on selected brands and varieties at various retailers. The process included selecting one or more popular brands (or, for fruits and vegetables, some varieties) for items selected from Chile's basic food basket; selecting supermarkets and street markets in the upper-, middle- and lower-income neighbourhoods;[22] and collecting prices on the selected items at each retailer. (Our study was done in late winter when fresh fruits and vegetables, especially those that are highly perishable, were less abundant.) Chile's basic food basket is based on a survey of greater Santiago's population consumption habits; it contains 483 products. It was updated in 1997 to take into account changes in consumer habits due to Chile's increasing exposure to globalization and modernization processes and to the steady increase in incomes that began in the mid-1980s.

Our research on prices corroborated earlier findings (OUR, 2002) that street markets in the higher-income neighbourhoods (Las Condes and Vitacura) tend to sell their fruits and vegetables at slightly higher prices than the nearby supermarkets. Fruit and vegetable quality tends to be substantially better in the street markets. On the other hand, street markets in the lower-income neighbourhoods tend to sell their fruits and vegetables at significantly lower prices than the nearby supermarkets (with the exception of lettuce).

Street markets in the upper- and middle-income neighbourhoods do not have stands with household supplies, while those in the lower-income neighbourhoods do. Such products tend to be sold at slightly higher prices at street markets than at nearby supermarkets, although not consistently. Prices vary, sometimes substantially, between supermarkets – even those of the same chain – with no clear pattern of products or neighbourhoods.

The earlier survey (OUR, 2002) showed that the virtues attributed to the supermarket, especially by higher-income consumers, were: quality of service, security (lack of petty crime), food safety, fair weighting procedures, homogeneous quality and ease of shopping (longer opening hours,[23] shopping carts, controlled temperature, parking space, credit cards and cheques accepted). The positive traits of street markets were fresh, natural products, personal attention from vendors and greater variety. The weight given to each aspect, and the importance of distance and prices, varied widely depending on buying habits (habitual supermarket or market-goers) and socio-economic level; lower-income groups tended to go to a market and to prefer street markets.

Initiatives taken to support linkages with the wholesale markets

Several attempts have been made to upgrade the traditional marketing system to improve its competitiveness with the supermarket chains. While these efforts have been directed at both upstream and downstream linkages, the downstream linkages have been most successful.

Upstream

Campocoop, a large cooperative of small farmers, has organized 7000 of its affiliates[24] to supply the Mersan market with a daily balanced supply of produce and has considered doing the same at Lo Valledor. Another small-scale farmers' cooperative, Coopeumo, found that organizational problems prevented it from competing successfully in LoValledor. These included getting the right mix of products at the right time to obtain a decent price, tracing the owners of the produce sold and reporting back to members on prices, margins, etc.[25]

Downstream

In 1997 a group from the Municipality of La Florida[26] started strategizing on how to counteract falling sales caused by supermarkets. They were later joined by Lo Valledor, which brought new ideas and more means; management at Lo Valledor had come to appreciate that the market is part of a value-chain and that it makes sense to promote street markets. This initiative eventually led to the founding, in 2001, of ASOF. Vendors were given economic support, and training courses were organized to 'modernize the micro-entrepreneur's head' in relation to marketing, organization, administration, food-handling, legal matters and consumer trends.[27] Customer relations training taught vendors to be accurate and honest when weighing wares, to let customers choose their fruits and vegetables and to wear aprons. Several street markets were spruced up with matching sunshades, uniforms, logotypes, private guards, chemical toilets, electronic scales, etc. Lo Valledor organized seminars, workshops and other activities for its owners, including co-organizing a large trade fair for small retailers in 2003.[28]

The result has been a substantial increase in the number of Lo Valledor clients, expanded and modernized services and security, and an increase in area from 7 to 25 hectares. This was accompanied by a campaign to 'prefer street markets for good health' in terms of food and contact with neighbours. Marketing efforts included advertising, product promotions and promotion of healthy foods, donations of fruit and vegetables, etc. These efforts were aimed at children in particular, with a view to improving their eating habits.

Since the beginning of this modernizing effort, street markets have received sporadic public support. FOSIS (*Fondo de Solidaridad e Inversión Social*, a public, decentralized, social investment fund) financed small projects to improve street markets and in 2000/01 financed a project for US$500,000 with counterpart funds from the municipalities, private institutions such as Lo Valledor and the vendors themselves. Sercotec (a Government technical cooperation service geared to micro- and small-scale enterprises) helped the street markets with several small projects totalling less than US$50,000. In several municipalities, the vendors are the most important group of entrepreneurs, but government support dropped off, one reason being the fact that most vendors do not form part of the 'extreme poor'. ASOF signed an agreement with the state development bank (*BancoEstado*) in 2001 for a package of financial services especially adapted to the needs of the vendors, and in 2004 a new agreement was signed that included new financial products (ASOF, 2004).

Conclusions and policy recommendations

We found that not only supermarkets and agro-industries but even most of the intermediaries of Lo Valledor and other wholesale markets tended to buy fruits and vegetables from medium- to large-scale farmers. Only occasionally did wholesale market suppliers use small-scale farmers to top up a truck. (Potatoes were a notable exception, as reported by Vargas and Foster, 2000.) One of the many reasons for this was the higher transactions costs for dealing with small-scale farmers and the difficulties in calculating and transferring costs to the farmers.

It was difficult to determine exactly where small farmers did sell their produce and whether those sales points would remain available in the future. A larger study is needed to ascertain what problems small-scale farmers face in selling their products and how to support them. We fully endorse the recommendation (OUR, 2002, p65) that government efforts be geared toward helping small farmers and intermediaries adapt their supply to the present and near-future standards and requirements of consumers and the changing demands of retail. In recent years government agencies have focused on initiatives for good farming practices (including standardization), agro-industry and packing, storage, transport and handling practices (including cleaning and classification), certification and quality assurances – and these should continue. There is an urgent need to encourage the formation of associations to pool production volumes, help with the administration of pooled volumes and continued support for improving productivity. The formation of more local value chains leading to the regional supermarkets – including small- and medium-scale farmers and processing industries – should be pursued more vigorously (OUR, 2002, p66).

While the lack of clear upstream linkages with the wholesale markets calls into question Lo Valledor's argument that it supports small farmers, in our opinion efforts to strengthen wholesale markets do merit support from government and municipal authorities, NGOs and international organizations given their downstream linkages with street markets and poor consumers. There are a number of good reasons for the government to help street markets and small shops adapt to the requirements of consumers and the rising competition of supermarkets. Prices in the street markets in the lower-income neighbourhoods (where it matters most) were found to be lower than at supermarkets. Fruit and vegetables sold there were fresher and more flavoursome and the service was more personal. In addition, the traditional chain provided higher levels of employment in comparison with supermarkets.

Specific measures to be taken should include discouraging mayors from issuance of more vendor permits around the time of an election than the market can sustain. ASOF should study the system of free sales of permits between vendors used by the Municipality of San Ramón and, if that system is advantageous for vendors, ASOF should lobby for its introduction in other municipalities. Given that a major factor detracting from the appeal of street markets is the higher likelihood of theft, public security at markets should be improved. Credit and training are needed to improve infrastructure and services, technology and management capabilities and to formalize businesses (OUR, 2002, p66). Initiatives taken in Santiago to support downstream linkages could well serve as an example for other countries.

Notes

1   The authors wish to thank Karen Darlington, Kristyn Feldner and Jessica Joiner for their work collecting information on street markets and prices.
2   These included representatives from ODEPA, RIMISP, Campocoop, Mucech, FAO and ECLAC.
3   Subsistence included those whose estimated yearly farm income was less than 12 times the monthly minimum salary; small-scale was distinguished from medium-scale by the government threshold for access to special programmes (the equivalent of 12 hectares of irrigated fertile land); and large-scale enterprises were those not requiring government intervention for access to credit.
4   Family budget survey (Encuesta de presupuestos familiares)
5   Internet article, Club Almacén, El Club de los Comerciantes de Chile (http://clubal-macen.com/lovalledor. html), and interviews in La Vega.
6   The weekly insert La Revista del Campo also contains pages on prices and traded volumes at cattle auctions, wholesale prices for agricultural inputs, international prices for the main exported fruit varieties, etc.
7   Conversation with Guilherme Schuetz, market specialist at FAO/Regional Office for Latin America and the Caribbean (22 August 2003).
8   Conclusion drawn by Riveros Bustos on the basis of the research and interviews done for article in *El Mercurio*, 5 June 2002.
9   See article by Joaquín Riveros Bustos, *El Mercurio*, 5 June 2002.
10   Since 1976, mobile markets (*ferias libres*) fall under the jurisdiction of mayors; extending permits is presumably one way to increase the incumbent's popularity.
11   In 1990 urban unemployment was 7.1 per cent among the economically active population with no technical or professional qualifications; in 2000 it was 10.1 per cent (ECLAC, 2002, p90). The official definition of unemployment is 'employed less than one hour in the past week'.
12   This section is based almost exclusively on the OUR study on supermarkets, completed in 2002.
13   See discussion above.
14   See Reardon et al, 2002 and the October 2003 FAO workshop presentations.
15   Between 1987 and 2000, the percentage of total households having a refrigerator increased from 57 to 82 and those with a car from 21 to 27 (OUR, 2002, pp55 and 13–14).
16   Several new supermarkets have opened in Santiago since the study was completed.
17   D&S with 29 per cent, Jumbo with 7 per cent and Unimarc with 5 per cent. The transnational Santa Isabel/Ahold accounted for 10.6 per cent of total sales and Carrefour for 2.4 per cent (OUR, 2002, pp17, 21).
18   See for example the Overseas Development Institute special issue on the subject (Reardon et al, 2002).
19   The authors gathered information for this part of the chapter through interviews with vendors, buyers and directors of Lo Valledor in August 2003.
20   Similarly, in a study on transaction costs in Peru, Escobal (2001) concluded that farmers' choice of markets is influenced not only by the cost and time it takes them to get to a market, but also by their experiences in particular markets, the stability of their relations with buyers and the resources they invest to obtain information and supervise implicit contractual arrangements.
21   The one exception is the permits extended by the Municipality of San Ramón.
22   From lower- to higher-income neighbourhoods: La Pintana, Estación Central, La Florida, La Reina, Las Condes and Vitacura.

23   Most supermarkets are open from 8 a.m. to 10 p.m., while street markets are usually open twice a week and only in the mornings.
24   Of a total of 280,000 small-scale farmers in Chile, two-thirds are subsistence farmers and the rest small commercial farmers.
25   Informant from Lo Valledor.
26   The group included street market union leaders, non-governmental organization (NGO) representatives, a Member of Parliament and government staff involved with micro-enterprise development.
27   The President of ASOF (personal communication).
28   See Club Almacén article at http://clubalmacen.com/lovalledor.html.

References

ACNielsen (2004) 'Changes in the Chilean market 2004: Understanding the consumer', ACNielsen, Santiago

ASOF (2004) 'El Feriante', Asociación Chilena de Organizaciones de Ferias Libres (ASOF), 1 May

Cornejo, V. (2000) 'Sin ferias libres mueren muchos pequeños y medianos agricultores', Diario Chile Riego, No 2, pp1–3, October

Development Policy Review (2003) Special issue on Food Policy Old and New, vol 21, nos 5–6, pp531–736

Economic Commission for Latin America and the Caribbean (ECLAC) (2002) Social Panorama of Latin America 2001–2002, ECLAC, Santiago, Chile

El Mercurio, Santiago, Chile (2003), 18 August

Escobal, J. (2001) 'The benefits of roads in rural Peru: A transaction costs approach', *Grupo de Analisis para el Desarrollo Working Paper*, November

Faiguenbaum, S., Berdegue, J. and Farrington, J. (2002) 'The rapid rise of supermarkets in Chile: Effects on dairy, vegetable and beef chains', *Development Policy Review*, vol 20, no 4, pp459–471

ODEPA/CIREN (2002) V Región: Catastro frutícola – principales resultados, ODEPA, Santiago, Chile

ODEPA/CIREN (2003) VI Región: Catastro frutícola – principales resultados, Oficina de Estudios y Políticas Agrarias (ODEPA), Santiago, Chile

ODEPA/University of Chile/RIMISP (OUR) (2002) 'Los supermercados en la distribución alimentaria y su impacto sobre el sistema agroalimentario nacional', final report, May, Santiago, Chile

ODEPA (2000) 'Clasificación de las explotaciones agrícolas del VI Censo Nacional Agropecuario según tipo de productor y localización geográfica', Documento de trabajo No 5, Ministry of Agriculture, Santiago, Chile

Reardon, T. and Berdegue, J. (2002) 'The rapid rise of supermarkets in Latin America: Challenges and opportunities for development', Development Policy Review, vol 20, no 4, pp371–388

Reardon, T., Berdegue, J. and Farrington, J. (2002) 'Supermarkets and farming in Latin America: Pointing directions for elsewhere?' *Overseas Development Institute Natural Resource Perspectives*, no 81, December

Vargas, G. and Foster, W. (2000) 'Concentración y coordinación vertical en la agricultura chilena', Santiago, Chile; paper presented at the workshop 'Concentración de los segmentos de transformación y mercadeo del sistema agroalimentario y sus efectos sobre los pobres rurales', Department of Agrarian Economy, Catholic University, Santiago, Chile, 27–28 November

Chapter 9

The Rapid Rise of Kenyan Supermarkets: Impacts on the Fruit and Vegetable Supply System

David Neven and Thomas Reardon[1]

Changes in end-consumer demand, ongoing trade and market liberalization, and increasing globalization have spurred a structural transformation process from traditional to modern in the agri-food systems of developing countries such as Kenya. At the forefront of this modernization process is the supermarket.

The spectacular growth of the market share of supermarkets in retailing is by no means an isolated phenomenon in the developing world. In Latin America for example, where 4 out of 10 people live in poverty, supermarkets increased their market share from 10–20 per cent to 50–60 per cent of national food retail markets from 1990 to 2000 (Reardon and Berdegue, 2002). To a lesser degree, similar observations were made in Asia (Reardon et al, 2003; *The Economist*, 2001). Emerging evidence now suggests that even in the poverty-stricken setting of sub-Saharan Africa, supermarkets are expanding rapidly (Robinson, 2001; *BusinessWeek*, 2001; *The East African*, 2001). South African supermarket chains have been the most active, with chains like Shoprite, Pick'n'Pay and Metro expanding throughout southern and eastern Africa (Weatherspoon and Reardon, 2003). This paper focuses on the case of Kenya, with 225 supermarkets, the second highest number of supermarkets in sub-Saharan Africa.

Supermarkets are very tough customers. They require higher and more consistent quality, consistent year-round delivery, larger volumes, more stringent payment terms and so on. Suppliers who are successful in meeting these criteria face great growth opportunities, but those who cannot make the grade are likely to be dropped. As the market share of supermarkets in food retailing grows, the effects of this supplier rationalization process will not be marginal. This has raised considerable concern about how small producers, processors, distributors and retailers will adapt. They may not adapt, leading to exclusion. Alternatively, some small firms and farms may adapt, through collective action, investments and learning, taking full advantage of the growth opportunities offered by supermarkets.

Domestic supermarket chains, as agents of change, have largely remained off the radar screen in the academic literature on African business and development. There has been work done on foreign chains: several studies have looked at the impact of the global strategies of UK supermarkets for sourcing fresh produce in Kenya (Barrett et al, 1997; Barrett et al, 1999; Dolan et al, 2000; Dolan and Humphrey, 2000, 2001). These studies have revealed the following important structural changes:

1   the competitive production and marketing of high-quality and value-added products for demanding markets (UK supermarkets with high quality standards);
2   the use of contracts rather than spot markets in the supply chain; and
3   the shift of horticultural export production in certain rubrics to larger, commercial farms where quality control and traceability are more practicable.

However, over 90 per cent of the volume, over 70 per cent of the value and the vast majority of the producers in the horticultural industry target the domestic market. This implies that a shift from traditional to modern in these domestic-market-oriented supply chains would potentially have a much wider impact than on just the minority that caters to the export market. Not hundreds but *thousands* of small farmers are challenged by this shift in Kenya. The main agents of change in the domestic horticulture market are the supermarkets. The latter have been mentioned only marginally in domestic market studies that have instead focused on traditional supply chain structures in which intermediaries play the key role (see, for example, Dijkstra, 1999b; 2001).

To help fill this void in the literature, this chapter focuses on the rise of domestic supermarkets and their impact on supply chains for fresh horticultural products in Kenya. It represents the findings based on data collected in 2003 and 2004. The primary data were collected through: a nationwide survey of retailers (210 supermarkets and 250 traditional retailers); a survey of 450 consumers in Nairobi; a survey of 116 farmers in the main production areas; field observations; expert interviews; and eight consumer focus groups in Nairobi.

The chapter proceeds as follows. The next section details the dimensions and growth patterns of supermarkets in Kenya and the drivers behind this growth and the following section analyses the procurement system for produce of supermarkets. The impacts of the supermarket's buying behaviour on traditional retailers, consumers and farmers are then examined while the next section discusses the implications of these impacts with regard to development programmes, government policy and private sector business strategies. The final section provides a summary and conclusions.

The rise of supermarkets in Kenya

Dimensions and diffusion patterns

While the supermarket is not new to Kenya (the first supermarkets arose in the 1960s), their rapid growth is a very recent phenomenon, having taken off since the mid-1990s. It is important to provide the definition of a supermarket that we use in this chapter because the definition varies from country to country. The terms 'self-service store' and 'supermarket' are used interchangeably in Kenya, irrespective of their size, as both have exploded on the retail scene together. Based on the Kenya branch of the international retail auditor ACNielsen, supermarkets are here defined as 'self-service stores handling predominantly food and drug fast moving consumer goods (FMCG) with at least 150m^2 (1625 sq ft) of floor space'. We define supermarkets of 15 times this size as hypermarkets (2250m^2 or 24,246 sq ft). Using these definitions, there are roughly 209 supermarkets and 16 hypermarkets in Kenya. At the same time, an estimated 900–1400 smaller self-service shops have entered the retail sector. These shops include mini-supermarkets in smaller towns and convenience stores in residential areas and at petrol (gas) stations. In small towns, the emergence of these mini-super-markets is just as radical a departure from the traditional shopping experience of consumers as hypermarkets are to consumers in Nairobi. Although this implies that small self-service shops are an important part of the supermarket revolution taking place in developing countries, this chapter focuses on the 225 supermar-kets meeting the size criteria outlines above.

Our research shows that in Kenya in 2003, 20 per cent of urban food retailing went through supermarkets.[2] In the main urban areas (Nairobi, Mombasa, Kisumu) are found the larger-format supermarkets (hypermarkets of up to 175,000 sq ft) and the larger chains. In the smaller towns and main crossroad towns, smaller supermarkets and smaller chains have emerged. The two clear market leaders in 2003 were Uchumi and Nakumatt, both large domestic-capital chains that together represent nearly 50 per cent of the supermarket sector, split between them about equally. Uchumi had 27 branches, including four hypermar-kets, in seven urban areas in Kenya, while Nakumatt had 12 branches, including eight hypermarkets, in three urban centres.[3] The following research findings indicate that the larger chains are gaining ground: the top five supermarket chains increased their combined floor space (a proxy for sales) nearly nine-fold between 1994 and 2003 (from 150,000 to 1,312,000 sq ft), while the other supermarkets increased their combined floor space only 150 per cent (from 300,000 to 737,000 sq ft).

The fruit and vegetable sub-sector provides a good example of how impor-tant supermarkets have become in Kenya. Based on our research, we estimate that in 2003 about 4 per cent (about 50,000 metric tons (mt)) of the fresh fruits and vegetables marketed to the urban consumer in Kenya was sold through supermar-kets. In 2002, 69,000mt of fresh fruits and vegetables were exported. Thus, even for important Kenyan export products such as fruits and vegetables, we estimate that supermarkets buy nearly the same volume of produce as is bought by the export market.

Supermarkets in Kenya are no longer the niche players they once were, catering exclusively to the high-income consumers in the capital. They have moved into intermediate cities (Mombasa, Kisumu, Nakuru) and are now expanding rapidly to smaller towns. For example, Uchumi opened two of its latest stores in the small towns of Karatina (125,000 inhabitants) and Kisii (75,000 inhabitants) and announced further expansion plans into other small towns such as Thika and Nyeri. A small town like Karatina is an attractive location for a supermarket chain because it is the bustling centre of commerce for a wider region of over 500,000 people who, before the arrival of Uchumi, had no modern supermarket available to them. Voids like these in Kenya's retail landscape are being filled up quickly as the major supermarket chains race to fill them first. The explosive expansion of the chains does not stop smaller players from arising in underserved areas. For example, in Bungoma town, a border town with Uganda (western Kenya), a major regional wholesaler moved into retailing, already announcing plans to set up shop in Kitale, another small town.

It is important to note that Kenya is also displaying clear signs of continued rapid expansion of supermarkets into the markets of middle- and low-income consumers. Emerging evidence indicates that while the relatively large high-income Asian/white/expatriate segment of the population (about 1.5 per cent of the total population, mostly residing in Nairobi) has played an important part in providing a nucleus from which supermarkets were able to arise (and these segments are still an important part of the customer base, especially for fresh produce), supermarkets have moved well beyond these segments. That the fastest growth is currently taking place outside the Asian/white/expatriate segment is made evident by the appearance of: smaller supermarket chains (such as Tusker and Ukwala, with eight and nine branches respectively) near the busy bus stops used by the middle- to low-income consumers in Nairobi (and other towns); the expansion of Uchumi to small towns like Kisii, Meru and Karatina; and the opening of Uchumi and Nakumatt branches in Nairobi's middle-income neighbourhoods (such as Buruburu and Kahawa Wendani). Some preliminary findings for Uchumi indicate that even in Asian estates in Nairobi, Africans make up a third of the customer base and in the other parts of Nairobi, Africans make up three-quarters of the customer base. Outside Nairobi Asian consumers are only marginally present. The latter gains in importance given our research finding that about 60 per cent of the supermarkets in Kenya are located outside of Nairobi (albeit mostly smaller ones).

Based on our Nairobi consumer survey, we found that 80 per cent of the households shop at supermarkets on a regular basis (at least once a month) and low-income consumers represent over 50 per cent of supermarket customers and over 30 per cent of supermarket sales. Our consumer focus group research in low-income neighbourhoods indicated that most of the residents shop at nearby supermarkets, although not frequently (mostly once a month) and for small values at a time. The low per capita expenditure is partially offset by the vast numbers of low-income consumers. The poor buy mostly easy-to-store bulk goods such as sugar or soap from the supermarket, while for their daily small and perishable purchases such as milk or produce they prefer to buy from nearby kiosks.

The growth of Kenya's supermarkets has also taken on a regional character with outward foreign direct investment (FDI) facilitated by the liberalization of regional investment regulations. Uchumi opened its first branch outside Kenya in Kampala (Uganda) in 2002. Their regional expansion plans make it appear that this is just the first drop of an upcoming flood of outward FDI by Kenyan supermarkets: Nakumatt plans to open two branches in Uganda, two in Tanzania, one in Rwanda, one in Burundi, one in Zambia and one in Zimbabwe; Uchumi's expansion plans include stores in Tanzania and Rwanda and more stores in Uganda. In these regional markets Nakumatt and Uchumi will face competition from the rapidly regionalizing supermarket chains from South Africa.

Drivers of growth

On the demand side, the key driver behind this rapid growth of supermarkets in Kenya is the equally rapid growth of the urban population and the change in lifestyle that accompanies it. Traditional retail outlets, with limited assortments, presented in drab decors, where consumers cannot pick up items to look at them at their leisure and where they have to scramble for the attention of the shop attendant behind the counter, leave consumers unsatisfied, creating a demand for better alternatives. The latter is provided by the emergence of shiny 'all-under-one-roof' store formats handling up to 30,000 different products, which offer consumers the convenience to buy practically everything that in the past involved a day of numerous errands.

Not only have consumers a strong incentive to switch to these more appealing retail formats, the number and concentration of consumers is growing as spectacularly as are the number and concentration of supermarkets. Between 1989 and 2002, Kenya's population grew from 21 million to 33 million and is expected to reach 42 million by 2010 (Mungai et al, 2000). Although only 37 per cent of Kenya's population lives in urban areas, population density is relatively high, with 80 per cent of the population living on 18 per cent of the land (Dijkstra, 1999a). In addition, the average urban population growth rate is double that of the overall population growth rate (UN Population Division, 2003). The populations of main cities like Nakuru and Eldoret doubled between 1989 and 2002 (*World Gazetteer*, 2002), trends which are predicted to continue in Africa. Kenya's capital Nairobi is on an especially sharp growth curve, with a recent study predicting that its population will grow from the current 2.5 million to 7.5 million over the next 20 years, an increase of almost 700 additional inhabitants every single day (African Population and Health Research Centre, 2003). Although the overwhelming majority of the people living in Kenya's urban areas are poor, their aggregated demand constitutes the effective demand that supermarkets can thrive on, with their low margin/high stock turnover strategy (Pralahad and Hammond, 2002).

With regard to fruits and vegetables, the impact of urbanization is further amplified by the change in consumption patterns. Fruits and vegetables are important items in the diet of urban consumers in Kenya. These consumers spend 11 per cent of their income on fruits and vegetables (Okado, 2001) and consume twice the volume of vegetables of rural consumers (Bawden et al, 2002).

With a downward trend in gross domestic product (GDP) per capita at constant prices over the last several years (CBS, 2002), there is no indication that consumer incomes are rising in Kenya, which in other parts of the world is a key explanatory factor behind the growth of supermarkets. Neither is consumer food safety an important driver. Unlike many other parts of the world, supermarkets in Kenya have not reached a stage of sophistication in their procurement methods where they can claim a guaranteed higher degree of food safety than the traditional shops. Our consumer survey furthermore indicates that price, quality, retailer location and freshness are the key decision criteria for deciding where to buy produce, but not food safety concerns (at least not yet).

On the supply side, trade liberalization/market reform and competition have been important factors driving the growth of supermarkets. Beginning in 1993, in collaboration with the World Bank and International Monetary Fund (IMF), the Government of Kenya started to stabilize and reform its economy (*Tradeport*, 1996). Import licensing and foreign exchange control were eliminated, the agricultural sector was liberalized, a process of privatization of parastatals was initiated and trade barriers were reduced. Import licensing removal led to increased product variety and shifted the retail market from a seller's to a buyer's market in which retailers had to fight for the consumer's 'dollar vote'. Both trade liberalization (more imports) and market liberalization (more competitors) increased product variety in the market place, thus favouring bigger stores that could stock a wider assortment of products (economies of scope). Furthermore, in 1992 Uchumi, which was state-owned, became a public company traded on the Nairobi Stock Exchange and its subsequent annual reports showed the retail industry that supermarkets can be highly profitable.

Competition, most notably between leading chains Uchumi and Nakumatt, has been an important growth driver in the industry. A new strategy by one competitor forces imitation and/or a counter-strategy by its competitor(s). For example, Nakumatt's introduction of large-format stores led to the introduction of hypermarkets by Uchumi. Conversely, Uchumi's subsequent introduction of fresh produce was followed by Nakumatt. Competition leads to low margin/high turnover strategies that imply economies of both scale and scope and thus fuel a never-ending need for supermarkets to increase the size of their operations while at the same time reducing costs.

Inward FDI, a key supply-side explanatory factor behind the rapid growth of supermarkets in other parts of the world, has not played a very important role in Kenya. South African supermarket chains have built up only a marginal presence in Kenya. Metro was the first supermarket chain from South Africa to move into Kenya in 1997; in Kenya it is a three-branch wholesale chain that organizes the 65-member voluntary trading organization 'Lucky 7'. More recently, its example was followed by the more upscale-oriented Woolworths (which in Kenya currently sells only clothing and furniture). Leading South African supermarket chains like Shoprite and Pick'n'Pay have not yet entered the Kenyan market but are likely to follow soon (Robinson, 2001; *East African*, 2001; *Business Report*, 2000), especially with a new trade protocol between Kenya and South Africa in the works (*Business Week*, 2002). FDI by global chains (such as Wal-Mart, Carrefour and Ahold) has not yet come to Kenya, although it would not be unreasonable to expect that it will begin in coming years. Such entry would greatly accelerate, deepen and extend the supermarket revolution as it has in other developing regions.

The key implication of the above trends is that if supermarkets were just a niche market – a tiny corner of the retail trade in just the capital city – it would be safe to ignore them. But a curent massive presence, growing quickly, implies that they are already, and will be increasingly, a major and even dominant force in food retail in Kenya. Moreover, they are growing fastest in the most dynamic markets in Kenya.

This means that supermarkets will increasingly influence the structure, conditions and performance of the agri-food system in Kenya. They will, to a large extent, determine the conditions – and the potential – for small farms and firms to sell agri-food products to the dynamic portions of the Kenyan economy: the urban markets that represent an important channel for the rural poor to escape from poverty. In order to assess the impact of supermarkets, we must understand their procurement strategy and its determinants.

Supermarket produce procurement systems and requirements

Supermarkets are much tougher customers – and present potentially much greater opportunities – than traditional buyers of Kenyan farm and food processing products. For small farmers and processors, supermarkets are far from 'business as usual'.

Not untypical for a developing country (Siamee, 1993; Sternquist, 1998), Kenya's traditional retail systems[4] are characterized by fragmentation, single units rather than chains, market power that lies with the wholesalers, long channels, direct payment to suppliers, a strong presence of women traders, little quality control, little grading, few standards and small inventories. Urban consumers buy their produce either directly from farmers or via collecting and distributing wholesalers and/or urban retailers (Dijkstra, 1997). Collecting wholesalers play a central role for small producers, from whom they buy their products via assembling wholesalers and purchase agents, because they create economies of scale, are very informed about the markets and assume most of the risk involved in moving produce from production to consumption areas.

The different nature of the supermarket industry implies that procurement strategies are not 'business as usual' for their suppliers. For example, relative to traditional retailers, leading supermarkets in Kenya demand from their fresh fruits and vegetables suppliers: higher, more consistent quality; consistent, year-round supply of larger volumes according to pre-arranged supply calendars; participation in promotions; lower transaction costs; new products (new varieties or value-added products, imports); food safety guarantees (which are very limited at present, for example inspection of cleanliness of water sources); adherence to specific logistical supply formats (transportation, crates); and more stringent delivery conditions (timing, payment terms, slotting fees, washing, grading, packaging, labelling). In order to reach all of these objectives supermarkets need to control their supply chains. Control (highly effective, highly efficient coordinated supply chains) is realized through standards and their enforcement mechanisms, contracts, centralized buying using distribution centres, sophisticated information technology systems for product flow management and communication, shorter supply channels with more direct links to farmers and fewer but larger suppliers (because like their customers, supermarkets prefer one-stop shopping for their procurement).

The analysis below shows that each of these measures has emerged and is increasingly important in Kenya. As supermarkets grow, they build the market power, financial means and geographic presence to realize all of these changes and to demand compliance from their suppliers, thus creating a fundamental structural change in agri-food supply chains.

As they grow, supermarkets tend to move from brokers to farmers to increase control over quality, supply reliability and price stability. Uchumi sources 35 per cent of its fruit directly from growers. This direct sourcing consists of 15 per cent from commercial farmers, 10 per cent from medium farmers and 10 per cent from small producers. Imports represent roughly 25 per cent of procured fruit and the remaining 40 per cent is supplied by brokers. For vegetables, roughly 50 per cent of the procured volume is sourced directly from growers. Medium-sized producers supply the largest share, with 25 per cent, followed by commercial farmers with 15 per cent, then small farmers with 10 per cent. Brokers supply 45 per cent of Uchumi's vegetables and the rest (5 per cent) is imported. Nakumatt, which started selling fresh fruits and vegetables a few years after Uchumi and with less conviction at first, utilizes the services of two specialized wholesalers who run the produce sections in each branch as a shop-within-a-shop. The first wholesaler is Mugoya Vegetable Shop, who supplies Nakumatt's nine stores in Nairobi and Kisumu and the second wholesaler is Shree Ganesh, who supplies Nakumatt's two more distant stores in Mombasa. The larger of those two brokers (Mugoya) in turn purchases 60 per cent of its vegetables from small producers. Small chains and independent supermarkets that are not able to undertake the above shift must continue to rely on traditional wholesale markets, or at best on the remaining non-dedicated brokers. As most horticultural producers in Kenya lack the scale of operations to provide large supermarket chains consistently throughout the year with the volume and quality of fresh produce they need, supermarket procurement managers, aiming to complete their orders, will purchase from a mixture of suppliers, including brokers, farmers, traditional and specialized wholesalers and processors, foreign suppliers and exporters diverting their produce (mostly that rejected for quality reasons) to the domestic market.

The supermarket produce procurement managers are under cost pressures to deal with fewer and larger suppliers. A larger supplier can be a collective of smaller suppliers or just larger individual suppliers. These tend to include agro-exporters (such as Sunripe) that add to their businesses a service of intermediation for supermarkets, or agroindustrial firms (such as Cirio Delmonte). The key is that both of these actors are already used to dealing in large volumes, assuring consistent and quality supplies either for export markets or processing plants that operate year-round.

As they grow regionally, supermarkets will look for suppliers from a wider pool. For example, Uchumi Uganda is closely linked in a bi-country procurement system with the same chain in Kenya and exports produce from its grower/suppliers in Kenya to its store in Uganda (40 per cent of Ugandan supplies). In fact, this is considered desirable by the Ugandan government, so that the arrival of a Kenyan chain does not further exacerbate trade imbalance and the flooding of the Ugandan market with agri-food products from Kenya, but rather represents a 'win–win' situation where Uchumi helps to build a procurement system that relies on growers in both countries.

Partly integrating the wholesale function, supermarkets tend to shift from per-store procurement to more centralized systems for their chain. In Kenya, centralized handling of produce items by supermarkets is mostly related to imported products (such as fruits from Israel, South Africa and Egypt). For the domestically produced fresh horticultural products, delivery usually takes place at the level of the individual store. However, Uchumi has completely re-engineered its existing distribution centre and will for the first time be moving domestic produce through it. Nakumatt has built a new distribution centre as well, but has no plans for moving produce through it and will continue to rely on specialized wholesalers. This move towards centralized buying and distribution centres simultaneously allows for economies of scale and greater control over product quality and distribution to individual stores. At the sector level, the combination of supermarkets both displacing great numbers of small retail outlets (such as open air market stalls) and centralizing their procurement implies a dramatic reduction in the number and increase in the size of procurement points.

Whether the procurement takes place directly from farmers, via specialized wholesalers as discussed above, or via distribution centres, supermarkets tend to have more stringent product quality standards as well as packaging and delivery timing requirements when compared to traditional intermediaries and retailers. Supermarkets like Uchumi demand the highest quality produce from their farmers and the chain is currently in the process of developing written quality standards for their produce items. At the moment product quality is visually inspected at the point of delivery (the supermarket branch) and produce not meeting the high standards is rejected on the spot. Over time suppliers learn the quality that is acceptable (which varies with seasonal availability) and they work towards supplying only this quality to supermarkets. Food safety standards (such as selection and the use of pesticides by farmers) are not employed by supermarkets in Kenya for the time being, nor are product samples tested for pesticide residues, although there are some emerging issues. For example, Uchumi inspects the farms of key suppliers, in part to make sure no sewage water is used for irrigation (a practice observed in urban agriculture). The brokers/wholesale markets cannot provide their customers with such a guarantee. The above standards and requirements are enforced with the greater bargaining/leverage power of consolidated buyers (relatively few chains), and so we come full circle back to the initial point about consolidation and increased scale of procurement.

Impact of supermarkets on Kenya's agri-food system

The impact of supermarkets can be assessed at the downstream level (retailer/consumer) and the upstream level (farmers and intermediaries).

The rise of supermarkets has a direct impact on traditional retailers. While there are no reliable statistics on the numbers of retail outlets per type, it is quite probable that thousands of small shops have been affected by the rise of supermarkets and hypermarkets. With a kiosk or an open air market stall in Kenya's cities having on average 100 sq ft of floor space and with the average size of Kenya's supermarkets at about 9900 sq ft (in 2003), and if one assumes a fixed ratio between floor space and sales, then one supermarket has 99 times the sales of a small shop (or stall in an open air market). The rise of 225 supermarkets would thus displace over 22,000 stalls or small shops. However, from interviews and the scarce statistics available, we learned that the rise of supermarkets in Kenya has mostly reduced sales rather than forced the market exit of traditional retailers. This can be explained by the notion that, during times of economic recession (as in Kenya in recent years), one sets up a small retail outlet as a survival strategy. As these small shopkeepers have no better alternative mode of employment, they stick to their market stalls and kiosks, even if they lose a large part of their revenues to supermarkets. At the same time some store types do go out of business because of the rise of supermarkets, most notably small self-service stores or other types of small retail outlets that are located close to supermarkets. For example, until a few years ago, most of 82 stalls of the City Municipal Market in Westlands (Nairobi) sold fruits and vegetables, but with three supermarkets now well-established nearby, only 12 fresh produce stalls remain (the other 70 having shifted to alternative products or services).

The increasing market share of supermarkets versus the more traditional retailers is a mixed blessing for urban consumers. On the one hand, the reduced importance of these traditional retail outlets can be problematic in terms of food security, not only because they provide a direct source of income to the low-income women and men who run them, but also because they are an especially important outlet for small producers (because they have less stringent requirements) and for poor urban consumers (because they are more familiar, more accessible and willing to sell in smaller quantities). On the other hand, the wide assortment and higher concern for quality at supermarkets positively affect food safety and the diversity of products available to poor consumers. Apart from higher, more assured quality, supermarkets offer a slightly cheaper food basket to consumers than do traditional retailers. Important food products like cooking oil and sugar, for example, are less expensive at supermarkets. While price differences are small (about 4 per cent on average), they are sufficient to influence consumer behaviour, especially for low-income households. Lower prices are observed not only for basic dry foods, but even for some fresh produce items. Preliminary data analysis indicates that for high turnover produce items that supermarkets procure directly from farmers (such as kale, green cabbage or spinach), supermarkets sell at prices 10–30 per cent lower than some traditional retail outlets such as greengrocers or city markets. With prices for many dry foods and some fresh produce items lower than traditional wholesalers, street hawkers and small shops have even started sourcing from supermarkets like Uchumi. These traditional retailers make their profit margin by dividing products up into smaller quantities and bringing them closer to the consumer.

The impact on the structure of agri-food supply chains follows from the challenges implied by the supermarket's procurement system. Farm-level compliance with supermarket demands implies that suppliers too have control over the production and marketing of their output. Control at the farm level is realized through new production and management practices. For fresh produce growers, new production practices include: working with year-round crop production calendars; investments in technology, most notably irrigation, transportation and communication technology; and farm management and post-harvest handling training (such as with regard to chemical usage, new technologies and packaging). New management practices (contracting, marketing, formal accounting and invoicing and working capital management) imply a more formal, businesslike approach to farm management. These changes affect small producers in particular. The formality of transactions, the need for investments, economies of scale associated with new technologies, working capital requirements and minimum volume demands all favour large, commercial farmers over smallholder producers. Quality and packaging requirements imply labour and capital investment requirements – often large relative to the capacities of the small producers. Small producers tend to face significant factor market constraints in overcoming the above obstacles, most notably access to credit markets to finance investments in cold chain technology, transport, drip irrigation, adequate processing equipment, packaging equipment and so on. Supermarkets often impose additional fees (such as for product breakage and promotion contributions) and often pay with significant delay (about two weeks) versus immediate payment (cash-on-delivery) to suppliers under the traditional system, which further magnifies the cash-flow and credit challenges faced by small producers who want to sell to supermarkets. Perhaps most importantly in the near term is the fact that supermarkets source from a variety of producers (large and small local suppliers, and via the procurement networks, from regional and global sources). Relative to traditional retailers, supermarkets also buy and sell more imported products. With respect to produce, imports are mostly fresh fruits (such as apples from South Africa) and processed fruits (such as orange juice from Israel). That means that supermarkets have brought and facilitated competition for local small producers right into their own backyard.

Suppliers who want to sell to the skyrocketing supermarket sector in Kenya face the above challenges, now or in the near future. Local rural retailers and traditional urban retailers are serving markets that are not growing quickly and are not primarily geared to middle-class consumers. If suppliers want to sell to growing markets with strong effective demand, and thus raise their own incomes, they would do well to target the supermarkets that are increasingly the gatekeepers for the dynamic urban markets.

Supermarkets are more demanding customers, and also offer great opportunities for growth. Relative to traditional retail outlets, supermarkets represent a more reliable, higher volume market for higher value produce (rather than accidental surpluses feeding into a thin market). Growth opportunities exist through market enlargement from zone to nation to region, as supermarkets expand their activities beyond country borders. Illustrations from other countries include a cheese cooperative in southern Chile that was selling to the local towns and rural areas in its zone before making deals with the supermarkets; these deals expanded the cooperatives' market from local to national, vastly increasing their incomes and the volume of their sales. Given that supermarkets in Kenya are still in full development, they represent an opportunity for gradual learning, capacity-building and adapting to continuously mounting requirements as supermarkets increase the level of sophistication of their operations. Supermarkets might also offer higher prices to small suppliers because of the higher quality of the products and/or a reduction in the number of intermediaries (implying fewer margins along the way). Additional opportunities exist to sell products with value added (such as cleaning, grading and sorting, packaging, organic or processed). Uchumi stores, for example, boast 11 varieties of potatoes; organically grown, pre-washed salads; and ready-to-cook stir-fry mixes – to name but a few of the value-added products that have appeared on its shelves. And finally, opportunities exist to sell fresh produce on promotion in case of a glut.

As illustrated in the following paragraphs, some smallholder producers do succeed in gaining access to the supermarket. In all three cases, key success factors are: a focus on quality products with a pre-identified market; the catalysing involvement of private and/or public organizations with a commercial basis; and sustainable group formation among farmers.

Family Concern

Family Concern is a private company that aims to combine development and business objectives in building horticultural linkages. Having identified (alongside Uchumi) the fact that there is a high, unmet demand for traditional African vegetables (such as spider plant, cowpeas, amaranth and black nightshade),

Family Concern assisted farmers who supplied Uchumi to increase their acreage under these crops. The International Plant Genetic Research Institute (IPGRI), the Kenya Agricultural Research Institute and FARM-Africa from the UK were key partners in setting up the project. With potential demand at Uchumi estimated at three times current supplies of 100 metric tonnes per month, Family Concern set out to build supply capacity for traditional African vegetables among smallholders. Starting with a group of 50 farmers with an average of one-quarter of an acre of available land, Family Concern initiated a production scheme for organically grown traditional African vegetables. These products are marketed under the brand name African Delicacies; they started to appear in the produce sections of selected Uchumi branches in 2004.

Horticultural Produce Handling Company

Some smallholder producers link up with supermarkets through the Horticultural Produce Handling Company (HPHC), which is managed by the Horticultural Crop Development Authority (HCDA). While HCDA is a parastatal organization, HPHC is run as a commercial enterprise. HPHC aims, through modern post-harvest handling systems, to improve the marketing system of horticultural produce (primarily with a focus on the export market). The facilities include seven satellite depots with pre-cooling units, the Nairobi Horticultural Centre (near Jomo Kenyatta International Airport) with cold-storage facilities and insulated trucks of various capacities to maintain the cold chain. Under the stringent quality and safety requirements of export markets, farmers produce and supply as groups of outgrowers to the Centre and from there to Uchumi supermarkets (among others). Although only operational since 2001 and still operating much below capacity, the potential impact of HPHC is large. Several other projects, for example an International Fund for Agricultural Development (IFAD)-funded irrigation scheme near Meru, have linked up with HPHC to create synergies.

Iga Muka

Iga Muka, a farmer's cooperative specializing in strawberries in the Sagana development scheme on the slopes of Mount Kenya, succeeded in linking up with Uchumi via the Kenya Agricultural Commodity Exchange (KACE). KACE is a private sector firm that facilitates linkages between sellers and buyers of agricultural commodities, mainly by developing marketing information systems that reduce the information asymmetry between farmer and broker. Part of these systems are the market information points that have small trading floors where buyers and sellers (like Iga Muka and Uchumi) can interact. The sustainability of this organizational structure is supported through commissions on trade transactions.

Implications for development programmes, government policy and private sector strategies

Development programmes can focus on pilot projects that link farmers with supermarkets through alliances. This can include strengthening marketing elements of the small farm and firm activities: packaging, labelling, quality, size consistency, information systems and cold chain logistics. One option is to model these projects as farmer field schools. It will also be critical to assist farmers' organizations in getting access to the credit needed to make the required invest-ments and help farmers to build organically the working capital required to cope with the payment terms of the supermarkets.

Government policy and programmes have a crucial role. There is a need to design and implement policies that encourage the institutional improvements required to integrate farmers into modern agri-food systems, such as:

1   establishing or reinforcing associations of farmers or firms that focus on scale increase and vertical integration (such as through association-owned cooling facilities, packing sheds and processing plants);
2   working with contracts (for example the Contract Farming Act and other commercial laws and regulations);
3   introducing food quality and food safety systems and the institutions to certify/police their implementation;
4   setting up specific partnerships between smallholder organizations in Kenya and supermarket chains;
5   providing or supporting changes in education/training to address the specific capabilities required for farmers to participate in consumer-driven markets; and
6   investing in logistical infrastructure (roads, cooling facilities) that make markets more reliably accessible and thus allow farmers to focus more on commercial markets.

Passable roads are a very critical element in market involvement and supermarket suppliers will be those who are closest to the roads. Some well-chosen investments in this regard can have a great impact in addressing poverty in selected rural areas.
Private sector associations could:

1   develop codes of best practices for suppliers to help them adjust to supermar-ket requirements;
2   develop codes of conduct between suppliers and supermarkets (as have recently been adopted in Spain and Argentina) to improve contract and trans-action conditions for the suppliers and meet the growing needs of supermarkets on win–win terms for both parties;
3   collect information on the domestic market to identify the most promising opportunities for smallholder producers (that is, those least sensitive to economies of scale);

4   work with business development services to train farmers and develop their organizational and management capabilities (including their ability to develop and implement marketing strategies); and

5   find international partners to complete year-round availability (critical to supermarket buyers), access export markets (over time) and learn from the sharing of best practices.

Summary and conclusion

Supermarkets are not business as usual for Kenyan suppliers. The presence of supermarkets induces challenges in the form of: the delivery of larger volumes and continuous supply throughout the year; higher and consistent quality requirements; more complex delivery formats (timing, packaging, refrigeration); and more challenging payment terms to suppliers, including longer gaps between delivery and payment, breakage fees and discounts for promotional sales of produce. These challenges are amplified by:

1   the new competition generated by supermarket chains offering attractive points of entry for diverted exports and foreign suppliers;

2   the smaller number of alternative procurement points remaining in the market as supermarkets increase their market share relative to traditional retailers, and as they consolidate; and

3   improvement of the value delivered to their consumers by surviving traditional retailers, which increases pressure on suppliers to comply with higher standards.

Overcoming these challenges requires substantial resources: managerial skill, information, physical and monetary capital, labour and technology. Small farms and firms are expected to have only limited access to these resources. Many farmers in Kenya may not be able to 'make the grade' and will be forced to exit horticulture altogether. There are many examples from other countries of small producers (farms and processing firms) that have been excluded from selling to supermarkets because they could not meet the challenges. Perhaps that would not be a problem – if it were not for the supermarkets taking over the dynamic markets. Small farmers may find jobs created in the new supply chains that feed into supermarkets or they may fall into subsistence agriculture.

Alternatively, a few case studies illustrate that some small farmers (or groups of small farmers) may find ways to overcome these challenges and grow with supermarkets, which represent great opportunities for growth through market enlargement and the introduction of higher value products into urban markets. Given that supermarket development in Kenya is still at an early stage in its development, the emphasis should be placed on the opportunities they create. Currently there is a (narrow) window of opportunity for smallholder producers to build partnerships with domestic supermarkets and grow along with them.

Development programmes, government policies and the strategies of private sector associations aimed at assisting small-scale producers in Kenya's agri-food sector need to take these supermarket-induced market dynamics into account.

Notes

1   The authors are grateful for support for this work from the Rockefeller Foundation and the United States Agency for International Development (USAID).
2   We focus on the urban market because this is where the dynamics in terms of population growth and retail market changes are taking place. The urban population is defined here as all people living in urban centres of 10,000 or larger. Based on the 1999 population census (CBS, 2002) and United Nations (UN) growth projections (UN Habitat, 2004; UN Population Division, 2003), we estimate the urban population in 2002 at 11.9 million (37 per cent of the overall population).
3   While this specific picture has changed in the years since the data were collected, the overall picture remains the same. Uchumi went through some financial problems, almost going out of business. However, other supermarkets, especially Nakumatt, have quickly filled the gap and strong growth of the supermarket sector has continued.
4   Traditional retail types include kiosks (small building structures alongside roads, usually located in or close to residential areas, handling products with high turnover), over-the-counter shops, greengrocers, market stalls in open air markets and in covered markets. Covered markets carry a broader assortment of higher-quality produce items at higher prices and have been, with upmarket greengrocers, the retailers of choice for the high-income consumers.

References

African Population and Health Research Centre (2003) *Population and Health Dynamics in Nairobi's Informal Settlements*, Nairobi

Barrett, H., Browne, A., Ilbery, B., Jackson, G. and Binns, T. (1997) *Prospects for Horticultural Exports under Trade Liberalisation in Adjusting African Economies*, Department for International Development (DFID), London

Barrett, H., Ilbery, B., Browne, A. and Binns, T. (1999) 'Globalization and the changing networks of food supply: The importation of fresh horticultural produce from Kenya into the UK', *Transactions of the Institute of British Geographers*, vol 24, no 2, pp159–174

Bawden, R., Aust Sterns, P., Harris, S. and Berdegue, J. (2002) *Increasing Rural Household Incomes in Kenya through Horticulture – A Design Proposal*, Partnerships for food industry development – fruits and vegetables, Michigan State University, East Lansing, MI

Business Report (2000) 'Shoprite checkers' tills prepare to ring in Kampala', 6 November

Business Week (2001) 'Giant supermarkets battle for supremacy', 11 December

Business Week (2002) 'Kenya and South Africa seek to establish a trade protocol', 26 November

Central Bureau of Statistics (2002) *Statistical Abstract*, Ministry of Planning and National Development, Republic of Kenya, Nairobi

Dijkstra,T. (1997) Commercial horticulture by African smallholders: A success story from the highlands of Kenya, *Scandinavian Journal of Development Alternatives*, vol 16, no 1, pp49–74

Dijkstra,T. (1999a) 'Commercial horticulture by Kenyan smallholders', in D. Grossman, L. M. van den Berg and H. I. Ajaegbu (eds) 'Urban and peri-urban agriculture in Africa: Proceedings of a workshop', Netanya, Israel, 23–27 June 1996, Ashgate, Aldershot, pp53–65

Dijkstra,T. (1999b) 'Horticultural marketing in Kenya: Why potato farmers need collecting wholesalers', in H. L. van der Laan,T. Dijkstra and A. van Tilburg (eds) *Agricultural Marketing in Tropical Africa: Contributions from the Netherlands*, Ashgate, Aldershot, pp169–184

Dijkstra,T. (2001) 'Applying marketing channel theory to food marketing in developing countries: Vertical disintegration model for horticultural marketing channels in Kenya', *Agribusiness*, vol 17, no 2, p227

Dolan, C. and Humphrey, J. (2000) 'Governance and trade in fresh vegetables: Impact of UK supermarkets on the African horticulture industry', *Journal of Development Studies*, vol 37, no 2, pp147–177

Dolan, C. and Humphrey, J. (2001) 'Governance and trade in fresh vegetables: The impact of UK supermarkets on the African horticulture industry', in O. Morrissey and I. Filatotchey (eds) *Globalisation and Trade: Implications for Exports from Marginalised Economies*, Frank Cass, London, pp147–176

Dolan, C., Humphrey, J. and Harris Pascal, C. (2000) 'Horticulture commodity chains: The impact of the UK market on the African fresh vegetable industry', Working Paper, Institute of Development Studies, University of Sussex, Brighton

East African, The (2001) 'Pick'n'Pay wooing Kenyan partner', Business Section, 7 May

Economist, The (2001) 'Asian retailing: A hyper market', 7 April, p68

Mungai, J., Ouko, J. and Heiden, M. (2000) *Processing of Fruits and Vegetables in Kenya*, GTZ-Integration of tree crops into farming systems project, GTZ, Nairobi

Okado, M. (2001) 'Background paper on Kenya off-season and specialty fresh vegetables and fruits', paper presented at the UNCTAD Diversification and development of the horticultural sector in Africa, Regional workshop for horticultural economies in Africa, 29–31 May, Nairobi

Pralahad, C. and Hammond, A. (2002) 'Serving the world's poor, profitably', *Harvard Business Review*, September, pp48–57

Reardon,T. and Berdegue, J. (2002) 'The rapid rise of supermarkets in Latin America: Challenges and opportunities for development', *Development Policy Review*, vol 20, no 4, pp371–388

Reardon,T., Timmer, C., Barrett, C. and Berdegue, J. (2003) 'The rise of supermarkets in Africa, Asia and Latin America', *American Journal of Agricultural Economics*, vol 85, no 5, pp1140–1146

Robinson, S. (2001) 'South African invasion', *Time Europe*, vol 157, no 14, 9 April

Siamee, S. (1993) 'Retailing and channel considerations in developing countries: A review and research propositions', *Journal of Business Research*, vol 27, pp103–130

Sternquist, B. (1998) *International Retailing*, Fairchild Publications, New York

Tradeport (1996) [online] www.tradeport.org/ts/countries/kenya/fdmrkt.html, accessed 25 October 2002

UN Habitat (2004) [online] www.unhabitat.org/habrdd/conditions/eafrica/kenya.htm, accessed 3 May 2004

UN Population Division (2003) *World Population Prospects: The 2002 Revision Population Database*, [online] http://esa.un.org/unpp/p2k0data.asp, accessed 3 May 2004

Weatherspoon, D. and Reardon, T. (2003) 'The rise of supermarkets in Africa: Implications for agrifood systems and the rural poor', *Development Policy Review*, vol 21, no 3, pp333–355

World Gazetteer (2002) [online] www.world-gazetteer.com/t/t_ke.htm, [online] accessed 25 October 2002

Chapter 10

Linkages Between Smallholder Farmers and Supermarkets: Lessons from Zambia

Hyde Haantuba and Jacques de Graaf[1]

Recent research shows that there has been a rapid expansion of supermarkets in several countries in eastern and southern Africa, which resembles similar phenomena in Latin America and Asia. According to Weatherspoon and Reardon (2003), supermarket chains such as Shoprite, Pick'n'Pay and Woolworths have established themselves in urban areas and have also opened retail outlets in smaller cities and poorer areas and neighbourhoods ('supermarkets for the poor'). Growth in the supermarket sector in southern Africa could have both positive and negative effects on the structure and conditions of the agri-food economy in the region. Some policy makers have argued that domestic producers may be increasingly marginalized by third-country imports of cheaper and often higher quality products. Others argue that these transformations may offer huge opportunities for integrating rural communities into the evolving local economic and trading system, thereby contributing to reducing poverty.

In Zambia there has been a significant increase in the number and the role of supermarkets in retail trade; in addition, supermarkets have added a new dimension to the way foods and foodstuffs are sold in the country. The effect of their presence, especially their impact on stimulating agricultural trade and retailing among rural producers, has recently received greater attention from policy makers and researchers. Market access and integration may offer opportunities for increasing food security and reducing poverty among small-scale rural farm households.

This chapter analyses the state of supermarket penetration in rural markets and their associated linkages with smallholder farm producers in Zambia. More specifically, it aims to increase understanding of the impact of supermarket expansion on two rural communities and the role that good agricultural practices (GAPs) could play in providing access for small-scale rural farmers to the changing food system. In order to adequately address these linkages, the chapter explores the procurement requirements and practices of supermarket chains to determine the nature of opportunities or constraints they pose to smallholder farm producers in rural areas. The collection of detailed quantitative data was hindered by supermarkets' hesitance to reveal corporate information.

The Zambia context

Zambia is a landlocked country of 750,000 km^2, most of which lies on a plateau ranging from 900 to 1500 metres above sea level. In 2002 it had a population of 10.9 million, with 3.4 per cent annual growth. The country suffered a drastic decline in its living standards during the last two decades with a gross domestic product (GDP) per capita estimated at US$289. Around 82 per cent of the rural population is classified as living below the poverty line and over two-thirds of the population live on less than US$1 a day. Population density is rather low, at 14.5 people per km^2, although the capital, Lusaka, and the Copperbelt urban centres are densely populated compared with many centres in the region. Over half of Zambians live in rural areas and are dependent on agriculture for their livelihoods.

Zambia's agricultural sector has become increasingly important and holds the key to the development of the Zambian economy. It employs 67 per cent of the labour force and in recent years has contributed 22 per cent of the GDP, enjoying an average annual growth rate of 2 per cent (which fluctuates a great deal depending on annual weather conditions). Zambia's agricultural resource base is immense. Of the total arable land (420,000km^2 or 42 million hectares), only 14 per cent is cultivated. Water bodies such as lakes and rivers are largely unexploited; only 5 per cent of the country's irrigation potential is utilized.

Until 1975, Zambia's economy was based on copper but as world prices fell, the government started focusing on agriculture as one of the alternative sources of economic growth, employment and foreign exchange earnings. Zambian farmers were to sell their produce to parastatal companies such as Namboard (for grains and legumes), Zamhort (horticultural products), Zambeef (beef and milk), Zambia Pork Products and Lintco (cotton). However, as a result of a constant decline in GDP per capita between 1980 and 1990, Zambia embarked on a comprehensive programme of economic reform and returned to a free market economy in 1991.

This led to radical changes in the policy and institutional environment governing the agricultural sector. Policies of liberalization and privatization entailed replacing services previously supplied by the state (notably agricultural marketing, credit and input supply) with provision by the private sector.[2] Both agricultural credit and marketing fell to the private sector, and coverage was unpredictable. The remaining public agencies providing agricultural services, such as extension, suffered from lack of staff, operational funds and transportation and were largely unable to respond to small farmers' needs. Nevertheless, liberalization policies led to some positive developments such as an increase in outgrower and contract farming, crop diversification, changes in land management practices and, in certain regions, increased private sector involvement in the provision of agro-services (ACF, 2002).

Zambia was transformed into one of the most liberalized economies in Africa and provides a model for the effective establishment of legal and institutional frameworks for the privatization of state-owned enterprises. The Zambia Privatization Agency (ZPA) was set up in 1992 to spearhead the process, and the country made substantial progress in creating an enabling environment for private investment through legal and regulatory reform and reduction of state intervention in various factor and product markets. This resulted in a fundamental change in the institutional structure of the economy.

The Zambia Investment Centre (ZIC) was established under the Investment Act of 1991 as part of the Government's strategy for economic reform and as an autonomous institution to promote local and foreign investment, facilitate the investment process and monitor the implementation of projects. ZIC estimated that US$1.4 billion worth of capital expenditure and more than 25,000 jobs were linked to foreign direct investment (FDI), with South Africa becoming the second largest foreign investor after the UK. Within the period 1993–1998, South Africa made significant investment commitments amounting to US$239 million, about 19 per cent of the total investment pledges in Zambia. Forming a critical part of this rush for Zambian investment was Shoprite Checkers, a large multinational chain of retail stores specialized in domestic groceries and consumables.

The policy environment and reforms that encouraged foreign investors like Shoprite to set up shop in Zambia included investment incentives such as an open market economy with little government interference; no price or exchange controls; no subsidies; and 100 per cent profit repatriation. The 1993 Investment Act provided incentives such as tax credits; entitlement to work permits for up to five expatriate employees for companies investing above US$250,000 and employing more than ten local people; acquisition of land for registered investors; and duty incentives. Guarantees were established for registered investors including compulsory acquisition only with an act of Parliament, adherence to Multilateral Investment Guarantee Agency (MIGA) and special bilateral investor protection agreements (Coffee Board, 2003).

Types of markets available to Zambian farmers

Zambian farmers have always had access to one or more types of markets for their produce. The nature, capacity and behaviour of such markets have determined to a large extent what produce could be sold, and smallholder access to the markets has not been straightforward. There are few systematic studies on this, but we provide here a synopsis of some of the market channels.

Farmers in Zambia often sell to local consumers within the vicinity of their farms, including neighbours, fellow farmers, local salaried workers and local traders. With increasing frequency, farmers along major highways establish rural roadside market centres, which are unpredictable markets with limited potential to stimulate commercialization. The main commodities sold include potatoes, cassava, squashes, fruits, poultry, goats, pigs, maize, beans and groundnuts. The trade involves cash, barter and credit transactions. Somewhere between 20 and 50 per cent of agricultural produce is traded in this way.

One of the oldest, time-tested market channels available to farmers in rural areas is intermediaries. In some cases, close family ties facilitate such trade because most urban-based intermediaries purchase produce on cash, barter or credit in their home villages. This channel is quite resilient although it is widely criticized by farmer organizations for 'exploiting' farmers. In studies in Monze, Bangwe et al (1997) underlined the increased importance of this channel after market liberalization and the collapse of parastatal institutions. In some communities, it was the only significant channel available to farmers to supplement local trade, and thus responsible for sustaining agricultural production. Bangwe et al demonstrated that the constraints that intermediaries face (such as price fixing and high marketing costs due to poor transport facilities) limit their ability to exploit farmers. He showed that when farmers decided to sell in urban markets themselves, low market margins meant they were likely to take a loss because of a range of accumulating marketing costs such as transport, living expenses, commissions and market fees.

The intermediaries have evolved and taken over most rural roadside markets selling chickens, goats, pigs, sweet potatoes, Irish potatoes, tomatoes, onions and watermelon along Kabwe Road, Mkushi, Kapiri Mposhi and Monze. CSO post-harvest studies estimate that intermediaries could be handling between 50 per cent and 75 per cent of produce sold in rural areas (CSO, 2001).

For many years, urban and peri-urban markets found in almost all residential compounds and in the central business district of major towns have provided the major market outlet for large, medium and smallholder farmers. Built-up market centres such as Soweto and Luburma in Lusaka, Kasanda in Kabwe, Chisokone in Kitwe and Chifubu in Ndola are commonly referred to as the 'stock exchange', because of their significant effect on the price and volumes traded.

The widespread occurrence of street vending and *ntembas* (temporary residential stalls) is also linked to the urban wholesale markets such as Soweto. These are well organized – despite what appears to a casual visitor as chaos and poor facilities – and popular with all classes of people. They sell almost all agricultural commodities except large livestock and are one of the most significant market channels in Zambia (although quantitative data are difficult to collect). Their main weakness has been the mistreatment of farm suppliers by a multiplicity of intermediaries due to weak control and regulation mechanisms by city authorities. This market channel might handle 10 to 25 per cent of produce sold directly by farmers around Lusaka and up to 75 per cent of produce sold by inter-mediaries in urban areas.

Schools, hospitals, prisons and other public institutions, hotels and lodges have also provided significant market outlets for smallholder farmers. Grains, legumes and vegetables are supplied to public institutions on behalf of the government. This channel handles 10–20 per cent of produce sold by intermediaries.

The emergence of supermarkets

Supermarkets are not a new phenomenon in Zambia, where, in Lusaka, they have been owned by local private-sector businessmen, especially from the Greek community (Kabulonga Supermarket, Melissa Supermarket, Konkola hypermarket and others). These are well stocked with imported goods, but are not as big as the new hypermarkets such as Shoprite.

The trend of establishing market chains under the same management throughout the country is a new phenomenon. Only large commercial farmers have successfully established forward contracts to supply agricultural products to supermarkets; trade access for smallholders has been difficult. Departing from this tradition, Shoprite has started to target the low and middle-income groups of consumers in Lusaka's residential neighbourhoods and medium-sized towns in rural Zambia.

In a number of countries the rapid rise of supermarkets has been associated with urbanization and the rise of the middle class. In Zambia, although just less than half of the population lives in urban areas, the growth of supermarkets is linked instead to market-oriented reforms that liberalized the economy and attracted substantial FDI, and which reached even remote parts of the country (COMESA, 2002; 2003).

One of the biggest South African investors in Zambia is Shoprite Checkers, which sought to expand further into southern Africa because of saturated South African home markets (see www.shoprite.co.za). Shoprite's investment in Zambia was related to liberalization and the favourable conditions negotiated with the government, which established that every province should have a Shoprite outlet and allowed for favourable import tariffs. Shoprite took full advantage of the investment climate and moved quickly to fill the vacuum left by the dissolution of parastatal institutions; in 1996 it purchased six buildings through the ZPA. Targeting low- and middle-income consumers, it set up a chain of supermarkets throughout the country. Shoprite's investment in Zambia has shown considerable growth, with turnover increasing from Zambian Kwacha (ZMK)19 billion (about US$5 million) in 1996 to ZMK276 billion (about US$72 million) for the year ending June 2002. Its network expanded to 18 retail supermarkets, one wholesale shop, seven fast-food outlets and a sister company, Freshmark Ltd, in charge of fresh food delivery and logistics.

Shoprite has maintained a lean but efficient management structure and good information and management systems. It entered into lease agreements with local companies (such as Zambeef for meat, milk and poultry products). Shoprite and

Freshmark have set up a central distribution system for non-perishable foods, household items and non-food products in addition to food, fruits and vegetables, with one main depot in Lusaka and the other in Kitwe.

Supermarkets still account for an insignificant proportion of produce sold by smallholder farmers in Zambia, in part because smallholders find it difficult to meet the necessary conditions set by Shoprite (and the retail sector in general) such as quality standards and grades. The unreliability of supply from smallholders, in addition to organization, marketing and transportation problems, means that supermarkets resort to importing from more reliable markets abroad or from local commercial farmers who are more likely to meet their standards and conditions. Supermarket executives interviewed during this study claimed that, until the capacity of local producers is raised to such a level that they can meet the standards and grades set and agreed with the supermarkets, trade links between the two will remain a pipe dream. As a tool for improving production processes, GAPs could play a role in establishing such links.

The emergence of good agricultural practices

The concept of GAPs has evolved in recent years mainly as a result of concerns about food safety and food quality raised by food scares in the industrialized world (bovine spongiform encephalopathy (BSE), dioxin, aflatoxin, campylobacter, etc.) and, to a lesser extent, the need for environmental sustainability of agriculture production. In 1997 the Euro-Retailer Produce Working Group on Good Agricultural Practices (EurepGAP, now known as GLOBALGAP) was formed as a platform of leading private sector retailers in Europe. It worked on a normative process for certification of fruits and vegetables and evolved a recognized standard with clear and transparent procedures for private and voluntary certification.[3] That standard sets out a framework for GAPs on farms that defines essential elements for the development of best practices for the global production of fruits and vegetables.

GLOBALGAP defines the minimum standards acceptable to the leading retail groups in Europe, but it does not set out to provide prescriptive guidance on every method of agricultural production. It is based on the principles of risk prevention, risk analysis and sustainable agriculture. Food safety is becoming increasingly important for retailers as they expand globally, because of both increased competition and tighter regulations. GLOBALGAP is playing a leading role in establishing production standards and verification procedures for fruits and vegetables, and intends to develop a global integrity and harmonization programme.

According to FAO (2002), the GAP approach can be compatible with developing sustainable domestic food systems to achieve food security at community level. In this context, GAPs are those practices that aim at producing sufficient, safe and healthy food in an economically viable, socially acceptable and environmentally sustainable manner. Many farmers around the world already apply GAP-related practices through sustainable agricultural methods. These GAPs apply to both on-farm production and post-harvest processes.

The GAP approach can be useful for attaining the standards and grades set by retailers and related features of the produce such as colour, size, taste, appearance, texture, uniformity and packaging. GAPs also include guidelines for animal welfare, water quality and labour standards, especially in industrialized countries. In Zambia, government extension programmes have been using the 'improved agricultural practices' and the 'recommended agricultural practices' terminology in their training programmes, particularly in the areas of conservation and organic farming, but use of the terms appears to be limited to production management practices rather than extending to consumer education.

Interviews with government officials in Lusaka, commercial farmers (Agriflora Ltd), training institutes and the Zambia Export Growers Association (ZEGA) revealed that many stakeholders are concerned about the development of GLOBALGAP. They worry that the standards could inhibit market access and reduce opportunities for domestic agricultural development and better integration of smallholders into the economy. The Zambian National Farmers Union (ZNFU) and ZEGA said that as of 2004 exports should have been compliant with GLOBALGAP standards. However, in Zambia little information is available on the technical details and procedures. ZEGA expects that private commercial farmers may well be able to comply with GLOBALGAP but that the small-scale farmers will find it very difficult to do so. The exporting commercial farmers and their organizations were aware of the development of GLOBALGAP normative standards, but argued that they lacked institutional and human capacity to meet them. They needed more information about what GAP really meant and how to apply them in the Zambian context. They thought that more time and resources needed to be invested to train small-scale outgrowers to adhere to GLOBALGAP standards. They feared they would lose export markets if the Zambian agricultural sector was not able to meet standards by 2004.

Some confusion arises from the fact that GAPs can have various connotations. GLOBALGAP grades and standards do not cover all on-farm and post-harvest practices and processes that contribute to achieving sustainable farming systems (see FAO, 2002). Commercial farmers are concerned about GLOBALGAP because its standards could restrict the overseas market access of those not able to meet them.

Case studies: Solwezi and Chipata Districts

The case studies discussed here analysed the effects of supermarkets in two rural areas (Solwezi and Chipata), including the perception of GAPs and how they could contribute to increasing smallholders' access to supermarkets. They are based on interviews conducted in August 2003 with commercial and subsistence farmers, supermarket representatives, trade experts, urban market traders and farmer organizations, along with a literature review on linkages between smallholder farmers and emerging supermarkets. Solwezi was selected following stakeholder consultation in Lusaka. Chipata was selected because of previous work done by the Business Forum to improve linkages between Shoprite super-market and smallholder farmers from Luangeni village.

Solwezi District, North-Western Province

Agriculture in North-Western Province (NWP) is still dominated by traditional subsistence farming systems. Off-farm activities such as trading, fishing, bee-keeping, hunting and timber harvesting are largely supplementary to farming. Commercial trade in agricultural products in NWP is relatively advanced only in Solwezi District; the other six districts are isolated outposts with no significant market potential. Solwezi District has a large number of small traders dealing in merchandise ranging from groceries to clothes. In spite of its large size, NWP has only one supermarket, the Shoprite Checkers in Solwezi, which opened in 1998. The coming of Shoprite was viewed as a threat to local businesses, which it was for many; some have since closed due to an inability to compete. But some farmers saw Shoprite as a window of opportunity to improve marketing oppor-tunities for their products.

Shoprite did not deal directly with farmers in the procurement of any farm produce, but engaged an intermediary company, Freshmark Zambia Ltd, for reasons related to logistics and chain management aspects, including quality control. Freshmark sometimes found it necessary to supply farmers with free seeds of the crops it wanted, and farmers were then obliged to sell their output to Freshmark, creating a kind of outgrower arrangement. (Farmers who used their own seeds could also sell to Freshmark.) Farmers reported occasional random visits from a Freshmark representative to check on crops and ensure that farmers kept up good management and agricultural practices. Most farmers interviewed indicated heavy use of synthetic pesticides in vegetable production (especially during the rainy season) and said that they lacked knowledge on the proper use of pesticides and good management and agricultural practices in general. However, no guidelines or checklists were made available to farmers about such practices; the representative mainly provided on-the-spot advice to ensure quality of the crop in the field.

The products delivered to Shoprite (mainly on bicycles or in wheelbarrows) included spinach, cabbage, Chinese cabbage, onions, tomatoes, eggplants and lettuce. The vegetables Shoprite bought most frequently were spinach and lettuce. The amount farmers could supply to Shoprite depended on customer demand. If demand was higher than local farmers could supply, Freshmark imported fruits and vegetables from Copperbelt Province. Farmers expressed satisfaction with Freshmark payment terms and modes because payments were made to suppliers punctually every week. Farmers were trading individually with no apparent signs of organized marketing, which meant they lacked bargaining power.

Constraints and opportunities for accessing (super)markets

Small-scale farmers had sufficient opportunities to sell their produce to Shoprite (via Freshmark) as long as they met Shoprite's required quality standards and demand. Shoprite's management expressed satisfaction with the quality of produce supplied by smallholder producers in the dry season but complained about poor quality in the rainy season. The company suggested that farmers would have to become better organized at marketing their produce to Freshmark to reduce the irregularity of supply. However, Shoprite had reportedly offered only half the farm-gate price for cabbage.

Alternatively farmers could sell to other markets within the district, including to urban traders who bought directly from the farms to sell on the open market, to hotels and restaurants, hospitals, teachers' training colleges and boarding schools. Although such markets had lower quality demands, the prices offered and the modes of payment were not sufficiently attractive, and farmers preferred to sell to individual customers who paid higher prices on the spot. Market intermediaries offered the lowest price among all the players in the marketing chain. Hotels, restaurants, colleges and hospitals tended to delay payment to farmers, but farmers said that such traders provided the biggest market.

As an alternative, the District Agricultural Co-ordination (DACO) and the ZNFU (Solwezi branch) advocated the establishment of a weekly 'green market' (open local vegetable market), which had been established with success in Lusaka and Chipata, with a view to enabling producers and traders to meet the quality, standards and prices set by Freshmark. Government officials also advocated the formation of a vegetable growers' association to coordinate the marketing of vegetables and arrange technical backstopping to farmers on vegetable production practices.

Although Shoprite had successfully established itself in Solwezi District and was slowly becoming an important outlet for some local farmers, traditional market outlets and players were still playing a dominant role. There were a variety of obstacles to linking small farmers to Shoprite in Solwezi, of which the most important were poor product quality, lack of consumer demand and unreliability of supply. Although GAPs were important, it was demand that played the critical role. GAPs were not yet reflecting market access to Shoprite because the channel was small and markets where GAPs were not followed continued to dominate.

In order to improve the mutual understanding between farmers and Shoprite, there was a need to engage in multi-stakeholder dialogues. Farmer organizations could play a role in improving bargaining power for farmers. There was also a need to look at ways to expand market horizons beyond what Shoprite offered and to diversify the products sold to it. With better processing and packaging, crops commonly grown in North-Western Province, such as beans, sweet potatoes and cassava, could be more easily traded with Shoprite.

Chipata District (Luangeni community)

The Luangeni project in the Chipata district of Eastern Province dates from a partnership programme set up in 2000 between Shoprite, ZamSeed, the Ministry of Agriculture, non-governmental organizations (NGOs) and the Luangeni community (with the support of the International Business Leaders Forum in the UK and the British Council and Danish Embassy in Lusaka). The main aim of the partnership was to build capacity among the people of Luangeni to produce high-quality horticultural products to be marketed to Shoprite in Chipata, backed by a well-established network of institutional support mechanisms.

The specific objectives of the partnership were:

*   to increase the capacity of the Luangeni community to produce adequate and quality horticultural products to be marketed to Chipata Shoprite;
*   to promote the forging of economically viable links between Chipata Shoprite and other businesses and the Luangeni community;
*   to enhance the ability of at least 50 per cent of the Luangeni community households to increase their annual income by 300 per cent by the end of 2001;
*   to facilitate increased access to health services for at least 50 per cent of the households in Luangeni village by earning enough to be able to pay health user fees; and
*   to facilitate access to education for 50 per cent of the children in Luangeni village by the year 2002, through increased household earnings.

The horticultural products being delivered to Chipata Shoprite by the Luangeni community on a weekly basis were tomatoes, cabbage, lettuce, green beans and onions. However, Shoprite was in most cases unable to buy everything the farmers were producing – indicating both limited market demand and lack of Shoprite trust in the ability of the community to supply all the quality produce it required.

Consultations were held between the Luangeni community's marketing committee (a locally selected group of farmers representing the community on marketing issues) and Shoprite before delivering the products, mainly on quantities to be delivered, quality and price. The quantity delivered in 2003 was still very low: on average Shoprite procured horticultural products worth about ZMK20 million (about US$5,300) per month. However, the Luangeni community was supplying only about 2.5 per cent of the value purchased by Shoprite because Shoprite relied more on external suppliers, through Freshmark. The rural market of Luangeni had yet to penetrate the supermarket chain, and the marketing committee was used only to fill supply gaps.

Shoprite required vegetables with high quality in terms of freshness, colour uniformity and incidence of disease. Vegetables had to be delivered on time and in agreed quantities. The farmers of Luangeni were able to meet most of the conditions because of training they had received from partners. Eastern Seed and Vet

Ltd supplied vegetable seed to Luangeni farmers as required by Shoprite, but farmers were not guaranteed a market and often had to find alternative outlets for their production.

According to the farmers of Luangeni, GAPs included pest and pesticide management, appropriate tillage methods, efficient irrigation methods, fertilizer regimes, rotation and organic matter management such as composting, manuring and biomass transfer. While they said they were practising these methods, there was no certification system. Farmers and Shoprite were most concerned with the use and management of pesticides. They had no evidence that GAPs were linked to expanded market access because there was no demand in the Chipata market to apply the practices. However, farmers and Shoprite perceived that good agricultural and management practices were important for producing fresh vegetables.

Opportunities and constraints

Luangeni farmers agreed that the main factors determining opportunities for access to markets included:

- willingness and ability of the communities to meet the production and procurement standards;
- ability of the community to source alternative markets (such as 'green markets') through its marketing committee;
- willingness of the community to work together through the cooperative society;
- direct payments to farming community on delivery; and
- the practising of GAPs.

Farmers also agreed that the main constraints to expanding access to markets were:

- limited quantities normally agreed with Shoprite compared to what was produced for the anticipated market;
- local overproduction of vegetables during the season;
- supply agreements that were not honoured, even when supplies met established conditions;
- prices set unilaterally by buyer; and
- failure of other partners in the forum to meet their obligations.

Farmers felt it necessary to increase their market share with the supermarket chain but recognized that demand for their products was limited. They recommended opening a 'green market' on Fridays where producers could sell their excess produce. Shoprite had provided the market space and would facilitate packaging.

The case study of the Luangeni project highlighted the importance of a multi-stakeholder approach to farmer mobilization in opening up market opportunities. It also illustrated the dangers of institutional failures, uncertainty and lack of mutual trust. Shoprite was still unable to trust farmers to comply with all their requirements and continued to maintain its mainstream suppliers, using local smallholder farmers as a backup. The excess supply from outside (including imports from South Africa) sometimes dampened local prices, further diminishing the ability of local farmers to compete.

Comparing the two districts

The case studies in Chipata and Solwezi show two different scenarios in which GAPs were applied in order to link with Shoprite. Whereas farmers in Solwezi had linked up with Shoprite in an ad hoc way that was uncoordinated and with limited institutional support, farmers in Chipata (the Luangeni community) were actively mobilized and assisted quite systematically to link up with Shoprite. Certain institutional and policy conditions were necessary to increase capacity at the community level.

Adopting GAPs was not a necessary condition for guaranteeing the Luangeni farmers expanded access to markets. While Shoprite's quality standards were relatively high, GAPs were not perceived as important in the alternative local markets through which farmers sold the largest portion of their horticultural crops. Because Shoprite's demand was limited, farmers were looking to explore ways to expand and consolidate other (local) markets.

Lessons learned

What needs to be done to improve and expand linkages between smallholder farmers and supermarkets? Figure 10.1 shows a framework for the discussion, whose main components are: (1) improved market penetration by smallholder farmers (white circle); (2) generating marketable surplus for smallholder farmers (light grey circle); and (3) building credibility and a sustainable environment for effective trade linkages (dark grey circle).

Improved penetration by smallholder farmers

Above we showed that in Chipata trade linkages between smallholders and supermarkets were weak, with supermarkets buying less than 2.5 per cent of total supplies from smallholder producers. We also noted that supermarkets are one among many outlets, efforts and policies are required that encourage the expansion of those alternative outlets. Farmers in both Solwezi and Chipata spoke favourably of 'green markets', which require support. Market infrastructure such as processing, transportation and storage facilities also need to be improved.

Experience shows that when markets are developed they can work for smallholders; farmers adjust their production patterns to tap market opportunities (FSRP, 2001). In order to make trade linkages more effective, there is a need to improve farmers' capacity to negotiate, understand contract terms and take remedial measures.

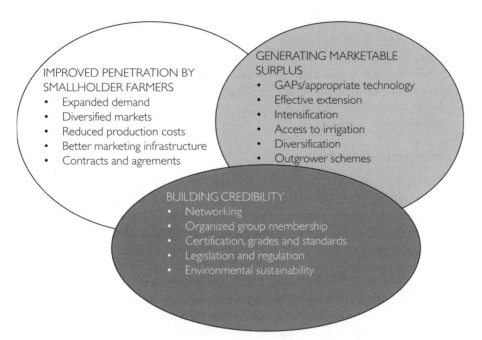

Figure 10.1 *Framework for summarizing effective linkages between smallholder producers and supermarkets*

Generating marketable surplus through improved production practices

Supermarket managers worry that smallholder farmers will be unable to guarantee required amounts and quality for changing consumer demands. Farmers are unable to respond quickly because of limitations in their production capacities. If farmers were able to apply GAPs it would help reduce Shoprite's (and others') rejection rates for smallholder produce. This could help raise income even if production levels remain the same.

Zambia has tremendous potential for the production of a wide range of crops and livestock, fisheries and forestry products. Prospects for growth in agricultural GDP are moderate to high in maize, legumes and oilseed, floriculture and horticultural crops. The livestock sector also offers potential for growth in the pork and poultry industries, hatcheries and meat processing, dairy and milk processing, as does the fisheries and fish processing sector. Most of these enterprises have been created by smallholder farmers.

Supermarkets can link up directly with farmer groups for production and trade relations, giving farmers important skills and experience in the process. Smallholders should be encouraged to grow high-value crops with low production costs, such as beans, groundnuts and rice. In order to intensify and diversify into products that meet consumers expectations, farmers need to be provided with total packages (seeds, inputs, financing, market demand and extension services) like those provided in outgrower models. Investments in irrigation, soil fertility management, on-farm processing and value addition are likely to benefit small-holders. Zambia needs to incorporate phytosanitary elements into its extension system to ensure that products sent to local supermarkets and export markets meet the standards demanded by consumers. This will reduce rejection rates, a frequent source of frustration among outgrowers. Effective extension systems are also needed to educate and train farmers on GAPs and appropriate and sustainable technology.

Building credibility

Sustainable business relationships are based on credible mutual relationships that recognize the need for both parties to survive (and make profits) in the long term. Farmers stand to gain by organizing themselves into groups with effective and well-trained leadership that can represent them in contract negotiations and market research. Local smallholder farmers are unlikely to benefit even with expanded market and consumer demand if they are disorganized. On the other hand, if supermarkets ignore capacity building for local producers they will miss an opportunity to source Zambian supermarkets with local produce. Acting with corporate social responsibility can improve supermarkets' public image and help them negotiate more favourable terms with governments.

Improved relationships between retailers and producers can be built on a solid foundation of laws regulating trade, grades and standards that are realistic to implement and consumer-driven. A credible system of certification to reward quality with premium prices may be desirable. Credibility in the trading system will be assured if an environmentally sustainable system of production and marketing is established. In Zambia there has been a surge of interest in the use of organic and conservation-minded farming practices. These have become accepted in many areas as the sustainable way to increase agricultural production and trade.

Conclusions and recommendations

The policy environment and reforms – especially the investment incentives provided through the 1993 Investment Act – have encouraged foreign investors like Shoprite to set up shop in Zambia. A necessary condition for effective trade linkages between smallholder farmers and supermarkets is for smallholders to adhere to established grades and quality standards.

The application of GAPs is limited by several factors at the farming level, such as a lack of knowledge and economic incentives for farmers. Declining purchasing power, combined with already low income levels and low consumer literacy levels, limit domestic demand for the application of GAPs. Because the domestic open market (which is still the dominant market for small-scale farmers) does not require specific standards or practices, there is no market-driven incentive for farmers to adopt GAPs. The adoption of GAPs is further hampered by constraints such as inadequate infrastructure and extension services. In such a scenario, it is difficult to see how smallholder farmers can be encouraged to adhere to GAPs unless the practices are directly linked to market expansion and incentives.

Attempts to link smallholder farmers to supermarkets by building human capacity for GAP application in the Luangeni community in Eastern Province showed potential for improving farmers' access to supermarkets. In addition, Shoprite successfully established itself in Solwezi District and was slowly becoming an important outlet for local vegetable farmers. In order to improve the mutual relationship and understanding between farmers and Shoprite, there is a need to form producer associations to link smallholders to supermarket chains.

The case study of the Luangeni project highlighted the importance of a multi-stakeholder approach to farmer mobilization in opening up market opportunities. Shoprite was still unable to trust that farmers could comply with its requirements and therefore still maintained its mainstream suppliers, using local smallholder farmers as a back-up system. This illustrated the dangers of institutional failures, uncertainty and lack of mutual trust: if a supermarket brings in excess supply from outside the area (including imports from South Africa), it could drive down local prices, further diminishing the ability of local farmers to compete. Less than 2.5 per cent of the total value of produce procured by Shoprite in Chipata was from smallholder farmers.

In order to improve linkages between smallholder farmers and supermarkets, we recommend that attention be given to the issues of building credibility and improving marketable surplus through, for example, good agricultural practices, better management, capacity building, outgrower schemes and chain management (Figure 10.1). This requires an enabling policy environment. Consumer demand should be increased by creating employment and diversifying the Zambian economy.

Notes

1   The FAO–Netherlands Partnership Programme (FNPP) facilitated this study through its project Making Market Integration and Economic Reform Work for the Poor.

2   Agricultural policy emphasized removing the government from direct involvement in agricultural marketing and input supply; freeing prices; removing subsidies; privatizing agro-parastatals; liberalizing trade in farm products, inputs and machinery; renting out and selling public storage facilities to the private sector; and removal of constraints and distortions to international trade in farm products.

3   GLOBALGAP is centred on a series of 24 'major musts', 70 'minor musts' and 54 'should/recommendations'. Of the 'major musts', one relates to site environmental risk assessment and 13 relate to the choice, use and storage of pesticides; 8 'minor musts' relate to nutrient applications. One 'minor must' and three 'should/recommendations' relate to environmental issues, while 6 'should/recommendations' relate to irrigation. The overwhelming emphasis of GLOBALGAPs 'major musts' is therefore food safety (see www.globalgap.org).

References

ACF (Agricultural Consultative Forum) (2002) 'Annual stakeholder consultation in Zambian agricultural development, (1998–2001), the concepts, process and impact', Report, Lusaka, Zambia

Bangwe, L. M., Hichaambwa, M. and Chiboola, M. (1997) 'Maize marketing under a liberalized environment, the case of Monze District', Report, Study Fund, Social Recovery Project, Lusaka

Chiwele, D., Pumulo Muyatwa-Sipula and Kalinda, H. (1996) 'Private sector response to agricultural marketing in Zambia: A case study of eastern province maize markets', Nordiska Africainnstitutet, Uppsala, Research Report No. 107

Coffee Board of Zambia (2003) *Zambia: Investment Opportunities in Agriculture*, CBZ, Lusaka

Common Market of Eastern and Southern Africa (COMESA) (2002) *Zambia Review*, 4th Edition

COMESA (2003) *Zambia: A Review of Commerce, Industry and Tourism*

CSO (Central Statistical Office of Zambia) (2001) *Annual Report 2001*, CSO, Lusaka, Zambia

Dolan, C. and Humphrey, J. (n/d) 'Governance and trade in fresh vegetables: The impact of UK supermarkets on the African horticulture Industry', Journal of Development Studies, vol 37, no 2

FAO (2002) *Programme: Development on Codes of Good Farming* [online] www.fao.org/prods/index.asp

Farina, M. (2002) 'Consolidation, multinationalization, and competition in Brazil: Impacts on horticulture and dairy products systems', Overseas Development Institute, *Development Policy Review*

FSRP (2001) *Food Security Research Project* [online] www.aec.msu.edufs2/Zambia/index.ht

Ghezan, G., Mateos, M. and Viteri, L. (2002) 'Impact of supermarkets and fast-food chains on horticulture supply chains in Argentina', *Development Policy Review*, vol 20, no 4, pp389–408

Giovannucci, D., Sterns, P. A., Eustrom, M. and Haantuba, H. (2001) 'The impact of improved grades and standards for agricultural products in Zambia', Michigan State University and United States Agency for International Development, PFID-F&V Report No. 3, East Lansing, MI

Gutman, G. E. (2002) 'Impact of the rapid rise of supermarkets on dairy products systems in Argentina', *Development Policy Review*, vol 20, no 4, pp409–427

Jayne, T. S., Govereh, J., Mwanaumo, A., Nyoro, J. K. and Chapoto, A. (2002) 'False promise or false premise? The experience of food and input market reform in eastern and southern Africa', *World Development*, vol 30, no 11, pp1967–1985

Jayne, T. S., Mukumbu, M., Chisvo, M., Tschirley, D., Weber, M. T., Zulu, B., Johansson, R., Santos, P. and Sorolo, D. (1999) 'Successes and challenges of food market reform: Experiences from Kenya, Mozambique, Zambia and Zimbabwe', MSU International Department Working Papers No. 72 East Lansing, MI [online] www.aec.msu.edu/agecon/fs2/chapters/idwp72.pdf

Laurian, U. J. (2000) 'Food safety issues and fresh food product exports from LDCs' *Agricultural Economics*, vol 23, pp231–240

Ministry of Finance and National Planning (2001) *Poverty Reduction Strategy Paper (PRSP), 2001*, Lusaka Zambia

Mwanaumo, A. (1999) 'Agricultural marketing policy reforms in Zambia', Tegemeo Institute/Egerton University, Njoro, Kenya, Eastern and Central Africa Programme for

Agricultural Policy Analysis (ACAPAPA), Entebe, Uganda and Michigan State University, East Lansing, MI

Olinto, P. and K. Deininger (2000) 'Why liberalization alone has not improved agricultural productivity in Zambia: The role of asset ownership and working capital constraints', Working Paper No.: 2302 World Bank, Washington, DC, [online] http://econ.worldbank.org/view.php?type=5&id=1056

Reardon, T. and Berdegue, J. (2002) 'The rapid rise of supermarkets in Latin America: Challenges and opportunities for development', *Development Policy Review*, vol 20, no 4, pp371–388

Reardon, T. and Timmer, C. (2002) 'Transformation of agrifood markets in developing countries: 1950–Now', Paper presented at the Agriculture Development Retrospective Conference, Yale University

Roekel, J., Willems, S. and Boselie, D. (2002) *Agri-supply Chain Management: To Stimulate Cross-Border Trade in Developing Countries and Emerging Economies*, Agri-Chain Competence Centre, 's-Hertogenbosch

Weatherspoon, D. D. and Reardon, T. (2003) 'The rise of supermarkets in Africa: Implications for agrifood systems and the rural poor', *Development Policy Review*, vol 21, no 3

Zambia Investment Centre (ZIC) (n/d) 'Investment opportunities in agriculture', ZIC, Lusaka

Part Three

Implications of Food Systems Transformation for Smallholder Farmers

Chapter 11

Overview of Case Studies Assessing Impacts of Food Systems Transformation on Smallholder Farmers

Ellen B. McCullough and Prabhu L. Pingali

Introduction

The following section of this book presents six empirical case studies on the implications and impacts of the transformation of food systems. The studies use a similar approach, but each addresses a specific set of questions according to the country context. Research was conducted in Kenya, Bhutan, India, China, Honduras and Mexico,[1] a set of countries that cover a wide spectrum with respect to the transformation of food systems. In Kenya and Bhutan, food systems are still somewhat traditional. In the rest of the countries, they are structured and modernizing. The studies in Kenya and Bhutan focus on market access and market participation across different market conditions. The studies in China and India draw comparisons between the traditional marketing system, which holds the majority of market share and is well structured, and alternative marketing chains that serve higher value urban consumers. Both Honduras and Mexico have higher urbanization rates and higher levels of food retail flowing through modern food chains. The studies in Honduras and Mexico (along with a few high-value export chains examined on a case basis in India and Kenya) address in detail the costs of participating in high-value chains for perishable products and compare different strategies to reduce these costs.

Research approach

The studies in Kenya, Bhutan, India and China began with a rapid rural appraisal at the village level to facilitate comparisons within and across countries. The study was designed to detect how production and marketing activities differed across different market access conditions. Facilitated group discussions were held in 15–20 villages per country, and they were designed to detect trends in cropping systems, production technology, market outlets, infrastructure and demographics over time. In each case, a second survey was conducted at the household level to follow up on problems related to market participation, as identified in the rapid rural appraisal. Specific sampling methodology, questionnaire content and site selection varied between studies based on the focus area.

The Kenya study focused on smallholder diversification out of low-value maize cropping systems (Omiti et al, this volume). This reflected the declining profitability of maize production and low market participation, as reported in the village surveys, along with the fast-growing opportunities to supply urban areas with dairy and horticulture products. The study consisted of household surveys and targeted interviews with traders, retailers and consumers. The study in Bhutan focused on road access and market participation for smallholders (Tobgay and McCullough, this volume). In the village surveys, road access and high transportation costs were identified as major constraints to market participation for smallholders in Bhutan. A household survey was conducted, with sampling stratified across walking distance to the nearest road point, to identify how marketing and production activities were influenced by road access. Traders, market agents and exporters were also interviewed to build a more complete picture of marketing chains.

In India, the rapid rural appraisal revealed that smallholders participated very actively in the traditional, structured wholesale market system but were not well represented in vertically integrated chains catering to the growing agroprocessing sector in the states of Punjab and Gujarat (Singh, this volume). Therefore, the study involved a comparison between terms of sale offered in the traditional wholesale market and those in the organized chains, with a particular focus on the contract farming mechanism. The comparison of terms of sale, distribution of risk and participation constraints drew upon household surveys and targeted interviews. The first phase of research in the China study traced the entire marketing chain of fresh fruits destined for Beijing consumers, concluding that traditional wholesale markets continue to dominate the fruit distribution system despite the rapid growth of supermarkets in the retail sector (Huang et al, this volume). Most fruit producers supplying Beijing were smallholders who sold to small procurement agents working on behalf of small wholesalers. The follow-up survey at the farm household level paid particular attention to representative sampling and compared the traditional channels to emerging alternatives.

As with most Latin American countries, Honduras' supermarket sector has long held a sizeable share of the food retail market, including for fresh fruits and vegetables. The Honduras study addressed different institutional mechanisms for linking smallholder vegetable producers with the specialized wholesalers that supply domestic supermarkets, drawing on interviews to facilitate a comparison between farmer organizations, the lead farmer model and individual linkages (Meijer et al, this volume). The final study also focused on modern marketing channels, in particular those for exporting high-value products to consumers in developed countries (Narrod et al, this volume). Since quality and safety standards are a major constraint for smallholder participation in high-value export chains, costs of compliance were estimated for different models of linking farmers with markets: cooperatives, farmer organizations and independent farmers with both small and large holdings. Using a case study approach and targeted interviews, comparisons were drawn within Mexico's cantaloupe export chain, Kenya's fresh and processed green bean export chains and India's fresh grape export chain.

Results

Across the board, and particularly for countries at the lower end of the agricultural transformation process, traditional market structures still account for the majority of food retail. In each of the countries, the strong majority of farmers surveyed participated in traditional, unorganized supply chains. Farmers who participated in modern, organized chains also participated in traditional markets, often for the same sub-products that were produced for modern chains. This finding underscores the importance of traditional markets for smallholders in developing countries. Even though traditional markets still dominate food systems, village surveys in all countries revealed that no village is static over time with respect to production and marketing. Among other factors, structural changes in agricultural institutions, commodity price trends and changing production technology have influenced the set of crops grown and the institutions that play a role in marketing them. Where available, modern chains offered higher returns but placed higher demands on producers. Participation was limited even where chains were well established.

In Kenya, a diversification trend among smallholder agriculture has been observed in peri-urban areas surrounding Nairobi. In villages with good market access, there has been decreased maize production in favour of dairy and horticulture. However, despite the declining profitability of maize-based agriculture, diversification was still limited in scope due to constraints posed by high input and transport costs, poor market infrastructure for horticulture and inefficiency in dairy cooperatives. In Bhutan, most farmers remain in subsistence cropping systems due to their remoteness, which leads to high marketing costs, especially relative to the small volumes of surplus production that are typically marketed. Farmers who are closer to the roads were more likely to participate in output markets and more likely to grow a crop mix reflecting their intentions to market produce. Along the southern border of the country, adjacent with India, traders have begun to bear transport costs and marketing risks in order to capture rewards from exporting to India.

In the Indian states of Punjab and Gujarat, multinational processing firms have moved in during recent years to procure raw materials from farmers with the intention of processing them into food products for marketing in Indian urban areas. The firms, procuring with contracts and on an ad hoc basis from preferred suppliers, imposed quality standards and exerted influence on farmers' production technology. Smallholder participation was limited, though, due to the investments involved and uncertainty surrounding interpretation and enforcement of contract terms. The Shandong province, in China, accounts for a large share of the country's fruit production. The research team traced trends in participation in market channels over time and observed a rise in the modern processing sector for grapes. Farm size and farm assets were not found to impact market participation, and price differences between channels could be attributed to quality attributes of the products flowing through them.

In the Honduras study, different institutional arrangements for linking smallholders with specialized wholesalers were compared on the basis of their effectiveness in creating linkages, costs of implementation and the number of producers included. Producer organizations were costly to manage, requiring external support, and reached a limited number of smallholders. The lead farmer model, whereby individual large landholders became preferred suppliers to the specialized wholesaler and filled their orders by procuring from smallholders, required no external finance and reached many producers but relied on the willingness of lead farmers to implement the system. It was not viable for smallholders to source the wholesaler individually as preferred suppliers because of the costs involved.

The cross-cutting study on high-value exports focused on the impact of international food safety standards on smallholders participating in chains for Mexican cantaloupe, Kenyan green beans and Indian grapes. In Mexico and Kenya, where farm systems are dualistic, the imposition of safety standards had a screening effect and led to some exclusion of smallholders. In Kenya, smallholders were able to reorient production towards the green bean processing sector, which had lower compliance costs. Smallholders in Mexico selling cantaloupes for export switched to production for domestic markets where standards were lower. In India, where producers were more uniformly small, size did not influence producers' ability to comply with safety standards, but capacity probably did. Smallholders earned high returns by participating in the high-value export markets for fresh grapes through a marketing umbrella organization for grape producing cooperatives.

Research challenges

Even considering the range of methodological approaches employed between the different country studies, a few challenges were common across them. The difficulty of identifying causal factors was perhaps the most problematic. For example, in Bhutan, it is difficult to determine if improved road access in fact causes smallholders to diversify or if smallholder diversification and improved road access are both impacted by some unobserved factor, such as a household's location in a low-lying, productive valley. Should one conclude that road access alone leads to improved market participation when, in fact, the latter is responsible, then one might send the wrong message to policy makers about the effects of their interventions. Similar endogeneity problems arise in assessments of the importance of household assets for participation in a marketing chain and vice versa. In India, farm incomes were compared across different marketing arrangements. In China, farm size and household assets were used to predict marketing choice. Clearly, household assets and market participation exert some simultaneous influence on each other. It is important that analytical frameworks seek out exogenous sources of variation to avoid problems of endogeneity.

Another challenge arises from the need to capture trends over time rather than static snapshots. Understanding changes that take place in individual households is important for understanding the full implications of the transformation of food systems. However, collecting such data at an acceptable quality is difficult. Household recollection of data over a period, such as five years, is biased and often limited. Very few panel datasets exist, and they are not likely to address marketing behaviour, transportation costs and transaction costs to be useful for analysis related to the transformation of food systems. Panel datasets take time and resources to build and require a commitment on the survey implementer. Price datasets with high temporal and spatial resolution are also in short supply. Price series are important for understanding price variability and its causes, price risk and the effect of transport costs on marketing margins. With better price data, price information products, particularly for high-value and perishable products, can be improved.

Measuring the distribution of impacts on households requires household level collection of data. But data collected at the village, market, district and national levels are useful for survey design and contextualizing trends. With respect to household sampling, the desire to target respondents efficiently must be balanced with the need for representative sampling and its associated costs. When a study focused on a particular marketing chain seeks to identify who participates and how participation impacts some measurement of welfare, it is important to target the place where the chain occurs and use some form of purposive sampling to compare participants with non-participants. This approach, when executed well, is effective for building a comparison between participants and non-participants. However, it is not appropriate for drawing regional or national conclusions if sampling is not representative of the population. For estimating the extent to which organized chains have penetrated the agricultural sector, or any sub-sector of interest, the case study approach cannot suffice.

In many of the country studies, researchers had difficulty collecting data from retailers and traders, particularly those participating in modern chains. Often, they considered their lists of suppliers to be proprietary and did not want competitors to access the lists. Or they wanted to avoid political and public relations problems that might arise from scrutiny of their practices for screening producers, setting prices and designing contracts. In some cases, retailers wanted to give the impression that their chains were completely integrated vertically, with full traceability, when in fact the retailers were found to be procuring from the traditional wholesale market. The country research teams employed several creative strategies for tracing products upstream from retailers, wholesalers and traders to the farmers responsible for production.

Full assessment of the implications of food systems transformation requires an expansion of the scope of analysis beyond production systems, with several topics emerging as particularly salient. One is a deeper look at the changing structure of the rural economy and its impacts on labour markets and off-farm incomes. Another centres around meeting the potential rise in demand for safe food, particularly in Asian countries, where the urban middle class is growing rapidly yet many retailers continue to procure through traditional wholesale systems with low traceability. Institutional mechanisms for upgrading the traditional wholesale system to basic public safety standards could avert large scale bypassing (McCullough et al, this volume).

Way forward

Across country studies, the transformation process in food systems has introduced many opportunities, particularly when it comes to meeting growing demands for higher quality and higher value produce in domestic food systems. In countries at the low end of the transformation process, organized chains account for a limited share of agricultural marketing and therefore offer limited opportunities for widespread poverty reduction by raising the incomes of participants. In some countries at the higher end of the transformation process, the scope for participation is larger, but higher participation costs can lead to the exclusion of smallholders. In countries where smallholders dominate agricultural production, modern retailers and processors have supported institutional innovations to lower the costs of procuring from smallholders. Because smallholders are small, by definition, linking them with larger modern retailers and processors introduces transaction costs associated with coordination. Each of the case studies came across successful attempts to lower transaction costs through coordination, either horizontally via production and marketing organizations, or vertically, via advanced agreement between buyers and sellers on terms of sale.

Because each of the countries addressed a slightly different set of research questions tailored to the salient issues, specific policy messages differ from country to country. For those at the lower end of the transformation process, such as Kenya and Bhutan, expanding and upgrading traditional markets remains the overall policy priority. It is virtually impossible for farmers engaged in subsistence production to join a high-value organized chain before first participating in the traditional marketplace. In many countries in sub-Saharan Africa, improving linkages with domestic urban markets will underscore agriculture's role in poverty reduction and can help to offset the rising food deficit. The Kenyan and

Bhutanese studies call for basic investments in transport and market infrastructure to overcome high transport costs, low access to inputs, and seasonal price gluts due to thin commodity markets.

In transforming countries with structured wholesale markets and low penetration of organized retailers, such as India and China, upgrading traditional markets is essential for meeting the needs of an urban population that is growing rapidly in terms of size and purchasing power. To avoid widespread bypassing by specialized wholesalers, traditional markets must be upgraded with basic safety standards, traceability, mechanisms for differentiating products based on quality and upstream flow of information to producers. The India study calls for an improved regulatory and institutional environment to lower the costs and risks associated with participation in modern chains. The China study advocates improved safety within China's traditional fresh fruit supply chains, citing regulation in pesticide markets as one strategy for reducing the incidence of pesticide poisoning.

In high-value, vertically integrated chains for domestic and export markets, there is a need for low-cost mechanisms to link producers into markets. These include pooling investments in specialized assets and certification costs, collecting market information, assuring product quality, obtaining inputs, and negotiating favourable terms of sale. The studies in Honduras, Kenya, Mexico and India advocate contextually appropriate institutional innovations to link smallholders with dynamic markets in a cost-effective way.

The transformation of food systems means different things in different contexts, varying according to the country, the place, the chain and the household. However, the organization of food systems is closely correlated with the development process. Over time, priorities will shift from promoting the commercialization of agriculture to upgrading traditional markets to facilitating smallholder linkages with modern retailers and processors.

Notes

1   The studies in Kenya, Bhutan, India, China and Honduras were commissioned by FAO and mostly supported under the FAO–Netherlands Partnership Programme. The Narrod et al study comparing costs of compliance for high-value chains in Kenya, India and Mexico was not originally designed as part of this set of cases, but was included anyway because of its relevance.

References

Huang, J., Wu, Y. and Rozelle, S. (this volume) 'Marketing China's fruit: Are small, poor farmers being excluded from the supply chain?'

McCullough, E., Pingali, P. and Stamoulis, K. (this volume) 'Small farms and the transformation of food systems: An overview'

Meijer, M., Rodriguez, I., Lundy, M. and Hellin, J. (this volume) 'Supermarkets and small farmers: The case of fresh vegetables in Honduras'

Narrod, C., Roy, D., Avendaño, B. and Okello, J. (this volume) 'Impact of international food safety standards on smallholders: Evidence from three cases'

Omiti, J., Otieno, D., Nyanamba, T. and McCullough, E. (this volume) 'The transition from maize production systems to high-value agriculture in Kenya'

Singh, S. (this volume) 'Marketing channels and their implications for smallholder farmers in India'

Tobgay, S. and McCullough, E. (this volume) 'Linking small farmers in Bhutan with markets: The importance of road access'

Chapter 12

The Transition from Maize Production Systems to High-Value Agriculture in Kenya

*John Omiti, David Otieno, Timothy Nyanamba
and Ellen B. McCullough*[1]

Introduction

In Kenya, agriculture supports the livelihoods of close to 80 per cent of the rural population. The sector employs nearly 70 per cent of the national labour force through forward and backward linkages to manufacturing, trade and services and provides food and direct incomes to households. Eighty-five per cent of the rural population are small-scale farmers with land holdings of less than 2ha, with not more than 20 ruminant animals (mainly cattle, sheep and goats) and a few chickens per household. Mixed crop/livestock production systems in small-scale farms generally involve limited use of purchased inputs and modern technology.

The share of Kenya's agriculture in gross domestic product (GDP) has been declining; it dropped from 42 per cent in 1977 to 26 per cent in 2006 (Figure 12.1). Maize is by far the most commonly grown crop in Kenya. Rapid urban growth combined with a major shift in urban consumption from maize to wheat means that there is decreased demand for maize. The decrease in demand, along with stagnating yields and cheap imports, means that smallholder maize systems are less viable.

There is growing evidence that many small-scale farmers stand to benefit from participation in commercialized agriculture, to varying degrees. In order to facilitate sustainable economic development with appropriate policy interventions, it is essential to understand the transformation process, what drives it and

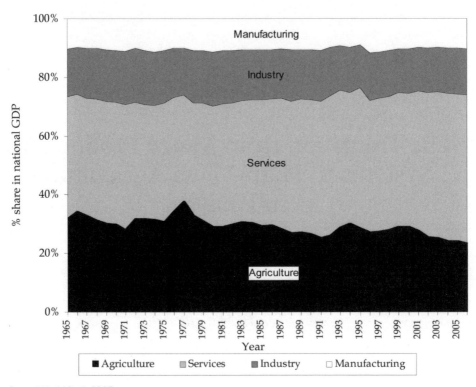

Source: World Bank, 2007

Figure 12.1 *Sectoral contribution to national GDP in Kenya, 1965–2006 (%)*

what its implications are. Population growth coupled with more demand for food and social amenities, changing lifestyles (such as more women in the work force) and rural–urban migration offer excellent opportunities to promote sustainable agricultural growth in Kenya.

In this chapter we evaluate the feasibility and desirability of smallholder diversification into higher-value crops, especially horticulture and dairy, and we examine evidence of diversification trends. Using data gathered across different market access conditions with surveys and interviews, we conclude that there are opportunities to further expand smallholder diversification, but constraints arise from high input costs, poor input quality, poor transport infrastructure, etc. Many of these constraints could be overcome with targeted interventions aimed at supporting the transition to higher-value commercialized production for Kenya's smallholders.

Smallholder diversification

Farming offers opportunities for broad-based expansion in tradeable agricultural commodities (i.e. cash crops or tradeable food crops) that provide direct and indirect employment and incomes for the poor. Extremely poor households and individuals in agrarian societies have considerable potential to benefit from such trade both directly (from increased labour demand owing to significant numbers of less-poor farmers producing tradeables) and indirectly (through increased demand for non-tradeables from these farmers). However, the challenge often involves determining the best strategies to improve the access of asset-poor farmers to skills, capital, inputs and output markets to allow them to utilize opportunities in the production of farm tradeables, and to improve their access to wage employment (Ellis and Freeman, 2004).

Poverty reduction requires increased productivity of both non-tradeables that have a high average budget share (mostly food crops) and non-tradeables with high marginal budget shares (which support consumption linkages). Institutional or technological changes in non-tradeable production may also have important redistributive effects if they minimize barriers to entry for poor producers (such as high transaction costs and institutional bottlenecks), allowing them to gain market and income shares from less-poor producers, and if they lower the prices paid by poor consumers (Dorward et al, 2002).

Integrating small-scale farmers into the exchange economy is important for stimulating growth, rural and overall economic development, food security and poverty alleviation (Von Braun and Kennedy, 1994). Small-scale farmers must commercialize and specialize in higher value activities in order to integrate into the high-value market economy. Agricultural commercialization could improve the welfare of smallholder farmers by enabling producers to reallocate their limited household incomes to high-value non-consumed agribusiness products, creating labour employment in production or post-harvest activities or other related enterprises and increasing the purchasing power of consumers (Figure 12.2). The main forces that drive commercialization at the farm level include high

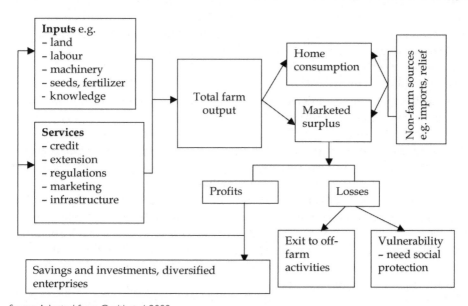

Source: Adapted from Omiti et al, 2000

Figure 12.2 *Decision-making dynamics in commercial and diversified agriculture*

opportunity costs of family labour (due to better alternative off-farm employment opportunities) and increased market demand for certain agricultural products, especially in urban centres.

Overview of agro-climatic areas and key agricultural sub-sectors in Kenya

Kenya has seven agro-ecological zones (AEZs) which vary in altitude, mean annual rainfall, temperature and evapotranspiration. These may be characterized as having high, medium or low agricultural potential, with distinct production systems distributed across the country. About 20 per cent of the country's total land (58 million ha) is suitable for crop cultivation (Republic of Kenya, 2007). The high-to-medium agricultural potential areas (26 per cent of total arable land) support the bulk of the population on mixed crop/livestock systems. The low potential areas cover 74 per cent of the arable land and, in the absence of irrigation or water conservation, are suitable only for pastoralism; they support about 20 per cent of the total human population. The most significant commodities for smallholders in Kenya are maize, horticulture and dairy.

Maize is a staple food, consumed in various forms by 96 per cent of the population (Nyameino et al, 2003). It is produced on 49 per cent of the arable land systems occupying about 1.9 million ha in 2006 (MoA, 2007). Maize production is characterized by high smallholder participation and is an integral part of a diversified cropping system. Although it is a relatively low-value commodity, maize is posited to have a considerable positive impact on rural incomes, poverty reduction and food security because it is less perishable (therefore relatively easy to market) and widely consumed by producer households.

Horticulture is an important source of income for smallholders, who account for over 70 per cent of its total production (McCulloch and Ota, 2002). It generates higher returns than most other commercially produced crops (especially important given declining farm sizes) and is suitable for production in varying agro-climatic zones (Minot and Ngigi, 2003). The main horticultural crops grown by smallholder farmers for both subsistence and commercial purposes include fruits, vegetables, herbs and spices. Common vegetables grown by small-scale households are cabbages, tomatoes, kales (*sukuma wiki*) and onions. The total acreage under horticulture has been expanding since 1980 and was estimated at 381,000ha in 2006. Out of these, 152,000ha were planted to fruits, 112,000ha to vegetables, 108,000ha to Irish potatoes, 3300ha to nuts, 2900ha to herbs and spices and 2400ha to cut flowers (MoA, 2007). Horticulture is the third most important source of foreign exchange earnings for the country, after tea and tourism, and employs more than one million people who are engaged in production, processing and marketing.

Dairy is a sub-sector that contributes a significant share of income and food for the majority of the population. It supports more than 650,000 smallholder farmers and an increasing number of small-scale entrepreneurs in the marketing system. Annual national milk production has risen steadily, from 2.8 billion litres in 2002 (Muriuki et al, 2003), to 3.2 billion litres by mid-2007, from a herd of 3 million dairy cattle. Kenya is the leading milk producer in the east African region. Consumer demand for milk is estimated to grow at 3.6 per cent per year. The increase in demand for dairy products such as milk, yoghurt, cheese and butter is largely due to population growth and improvement in purchasing power as a result of rising incomes. Growing demand for milk offers scope for income generation among small-scale farmers and poor households. Effective participation in the production of milk for emerging lucrative markets is associated with consistent increments in household wealth among farmers in the country (Burke et al, 2007).

Historical changes in Kenya's food systems

Important changes in Kenya's agri-food systems can be grouped into three time periods: colonial, post-independence and post-liberalization periods. In the colonial era (1920–1960), commercial agriculture was limited to foreign-owned land (commonly referred to as the 'white settler farms'). Maize marketing was governed by the Native Foodstuffs Ordinance of 1922 (which restricted rural (African) maize sales across district boundaries), the Marketing of Native Produce Ordinance of 1935 and Provincial Maize Boards in 1941–1962 (Thomas et al, 1997). The State Maize Board was also established, which purchased maize from European settler areas at higher prices than those offered to native Africans by the Provincial Boards. The colonial government initiated measures to encourage production of horticultural crops, but marketing was done only by private individuals (Minot and Ngigi, 2003); any impetus for expanding the production and marketing of horticulture came from the private sector. In dairy farming, there was commercial orientation by European settlers in the high potential areas of Central, Rift Valley and Eastern provinces as early as the 1920s. However, the indigenous Kenyans were not permitted to engage in commercial agriculture. This continued until 1954 when the Swynnerton plan for agricultural commercialization by indigenous Kenyans was initiated (Conelly, 1998).

Substantial changes occurred during the post-independence period (1963–1980). With political independence in 1963, the policy focus shifted to increased participation by indigenous Africans in commercial agriculture (Republic of Kenya, 1965). There was also increased state control over the production and marketing of commodities. For cereals, the National Cereals and Produce Board (NCPB) was established with the mandate to achieve price stability and food security, and with the responsibility to import and distribute inputs for major cereals, especially maize, wheat and rice, at subsidized prices. The Board procured and marketed about 70 per cent of maize; the rest was sold by farmer cooperatives and private traders. However, the Board's market share started to decline due to the emergence of vibrant and competitive private trade channels, both legal and illegal (Winter-Nelson, 1995).

At the time of independence, the commercial horticulture sector was still very limited. But three significant changes in the sub-sector occurred during the post-colonial period. First, the government gave higher priority to improving conditions for the African farmers, for instance by launching a land reform programme whereby the government purchased most of the land owned by Europeans and distributed it to African smallholders. This move is widely considered to have significantly expanded opportunities for smallholder involvement in horticulture and other forms of commercial agriculture (Dijkstra, 1997). Second, the Horticultural Crops Development Authority (HCDA) was created in 1967, with the sole purpose of providing advisory and regulatory support. HCDA facilitated private sector development through a wide range of institutional and marketing arrangements, including the use of contract farming, in which traders provided funding for the purchase of inputs, price information and overall marketing services to farmers. This allowed the sector to develop more rapidly. Third, there was growth in foreign direct investment (FDI) in both the production and processing of horticultural products in Kenya (Swanberg, 1995).

Following independence, a large numbers of smallholder farmers started engaging in dairy farming. To encourage dairy production, the government provided subsidized and efficient livestock services including clinical services and artificial insemination (Omiti et al, 1993). Active public support for these services soon resulted in a rapid increase in the amount of milk produced nationally (Muriuki et al, 2003). Over 60 per cent of the milk market was then dominated by Kenya Cooperative Creameries (KCC), a dual parastatal and private company. The government subsidies continued until the early 1980s, when efficient delivery of these services became impossible due to government budgetary constraints. This led to a restructuring of the industry with the aim of increasing the role of the private sector (Omiti and Muma, 2000). As a result of the restructuring, KCC collapsed and many of the systems that had controlled the supply of milk through the formal dairies broke down.

Beginning in the 1980s, liberalization opened both the input and output markets to forces of demand and supply in most agricultural commodities. In general, liberalization led to increased input sources, increased output market channels, wide variations in both input and output prices and wide fluctuations in seasonal commodity production (Freeman and Omiti, 2003; Nyangito, 2001). Liberalization also contributed to increased enterprise competition and farm commercialization by permitting private sector participation into the sectors that had been dominated by state trading enterprises.

Maize market liberalization policies began in 1988 and were implemented in the structural adjustment programmes (SAPs) with the objective of increasing economic efficiency by allowing market forces to play a major role in determining prices and guiding resource allocation (Jayne et al, 1997). Due to a number of factors, there was a gradual increase in maize production following liberalization. A major driver was the emergence of many new seed providers, thus widening farmers' choices on seed varieties. The introduction of new production technologies, like the use of early maturing maize varieties, also increased maize production. Furthermore, the strengthening of seed quality monitoring by the Kenya Plant Health Inspectorate Service (KEPHIS) contributed to improved seed performance.

Another factor that contributed to the increased focus on maize production in Kenya was the involvement by several development actors (non-governmental organizations (NGOs), research institutes and donor organizations) in the activities of the maize industry, in the interest of both producers and consumers. Other forces of change in maize included rapid urbanization, especially of poor people who consume primarily maize, and increased consumption of fortified maize flours, which led to expansion of the milling capacity. Lele (1992) also observed that maize grain market liberalization in Kenya greatly increased marketing channels for producers. Although the growth in maize production was concentrated among large-scale farms owned by a few less-poor individuals and private companies, resource-poor small-scale farmers in remote villages benefited from the transformations due to improvements in marketing and better price regimes.

The horticultural sub-sector experienced rapid growth arising mainly from increasing incomes in some population segments, increased demand for quality products, an increased number of women in the work force, changes in eating habits, better infrastructure, improved technologies and the emergence of various market outlets for fresh fruits and vegetables (supermarkets, wholesalers, retailers, assemblers, etc.). With improved access to inputs, small-scale horticulture farmers in high-potential areas were able to reap moderate benefits from rising demand.

The dairy market underwent a major transformation following the ending of KCC's monopoly in urban areas in 1992. That liberalization measure opened up the dairy industry to private sector investors in input provision and marketing, with a resultant redistribution of socio-economic pay-offs to smallholder farmers, traders and consumers (Omiti and Muma, 2000; Staal and Shapiro, 1994). Other structural changes in the dairy sub-sector included privatization of artificial insemination and other health services, which led to higher costs for these services. Some farmers responded by shifting to inferior bulls, which had the effect of lowering their milk yields. The liberalization of the milk market also opened up the sale of fresh whole milk to different channels. Demand for milk and other processed dairy products such as cheese, yoghurt, butter and ghee increased due to urbanization, changes in consumer preferences and increasing purchasing power, especially among newly employed people in previously disadvantaged categories such as women, youth and those in poor remote areas.

Recent agricultural production in Kenya

This section of the chapter is based on our research and analysis at the village and farm levels, conducted through participatory rural appraisals at village level and a household survey.

Participatory rural appraisal

To illustrate current conditions and trends in Kenya's small-scale agricultural sector, we used village-level data obtained through a participatory rapid rural appraisal (RRA) conducted through focus group discussions with 8–12 persons per group in one peri-urban and one rural district (Kiambu and Kisii, respectively). The two districts have differential levels of poverty and degrees of commercialization (CBS, 2005), and therefore provide a sampling across localities that differ widely with respect to resource endowment and access to urban markets. Kiambu district in central Kenya is in close proximity to the capital city of Nairobi, where there is a potentially huge lucrative urban market for maize meal, dairy and horticultural products. Generally, food production systems in peri-urban areas such as Kiambu are relatively commercialized, with good infrastructure as compared to other parts of the country. On the other hand, Kisii district, about 400km from Nairobi in southwestern rural Kenya, is characterized by a modest level of commercialization and comparatively worse state of infrastructure (roads, water, energy, etc.).

The selected study areas are representative of the salient features of Kenya's agricultural systems in terms of agro-ecological zones, demographic changes, resource re-allocation decisions and emerging prospects for high-value commercial diversified crop/livestock production. Some high-potential areas (such as Uasin Gishu and Trans Nzoia districts) were omitted from the analysis due to relatively smaller proportions of smallholder maize farms compared to large-scale plantations. Districts with extreme levels of poverty and bad infrastructure (particularly the pastoral northeast) did not fall within the scope of this analysis due to their low levels of agricultural potential and absence of maize, horticulture and dairy. Still other districts were potentially relevant but omitted because of the limited scope of the project.

A matrix representing four possible combinations of market access and market integration was used in selecting villages in each of the two study areas (Table 12.1). Differential poverty indicators, biophysical, environmental and agro-climatic features, infrastructure networks (CBS, 2005) and expert views of agricultural officers in the Ministry of Agriculture and Ministry of Livestock and Fisheries Development at the district and divisional levels were also taken into consideration in the selection of the villages. The surveys were conducted in a total of 16 villages: eight villages in each study area, with two villages each for all four types (Annex 12.1).

Table 12.1 *Village selection criteria in each study area*

| | | Integration into commercialized food systems | |
		Low	High
Market Access	Bad	Type one (2 villages)	Type three (2 villages)
	Good	Type two (2 villages)	Type four (2 villages)

Household survey

A household survey was also used to trace individual farmers' participation in emerging market channels and consumer institutions. It was conducted primarily to enable characterization of the existing points of sale. Identification and selection of farm-level respondents was through purposive snowball sampling technique, while market channels were drawn by purposive quota sampling in various representative production and consumption regions spread across the two districts and adjacent areas.

A truncated regression model was used to analyse determinants of percentage of farm output sold. In the model, the degree of market participation is unobservable, but is implied when a decision to sell output is made by a household and positive quantities are actually sold. Market participation was proxied by the observed percentage of output that is actually sold in the market. The truncated regression model (1) assumes normal distribution with constant variance (Greene, 2003).

$$Y_i^* = \beta_i X_i + \mu_i \tag{1}$$

where Y_i^* is the percentage of output sold, β_i is the vector of parameters, X_i is the set of exogenous explanatory variables and μ_i is the error term. The specific regressors in the estimated model are gender, distance to point of sale, unit price, market information arrangement (formal or informal), proportion of non-farm income in total household income and quantity of output for the particular commodity. A separate equation is estimated for each of the three commodities (maize, dairy and horticulture).

Recent agricultural production trends in Kenya

At the national level, the production of maize, horticulture and dairy remained fairly stable in the 20 years between 1990 and 2005 (Figure 12.3). However, our RRA showed that no single village remained static with respect to production over the same period. Population growth contributed to a decline in average land holdings (from over 20 acres to fewer than 5 acres per farm-family) and led to changes in land tenure systems from a largely communal system to individual (private) ownership. The average acreage of traditional export crops, particularly coffee, declined due to declining sizes of land holdings.

Changing enterprise competitiveness (at farm level, driven mainly by market prices) occasioned significant resource re-allocation patterns and shifts in farm enterprise choices. For instance, pyrethrum, a once profitable crop, was largely substituted with high-value horticultural crops (partly due to various institutional bottlenecks, including high overhead costs and poor management). The rising demand for housing in the peri-urban areas also led to shifts from farm production to more profitable rental estate construction, thus limiting arable land. Within

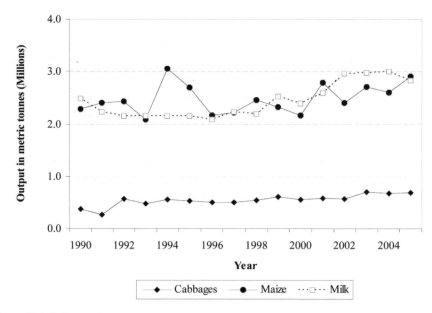

Source: FAOSTAT data, 2006

Figure 12.3 *National agricultural production trends in Kenya, 1990–2005*

small-scale agriculture, there was evidence of a transformation from relatively low-value maize to high-value horticulture and dairy production.

Despite an increased uptake of hybrid maize varieties, average yields are declining in both rural and peri-urban farms, due mainly to land fragmentation resulting in uneconomic land sizes, and the inherent poor quality of seeds and fertilizer used by the majority of resource-poor small-scale farmers. Production of key horticultural crops (kales, cabbages and tomatoes) is on an upward trend in the peri-urban areas due to high demand arising from a rapid increase in the urban population. In the rural areas, horticultural production continues to drop because of the high cost of inputs (such as seeds, fertilizer and pesticides) and motorized transportation, and the limited number of buyers at farm level (consumers and traders).

In the dairy sub-sector, milk production is steadily rising in both rural and peri-urban areas, ostensibly in response to increasing market demand. Marginal growth in per capita incomes, especially due to the implementation of an economic recovery strategy beginning in 2003 (Republic of Kenya, 2003) and increased education on the benefits of good nutrition have helped to improve milk consumption in various forms (especially in tea, yoghurt, cheese, butter, porridge and vegetables or as fresh milk). Small-scale farmers have embraced improved technology to facilitate their effective response to the growing demand for milk. For instance, there is evidence of an increased uptake of improved zero-grazing methods and the use of high-quality purchased dairy feeds on increasingly fragmented land holdings. More high-yielding milk cattle breeds (especially

Table 12.2 *Farm-level production trends in Kenya, 1985–2005*

	Maize	Kales	Enterprise Horticulture Cabbages	Tomatoes	Dairy
Changes in production systems	• Introduction of hybrid varieties on pure stand • Limited intercrop	• Increased production of kales	• Reduction in cultivation of capsicum and Copenhagen varieties of cabbages	• No major changes	• Adoption of improved zero-grazing technology and artificial insemination services • Increased adoption of Friesian and its crosses, while Guernsey and Zebu breeds declined
Changes in average yields	• Drop in yields from 5560 to 2220kg/ha in Kisii • Drop from 1110 to 440kg/ha in Kiambu	• Yields of kales in Kisii dropped from 18,530 to 14,830kg/ha • Yields of kales increased from 3710 to 14,830kg/ha in Kiambu	• Yields of cabbage in Kisii declined from 123,550 to 74,130kg/ha • Cabbage yields increased from 24,710 to over 148,260kg/ha in Kiambu	• Tomato yields declined from 2960 to less than 2470kg/ha in Kisii • Tomato yields increased from 990 to over 3950kg/ha in Kiambu	• Increase in milk yields from 3 to 6 litres/day in Kisii • Increase in milk yields from 8 to 12 litres/day in Kiambu
Main forces of change	• Decline in land holdings • Decline in productivity due to poor quality of seeds and fertilizers	• Increased demand for cheap nutritious food in peri-urban areas (and high cost of other foods e.g. meat) • High cost of pesticides, fertilizers and seeds for rural farmers • High cost of motorized transport and poor road infrastructure in rural villages	• Increased demand for cheap vegetables as prices of other foods escalate • Declining farm sizes and unreliable rainfall patterns	• Increased incidence of pests, high transportation costs and illegal market charges • Increased population and demand for food in urban areas, and changing preference in favour of nutritious foods (in hotels, hospitals, residential estates, etc.)	• Rise in demand for milk • Change in frequency of milking from 1–2 times a day to 2–3 times a day • Increased use of high-quality purchased dairy feeds

Note: These yield estimates were provided by village elders and may vary from actual yield averages from farms in the same locality; however, they represent the elders' perceptions.

Friesian and its crosses) are being adopted, and the frequency of milking is also being optimized by most dairy farmers (from twice to thrice per day where possible) under better animal husbandry practices including optimal feed rations, mandatory veterinary care and suitable housing (Table 12.2).

Commercialization

The proportions of output sold and the percentage of farmers participating in markets are important indicators of agricultural commercialization and rural development. Our village-level analysis showed a higher degree of commercialization in peri-urban villages compared to remote rural villages (about 67 per cent and 52 per cent, respectively). With regard to the market access/integration grid, there is an upward trend of commercialization for all commodities investigated in all the rural villages (Figure 12.4). However, fewer smallholder farmers participate in commercial farming: about 55 per cent in peri-urban areas and 50 per cent in rural areas. The degree of enterprise competitiveness varies from place to place depending on market prospects, production costs and marketing costs. Some enterprises (such as maize) in the farming systems have diminished in relative importance over time in terms of income generation. This is evidenced through the declining acreage allocated to such enterprises.

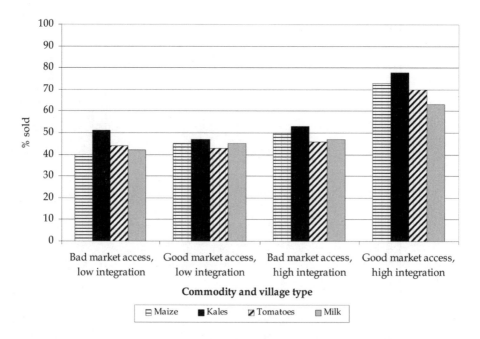

Figure 12.4 *Extent of commercialization in rural areas of Kenya (%)*

Irrespective of the commodity, it is evident that improvements in either market access conditions (e.g. infrastructure) alone or market integration features (connectedness) alone will not substantially improve the degree of market participation by smallholder farmers in rural areas. When factors influencing both market access and market integration are favourable, the degree of participation by smallholder farmers is higher than it is when only one (or neither) factor is favourable.

In the peri-urban areas, there is a positive correlation between commercialization and market access/integration for high-value enterprises like horticulture and dairy (Figure 12.5). Marketing costs decline with improvements in market access and degree of market integration because of increased competition by buyers, while enterprise competition intensifies. Because of proximity to high-value urban markets, there is a shift from low-value and less-perishable commodities such as maize to more profitable enterprises such as dairy and horticulture.

The degree of market orientation by smallholder farmers is higher in peri-urban areas than in rural areas, primarily due to shorter distances to urban markets. However, there are variations in the extent of market participation depending on the nature of market access and degree of market integration. The degree of market participation is highest when both market access and market integration are optimal (most improved). Therefore, it is necessary to improve both market access (roads, telecommunications, etc.) and market integration (market intermediation, institutional linkages, etc.) in order to enhance market participation by smallholder farmers.

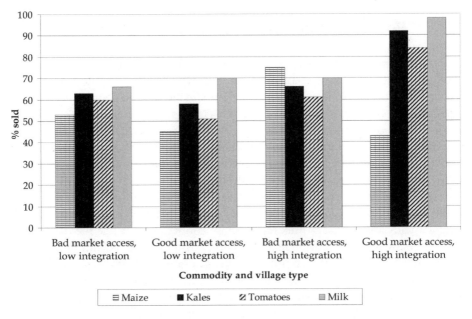

Figure 12.5 *Extent of market orientation in peri-urban areas in Kenya (%)*

Farm household level

The results of our truncated probability regression show that within individual farm households, the percentage of maize, horticulture and dairy produce sold is significantly increased by producer prices, access to formal market information and quantity of output produced (Table 12.3). The positive coefficients of producer price and production capacity in the model reflect the motivation for supply response in a rational economic system and the basis for stability in market participation, respectively. Other things being equal, more is sold when more is produced. Formal market information arrangements guarantee producers a steady flow of insights on market requirements and opportunity sets that enable farmers to plan effectively on enterprise choices and efficient resource allocation. However, the longer the distance between farm households and points of sale, the lower the percentage of output sold in all three sub-sectors. Distance naturally acts as a barrier to market participation by imposing transportation costs. Earning non-farm income is significantly and negatively associated with the degree of market participation, particularly in maize and dairy.

The results also show that a greater percentage of high-value farm output (e.g. dairy) is sold in male-headed households compared to female-headed households. This could be explained by the inherent skewed resource endowments (e.g. ownership of land, capital), access to information, membership in development associations and benefit-sharing schemes, which often favour men and disadvantage women, irrespective of the latter's level of effort and multiple roles.

Points of sale and market arrangements

The main points of sale in peri-urban villages are brokers/assemblers and in the rural areas retailers in open-air markets. For maize and horticultural produce, wholesalers and assemblers are the key points of sale, while cooperatives are the main market channels for milk (Table 12.4). Nearly 90 per cent of all market arrangements on quantities traded, delivery mechanisms, mode and frequency of payment are informal and prone to violation by both parties especially during periods of glut or extreme scarcity. However, it is important to note that dairy cooperatives are not really informal although there are no formal arrangements with the cooperatives on quantity and milk delivery mechanisms. In addition, this is the fundamental basis for assertions by farmers regarding violation of the arrangements and arbitrary milk rejection by cooperatives. While the dairy enterprise is characterized by relative asset fixity, farmers in maize and horticultural crops (mainly vegetables) respond to challenges in market channels and arrangements through seasonal changes in cropping patterns, particularly by switching into low-input crops like beans, cassava and sorghum.

In the dairy sub-sector, cooperatives determine prices and payment is made on a monthly basis. Cases of lack of transparency in milk testing during purchase

Table 12.3 *Determinants of farm households' degree of market participation in Kenya*

Variable	Variable description	Maize			Horticulture (Kales)			Dairy		
		Coeff	Std error	t-ratio	Coeff	Std error	t-ratio	Coeff	Std error	t-ratio
Constant		0.476	0.288	1.653	0.395	0.232	1.703	0.413	0.274	1.507
Price	Unit price, in Ksh[a] per Kg	0.197	0.025	7.880**	0.134	0.027	4.963**	0.317	0.139	2.281*
Market information source	1 if formal, 0 if informal	0.271	0.104	2.606*	0.325	0.141	2.305*	0.538	0.271	1.985*
Quantity	Output quantity, in kg	0.730	0.180	4.055**	0.532	0.157	3.389*	0.528	0.269	1.963*
Distance	Distance to nearest point of sale, in km	-0.508	0.116	-4.379**	-0.597	0.124	-4.812**	-0.249	0.105	-2.371*
Non-farm income	As percentage of total farm income	-0.494	0.134	-3.687*	-0.067	0.039	-1.718	-0.068	0.007	-9.714**
Gender	1 if male, 0 if female	0.818	2.754	0.297	-0.055	0.028	-1.964*	0.502	0.148	3.392*
		N = 76			N = 77			N = 71		
		Log likelihood = -86.35			Log likelihood = -77.93			Log likelihood = -61.58		
		R^2 = 0.401			R^2 = 0.437			R^2 = 0.483		

Note: [a] Ksh = Kenyan shillings; * Significant at 5 per cent; ** Significant at 1 per cent.

Table 12.4 *Points of sale by farmers in Kenya*

Commodity and market channel/point of sale	Average sold to each channel by area (%)	
	Peri-urban	Rural
Maize	**n = 58**	**n = 18**
Wholesalers	54	6
Assemblers	26	21
Individual buyers in the village	8	37
Retailers in open air markets	6	24
Schools	4	8
Others (millers, individual buyers in other village, NCPB)	2	5
Dairy	**n = 64**	**n = 7**
Assemblers	35	14
Cooperatives	33	29
Individual buyers in the village	17	23
Wholesalers	9	0
Hotels or restaurants	2	34
Others (individual buyers in other village, retailers in open air markets, schools)	5	0
Horticulture	**n = 65**	**n = 12**
Assemblers	36	48
Wholesalers	35	14
Retailers in open air markets	15	22
Individual buyers in the village	11	16
Others (individual buyers in other village, hotels or restaurants)	3	0

lead to complaints of frequent milk rejection on the basis of claims of false quality distortion. About 20 per cent of farmers have experienced rejection of their milk at the time of sale and, on average, these farmers lose 30 per cent of their production due to such rejection. This is particularly evident during periods of glut and also during the wet season when roads are generally in poor condition. In addition, farmers report payment delays of up to three months after delivery of farm produce; this leads them to side-sell at lower prices in order to overcome cash constraints. However, this does not yield optimum returns because seasonal gluts in milk supply lead to price fluctuations. Better and innovative marketing arrangements are required in order to streamline operations of milk cooperatives and facilitate linkages between small-scale producers and growing market segments. These may entail examining the contractual obligations under the existing and potential marketing arrangements to see which can best serve smallholder farmers.

Policy and institutional frameworks for diversification

The creation of a facilitative business environment, which encourages local investors to put their resources into productive use and attracts foreign investment, has been an important aspect of public policy in Kenya since economic liberalization in the early 1990s. A conducive business environment allows competition and promotes new investment and productivity growth (KIPPRA, 2006). This leads to increased production and marketing of farm produce and ensures that consumers receive high-quality products and services at remunerative prices. It is important to provide supportive regulation and institutional services to enable trade expansion in profitable enterprises, which in Kenya includes small-scale dairy enterprises in particular. Some of the issues in the current policy framework include those described below.

Licences and business permits

In order to engage in trade in milk in Kenya it is necessary to obtain legal approval from relevant authorities (licences and permits). Amounts paid for the legal documents vary depending on area of operation, and it may take up to two months to obtain them. Until recently many small-scale milk producers and/or traders sought entry into commercial systems (through informal channels within their means, such as hawking) without being registered and often faced the wrath of the law through harassment by government departments (mostly the local authorities and police). This was essentially a government policy to maintain the monopoly status of the quasi-governmental KCC, a status it had held since the colonial period (1935). But due to growing public pressure for change in the policy and the government's realization of the immense potential for economic growth in small-scale milk production and trade, small-scale milk trade permits were introduced in 2003 and 2004. This move was driven by various actors in the dairy industry, drawing on evidence-based research from the International Livestock Research Institute (ILRI), the Institute of Policy Analysis and Research (IPAR), Tegemeo Institute of Agricultural Policy and Development and other groups. Such shifts re-affirm the important role of collective advocacy by stakeholder groups in policy formulation for improved farm livelihoods, a trend that contributed to significant agricultural reforms in, for example, Ghana.

Market charges

For small-scale farmers with the ability to sell their produce at the higher-paying markets (as opposed to farm-gate), market charges (both legal and illegal) constitute a key barrier. Vendors are required to pay on average US$0.60 in legal fees and US$1 in stall charges on a weekly basis. In addition, numerous illegal charges are levied at various points of transit and sale. For instance, there are about five roadblocks on the highway from Kisii to Nairobi where the police, under the pretence of quality/minimum load inspection, charge, as a bribe, not less than

US$10 per vehicle of maize, cabbage, kales, tomatoes or milk that passes from farming areas to the market. At the open-air retail markets, daily operating fees of about US$0.50 are charged per trader, with no receipts issued; some producers unable to afford the charges have their merchandise confiscated. These exorbitant and uncoordinated market charges mean that small-scale producers hoping to trade their produce begin to count their losses even before they engage in price negotiations.

Agricultural credit

The role of credit in facilitating access to both production inputs and marketing services is paramount, especially among small-scale farmers. Generally, credit provision to agriculture in Kenya is still very limited due to the risky nature of farm enterprises. Even the few credit providers that offer substantial amounts to agro-based investments (e.g. cooperatives, the state-run Agricultural Finance Corporation (AFC) and micro-finance institutions) focus mainly on dairy and export commodities such as tea, coffee and cut flowers. Small-scale farmers who produce maize or vegetables, and particularly highly perishable crops such as tomatoes, lack considerable institutional credit support, public or private.

Agricultural extension services

Improving farm-specific skills through extension visits is important in precipitating entry into commercial farming and participation in high-value agricultural enterprises, by giving farmers the capacity to grow and market high-value crops (Lapar et al, 2003). To a greater extent, provision of extension services is by the government, supplemented by a few private entities. Extension services from government are coordinated by the Ministries of Agriculture, Livestock and Fisheries Development, while private crop/livestock input companies provide extension services through field demonstrations and product promotion campaigns. The frequency and quality of extension service provision is relatively better in peri-urban areas (especially for commercial milk producers due to the high value of their production and their willingness to pay for better services) than in rural areas and for low-value crops such as maize, kales or cabbages.

Potential for high-value smallholder commercial agriculture

Recent transformations in Kenya's agricultural systems mean that there is a vast potential for farmers to diversify into high-value agriculture, such as dairy and horticulture. Considering the global forces of urbanization, population pressure and changing consumer preferences, enterprise diversification (particularly involving dairy and maize fodder production) is likely to be a profitable and sustainable agricultural occupation strategy among small-scale farmers in rural Kenya.

The rapid growth in milk demand in Kenya and other east African countries, positive uptake of modern technology (such as zero-grazing) and the optimization of milking frequency all provide evidence of a stable dairy sub-sector that could contribute significantly towards better livelihoods for small-scale farmers. Recent policy reforms in the dairy industry (such as the Kenya Dairy Board's introduction of small-scale traders' licences) and the feasibility of maize fodder cultivation in some agro-ecological zones of Kenya, including the semi-arid lands, also provide a sound basis for upscaling the diversification approach. On the other hand, declining average farm yields and market returns for maize, along with land scarcity and seasonal gluts in vegetable supply, require decisive interventions in order to support the rural livelihoods of small farmers who are unable to diversify. Policies to promote value addition through agro-processing of horticultural products could ease the problem of seasonal glut. Furthermore, the economics of fodder production need to be set against a background of uncertain milk prices and availability of water resources. When there is an inherent risk of drought, farmers resort to fodder production.

In order to facilitate smallholder farmers' adjustment to transformations in agricultural systems, priorities for public expenditure should change over time to reflect the changing patterns of their returns on investment. Policy interventions should address the differences in market integration that arise from poor infrastructure and technology adoption. Equally important for promoting market integration is improving governance within the relevant institutions in commodity value chains in the agricultural commercialization process. It would be prudent for Kenya to improve the targeting of agricultural investments (toward research and technology that meets diversified product needs in the markets), promote market deregulation and stabilize the macroeconomic framework to foster the ongoing transformation of the rural economy.

Way forward

The following interventions are necessary in order to facilitate the development of sustainable diversified small-scale crop/livestock systems in Kenya:

(a) Investment

* public development of infrastructure (especially roads, energy, markets, security, etc.) in order to encourage private sector provision of affordable inputs and extension services, facilitate the delivery of marketed surpluses and enhance farmer interaction with the rest of the economy;
* strengthening of market information provision through the establishment of more affordable formal channels and the enrichment/targeting of message content to serve the diverse production and marketing needs of different types of agricultural producers and traders;

- establishment of programmes to enhance accessibility to improved technologies and inputs, which calls for public/private partnerships.

(b) Regulation

- exploration and implementation of innovative mechanisms to strengthen/deepen market integration, which may include institutional linkages to formal markets through producer marketing groups, farmer associations, etc.;
- harmonization of legal market charges and establishment of 'rules of the game' for vendors, such as operating at designated areas, maintaining hygiene, etc.; corresponding elimination of all illegal fees in commodity transit routes, points of sale and police roadblocks (particularly critical for perishable commodities such as horticultural produce) and curbing of harassment by authorities;
- elimination of discrimination and other forms of harassment of small-scale agricultural traders, either during licence/permit provision processes or in the course of their trade operations;
- institution of mechanisms to minimize contract violations in order to streamline enforcement of market arrangements among producers, and between producers and marketing agents; these included low-cost arbitration channels so that penalties could be enforced on behalf of small farmers.

(c) Cross-cutting

- provision of sustainable exit options to small-scale farmers who suffer from declining profitability of maize and declining horticulture production. Affordable credit and entrepreneurial skills for engaging in small and medium enterprises such as bicycle transport (*boda boda*) are possible strategies, as long as the agricultural economy is able to support opportunities to earn off-farm income;
- establishment of cost-effective and equitable social protection policies in order to fully cushion groups (e.g. widows on rented land, squatters and victims of natural disasters such as prolonged droughts) that are made extremely vulnerable by declining returns from the transformations in maize and horticulture and have no means of venturing into any other profitable alternatives.

It is necessary for both the government and the private sector to continue designing policies and implementing programmes that further promote smallholder agricultural commercialization; promoting agricultural transformation to high-value products will support vibrant rural livelihoods and boost rural economic prosperity.

Annex 12.1 *Villages sampled in the participatory rural appraisal (PRA) in Kenya, 2006*

Quadrant	Village	Location	Division	District
Bad market access, low	Gituamba	Kirenga	Lari	Kiambu
commercialization	Matimbei	Kamburu	Lari	Kiambu
	Obosando	Kegogi	Marani	Kisii
	Bonyunyu	Keera	Nyamaiya	Kisii
Bad market access,	Miumia	Githunguri	Githunguri	Kiambu
high commercialization	Ngenia	Ngewa	Githunguri	Kiambu
	Kionganyo	Sensi	Marani	Kisii
	Mwogeto	Sensi	Marani	Kisii
Good market access,	Kamungaria	Ndeiya	Ndeiya	Kiambu
low commercialization	Ndiuni	Ndeiya	Ndeiya	Kiambu
	Bomwancha	Bomariba	Suneka	Kisii
	Ititi	Bogeka	Mosocho	Kisii
Good market access,	Gachie	Kihara	Kiambaa	Kiambu
high commercialization	Kabae	Ndumberi	Kiambaa	Kiambu
	Matongo	Kiangeni	Borabu	Kisii
	Amaiga	Kegati	Kiogoro	Kisii

Notes

1   The authors are grateful to the FAO–Netherlands Partnership programme (FNPP) for funding the study. Technical inputs from researchers at the Kenya Institute for Public Policy Research and Analysis (KIPPRA) and from other public and private sector institutions are also acknowledged. The authors remain responsible for any errors and/or omissions.

References

Burke, W. J., Jayne, T. S., Freeman A. H. and Kristjanson, P. (2007) 'Factors associated with farm households' movement into and out of poverty in Kenya: The rising importance of livestock', International Development Working Paper No. 90/2007, Michigan State University, East Lansing, MI

CBS (2005) 'Geographic dimensions of well-being in Kenya: Who and where are the poor'? A constituency-level profile, vol II, Central Bureau of Statistics (CBS), Ministry of Planning and National Development, Regal Press Kenya Ltd, Nairobi

Conelly, W. T. (1998) 'Colonial era livestock development policy: Introduction of improved dairy cattle in high-potential farming areas of Kenya', *World Development*, vol 26, no 9, pp1733–1748

Dijkstra, T. (1997) 'Commercial horticulture by African smallholders: A success story from the highlands of Kenya', *Scandinavian Journal of Development Alternatives*, vol 16, no 1, pp49–74

Dorward, A., Poole, N., Morrison, J., Kydd, J. and Urey, I. (2002) 'Critical linkages: Livelihoods, markets and institutions', Seminar Paper, Imperial College, Wye, Kent

Ellis, F. and Freeman, H. A. (2004) 'Rural livelihoods and poverty reduction strategies in four African countries', *Journal of Development Studies*, vol 40, no 4, pp1–30

Freeman, H. A. and Omiti, J. M. (2003) 'Fertilizer use in semi-arid areas of Kenya: Analysis of smallholder farmers' adoption behaviour under liberalized markets', *Nutrient Cycling in Agro Ecosystems*, vol 66, pp23–31

Greene, W. H. (2003) *Econometric Analysis*, 5th edn, Prentice Hall, Upper Saddle River, NJ

Jayne, T. S., Jones S., Mukumbu M. and Jiriyengwa S. (1997) 'Maize marketing and pricing policy in eastern and southern Africa', in D. Byerlee and K. C. Eicher (eds) *Africa's Emerging Maize Market*, pp213–262, Lynne Reinner Publishers, Boulder, CO

KIPPRA (2006) 'Improving the enabling environment for business in Kenya', Policy Brief No. 11, Kenya Institute for Public Policy Research and Analysis (KIPPRA), Nairobi

Lapar, M. L., Holloway, G. and Ehui, S. (2003) 'Policy options promoting market partici-pation among smallholder livestock producers: A case study from the Philippines', *Food Policy*, vol 28, pp187–211

Lele, U. (1992) 'Structural adjustments and agriculture. A comparative perspective on response in Africa, Asia, and Latin America', in F. Heidhues and B. Knerr (eds) *Food and Agricultural Policies under Structural Adjustment*, Proceedings of the 29th seminar of the European Association of Agricultural Economists, Hohenheim, p35

McCulloch, N. and Ota, M. (2002) 'Export horticulture and poverty in Kenya', Working Paper No.174, Institute of Development Studies, University of Sussex, Brighton

Minot, N. and Ngigi, M. (2003) 'Are horticultural exports a replicable success story? Evidence from Kenya and Côte d'Ivoire', Paper Presented at the InWEnt, IFPRI, NEPAD, CTA Conference on Successes in African Agriculture, 1–3 December, Pretoria

MoA (2007) 'Economic review of agriculture', Central Planning and Monitoring Unit, Ministry of Agriculture (MoA) of Kenya, Nairobi

Muriuki, H., Omore, A., Hooton, N., Waithaka, M., Ouma, R., Staal, J. and Odhiambo, P. (2003) 'The policy environment in Kenya dairy subsector: A review', Smallholder Dairy Project (SDP) Research and Development Report, No. 2, International Livestock Research Institute (ILRI), Nairobi

Nyameino, D., Kagira B. and Njukia, S. (2003) 'Maize market assessment and baseline study for Kenya', Consultancy report, Regional Agricultural Trade Expansion Support (RATES), Nairobi

Nyangito, H. O. (2001) 'Policy and legal framework for the coffee sub-sector and the impact of liberalization in Kenya', Policy Paper No. 2/2001, Kenya Institute for Public Policy Research and Analysis (KIPPRA), Nairobi

Omiti, J. M. and Muma, M. (2000) 'Policy and institutional strategies to commercialize the dairy sector in Kenya', Occasional Paper No. 006/2000, Institute of Policy Analysis and Research (IPAR), Nairobi

Omiti, J. M., Mbogoh, S. G. and Odhiambo, M. O. (1993) 'An economic analysis of marketed milk production in Kenya over the 1957–1985 period', *East African Agriculture and Forestry Journal*, vol 58, no 4, pp141–153

Omiti, J. M., Parton, K. A., Ehui S. K. and Sinden, J. A. (2000) 'Some policy implications of the resurfacing of rural factor markets following agrarian de-collectivisation in Ethiopia', *Human Ecology*, vol 28, no 4, pp586–603

Republic of Kenya (1965) 'African socialism and its application to agriculture', Sessional Paper No. 10/1965, Nairobi

Republic of Kenya (2003) 'Economic recovery strategy for wealth and employment creation', Government Printer, Nairobi

Republic of Kenya (2007) 'Economic Survey report', Ministry of Planning and National Development, Government Printer, Nairobi

Staal, S. J. and Shapiro, B.I. (1994) 'The effects of recent price liberalization on Kenyan peri-urban dairy', *Food Policy*, vol 19, pp533–549

Swanberg, K. (1995) 'Horticultural exports from Kenya', *Horticultural Trade Journal*, vol 3, pp3–5

Thomas, S. J., Jones, S., Mukumbu, M. and Jiriyengwa, S. (1997) 'Maize marketing and pricing policy in eastern and southern Africa', in D. Byerlee and K. C. Eicher (eds) *Africa's Emerging Maize Market*, Lynne Reinner Publishers, Boulder, CO, pp213–262

Von Braun, J. and Kennedy, E. (1994) 'Agricultural commercialization, economic development, and nutrition', Food Policy Statement No. 19, International Food Policy Research Institute (IFPRI), Washington, DC

Winter-Nelson, A. (1995) 'Expectations, supply response, and marketing boards: An example from Kenya', *Agricultural Economics*, vol 14, pp21–31

World Bank (2007) *World Development Indicators*, Green Press Initiative, Washington, DC

Chapter 13

Linking Small Farmers in Bhutan with Markets: The Importance of Road Access

Sonam Tobgay and Ellen B. McCullough[1]

Introduction

Bhutan's mountainous terrain presents a major obstacle for marketing agricultural products. Furthermore, transportation facilities are limited in number and constrained by high costs due to low passenger and freight volumes. For example, it takes almost three days for fresh chillies (which command higher prices at the start of season) to cover a distance of little over 400km from Trashiyangtse to Thimphu. The Poverty Assessment and Analysis Study of 2000 showed that, out of all 201 *geogs* (sub-district blocks), 33 per cent are not at all connected to feeder roads and another 33 per cent are only partly connected to feeder roads (Planning Commission, 2000).

Limited access to markets contributes to high marketing costs and poses a major deterrent to commercialization. Bhutan's poor road infrastructure and a lack of market institutions have deterred market participation for smallholders. Price transmission is low and price changes in urban markets are not fully transmitted to producers and traders, whose prices are volatile and drop drastically even with a small increase in market arrivals. Without effective competition among market agents, those with larger market power control prices. This is evident in the case of mandarin exports to Bangladesh where importers negotiate prices prior to the trading season.

In this study, we use village and household surveys to explore trends in smallholder commercialization. We present new quantitative evidence highlighting road access as a major constraint to market participation. However, limited market infrastructure and institutions further constrain market behaviour and influence production decisions. As long as marketing costs remain high and marketed volumes remain small, market participation will be a risky prospect for Bhutan's smallholders, particularly those located in remote areas.

Background

Smallholder agriculture in Bhutan

Smallholder farmers continue to be the backbone of the Bhutanese food system. Their importance derives from their prevalence, their role in agriculture, food security and economic development and the concentration of poverty in rural areas.[2] While the definition of a smallholder may differ between countries, regions and agro-ecological zones, for the purpose of this study, smallholder farmers are defined as farmers with less than the average agricultural landholding of 0.89 hectares[3] (Table 13.1). Typically, these households are characterized as low income and resource poor, with relatively high vulnerability to economic and climatic shocks.[4]

Agriculture constitutes the core of the Bhutanese economy with 79 per cent of the population living on subsistence agriculture, sparsely scattered in far-flung isolated villages. Cultivable land, which is a main asset for smallholder households, is already in short supply. Per capita availability of agricultural land in Bhutan is one of the lowest in the world, even though the population density is also one of the lowest. Consequently, the prospects for agricultural expansion are constrained by a lack of arable land (5.4 per cent of total land area in the country is fit for cultivation), along with inadequate technology, poor road access and high transaction costs.

Such realities have resulted in mounting concerns about the conditions of Bhutan's smallholders as the country makes new commitments to trade liberalization and explores opportunities to meet increasing demand for new and higher

Table 13.1 *Agricultural land holdings of farm households*

Size group (hectares)	Percentage of households	Percentage of land area
0.0 – 0.5	13.7	1.4
0.5 – 1.0	33.7	14.7
1.0 – 2.0	22.0	19.2
2.0 – 3.0	13.5	17.4
3.0 – 4.0	8.4	15.7
4.0 – 10.0	8.0	25.8
> 10.0	0.6	5.9

Source: Adapted from Ministry of Agriculture, *Renewable Natural Resource Census* (Ministry of Agriculture, 2002)

quality products in a global economy. Production in Bhutan has barely managed to keep pace with population growth, leading to increasing imports from India. Bhutan trade statistics show that in 2004 imports from India in rice alone reached 39,000 metric tonnes (mt), with a value of US$7.1 million (or 309 million Nu[5] at that year's exchange rate) (Department of Revenue and Customs, 2004).

Several marketing systems are present in Bhutan, with options varying for different products (Table 13.2). The most common market outlet is direct sale to traders or consumers at the farm gate. The second most popular channel is the weekend markets, which can be found in all districts at least once a week according to government mandate. Due to increase in demand from the growing population, the vegetable market in Thimphu now operates up to three days a week. Other major vegetable markets are located in Paro and Phuentsholing. Finally, auction markets in the south, where produce is purchased by traders for ongoing sale in India, are the smallest of Bhutan's major chains. In the auction yard, it is mostly the Indian traders who purchase for onward sale to various parts of India. Cash crops like potatoes are sold primarily through the auction market, whereas other vegetables are sold in the district and weekend markets, typically in small volumes.

The office of the Agricultural Marketing Services (AMS), a government institution within the Ministry of Agriculture, is responsible for identifying markets and conducting trial shipments in liaison with the private sector. The AMS is also responsible for constructing marketing-related infrastructure and putting in place appropriate institutions to facilitate effective and efficient marketing of agricultural produce. The Food Corporation of Bhutan (FCB), a state-operated company, is the main marketing agent for agricultural produce. The FCB, in collaboration with AMS, has installed infrastructure, such as warehouses, storage and auction house facilities, in major trading districts.

Auction yards have been constructed to encourage the marketing of cash crops and to facilitate diversification into potatoes and other vegetables, ginger and cardamom. Farmers bring their produce to the auction yards where it is auctioned off (immediately or the day after delivery) to buyers from India and Bangladesh. FCB retains a percentage of sales revenues as a service charge. Mobile temporary auction yards are also set up in the main production areas during harvest seasons. These facilities are supervised by government agencies.

Table 13.2 *Popularity of different points of sale, by region*

Region	Direct marketing	Auction market	Cooperatives	Traders
Central	68%	20%	n.a.	28%
Eastern	90%	n.a.	3%	21%
Southern	66%	n.a.	n.a.	65%
Western	90%	33%	n.a.	89%

Trade

Bhutan is party to a free trade agreement with India and is a member of the South Asian Free Trade Area (SAFTA), Bay of Bengal Initiative for Multi-sectoral Technical and Economic Cooperation (BIMSTEC) and, soon, the World Trade Organization (WTO). With the liberalization of markets, there is an increasing trend towards outward-oriented policies, with export markets seen as an important source of economic growth. Foreign markets provide new opportunities and challenges for poor smallholder farmers in Bhutan. However, to take advantage of these opportunities, smallholder farmers must be able to participate in productive activities in which they have a competitive advantage. This implies access to well-organized marketing, distribution and post-harvest systems, effective market information and technologies that allow them to be competitive in price and quality.

Free access to the Indian market provides Bhutan with a major export opportunity, but it has also caused India to dominate Bhutan's trade relationships; India is by far the most important trading partner of Bhutan. As can be seen from Table 13.3, in the early 1990s about 88 per cent of all exports from Bhutan were destined for India; a decade later, that proportion had increased to 95 per cent. During the same period, India's share in imports increased from 74 per cent to 81 per cent. A number of factors have contributed to the predominance of India in Bhutan's external trade scenario. The most important of these are geographical proximity, the free trade agreement between the two countries and the financial and technical assistance India provides to Bhutan. Bangladesh is the second largest export market for Bhutan, with a share of about 4 per cent and Japan is the second largest source of imports, also with a share of 4 per cent.

Table 13.4, which traces Bhutanese agricultural exports, shows that agricultural exports accounted for between 8 and 12 per cent of total exports to India for the period 1998–2003.

Agricultural exports are confined to potatoes, oranges and apples for the Bangladeshi and Indian markets. Small quantities of highland red rice are being

Table 13.3 *Percentage share of total imports and exports held by Bhutan's major trading partners (periodic annual averages)*

	1990–1994	1995–1999	2000–2003
Exports			
India	88.4	93.1	94.6
Bangladesh	9.5	5.2	3.9
Others	2.1	1.7	1.5
Imports			
India	73.7	69.2	81.2
Japan	10.7	10.4	4.0
Singapore	0.7	7.1	2.5
Others	14.9	13.3	12.3

Source: Royal Monetary Authority of Bhutan (2003, 2004)

Table 13.4 *Agricultural exports, 1998–2003*

	1998		2003	
	India	Others	India	Others
Value (in million US$)	487.6	192.1	648.3	170.9
Share in Total Exports	11.6	68.6	10.9	64.7

Source: Royal Monetary Authority of Bhutan (2003, 2004)

exported to the US, UK and Germany; and high-value mushrooms are exported to premium markets in China and Japan by individual Bhutanese entrepreneurs. Oranges, with an earning of US$3.39 million, were rated the seventh top commodity export in 2003. Juice mixtures were the ninth top commodity export, with export earnings of US$2.33 million (Royal Monetary Authority of Bhutan, 2004). Taken together, the aggregate volume of cash crop exports increased impressively, by 126 per cent, between 1997 and 2004 (Table 13.5). Most of the growth occurred in the potato sub-sector, however, with apple and orange exports even declining during the period.

Despite a high concentration of exports into India and Bangladesh, the sheer size of Bhutan's south Asian trading partners means they still have great absorption capacity for Bhutanese production, particularly during off-peak production months in the receiving countries. During the summer and autumn, vegetables are in short supply in the lowlands of India and Bangladesh, but at peak production levels in the highlands of Bhutan. There is also great potential to expand exports of high-value, low-volume specialized products to these markets. However, as mentioned earlier, the challenge for benefiting fully from such niche markets will depend on overcoming bottlenecks arising from production and marketing constraints associated with a lack of marketing skills, product standards, post-harvest infrastructure and technology.

Due to the free trade relations between Bhutan and India, Bhutanese farmers must compete with cheap imports from India of staples and cash crops. The extent of rice insufficiency is shown by the increasing quantity of rice imports. Imported rice is not only destined for towns and municipalities, but also for the

Table 13.5 *Export of major cash crops*

Crops	Quantity (mt)			Value (millions)		
	1997	2000	2004	1997	2000	2004
Oranges	18,647	11,305	18,578	178.928	105.485	219.070
Potatoes	13,016	11,356	22,835	43.109	46.968	162.610
Apples	4,103	470	2,439	81.669	22.183	37.870
Ginger	1,150	676	250	4.609	6.868	3.257
Cardamom	527	402	818	36.922	75.045	81.180
Vegetables	1,660	4,235	1,994	22.536	26.741	12.540

Source: Bhutan Trade Statistics, Ministry of Finance

rural heartlands in the countryside through a network of food distribution outlets, both private and state-sponsored (Ura, 2005). Large suppliers from Indian border towns have been successful in meeting Bhutanese horticulture demands, with respect to quality and quantity, by developing successful partnerships with Bhutanese vendors. Imports on an annual average amount to 261 truckloads of vegetables and fruits at the Thimphu market alone. Of eight large vendors surveyed in the Thimphu weekend market, seven sourced their produce largely from Indian suppliers (Agriculture Marketing Services, 2006).

Production overview

Farmers in Bhutan grow a wide variety of field crops and tree fruits depending on the agro-ecological zone in which they live and the availability of cultivable land. Rice and maize are the most important cereal crops and are grown widely for subsistence. The following paragraphs outline crop production activities.

Rice

Rice production occupies the vast majority of Bhutanese farmers, with 28,930 households (74 per cent of farming households) engaged in rice cultivation. Bhutan's rice production, 55,762mt in 2006, meets about half of national demand. Total cultivated rice area is estimated at 19,410ha and represents 74 per cent of all farming households (Ghimiray and Wangdi, 2006). Production of rice on a commercial scale is limited – total paddy cultivation is limited to only 19,410 hectares – due largely to a shortage of arable land and farm labour, low cropping intensity, inadequate irrigation and crop losses to pests, especially wild animals. Studies have shown pest damage from boars, monkeys and elephants ranging from 18 to 71 per cent of crop values. The problem has been difficult to tackle because of the Royal Government of Bhutan's zealous enforcement of nature conservation laws and the religious sentiments against killing such animals. Farmers pay the costs in direct yield losses due to pest damage and the labour burden of guarding crops at night.

As a consequence, the domestic supply of rice has not kept pace with rising demand, and increased domestic demand is met with imports from India rather than local production. Imports from India alone increased to 71,000mt in 2005, about 74 per cent of the rice consumed. Rice imports have increased in recent years with the government importing 49,000mt constituting about 40 per cent of domestic demand (Shrestha, 2004). However, there are substantial quality and price

Table 13.6 *Consumption of rice in Bhutan's urban areas*

Rice type	Percent share
Local red rice	22
Local white rice	4
Imported Indian rice	74

Source: Ghimiray and Wangdi, 2006

differences between locally grown red rice and imported white rice from India. Red rice is a nutritious and traditional component of the Bhutanese diet, while white rice is cheaper and readily available. Table 13.6 shows the differentiation of rice consumption in urban areas.

Maize

Maize is the next most important crop after rice, by area of cultivation. It is cultivated predominantly in the eastern region of the country. The area harvested averages 0.7 hectares and production at less than 2mt per household. According to the Renewable Natural Resource (RNR) census 2004, overall maize yield has increased from 2480kg per ha in 2000 to 4150kg per ha in 2004.[6] Maize constitutes 49 per cent of the national food basket and represents 42 per cent of the total cultivated area. According to the RNR survey, 69 per cent of Bhutanese farmers grow maize for subsistence.

Potatoes

Potato is the most important horticulture crop in Bhutan, accounting for 60 per cent of vegetable production and the number one exported commodity by volume. Since potatoes are harvested earlier in Bhutan than in most parts of India, they fetch higher prices in nearby export markets. Wangduephodrang, Trashigang, Chhukha, Bumthang, Paro and Mongar together contributed 79 per cent of total production in 2000, with 3523 hectares planted to potatoes and a total production of 47,403mt (Royal Government of Bhutan (RGOB), 2004). The national average yield of potato is 5606kg per acre with yields upwards of 11,010kg per acre in Bumthang district (Figure 13.1) (Department of Agriculture, 2006). Most exports go to India and are sold through auction markets located in the southern towns of Phuentsholing, Samdrupjongkar and Gelephu.

Fruit crops

Apples, oranges and mushrooms have had a major impact on farmer income. Total fruit crop production from bearing trees was recorded at 44,755mt in 2004. Apples and oranges account for 90 per cent of Bhutan's fruit production (Department of Agriculture, 2006). The bulk of production comes from the southern *dzongkhags* (districts) of Chhukha, Sarpang, Samtse, Tsirang and Samdrupjongkhar. Apples account for 14 per cent of all fruit trees, with growth highly concentrated in Thimphu and Paro, which account for 90 per cent of apple production. Areca nut is an important tree crop in Samtse and Sarpang *dzongkhags* and walnuts are grown in Trashigang, Trashiyangtze, Mongar, Paro, Chhukha and Thimphu. Citrus production is expected to decline in the near future unless swift remedial measures are taken to correct the citrus greening disease *phytophthora*. Orange exports to Bangladesh, comprising 90 per cent of total orange exports, have decreased by more than 50 per cent recently. This decrease can be attributed to recent strikes in Indian border towns, poor road infrastructure, low fruiting volume and uncoordinated efforts in the entire supply chain (Figure 13.2).

Potato yields (average per household in kg/ha)

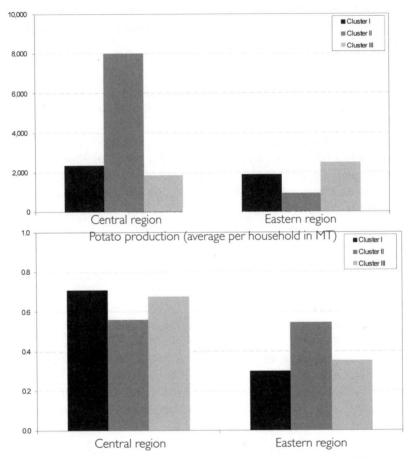

Potato production (average per household in MT)

Figure 13.1 *Average potato production (in mt), percentage sold and yield by region and cluster*

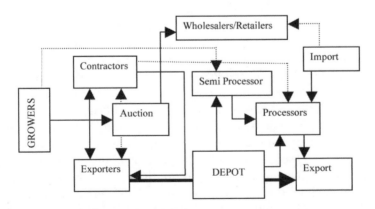

Figure 13.2 *Flow of oranges and apples from farm to markets*

Market access in Bhutan

In the context of this research, market access means access to roads, output markets, input markets, financial markets (e.g. credit) and market information.

Road access alone cannot suddenly create market access where it did not exist before. A broader set of conditions must complement transport infrastructure. Improving marketing systems for both farm produce output and agriculture inputs necessitates appropriate policy and legislative frameworks and effective government support services backed by strong marketing institutions and market infrastructure. Such services can include provision of market infrastructure, supply of market information and agricultural extension services to advise farmers on marketing. Bhutan suffers distinct disadvantages in all of these areas. Traders must have clear incentives to develop partnerships with farmers, which require them to assume high costs per unit procured. Low, unreliable and scattered production volume and post-harvest losses are some persistent constraints.

Methods and approach

This paper presents an analysis of data collected during two phases of field-based research. The first consists of a series of focus group discussions conducted at the village level in the districts of Chukha, Wangduephodrang, Paro, Bumthang, Lhuentse and Tsirang. The questionnaire was broad in scope, addressing many aspects of marketing and production of agricultural crops, livestock and forestry products. After obtaining information from secondary sources, the research team identified a group of informants to answer the survey questionnaire. The village informants in most situations included the people's representative, or the *Gup*, who is an elected member to that post. Other group respondents included the *Chimi, Tshogpa* and *Mangmi*, who also hold leadership roles in the village.

A second survey, involving a detailed household interview using structured questionnaires, was designed to supplement preliminary findings from the rapid rural appraisal survey. This survey focused on the importance of road access, so sampling of respondents was stratified by road access clusters. Households were categorized by their travel time to the nearest road point (less than 30 minutes, between 30 and 60 minutes, more than 60 minutes). Village sampling was conducted within these road access 'clusters'. Sample clusters are defined as follows:

1 Cluster I   Villages less than 30-minute walk from road point;
2 Cluster II Villages more than 30-minute walk, less than 1-hour walk from road point;
3 Cluster III Villages with no road access, more than 1-hour walk from road point.

In each of the districts, two representative *geogs* were chosen in consultation with the District Agriculture Officers (DAOs) and local extension agents. Within the identified *geogs*, three villages were selected, each fitting into a road access cluster. Upon identifying the cluster villages, 30 households in each *geog* were chosen (10 households per village per cluster). In total, 408 farmers were interviewed across 7 and 13 *geogs*. The *dzongkhags*, spread throughout eastern, central, western and southern Bhutan, were Samtse, Paro, Bumthang, Zhemgang, Trongsa, Mongar and Trashigang.

The study was designed with the intent of creating a profile of farmers' marketing and production systems by degree of market access. Using these profiles, we aim to determine the relationship between road access and other components of market access. We then establish the relationship between road access and production and marketing behaviour. The commodity focus was limited to rice, maize, potatoes and oranges to facilitate the comparison of impacts on similar commodities across regions along with the comparison of impacts across different levels of market access.

Current status and policy initiatives

Because there is limited domestic transfer of agricultural produce within Bhutan, one of the main priorities of the government is to improve the domestic marketing system. Roads in Bhutan are the only means of surface transport for goods and passengers. Road corridors follow the major north–south waterways, which serve as the main channels for population settlements and transport and provide access to the most fertile wetlands found in valley floors. Certain roads become difficult to drive on during winter months on mountain passes and during the rainy season (July, August and early September). Landslides are common during the monsoons, further hindering access. For example, the Phuentsholing–Thimphu highway, the main lifeline for supplies coming from India, often gets blocked for several days. Similarly, the highways connecting Wangduephodrang, Trongsa, Mongar and Trashigang are often closed due to snowfall and landslides.

In view of road access as an important catalyst for development, the tenth Five-Year Plan, (2008–2013) placed a high priority on infrastructure expansion, particularly with respect to feeder roads and farm roads to improve rural access and urban linkages. The Ministry of Agriculture was given the mandate of constructing farm roads linking potential surplus areas to markets and facilitating the movement of inputs to farmers. The Royal Government of Bhutan contributes to this initiative by providing construction and maintenance equipment and technical support, while farmers contribute voluntary labour. Mule tracks are another important means of communication for rural farmers.

In order to strengthen the overall national policy objective of attaining a self-sufficient economy, in 2004 the Ministry of Agriculture introduced a three-pronged strategy, the 'triple gem' policy guideline of production, access and marketing. The 'triple gem' underlies all programmes and projects implemented by all departments and agencies within the Ministry of Agriculture. Here we look at policies related to food self-sufficiency, road accessibility and market development. Current policies focus on:

- enhancing production through the use of best practices and increasing arable area;
- accelerating accessibility by bringing more roads into the interiors of the country; and
- increasing markets by concentrating on high-value and low-volume niche markets such as capturing off-season markets in India and neighbouring countries.

With accessibility as one pillar of the 'triple gem' approach, the Ministry of Agriculture as of June 2006 had completed 484km of farm roads, 71km of power-tiller tracks[7] and 4300km of mule tracks. This brought Bhutan's road network to 4545km, including 1556km of national highway and 597km of farm roads (Department of Roads, 2007). Road length has increased by 67 per cent since 1987, with more than 249 bridges and 366 suspension bridges (triple the number in 1987). The main road consists of the east–west highway connecting Thimphu with Trashigang and four north–south highways running from the Himalayas down to the Indian border. Although this network connects all districts, some areas are accessible only by mule, horse or yak.

Apart from the road network, mule tracks and footpaths provide the only means of transport. Most of the road network needs significant repair; during monsoons some important sections of the main highway are almost impassable and access to some interior areas severely curtailed, especially along the east–west national highway.

The RGOB is engaged in improving access to markets and marketing facilities through the construction of farm roads and other marketing infrastructure, such as post-harvest storage, primary processing facilities and weekend markets. Efforts to improve the economic efficiency of production and marketing have included facilitating the formation of cooperatives and farmer associations.

Improvements in marketing, the third 'gem', have centred on developing services and capacity. However, many hurdles must be overcome before Bhutanese products can compete more readily in the bigger markets of India and Bangladesh. In general, Bhutanese agriculture is not cost competitive compared to Indian products because of high production and transaction costs, in part an outcome of the shortage of labour in the rural areas willing to engage in agricultural activities. Bhutan has relatively high labour costs and most labour is performed by contracting Indian labourers at a lower wage rate than the national standard.

The government has made unprecedented efforts to add new market infrastructure with the construction of a new weekend market complex in the capital, Thimphu. There are weekend markets in each district, but prices are not attractive and there is a lack of buyer volume, particularly in the district markets of the eastern region. Policy support is under way to develop an efficient marketing infrastructure including retail, wholesale, assembly markets and storage facilities. The system also aims to improve the efficiency of transactions throughout the supply chain to minimize post-harvest losses and reduce health risks from contamination.

Policies are being implemented to ensure equitable distribution of the benefits of development, particularly among small and marginal farmers. Priority has been accorded to increasing accessibility to markets and other services to help facilitate rural income generation outside of the RNR sector. As of June 2006, a total of 1570km of rural feeder, farm and forest roads had been constructed to improve access for small farmers in rural areas. Other interventions include assisting farmers with sales of surplus maize in the eastern region through collaborative efforts with the World Food Programme (WFP). Another project promotes the marketing of eggs from Tsirang district and yak butter and cheese from the isolated districts of Merak and Sakten. Trials on marketing green chillies from Trashiyantse and cheese from Sha Gogona have also been undertaken. Despite a concerted effort to improve the domestic marketing system, it remains quite limited across crops and districts.

Are small farmers in Bhutan linking to markets?

Regardless of its efforts to construct new roads, Bhutan still suffers significant difficulties in connecting scattered villages into a road network. The present road network comprises 4545km of mostly paved road and roughly 4300km of mule tracks; the lack of road access continues to persist as one of the major shortcomings towards linking small farmers to markets. According to the recent Population and Housing Census Survey 2005, 21 per cent of Bhutanese households live one to four hours' walking distance from the nearest all-season road and another 21 per cent live more than four hours' walking distance away.

In addition, Bhutan's terrain of rugged mountains and steep slopes means that farmers' fields are widely spread out from each other and far from consumption centres. Transport costs are high and account for a significant proportion of total production and marketing costs. Due to low coverage and poor quality of road infrastructure, travel times are high, as are the costs of running and maintaining vehicles. Farmers' profit margins are affected at both ends, with high input costs and lower farm-gate prices. The absence of good quality roads limits incentives to produce and restricts rural–urban links. The isolation of the many villages in high mountain areas is one of the greatest barriers to developing marketing links for perishable food products. With only one airport in the entire country, air freight is not viable for reaching high-value export markets. The border with India is closed at night, restricting timely movement of goods between the two countries.

Smallholder farmers in Bhutan continue to face many obstacles to joining the ranks of preferred suppliers for weekend and auction markets. Besides the challenges of delivering products to the bigger markets of India and Bangladesh, satisfying quality and quantity standards requires substantial investments in production technology, transportation trucks, post-harvest equipment and packaging. There is scarcely a farmer in Bhutan who has succeeded in overcoming these impediments. Deficiencies in Bhutanese ability to supply domestic markets are increasingly overcome by vegetable and fruit imports from India.

Because Bhutanese farms are highly dispersed and diversified, there is apprehension about the ability of smallholders to expropriate niche market opportunities. Most high-value food commodities are perishable and prone to high production and market risks, which may act as a deterrent to smallholder participation. The rapid rural appraisal survey and the household survey confirmed the existence of imperfect market knowledge and price volatility in high-value markets. Local markets for high-value commodities are thin and the marketable surplus of an individual smallholder is too small to be traded remuneratively in distant urban markets. Production is constrained by a lack of adequate access to improved technology, quality inputs, credit and information.

Although the authorities still consider marketing and markets problematic due to poor transport arrangements, cash crop marketing is gradually emerging as a result of improved transport facilities and access to export markets. Also, a small domestic food processing industry, including Druk Fruit Products and Bhutan Agro Industries Ltd, is boosting demand. There are success stories of producers, traders and marketing agents managing to build successful supply chains (Bellotti and Cadilhon, 2007). BioBhutan, a local agri-food company, is a private firm that has managed to build consensus among processors on common standards and production practices so as to benefit all supply chain actors, including households that collect natural lemongrass in the forests for export. Another example is the Bumthang Gouda cheese enterprise, which rewards quality improvement at the farm level by differentiating milk prices according to protein content levels.

As for public enterprises, the Druk Seed Corporation, a state-owned and subsidized corporation, has developed and trained a network of seed farmers all over the country to produce high-quality seeds for many vegetables demanded in the Indian market. The National Mushroom Centre, another government entity, trains mushroom producers in quality improvement practices that bring price rewards. Finally, the initiative taken by the Department of Trade of the Ministry of Economic Affairs (formerly the Ministry of Trade and Industry) to seek funding for marketing missions of Bhutanese exporters to the US and the EU are commendable as they expose Bhutanese entrepreneurs to the reality of export markets.

Road access and market orientation

Market participation results

According to regressions performed with survey data, road access is indeed a significant determinant of a household's decision to participate in markets and to adopt more market-oriented cropping patterns. A logit regression was used to predict the influence of road access, along with other household characteristics, on the likelihood of selling any farm output (Table 13.7). A 1-hour decrease in walking time to the nearest road point corresponded with a 33 per cent increase in the relative probability of selling farm output.[8] The relationship between road

Table 13.7 *Impact of road access on likelihood of selling farm output*

Variable	Variable description	Coeff	Std error	z
Road access (hours walking to nearest road point)	negative, so larger value corresponds with better road access	0.282	0.170	1.66*
Production and marketing costs (excluding transport)	natural log of, in local currency (Nu)	0.470	0.201	2.34**
Number of HH workers	Residents aged 15–60	−0.326	1.122	−2.68***
Education level of HH head	Categorical (1–5)	0.030	0.109	0.27
Average age in HH	Age	0.304	0.106	0.29
Average age in HH squared	Age^2	−0.000	0.002	−0.17
East (regional dummy)	1 if true, 0 if false	0.382	0.371	1.03
South (regional dummy)	1 if true, 0 if false	−1.635	0.552	−2.96***
West (regional dummy)	1 if true, 0 if false	2.026	0.479	4.23***
Constant		−5.029	2.798	−1.80*
N = 262				
Likelihood ratio chi^2(9) = 106***				
Pseudo R^2 = 0.278				

Note: * = 90% confidence intervals (CI); ** = 95% CI; *** = 99% CI.

access and the likelihood of participating in markets was robust despite different forms of model specification.

These results suggest that, in the event of generating farm surplus, households located near road points find it worthwhile to transport their surplus to markets, while those located further away do not. While only 40 per cent of households in the survey dataset participated in output markets, virtually all purchased some food items for household consumption. At the household level, food expenditures per capita are not explained by road access but by land holdings, irrigation and credit access. Improved road access, therefore, would allow more households to sell farm output while lowering their expenditures on necessities.

The household survey showed that improved road access corresponded with higher specialization of cropping systems (Table 13.8). Specialization of cropping systems was quantified using the Herfindahl concentration index, which ranges from 0 in a highly diversified cropping system to 1 if landholdings are entirely planted to one crop. Concentration increased significantly (and robustly) with improved road access. Human capital variables caused specialization to increase, but credit and production costs did not. Households located closer to a road point may choose to sell surplus simply because it is worth their while. Evidence of increased specialization of cropping systems with better road access, however, suggests that road access causes households to be more market-oriented when they make their investment decisions. Households with good road access are able to specialize because they can rely on their ability to market their produce.

Table 13.8 *Impact of road access on specialization of cropping systems*

Variable	Variable description	Coeff	Std error	t
Road Access (hours walking to nearest road point)	negative so larger value corresponds with better road access	0.037	0.012	3.17***
Production and marketing costs (excluding transport)	natural log of, in local currency (Nu)	−0.019	0.014	−1.36
Credit Access Dummy	1 if credit availed, 0 if not	−0.007	0.026	−0.27
Education level of HH head	Categorical (1-5)	−0.004	0.007	−0.52
Average age in HH	Age	−0.014	0.007	−1.94**
Average age in HH squared	Age^2	0.000	0.000	1.97**
East (regional dummy)	1 if true, 0 false	−0.043	0.028	−1.54
South (regional dummy)	1 if true, 0 false	−0.032	0.030	−1.06
West (regional dummy)	1 if true, 0 false	0.210	0.036	5.86***
Constant		0.987	0.190	5.19***

N = 376
Likelihood ratio chi^2(9) = 64***
R^2 =0.148

Note: * = 90% confidence intervals (CI); ** = 95% CI; *** = 99% CI.

Households with poorer road access display more subsistence-oriented, diversified cropping patterns that reflect aversion towards the risks of market-oriented production.

Transportation

In most parts of the study area, respondents complained that transport availability was inadequate and also highly unpredictable. There is no regular form of transportation to ensure reliable movement of produce from farm to market. For instance, in the household survey almost 90 per cent of the farmers reported waiting between 30 minutes and 5 hours for transit at the nearest road point. Dirt roads connecting villages and farms to markets are usually inadequately maintained and left in poor conditions, making them costly to use. Because of high costs, farmers rely heavily on walking and human porters to deliver produce to markets and to procure household goods. The cost of transport depends on road access and distance to markets. In the eastern region the cost of transport by foot ranges from Nu50 to Nu390 per trip, depending on their choice of markets (between US$1.20 and US$9). Other means of transport include ponies, trucks, public buses, small engine power tillers and in some cases private cars, as shown in Table 13.9.

The delivery of farm produce to markets varied depending on road access, farmer resources and the availability of market related infrastructure (Figure 13.3). For example, the majority of farmers in the eastern region carry farm produce by foot to the nearest markets, whereas in the most remote areas farmers use ponies because of long distances to the nearest road point. In the central

Table 13.9 *Types of transport used (%)*

Region	Horses	Human porter	Power tiller	Public transport	Taxis	Tractors	Trucks	Self-carried
Central	11	1	5	1	5	40	28	40
Eastern	31	3	1	5	0	0	16	131
Southern	1	22	0	0	2	0	0	65
Western	12	10	6	1	6	0	87	52

region, irrespective of road access, almost half of the farmers arranged transport with private truck owners.

Traders and intermediaries are important players in providing transport linkages for small farmers. Traders are also often transporters in their own right, owning and operating a vehicle to conduct business. Transport providers and traders alike profit from poor rural roads. When roads are bad, theirs is often the only truck visiting a remote village and they can establish a monopoly position, buying primary products at prices they themselves dictate. When roads are better, transporters save on transport costs but earn lower margins. With more traders visiting remote areas, farmers are likely to receive better terms of sale. These inadequacies bring significant non-monetary costs to farmers, both in terms of production and marketing. Costs increase rapidly with distance. Small-scale marketing leads to high unit costs in terms of time and energy. These factors have limited production to levels considerably below the potential of rural areas. They have also constrained efforts to move from subsistence agriculture to market-oriented production systems.

The mandarin orange export model

The mandarin orange and apple export model has been successful at mediating market risks and could be suitable for replication in other sectors. Amid risks of crop deterioration from road blocks and long distances to markets, enterprising traders have contributed towards the development of the supply chain while also generating foreign exchange earnings for the country. According to FCB export data, mandarin and apple exports in 2006 were worth US$541,219.

The supply chain is comprised of four principal players: (i) the farmer who sells to (ii) the supplier for onward delivery to (iii) the exporter and the ultimate buyer, (iv) the importer. The supplier engages in most of the activities, starting with informal agreements or contracts with farmers prior to the harvesting season. Agreements consist of a written guarantee between parties, with the farmer agreeing to sell his harvest to the supplier who advances cash payments ahead of the season to ensure a commitment to honouring the contract. Similar contracts take place between the supplier and the exporter, where the former agrees to supply the latter the agreed quantity of the crop at the time of harvest. In return, the exporter grants cash advances to the supplier ahead of the season in order to ensure the agreed quantity.

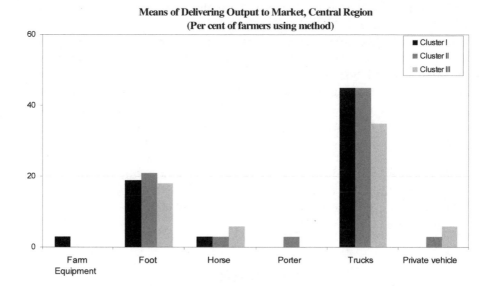

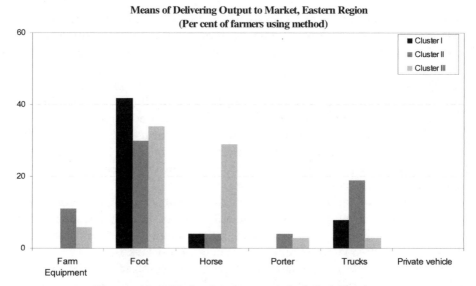

Figure 13.3 *Mode of transport used while delivering farm surplus to market*

Price negotiation occurs between the farmer and the supplier based on the supplier's judgement of fruit density somewhere between flowering and full maturity. Upon negotiating the farm price, the supplier then performs all downstream marketing activities including harvesting, packaging and transporting produce to the collection depots. Farmers who are not engaged in contract obligations with suppliers have the option to sell their produce in the auction market, but this entails carrying out all downstream logistics themselves. Few suppliers are engaged in procuring from the auction market in order to top up the required volume to be delivered to exporters.

Upon receiving consignments from suppliers, exporters grade and repackage into sizes categorized as *meel* (larger) or *keel* (smaller). Average export price fluctuates between US$8 and US$14 for meel sizes and US$6 and US$12 for keel sizes depending on the value of the dollar in the international market. Most of the fruit from the mandarin-growing regions (Dagana, Tsirang, Sarpang, Gelephu, Chukha, Samtse) flow to Phuentsholing, the main exit point in the south where the exporters are based. Exporting of the crop starts in mid-November and lasts until early February. In a recent season about 20,000mt were exported, a 70 per cent increase over previous years. Traders are essential to the feasibility of this export model. Although they offer farm-gate prices that are considerably lower than the auction price, they make accessible to smallholders an export chain that would otherwise be inaccessible.

Conclusions

Bhutanese agriculture is at a crossroads, with expanding opportunities and new competitive pressures. To harness export opportunities, small farmers must first become more market-oriented, producing the right commodities at the right time in the volumes required and at competitive prices. Commercialization into high-value agriculture will bring significant benefits in stimulating agricultural and economic growth, agribusiness and farmers' incomes. However, to take advantage of Bhutan's agro-ecological potential and proximity to vast consumer markets, major structural problems in the rural sector must be addressed. Stronger marketing and transport infrastructure will lead to improved price signals to producers, lower transaction costs and increased private sector investment.

Since a consolidation of farms is unlikely because of farmers' sentimental attachments to their plots and land policies in Bhutan, farming households must maximize their revenue per land area by pursuing higher value products. However, supply-side constraints associated with a lack of marketing skills, technology and high transportation cost need to be resolved in order for small-holders to benefit fully from such markets (Tobgay, 2006). Small farmers in Bhutan must also cope with the reality of its landlocked position, mountainous terrain and dispersion of farms. The government and policy makers need to recognize the enormous changes taking place in Bhutan's food systems and their implications for small and marginal farmers. Development models, policies and programmes should help smallholders capitalize on opportunities amid a liberalizing agricultural sector.

Road access will improve rural households' access to input and output markets and to consumer staples; it is necessary but not sufficient for improving the market integration of smallholders. Entire marketing systems must be upgraded to allow for cost-effective movement of goods between producers and consumers. Due to cost constraints and the government's stance on conservation, improved road access is not likely to occur in many areas in the near future. For these areas, the best prospect is to develop high-value but low-volume enterprises, where perishability is not a major concern and transport costs are not prohibitive, as they are for bulky commodities in remote areas.

Notes

1   The authors are grateful to Alessandro Porpiglia for performing the econometric analysis reported in this paper.
2   Incidence of poverty is a mostly rural phenomenon, with 38.3 per cent of the rural population falling below the national poverty line compared to 4.2 per cent of the urban population.
3   Not including less productive types of landholdings.
4   According to Dixon et al (2003), the term 'smallholder' refers to limited resource endowments relative to other farmers in the sector. On the other hand, Narayanan and Gulati (2002) characterize a smallholder as 'a farmer (crop or livestock) practising a mix of commercial and subsistence production or either, where the family provides the majority of labour and the farm provides the principal source of income'. Further, Lipton (2005) defines family farms as 'operated units in which most labour and enterprise come from the farm family, which puts much of its working time into the farm'. The World Bank's Rural Strategy defines smallholders as those with a low asset base, operating less than 2 hectares of cropland (World Bank, 2003).
5   The Ngultrum (Nu) is the Bhutanese currency, with a fixed exchange rate against the Indian rupee.
6   This was due mainly to the introduction of new improved varieties and the use of fertilizers.
7   Powertiller tracks are narrow roads wide enough to accommodate small farm tractors but not other vehicles.
8   A one unit decrease in the regressor (walking time to road point) can be interpreted as an increase in the odds ratio by 0.282, the regression coefficient reported in Table 13.7. Therefore, the relative probability of selling increases by $1 - \exp(0.282)$, or 0.326 (see Cameron and Trivedi, 2005).

References

Agriculture Marketing Services (2006) *AMS Vendor Survey in Thimphu Vegetable Market*, A periodical research study carried out for data update in the marketing information systems of the Ministry of Agriculture

Bellotti, P. and Cadilhon, J. (2007) 'A summary analysis of high mountain products sector: Appraisal mission for high value products in Bhutan'

Cameron, A. C. and Trivedi, P. K. (2005) *Microeconomics: Methods and Applications*, Cambridge University Press, Cambridge

Department of Agriculture (2006) 'Walking the extra mile', in Ministry of Agriculture, *Agriculture Statistics 2004*, vol 1 and 2, Royal Government of Bhutan, Thimphu

Department of Revenue and Customs (2004) 'Bhutan trade statistics', Department of Revenue and Customs, Royal Government of Bhutan, Phama Printing and Publishers, Thimphu, Bhutan

Department of Roads (2007) Department of Roads website, [online] www.dor.gov.bt, Department of Roads, Royal Government of Bhutan

Dixon, J., Taniguchi, K. and Wattenbach, H. (eds) (2003) 'Approaches to assessing the impact of globalization on African smallholders: Household and village economy modeling', Proceedings of a working session on Globalization and Small Farmers, Rome

Ghimiray, M. and Wangdi, K. (2006) *Rice Commodity Chain Analysis: Irrigated Rice in the High, Mid and Low Altitudes of Bhutan*. RNR-RC Bajo, Wangduephodrang, Bhutan

Lipton, M. (2005) 'The family farm in a globalizing world: The role of crop science in alleviating poverty. 2020 vision for food, agriculture, and the environment initiative', Discussion Paper No. 40, International Food Policy Research Institute, Washington, DC

Ministry of Agriculture (2002) *Renewable Natural Resource Census 2000*, Thimphu, Bhutan

Narayanan, S. and Gulati, A. (2002) 'Globalization and the smallholders: A review of issues, approaches, and implications', Markets and Structural Studies Division Discussion Paper No. 50, International Food Policy Research Institute, Washington, DC

Planning Commission (2000) 'Poverty assessment and analysis report 2000', Planning Commission, Royal Government of Bhutan

Royal Government of Bhutan (2004) Comparative Socio-economic Indicators for Bhutan, Royal Government of Bhutan

Royal Monetary Authority of Bhutan (2003, 2004) RMA Selected Economic Indicators, December 2003, 2004

Shrestha, S. (2004) *An Economic Impact Assessment of the Rice Research Program in Bhutan*, International Rice Research Institute, Los Banos, Philippines

Tobgay, S. (2006) 'Small farmers and food systems in Bhutan', Food and Agriculture Organization, Rome

Ura, K. (2005) 'Food security a national concern', Research paper written for World Food Programme

World Bank (2003) 'Reaching the rural poor: A renewed strategy for rural development', Washington, DC

Chapter 14

Marketing Channels and their Implications for Smallholder Farmers in India

Sukhpal Singh[1]

Introduction

Agricultural markets in India, as in most countries, are inefficient and imperfect, with temporal and spatial price variations. The producers' share in the consumers' rupee is low, except in a few commodities. In fact, under some circumstances, producers end up with net losses when traders make substantial profits from the same crop; this is the case with potatoes in some parts of India (Mitra and Sarkar, 2003). On the other hand, processors and/or marketers cannot always obtain timely, cost-effective and adequate supplies of quality raw materials. In the current environment of liberalization and globalization, the role of the state in agricultural marketing and input supply is being reduced, with increasing space provided to the private sector to bring about more efficiency in markets.

The procurement practices of supermarkets and large processors have a huge impact on farmers and present them with an important challenge. Through their coordinating institutions and mechanisms such as contracts, private standards, sourcing networks and distribution centres they are reformulating the rules of the game for farmers and first-stage processors (Reardon and Berdegue, 2002). An important issue in globally oriented supply chains is whether small producers can participate and benefit from these chains and markets – which is crucial for their survival as traditional marketing channels weaken or disappear (Pingali and Khwaja, 2004). Small farmers have some advantages for integrating with the supply chains, as they can supply better quality with intensive management attention to each output unit. However, they lack the size to benefit from economies of scale. The net effect of integrated markets on small farmers depends on the nature of the commodity and its market, as well as the ability of small farmers to coordinate marketing activities (Barghouti et al, 2004). In this context, smallholder farmers in India face a number of challenges and can adequately respond to them only if supported by policies and institutions.

In order to examine the situation for small farmers in the context of the commercialization and globalization of Indian agriculture, this chapter explores potato marketing in the Gujarat and Punjab states of India. It identifies mechanisms of small producer inclusion and their implications; examines both production and marketing sectors, with a primary survey of supply chain participants from farmers to retail chains; and looks at risk aspects and the channels for reducing risks. It compares the working of three major market channels for potatoes in Punjab and Gujarat: farm-gate sales, sales through regulated markets called Agricultural Produce Marketing Committees (APMCs) and contract farming, with special focus on case studies of contract farming in potatoes. Finally, the chapter points out policy priorities for facilitating smallholder farmers' adjustment to changing food systems.

Trends in food systems in India

Food retail

Organized retailing accounts for less than 2 per cent of the food retailing industry in India. However, with a projected annual growth rate of 8.3 per cent, it is expected to grow to 20 per cent of total retail by 2008. Food is the largest retail sector, with food and groceries representing 48 per cent of consumer spending. The number of retail outlets grew at the rate of 26 per cent per annum during the period 1996–2001. Food retail outlets account for one-third of all retail outlets and 63 per cent of total retail sales (Chengappa et al, 2005). Most retail outlets are still small, family-owned operations. In recent years, a number of corporate players have entered the organized food retail sector, including large food retailers like RPG, Nilgiris, Viswapiya and Pantaloon, and others that deal in food and fibre products (Table 14.1).

From the demand side, the major drivers of growth in the retail sector and its constituents have been the changing age structure of the Indian population, rising incomes, increasing numbers of employed women, changing food habits (increasing popularity of convenience and western foods) and growing health and food quality consciousness among food buyers and consumers. The growth of large food retailing outlets has contributed to this change from the supply side (Cygnus, 2007). One firm examined in this study, McCain Foods, produces frozen western-style potato-based products such as French fries, wedges and bite-sized nuggets for the Indian market. A new processing facility allows it to displace imports from Holland, New Zealand and Canada. It serves leading fast food

Table 14.1 *Major food retailers in India, by retail format*

Group name	Store brand	Number of stores	Sales (US$ millions, where available)
Hypermarkets (typically 106–1524m²)			
Tata Trent	Star India Bazaar	1	
Shoprite Checkers	Shoprite	3	
RPG	Spencer's	11	8.25
Reliance	Reliance Mart	1	
Supermarkets (typically 305–610m²)			
Pantaloon	Food bazaar	77	225
Nilgiris	Nilgiris	32	19.5
RPG	Spencer's	190**	75
Apna bazaar	Apna bazaar	24	
Zakaria shahid group	Sabka bazaar	92	62.5
Birlas*	More*	170	
Fab Mall		110	
Valdel Retail (Family Mart)		100	
Reliance Fresh (franchised)		175	
ITC Choupal Fresh	Choupal Fresh	3	
Pyramid Retail	True Mart	10	
Namdhari Seeds	Namdhari Fresh	19	17.5
Heritage Foods	Fresh@	24	
Wadhwan Group	Spinach	23	
Discount stores			
Viswapiya	Subhiksha	800	300
Margin Free Markets	Margin Free	300	

Notes: * Formerly Trinethra.
** 7 supermarkets, 3 fresh, 55 express, 125 dailies.
Sources: Author compilation based on Chengappa et al, 2005, various newspaper reports and personal communications

restaurants, hotels and catering companies, while its branded retail products for home consumption are increasingly sold in modern grocery stores and supermarkets across India.

Among the domestic fresh food chains, only a few procure a small part of their requirements directly from farmers. More recently, several European supermarket chains (including Sainsbury's, Safeway [now Morrisons] and Tesco) have begun to procure in India with standards set by GLOBALGAP (good agricultural practices specified by the European Union Retailers Association). Tesco procures greens from India through Mahindra Ltd and Field Fresh Foods and has its own global standards for food, with more than 400 farmers in India supplying the chains with crops that include lychees, mangoes, grapes, potatoes and gherkins (Srinivas, 2005). Other firms such as Radhakrishna Foodland, Adani Agri Fresh Limited and Trikaya Agriculture work as specialized wholesalers providing supply chain support to the retail chains and fast food outlets.

The food processing sector in India

The processed food industry in India was estimated to be worth US$126.5 billion in 2004/05, with a growth rate of 10 per cent (Cygnus, 2007). Processed food exports grew at a rate of 9.8 per cent between 2000 and 2005. The fruit and vegetable processing industry was estimated to be worth US$890 million in 2004/05 (divided equally between organized and unorganized sectors); the level of processing as a percentage of total production was just 1.7 per cent. Levels of processing for other sectors ranged from 37 per cent for milk, 21 per cent for meat, 10.7 per cent for marine fisheries and 6 per cent for poultry to 1.4 per cent for shrimp (Cygnus, 2007). In the Indian food market overall, the processed food segment is only 10 per cent and semi-processed 15 per cent. The food processing sector is dominated by unorganized sector units (42 per cent); the small-scale sector takes another 33 per cent and the organized sector only 25 per cent of all food industry units (CII and McKinsey & Co. Inc., 1997). The food processing sector accounted for 3.3 per cent of total foreign direct investment (FDI) in India between 1991 and 2005. FDI in food processing is fully permitted and has been sought by both the union and the provincial governments since the late 1990s through various incentives. In retail chains, however, only up to 51 per cent foreign equity is allowed in a single retail brand.

Food processing has been promoted recently by such policies as temporary removal by some state governments of licensing requirements for stocking and movement of various grains and oilseeds, removal of plant scale restrictions and licensing requirements for most food processing activities, removal of restrictions on futures trading in 54 commodities, setting up of new commodity exchanges, amendments to the APMC Act in some states to facilitate direct procurement from farmers by the agro-processing entities and development of private markets (Landes and Gulati, 2004).

Potatoes in India

India is one of the top three potato-producing countries of the world, contributing almost 8 per cent of the world's total produce, in spite of low yields. Potato is one of the major traditional and potential commercial vegetable crops in many regions of India, accounting for the largest area and the largest percentage production of vegetables in India (Mittal, 2007). Demand for potatoes has increased in recent years due to new processing plants, product innovations and increased consumption of products like potato chips; consumption of chips/crisps, frozen foods and pasta had double-digit compound annual growth rates between 1998 and 2003 (Cygnus, 2007).

Potato prices are based on size, purpose of use and quality (quality seed, table and undersize). There are significant fluctuations in price (and, therefore, production). Potatoes do not have a minimum support price (MSP) the way many cereal and oilseed crops in India do. There has been a potato futures market in India since 1985, and Indian potatoes are exported to Bangladesh, Nepal, Sri Lanka, the United Arab Emirates, Malaysia, Syria and Mauritius (Mittal, 2007).

Potatoes are consumed widely in India as a vegetable in their cooked form and as raw materials in various snacks prepared at home. They are retailed from every vegetable outlet and available in food outlets ranging from roadside vendors to international chains like McDonalds and Subway. There are opportunities for value addition in potatoes with the setting up of many potato chip and French fry facilities by both national firms and multinational corporations. More recently, low-sugar potato varieties are being grown that have higher yields and good demand from processors and domestic retail chains, who offer a higher price for the variety (Singh, 2007).

The potato crop supply chain is coordinated by private market players using APMC and farm-gate procurement or the more closely coordinated arrangements of contract farming with growers. Contract farming is becoming more common due to the increased presence of food processing firms and retail chains.

Smallholder farmers and Indian agriculture

Agriculture still provides employment to almost 58 per cent of India's work force and contributes 18 per cent of its gross domestic product (GDP). Small farmers with holdings of less than 2ha accounted for 82 per cent of all operational holdings in 2000/01, on 39 per cent of the total area. Large holdings of more than 4ha declined to only 6.4 per cent by 2000/01 and accounted for 37 per cent of the area. The average holding size came down to 1.32ha in 2000/01, with the average size of marginal holdings being only 0.4ha and that of small holdings 1.41ha (Sharma, 2007b). Fragmentation and subdivision of holdings is leading to an increasing amount of area being cultivated by small and marginal holders. Small farmers (including landless) had higher livestock ownership (60–80 per cent of the total livestock population); 12–20 per cent of small-farm and landless households owned livestock compared with only 8–15 per cent of larger-farm households (Jha, 2001). Dairy accounted for more than 50 per cent of the household income of the landless and 30 per cent of that of marginal and small landholders.

Small and marginal farmers are oriented largely toward cereals. A shift towards higher value non-cereal crops could increase income and employment among small and marginal farming households (Sen and Raju, 2006), and the New Agricultural Policy in India emphasizes diversification towards such high-value commodities as fruits, vegetables, livestock and fisheries (and local agro-processing). While the overall GDP growth in agriculture was largely unchanged between the 1980s and 1990s, the composition of the product mix shifted in favour of high-value commodities (Gulati and Mullen, 2003).

Risks in production and marketing

Commercial farming has risks in addition to the natural phenomena that are the intrinsic risks of farming everywhere (Tomek and Peterson, 2001). Whereas production risks can derive from weather, pest and disease attack, low-yielding seeds or increased costs, marketing risks involve market demand, price volatility, seasonality and quality standards. Risks in agriculture can also be institutional, legal or financial (availability of credit, sudden rise in interest rate, unexpected demand to repay or inadequate amount of credit).

In India, large farmers cultivate many crops and prefer highly remunerative crops involving higher costs and more risks due to thin markets, relatively uncertain yields and high perishability (Simmons et al, 2005). Small farmers are typically more cautious, concentrating on fewer and lower-risk traditional crops essential for their survival (Sengupta and Kundu, 2006). The prices of onion, tomato and cabbage varied highly in India in 2006, and the price of potato moderately, compared with low variation for basmati paddy, non-basmati paddy, castor seed and wheat. Some of the latter crops also enjoy MSP protection, which the more perishable crops do not (Sharma, 2007a). While smallholders generally produce higher yields, they are usually paid lower prices. For example, in wheat, marginal holders in India had higher yields per hectare than all other holders, but they realized the lowest prices per quintal and sold the lowest percentage of their output in grain markets (Gandhi and Koshy, 2006).

Risk-reduction options include crop/weather insurance against yield/production risk; state-sponsored tools such as MSP for 24 crops, with market intervention schemes (MIS) for other crops; futures markets and warehouse receipt systems; and diversification of crops and use of risk-reducing inputs (Acharya, 2006). But these risk-reduction measures all have drawbacks. Crop insurance offers a potential for production risk reduction, but has not worked well in India, in part because it does not address market risk (Witsoe, 2006), while MSP and MIS require state interventions that are likely to decrease as the state continues to liberalize the agricultural sector. Futures markets are impractical and risky mechanisms for small and marginal farmers who lack the capacity to store produce.

Public/private partnership is the main route being taken through India's agricultural policy to bring about a transformation in agriculture; the state provides incentives like tax concessions and subsidies, including land, to corporations to enter the agribusiness sector – including through contract farming.[2] Contract farming is seen as a risk-reduction option or policy strategy and is an increasingly utilized model of agricultural coordination, especially in well-endowed states like Punjab and Gujarat. It can be defined as a system for the production and supply of agricultural and allied produce by farmers/primary producers working under advance contracts. In essence it is a commitment to provide a specified quantity of an agricultural commodity at a specified time, price and place to a known buyer; it may involve some or all of these aspects (Singh, 2002).

Both farmers and those who purchase farm products (for processing or marketing) have good reasons to choose contracts over other alternatives (complete vertical integration or spot market participation). For farmers, contracting gives access to additional sources of capital, inputs and technology, and shifts part of the risk of adverse price movements to the buyer (Glover, 1987). For a processor or distributor, contracts are more flexible and reliable in the face of price and supply uncertainty, make smaller demands on scarce capital resources and impose less burden on management in terms of labour relations, land ownership and production activities. Contract farming can be an effective alternative to corporate farming which may be costly, risky and difficult to manage. Contracts also help improve product quality by directly introducing incentives (Wolf et al, 2001). Given that contract farming involves so much diversity in the type of firms, farmers, nature of contracts, crops and socio-economic environment, it is more useful to focus on specific than on generic contract farming situations (White, 1997).

Areas of study: Gujarat and Punjab

In order to examine issues of risk for smallholder farmers in India, and whether contract farming is an appropriate risk-reduction tool, a study was conducted to compare contract market outlets with other outlets from the smallholder's perspective. The states of Gujarat and Punjab were selected because of the presence of contract farming and other factors that characterize the two states.

The western state of Gujarat is the seventh largest state in India. It is a major producer of groundnut, castor, sesame and millet and also produces cotton, tobacco, psyllium, cumin, fennel, sugarcane, sorghum, rice, wheat and red and black gram (pulse crops) (Gujarat, 2006). One-fifth of India's dry lands are located in Gujarat; they are fragile and prone to desertification (Singh et al, 1996). Gujarat is known for its agricultural diversity, which is dominated by non-food crops. It has a high degree of commercialization in these crops and well-established market linkages. Different agro-climatic regions specialize in different crops. Although a relatively late entrant to contract farming of perishables, Gujarat now has quite a few firms engaged in it in various regions and across crops.

Punjab in the east has been at the forefront of the Green Revolution in India, with a high degree of commercialization in food crops (mainly wheat and paddy). It was the first state to actively promote contract farming mechanisms for agriculture, beginning in 2002. Farming in Punjab is highly mechanized and intensive, with farmers taking three crops a year in many districts. Punjab leads India in potato and maize yields (Punjab, 2005) and produces 6 per cent of the

Table 14.2 *Agricultural conditions in Punjab and Gujarat*

Parameter	Punjab	Gujarat	India
Rural poverty ratio, 1999	7%	14%	27%
% of GDP from agriculture	36	16	18
Average size of holding (ha)	3.6	2.6	1.3
% marginal/small landholders	35	55	86
% area under small and marginal holdings	9	21	36
Change in marginal holdings between mid-1980s and mid-1990s	Declined (from 23.5% to 18.7%)	Increased (from 26% to 27%)	Increased
Credit/capita (US$)	310	225	166
Area (km²) per regulated market	74	495	459
NGO presence and social networks	Almost absent	Very high	High
Irrigation (net irrigated area)	95% (gross 97%)	32% (gross 36%)	40%
Reliance on groundwater (% of irrigation water)	80	68	65
Average rainfall (mm)	460	859	1196
Crop diversity	Low	High	High
Production (yield) risk in existing crops	Low	High	High
Staple vs non-staple crop dominance	Staples (but for cash)	Largely cash and non-staples	Largely staple
Cropping intensity	188	111.3	135
No. of tractors/'000ha	104	15	22
No. of tube wells/'000ha	275	99	111
Road density (km road/km²)	0.92	0.38	0.75
Number of rural storage facilities (capacity in million mt)	301.5 (34.98)	52.8 (2.92)	948.3(141.8)
Number of cold storages (capacity in million mt)	35.1 (8.74)	38.2(12.31)	477.9(196.25)

potatoes, 3 per cent of the maize and 2 per cent of the sugarcane produced in the country. The average size of holdings in Punjab increased over five years to 4ha by 2000/01, compared with the Indian trend toward decline. The consolidation of operational holdings in Punjab (due to reverse tenancy) meant that by 2003/04 the average size of marginal and small holdings in Punjab was estimated to have increased to 0.65ha and 1.5ha, respectively (IFPRI, 2006a). Table 14.2 provides further details on agricultural conditions in the two states and in India.

Jalandhar is a top-ranking district in agricultural development in Punjab, traditionally known for potato (especially seed potato) production and trade. It has more than one-quarter of Punjab's area and production of potato and the largest area under vegetable crops in the state, with 90 per cent net sown area and 100 per cent of its area irrigated with tube wells. Jalandhar has more marginal and

Table 14.3 *Distribution of operational holdings in the areas under study*

Place	Farm category					
	Marginal *(<1)*	*Small* *(1–2)*	*Semi-medium* *(2–4)*	*Medium* *(4–10)*	*Large* *(over 10)*	*Average*
Gujarat	27 (6.7)	28 (16)	26 (27.3)	17 (38)	2 (13.6)	2.6
Banaskantha	15 (2.5)	25 (11)	30 (24.7)	26 (45)	4 (17.3)	3.5
Punjab	12 (1.9)	17 (6)	33 (21.8)	30 (43)	7 (27.3)	4.0
Jalandhar	25 (5.4)	16 (7)	30 (23.4)	23 (38)	6 (26.3)	3.5

Note: Figures in parentheses are percentage share of the total area.

Sources: Centre for Monitoring Indian Economy (CMIE), March 2006; *Statistical Abstracts* of Gujarat and Punjab (various issues); figures for Punjab are from 2000/01

small land holdings (45 per cent) than the state average of 35 per cent (Punjab, 2005) but higher than average literacy levels (78 per cent).

Banaskantha is one of the northern districts of Gujarat; it is known for potato, spices and dairy production and has a modest level of agricultural commercialization in general due largely to a lack of canal irrigation and depleted groundwater levels. Its Deesa region previously produced river bed potatoes and now produces more groundwater-irrigated potatoes. Banaskantha has a much lower proportion of small and marginal holdings (13 per cent) compared with the state average (21 per cent) and much larger average land holding size (3.5ha) compared with the state average (2.6ha). It has relatively modest infrastructure (roads, water, etc.) compared with the rest of India.

The two districts selected for study – Banaskantha in Gujarat and Jalandhar in Punjab – are major centres of potato production in India. Both districts have low rainfall and depend heavily on groundwater for irrigation. Banaskantha is linked with Jalandhar via potato seed supply systems. Table 14.3 shows how the districts compare with their respective states with respect to various indicators.

The study involved interviews with various supply chain participants including 126 growers in all (81 in Gujarat and 45 in Punjab). The growers, whether engaged in contract farming or not, were from the same villages, faced similar production and marketing situations and represented proportionally the size of land-holding categories. The cold-storage owners, traders and processors interviewed were from local APMC markets or based in local towns. The only retail chains included in the study were in Ahmedabad (Gujarat).

Potato production overview in Gujarat and Punjab

Gujarat has the highest average yield of potatoes and in 2003/04 produced 3.4 per cent of the total production in India (Sherasiya, 2007). Potato is the largest traded vegetable in APMC markets in Gujarat by volume. There are more than 100 licensed commission agents in each of the vegetable APMC markets in Ahmedabad with a few cooperative societies in some markets. All of the farmers sell to commission agents, who also buy from other traders and cold storages and sell to retailer-traders. The main system of sale is secret bidding (57 per cent) followed by simple transaction (27 per cent) and open auction (16 per cent). The primary producer of potatoes receives about 60 per cent of the consumer price (Gandhi and Namboodiri, 2005). There are large seasonal fluctuations in arrivals of potatoes.

Potato is the most commonly grown vegetable of Punjab, with farmers taking two crops a year (rotating with a third crop of wheat). During the early 1990s, 87 per cent of the cold storage capacity in Punjab was being used for potato only (Singh and Singh, 1996).

In Jalandhar, because potato production is highly capital-intensive (requiring investments in farm machinery such as tractors, potato planters and diggers), small farmers avoid potatoes and prefer wheat/paddy rotation. However, potato was one of the first crops in the state to be grown under contract farming arrangements (IFPRI, 2006a). In 1992/93, the marketed quantity of table potato was around 84 per cent, most of which (93 per cent) was sold in the local market, followed by sale in the farmers' market (6 per cent) and on-farm (1 per cent). The unmarketed amount was used for seed or household consumption or sold locally. The producer's share of the final consumer price was 38 per cent when sold to a retailer directly and 33.5 per cent when sold through a wholesaler (Singh et al, 1996).

Large retail chains for raw potatoes

This section describes two large retail chains in Gujarat: Food Bazaar and Subhiksha. Food Bazaar is a part of the Futures Group (formerly Pantaloon Retail), which runs the Big Bazaar hypermarket chain; it had 77 outlets in 2004 with sales of US$225 million and 2500 employees. It procured mainly through APMC or wholesale traders at vegetable markets (1000–1500kg of vegetables daily). Two registered suppliers procured fruits and vegetables from the local market for all four outlets in Ahmedabad; vendors sorted and graded produce as per specified quality standards to minimize wastage losses (Figure 14.1). The Bazaar paid a 20 per cent commission on procurement price to vendors. Farmers generally avoided selling directly to such a big retail outlet because of difficulties in meeting quantity and quality requirements and fear of losing regular buyers. The Bazaar did not have its own food processing facility, but sold under its store label processed products (like potato chips) manufactured by small private companies in India.

Subhiksha is a discount retail chain of the Chennai-based Viswapriya group, with 800 outlets throughout India (30 in Ahmedabad) and a turnover of US$300 million in 2007. It also runs smaller-sized functional stores and operates four verticals – fruits and vegetables, pharmaceuticals, fast-moving consumer goods and telecommunications. It uses a centralized purchasing system for all its stores. During the months of February and March potatoes were procured directly from the farmers through farm-gate traders (20 per cent) and APMC (10 per cent); between April and October from cold storage in Gujarat; and between November and late January from cold storage in Punjab (all together 70 per cent) (Figure

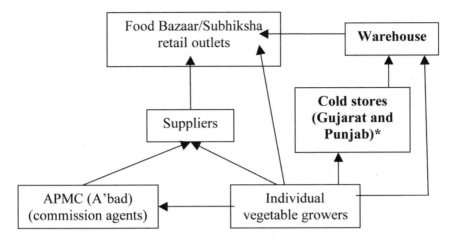

Note: * The bold marked channel is for Subhiksha alone.

Figure 14.1 *Potato procurement system of Food Bazaar and Subhiksha in Gujarat*

14.1). The farmers who supplied Subhiksha agents directly got a higher price than they did selling through a wholesaler. There were several farmers supplying 27 varieties of vegetables directly to retail chains, especially to Subhiksha in cities; retail chains generally took up to 3 metric tons (mt) of vegetables every two weeks. Farmers were hesitant to supply directly to retail chains as they rejected any produce that was not A-grade and did not use preferred supplier lists. Per-day procurement for the entire state of Gujarat was about 5mt. Grading of potatoes was done at Jetalpur before they were sent to retail outlets by 16 labourers who were paid the equivalent of US$1.50–US$2.00 per day. Potato produce loss due to grading was just over 10 per cent. Subhiksha was not engaged in contract farming.

Traders

In Gujarat, the APMC markets in Deesa and Ahmedabad had 50 traders each, either licensed wholesalers or commission agents. For the latter trading was a family business and most did not belong to any trade association; three of the wholesalers participated in the futures market for potatoes. Produce was procured from farmers through auction in the APMC, farm-gate and other traders (in that order); procurement ranged from a high of 300,000mt to a low of 60,000mt per season. Major considerations in procurement were price and quality by visual inspection (dryness, cleanliness, colour and brightness). Most Ahmedabad APMC traders procured from cold stores. Figure 14.2 shows the various potato marketing channels in Gujarat.

Transaction costs (transport, packing and loading/unloading costs) were borne by farmers if brought to the APMC but by traders at farm-gate (who recovered their costs by offering lower prices). However, if the produce was bought

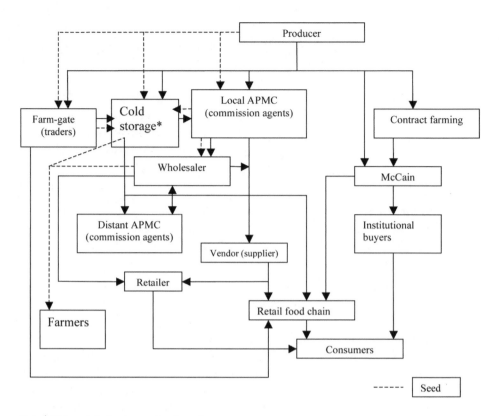

Note: * Only an infrastructure, not a channel.

Figure 14.2 *Marketing channels for potatoes in Gujarat*

from outside Gujarat, farmers bore the costs (excluding market fees and transport). Although there were no formal agreements between traders and farmers, there was significant interlinking of markets as many traders provided seeds and other inputs. Some traders also provided cash advances to farmers, providing 60–70 per cent of the value of potatoes in cold stores before the produce changed hands; final payments were made within a week of (or even upon) delivery. Most traders also stored produce for 7–8 months to realize better selling prices. Many had their own cold stores in the area, although with small capacity (5000–20,000mt each) and others hired facilities. Local traders and supermarkets were major buyers of potato from these traders. Every week, 6–9mt of potato was sold to Subhiksha and Big Bazaar in Ahmedabad. Deesa-based APMC traders sold most of their produce directly to traders, with verbal agreement about quantities, quality and price. Prices were determined on the basis of market demand, quality of the produce and prevailing market prices. Payments to traders came within 15–30 days by cheque or cash. Seed potato purchases by farmers accounted for 20 per cent of the total sales on an average. Typically, a trader had 15–20 retailers as regular buyers who purchased 80 per cent of the quantity sold.

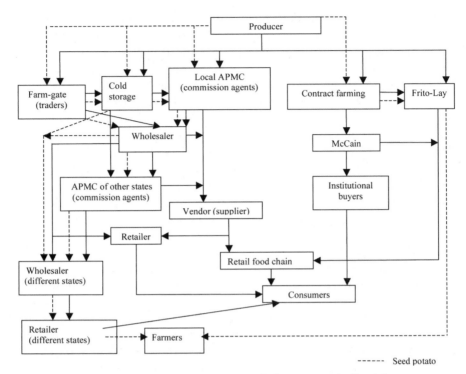

Figure 14.3 *Marketing channels for potatoes in Punjab*

In Punjab, five traders were interviewed who dealt in multiple varieties of potato. Almost 90 per cent of the total procurement of potatoes took place through farm-gate deals, because traders needed to ascertain the quality of the produce purchased, which they could not do in the APMC market where produce was bagged. They normally collected potatoes from villages within a radius of 60km and paid farmers in cash within five days of procurement. They cold-stored the produce from March to December and sent it on to traders in other states; more than 98 per cent of the procured produce was sold outside Punjab (Figure 14.3). Sale of the produce was through advance order, with transaction costs borne by the buyer.

Processors

A major alternative marketing chain is emerging in India with the arrival of large processing firms that have reached agreements with state governments to procure directly from farmers rather than using the official state marketing system. In Gujarat, the potato processing firm is McCain, while in Punjab it is Frito-Lay.

Gujarat: McCain Foods

McCain Foods India (Private) Ltd, a subsidiary of the Canada-based McCain Foods, was established in 1997 and its potato processing facility in Gujarat (Mehsana) became operational in 2007, with a processing capacity of 30,000mt per annum or 4mt per hour. The facility aims to produce French fries and other potato specialties such as flakes, patties, mashed potatoes, *aloo tikki* and wedges for retail and food service businesses across the Indian subcontinent and is expected to employ between 100 and 125 people at full capacity. In addition, it will create indirect employment in storage, supply chain and outsourced services.

Farmers have three options for selling to the company: fixed-price, linked to market price and non-contract sale (Annex Table 14.A). McCain operated in 10 villages of Bansakantha district with 100 contract growers; it also had 10 growers in three villages of Mehsana district and 30 growers in seven villages of Anand district. Contract procurement was divided evenly between fixed price and market-linked price. McCain has been buying its potato stock for processing without contracts, of which 85 per cent was from Gujarat and 15 per cent from Punjab. McCain gets potato seeds produced from seed contract growers.

Punjab: Frito-Lay India

Frito-Lay India, a subsidiary of PepsiCo, has a potato chips unit in Punjab (Channo village, Sangrur district), with the capacity to process 36,000mt of potatoes annually. It employs 50 technical workers in the plant and 25 supervisory and managerial staff. Frito-Lay started contract farming in potatoes in 1997/98 with five varieties imported from the US, which were later reproduced locally and at the company's 12-acre farm. It later set up two more plants in other parts of India (where the contract farming system followed is different than in Punjab).[3] In 2006, contract procurement accounted for about 40 per cent of total procurement. Potato cultivation was phased across regions depending on climatic conditions. Frito-Lay also had 300 potato seed growers and supplied 150mt of seeds to its growers in Jalandhar and more than 2000mt in other places.

Frito-Lay expected a minimum of 5 acres for contract production (although in practice, smaller contract areas were allowed if they fell in a given cluster), plus commitment by the farmers and a progressive attitude to farming. Leased areas could also be put to contract production. Contract prices were generally lower than non-contract (market) prices. The quality for both contract and non-contract produce was determined at the local chip-frying test lab; farmers delivered produce to the factory, where another quality test was carried out. The farmer was not permitted to do contract farming in potatoes for any other company or agency, and defaulters on delivery were blacklisted (Annex Table A.1). The company had established cultivation practices such as size, distance and shape of raised beds, depth of sowing and new varieties of seeds.

Potato procurement with contracts

Both McCain and Frito-Lay worked directly with growers to manage contracts with them, specifying very clearly the quality parameters. They had shifted from acreage contracts toward some hybrid acreage/quantity contracts that specified the minimum quantity to be delivered per area under contract. Both firms expected delivery at a specified place, with growers bearing the delivery costs. There were differences between the two firms: McCain had a smaller area of operation due to its recent entry into India and a more specialized market for its products, and while Frito-Lay paid market prices, McCain offered a range of pricing options to its growers (as long as they kept a certain amount under fixed pricing). Frito-Lay contracts offered only one price for all rejected chip-grade potatoes and could reject produce at its own discretion to buy it at the lower price stipulated for rejected produce; the final quality tests were done at the factory at Channo and undersized potatoes were not returned to the farmer. The McCain contract specified that if there was a deviation of more than 2 per cent in some quality parameters (size, machine damage, mixing of varieties, presence of solid matter), the company could reduce the prices paid by an unspecified amount. The quality aspects generated uncertainty and risk for growers due to information asymmetry and the growers' lower bargaining power.

The contract documents were replete with various obligations on the part of the farmer with regard to quality maintenance, quantity, cultivation practices, post-harvest care of the produce, etc., but with very little obligation on the part of the company. All production risks were borne by the farmers and neither firm provided any reprieve to a contract farmer in case of crop failure. Even having entered into a contract and followed all instructions, there was uncertainty about whether the producer would have a market because neither firm's contract obliged the company to buy the produce.

Potato contracts in practice: Small farmers

Aspects of contracting that can contribute to the exclusion of small producers (directly or indirectly) include high transaction costs for procuring firms; quality standards and high rates of product rejection; delayed, reduced or absent payments; and the weak bargaining power of the small growers (Kirsten and Sartorius, 2002). Contracting firms can impose eligibility conditions for contract participants such as minimum or maximum land holdings, prohibitions on non-contract crop production in neighbouring fields and certification requirements, especially in seed production (Simmons et al, 2005), all of which can directly or indirectly exclude small farmers from participating. In contract farming every-where, agribusiness firms have less interest and ability to deal with small-scale farmers on an individual basis (Hazell, 2005), preferring large farmers because of their efficient and business-oriented farming methods; large production volumes that reduce the cost of collection; better traceability of produce; capacity to bear risk in case of crop failure; and various services such as transport and storage (Key and Runsten, 1999; Simmons et al, 2005).

By and large, both of the firms studied worked with large or very large growers by Indian standards. Among the sample farmers only one contract grower with McCain had operational land holdings of less than five acres (although McCain did buy from some small growers without contracts) (Table 14.4). A recent Punjab-based study of contract farming showed that the average size of the operational holding of contract growers was more than one and a half

Table 14.4 *Potato growers in Gujarat, by marketing channel*

Contracting agency parameters (average per farmer)	McCain CF	McCain NCF	Farm-gate growers	APMC growers
No. of farmers surveyed	21	17	20	23
Operational holding (acres)	19.2	22.8	4.6	8.9
Owned land (acres)	18.9	21.8	4.4	8.0
Leased land (acres)	0.29	0.97	0.16	0.83
Plots per farmer (number)	1.9	1.8	1.1	1.3
Land under sprinkler (acres)	12.5	8.0	0.2	2.8
Percentage of farmers with sprinkler	100	41	10	26
Tube wells per farmer (number)	1.9	1.6	0.95	1.4
Tractors per farmer (number)	1.1	1.1	0.4	0.6
Area under potato (acres)	15.4	17.9	3.6	7.7
Area under contract potato (acres)	4.0	5.8	—	—
Area under potato as % of operational holding (average)	81	78	79	86
Area under contract as % of operational holding (average)	21	26	—	—
McCain potato area as % of total potato area	26	33	—	—

times that of the non-contract growers. It found 'no marginal farmer in the size group of below one hectare ... operating under contract farming. A handful of small farmers in the size group of one to two hectares were operating' (Kumar, 2006, p5369). Another study noted that 'the majority of the acreage registered in the project (contract farming by Punjab Agro Foodgrains Corporation) is held by larger farmers, who tended to receive greater benefits from participation (in contract farming)' (Witsoe, 2006, p16).

Comparison across Gujarat's marketing channels

Producers growing on contract for McCain owned most of their holdings, all of them had sprinkler systems (compared with only 40 per cent of non-contract growers) and more than half of their land was under sprinkler irrigation, with an average of almost two tube wells per holding.

Growers spread their risk by choosing to put only limited areas under contract and keeping other marketing options open for the rest of the produce. Farmers selling to McCain, with or without a contract, devoted only 20 per cent and 25 per cent of their total holdings, respectively, to such production. Another recent study in India reported other contract growers putting only 15 per cent of their total cropped area under contracts to cover the risk of rejection of contracted produce on quality grounds (Kumar, 2006).

Seventy per cent of McCain growers were involved in some non-farm occupation besides farming, including dairying, ownership of cold stores, grain

Table 14.5 *Reasons McCain suppliers chose non-contract option over contracts*

Reasons	% of farmers
Lower prices under contract	50
Lower prices under contract; no sprinkler	6
Waiting to see experience of fellow farmers	6
Not happy with contract farming in past	31
Could not say	6

market operations (trading or commission agency), input dealing and diamond polishing. Most (85 per cent) had Kisan Credit Cards (KCCs), a credit delivery mechanism for farmers. All of them owned tractors and most of them (90 per cent) also had diggers and planters, threshers, cultivators and rotovators, which are needed in potato cultivation. McCain non-contract farming growers also owned tube well(s), had credit cards and owned tractors and other mechanical farm equipments. They chose the non-contract farming option because they perceived contract prices to be lower than market prices or had bitter experiences with contract farming in the past (Table 14.5).

Most farm-gate growers in the Deesa region of Bansakantha district were involved in other occupations such as dairying, diamond-cutting work, manual labour, shopkeeping or trading in the towns. More than two-thirds of them did not own a tractor and fewer still owned potato planters, cultivators and threshers. Most of the growers did not have KCCs for credit but three-quarters of them did have credit, mostly from banks and traders who bought their produce. All medium and large APMC growers owned at least one tube well, half owned a tractor, one-third owned potato planters and about half (the medium and large farmers) owned cultivators. Only about half of them had non-farm occupations. The major sources of inputs (mostly fertilizers) were from the Primary Agricultural Co-operative Societies (PACS) and local dealers. Small farmers used only APMC and farm-gate channels whereas medium and large farmers also used cold-storage facilities and sold in distant markets. A major problem for APMC potato growers was the sale of spurious potato seed by local input dealers claiming that it was high-quality seed from Punjab.

Comparison across Punjab's marketing channels

Contract growers for Frito-Lay in Punjab had average operational holdings of 63 acres, with only 22 acres owned and the rest leased. None of the contract growers with Frito-Lay that we interviewed had less than 10 acres of land, in spite of the fact that the average size of holdings in the state is 9 acres and 70 per cent have holdings below 10 acres each.[4] Growers had as many as seven plots, with two tractors per holding and more than six tube wells. They devoted 50 per cent of their area to potato and 26 per cent of the potato area to the contract crop (34 acres to potato and 16 acres to contract potato for Frito-Lay) (Table 14.6). They were generally quite literate and more than 50 per cent made use of PACS

Table 14.6 *Potato growers in Punjab, by marketing channel*

Parameters (all average)	Contracting agency		
	Frito-Lay contract growers	APMC growers	Farm-gate growers
Number of farmers	14	15	16
Operational holding (acres)	63	39	34
Owned land (acres)	22	19	22
Leased land (acres)	41	20	12
Number of plots per farmer	7	5	3
Number of tractors per farmer	2	1	1
Number of tube wells per farmer	6.4	5.7	4.1
Area under potato (acres)	34	23	20
Area under contract potato (acres)	16	–	–
Area under potato as % of operational holding	53	59	60
Area under contract potato as % of operational holding	26	–	–

services, mostly to buy fertilizers and credit. All of the sampled growers had a history of selling to Frito-Lay before the company took up potato contracting and many were now growing new varieties for the company. Major reasons for contracting included an assured market and stable and better prices.

APMC growers in Punjab had average holding sizes of 39 acres, about half of it owned and half leased. They had an average of six tube wells each and put almost 60 per cent of their area to potato (Table 14.6). These farmers were involved mostly in potato seed production, a high-cost operation that only such growers could afford. The main reason for not engaging in contract farming was that they had not been approached by any company; they were willing to enter into a contract if fixed prices were offered, in order to achieve higher and more stable prices, an assured market and better quality seed (Table 14.7). Major reasons for the purchase of input from given sources was proximity, timeliness, credit facility and quality. The major problems they faced were price fluctuations,

Table 14.7 *Reasons contract growers took up contracts (% per firm)*

Reason	Firm	
	McCain	Frito-Lay
Need for stable prices	95	36
Assured markets	–	71
Better prices	–	36
Services provided by the company	5	14
Demonstration effect of fellow farmers	86	–

Note: Total adds up to more than 100 per cent because some respondents gave multiple reasons.

Table 14.8 *Risk, reward and cost profiles of various channels in potatoes*
(CF=contract farmers)

| | Marketing channel | | | | |
	McCain CF	McCain Non-CF	Frito-Lay CF	APMC	Farm-gate
Risk (More stars = higher risk)					
Input price	*	***	*	***	***
Input quality	*	***	**	***	***
Yield	**	*	***	***	***
Output price	*	**	*	***	***
Output quality	*	**	**	***	***
Marketing costs	*	*	*	*	*
Policy/institutional/legal	***	*	***	*	*
Ecological/environmental/natural resource-related	*	*	*	*	*
Reward (More stars = higher reward)					
Input quality	***	**	**	*	*
Extension	***	NA	***	NA	NA
Credit	NA	NA	*	***	***
Mechanization	***	***	***	**	***
Degree of production control	***	*	***	*	*
Yields	***	***	*	*	*
Prices	**	***	**	*	*
Timeliness of payment	*	***	*	***	***
Quality price incentives	***	**	***	*	*
Costs (More stars = lower costs)					
Production	***	**	***	*	*
Inputs	*	*	*	***	***
Grading and packing	***	***	***	*	*
Transport	*	*	*	*	***
Storage costs	NA	NA	NA	**	*

low prices, high marketing costs and lack of farm-gate sales. The farmers agreed that the demand for potato was increasing due to the entry of new companies into the market. Almost half of them sold produce immediately after harvest and others within four months (after cold storage).

Most farm-gate growers in Punjab had operational holdings of 34 acres with two-thirds owned and the rest leased (Table 14.6). They had high rates of tube well and tractor ownership but lower rates of ownership of diggers, planters, threshers and drillers. Potato, paddy and to some extent mint were important crops for these growers. Major non-farm sources of income included dairy and non-resident Indian remittances, but 43 per cent had no non-farm occupation.

Two-thirds of the growers had membership in PACS. The major sources of fertilizers and seeds were input dealers, followed by PACS. The major problems for potato cultivation for this group were blight, shortage of fertilizers, high cost of inputs and low-quality seed.

Growers who marketed through farm-gate sales said they received better prices than through other channels and saved on transportation and other trans-action costs. However, they cited the marketing problems of price fluctuations and high marketing costs. Produce rejected at the farm gate was sold in the APMC. Unlike in Gujarat, none of the growers got pledge finance from traders. The major reason they gave for not engaging in contract farming was that they had not been approached by any company. See Table 14.8 for risk, reward and cost profiles of various channels in potatoes.

Results and experiences

One difference across channels and states was the role the farmers wanted the state to play: in Punjab, farmers called for an MSP for potatoes, which they have enjoyed for wheat and paddy for decades. They also wanted monitoring of contract farming. In Gujarat, farmers wanted the state to play a role with regard to monitoring the quality of seeds and other inputs (Table 14.9).

We found a clear trend of operational consolidation in Punjab; contract farming is likely to further reinforce the trend, leading to a decline in the number of operational holdings (Singh, 2002). The proportion of small and marginal holdings in Punjab declined from 45 per cent of the total in 1990/91 to 30 per cent in 2000/01 (Gill, 2005). Reverse tenancy provides some income for small-holders and allows larger farmers to increase their economies of scale, but in areas that are less developed in agriculture, this practice may alienate marginal and small farmers from land altogether, without alternative sources of employment

Table 14.9 *Where growers want the state to play a role in agriculture*

	Minimum support price	Crop insurance	Contract farming	Quality input supply, extension	Monitoring of contract farming
Contract farmers (Gujarat)	No	No	Farm-gate procurement	N/A	No
Contract farmers (Punjab)	Yes	Yes	Purchase of rejected/lower quality produce	N/A	Yes; should guarantee price
Non-CF (Gujarat)	No	No	No	N/A	N/A
APMC (Gujarat)	No	No	No	Yes	N/A
APMC (Punjab)	Yes	Yes	Yes	Yes	N/A
Farm-gate (Gujarat)	No	No	No	Yes	N/A
Farm-gate (Punjab)	Yes	Yes	Yes	Yes	N/A

(Haque, 2000). While contract farming can reduce some risks and transaction costs for small farmers, it can also hurt them because of their lack of bargaining power (small farmers in India are not well organized[5]), a lack of alternative markets and because of ineffective regulation and enforcement of contracts by the state. Thus, the role of contract farming in agricultural development is limited.

Economics of potato production

The cost of production for McCain potato contract growers was found to be slightly lower than the McCain non-contract growers but much higher than the APMC and farm-gate sellers. The yield and transaction costs for McCain contract growers were higher than in all other channels; net income per acre was higher than the farm-gate and APMC sellers but lower than that for McCain non-contract sellers (Table 14.10). Marketing costs were higher for growers involved with McCain than they were for the APMC alternative, while net income from McCain was higher compared with income from alternative channels. Variation in net income between growers in the same category was much less in the case of contract growers because of fixed prices. The McCain contract farmers found that the use of sprinklers rather than flood irrigation reduced their labour requirements, improved soil quality and increased potato yields and quality, besides saving on water and its extraction cost. These advantages extended to other crops as well.

In the case of Frito-Lay, the cost of production was higher and transaction costs somewhat lower than for APMC and farm-gate growers despite the fact that contract growers had to deliver to a factory. Gross and net income was lower than that of growers using other channels due to lower yields; contract prices for high-quality produce and rejected produce were lower than post-harvest and off-season prices (Table 14.11). The trend was for farmers directly supplying the

Table 14.10 *Average costs, yields and income from potatoes in Gujarat, by channel*

	Contract farming (CF)	Non-CF	Farm-gate	APMC
Production costs (rupees/acre)	42,852	43,813	36,276	37,914
Yield (quintal/acre)	163	150	115	122
Price* (rupees/quintal)	450	512	465	452
Transaction costs (rupees/acre)	9,037	5,671	0	4,518
Gross income** (rupees/acre)	71,918	74,831	53,650	52,210
Net income (rupees/acre)	20,029	25,346	17,375	12,278

Notes: 39 Rupees = US$1.

* Price shown is for the main channel. Farmers invariably sold a portion of their production outside of the main channel for various reasons.

** For produce sold to McCain, it is assumed that 95 per cent of produce is sold at the specified price, and 5 per cent is rejected and sold at the price of Rs250/qtl. For farm gate producers, 100 per cent of produce is sold at the main price. For APMC growers, gross income calculations considered prices and sale in both channels.

Table 14.11 *Average costs, yields and income from potatoes in Punjab, by channel*

Channel	CF	APMC	Farm-gate
Production cost (rupees/acre)	30,504	28,878	28,758
Yield (quintal/acre)	84	91	105
Price* (rupees/acre)	596	481	394
Transaction costs (rupees/acre)	6800	7184	4342
Gross income** (rupees/acre)	40,718	49,700	43,706
Net income (rupees/acre)	3414	13,639	11,149

Notes: * Price shown is for the main channel. Farmers invariably sold a portion of their production outside of the main channel for various reasons.

** For produce sold to Frito-Lay, 95 per cent of produce is sold at the specified price, and 5 per cent is rejected and sold at the price of Rs250/qtl. For farm gate producers, 100 per cent of produce is sold at the main price. For APMC growers, gross income calculations considered prices and sale in all the four (APMC, distant market, cold store, and farm-gate) channels.

companies to have higher production costs, regardless of whether a contract was involved, than those with other market outlets.

According to this study, in Punjab the net income was lower for growers working with Frito-Lay, although marketing costs for contract farmers with Frito-Lay were lower than the APMC alternative. Another study of Frito-Lay growers in Punjab showed that potato yields under contracts were lower and the cost of production higher, but reported that net returns were still higher than they were on non-contract fields due to better prices and quality-linked incentives (IFPRI, 2006a). An input supply and contract farming programme for potatoes in Haryana also showed higher net returns for contract growers compared with those for non-contract growers due to higher yields and higher prices, although the cost of cultivation was also higher (Tripathi et al, 2005); a more recent study across crops, companies and locations in Punjab confirmed similar results (Kumar, 2006).

Farmer experiences with potato contracts

Farmer defaults for both companies were 10 per cent; default rates were lower when the firm was involved with input supply and support for micro-irrigation. In case of delayed procurement for various reasons, Frito-Lay growers sold the produce in the open market and the company blacklisted defaulters.

Farmers' main concerns were payment, input supply, extension, credit, market assurance, better technology and yields, and profitability of the crop under contract. McCain contract farmers complained about high transport costs of delivering to the company, while the fact that McCain stipulated verbally that the contract growers adopt micro-irrigation systems has important implications for both farmers and society at large. One major problem faced by Frito-Lay contract growers was the variety used (Atlanta), which was susceptible to seed cracking problem and blight disease; farmers suffering from blight infestations received no support from the company.

Another problem was rejection rates: farmers reported that Frito-Lay rejected 46 per cent of produce marketed to it, with some farmers experiencing a rejection rate as high as 62 per cent. This raised the question of whether extension is weak, varieties being promoted are not suitable to the local growing conditions, or even if rejection is a ploy to buy the rejected produce at lower cost. Farmers argued that the quality check should be final before produce is loaded from the farm, given that the rejected potatoes are a processing variety that cannot be used for seed purposes.

Furthermore, the Frito-Lay contract stipulated farmer payment within 15 days of produce delivery, but payment was often delayed for up to two months. Frito-Lay had introduced new technologies and practices like spacing in planting and storage on farm after the harvest, but in case of excess production during a good crop year, the company increased the quality parameters and rejected the contract growers' produce. Farmers resented that the company set strict rules but was not required to adhere to any agreements. Growers said that growing for Frito-Lay was initially profitable but that stagnant contract prices and the rising costs of cultivation of new varieties with lower yields had led to losses.

Public policy for contract farming

Because the objectives of contract farming are sometimes conflicting, it is difficult to design effective public policy interventions for it and organize growers around it (Glover, 1987). Contract farming performance is determined not only by resources and technology but also by the relationship among state, companies and farmers, which interact with formal and informal institutions (Ornberg, 2003). Legal and institutional provisions are required to regulate and monitor contracts and facilitate their smooth functioning, in order to reduce the negative effects of the system on some farmers.

Legal frameworks

It is difficult to regulate contract farming because of the multiple variables involved, including output price, input prices and supply, payments and quality standards (Glover, 1987; Wolf et al, 2001). Typically, terms are written in such a way that firms ultimately have leeway in how the contracts are implemented and governments cannot do much to enforce them – nor can they (or should they) impose contracts on an unwilling firm. The state/government may not always support small growers due to pressures from agribusiness interests or because of the conflicting objectives of its various agencies. Policy interventions at the margin are unlikely to turn contract farming into a silver bullet for the reduction of poverty among smallholders; therefore, expectations for the role of policy in contract farming should be revisited and an appropriate niche for smallholder contract farming should be defined, using experiences elsewhere as a reference (Glover, 1987).

Legal protection to contract growers as a group must be considered to protect them from the harmful effects of contracting as practised by some supply chain actors. Japan provides examples of cases of legal protection provided to subcontracting industries in relation to large firms. These laws specify duties (including a clear written contract) and acts that are forbidden for the parent firm, such as a refusal to receive delivery of commissioned goods, delaying payment beyond the agreed period, discounting payment, returning commissioned goods without good reason, forced price reduction, compulsory purchase by subcontractors of the parent firm's products and forcing subcontractors to pay in advance for materials supplied by the parent firm. These provisions are monitored by the country's Fair Trade Commission. Most violations by parent firms were on the the form and terms of the contracts (Sako, 1992).

If contract farming is the application to farm production of the flexible production systems prevalent in industry, then it is logical to extend the legal provisions of industry to farming contracts (with the necessary modifications). There are also lessons to be learned from legislation designed specifically to make contract farming more transparent and fair. One example comes from the State of Minnesota (US): the Model Producer Protection Act of 2000 requires contracts to be in plain language and disclose material risks; provides a three-day cancellation period for the producer (allowing time to discuss production contracts with advisers); gives producers first priority in case of company bankruptcy; protects against the undue cancellation of contracts; and prohibits 'tournaments' (contracts where compensation to growers is determined by performance relative to other growers) (Stokes, 2006). Vigorous bargaining by cooperatives or other agricultural producer organizations is needed to negotiate equitable contracts and to facilitate the involvement of state regulatory agencies.

The APMC Act

In India, the State Agricultural Produce Marketing Committee (Development and Regulation) Act of 2003 (APMC Act) contributed to the legal reform process for agricultural marketing. The amended APMC Act includes mandatory and optional provisions regarding contract farming. Mandatory provisions cover who can undertake contract farming (as a buyer or seller), details about the land under contract, duration of contract, description of farm produce and other specifications in contracts. The optional aspects include quantity or acreage of crop, quality specifications for produce and penalties for inferior quality, crop delivery arrangements, pricing and credit mechanisms, farmer asset indemnity, compulsory registration of contracts with the local authorities and a procedure for dispute resolution.

The model contract agreement is quite fair in terms of sharing of costs and risks between sponsor and grower (GoI, 2003). But the Act does not offer farmers penalties for delayed payments and deliveries or contract cancellation, even if they make firm-specific investments or are pressured into entering a contract; does not require sponsors to disclose material risks or share in production risks; and does not prohibit competitive performance-based payment schemes.

Organizational mechanisms

In India there is a striking absence of the farmer/producer organizations at the village level necessary for promoting and protecting small producers' interests. Collective purchase and sale can lower transaction costs both for producers and buyers and give producers bargaining power. Producers' organizations create opportunities for producers to get more involved in value-adding activities such as input supply, credit, processing, marketing and distribution. In contract arrangements with small producers in west African countries during the 1970s, cotton contract farming companies transferred some operational and functional responsibilities to village associations organized by traditional village authority structures, providing the associations with capacity building to perform these tasks. This arrangement was highly successful (Bingen et al, 2003). In India, RPG Spencers passed on all the post-harvest value-adding activities (cleaning, grading, cutting, pre-packing fruits and vegetables and bar coding) to farmer groups, with products sent directly to retail stores. Farmers share in value addition opportunities while companies save on the costs of running a distribution centre.

Group contract farming can prove beneficial for both growers and companies by reducing defaults by either of the parties because of the mechanisms of social pressure, incentive structure and group incentives (Ornberg, 2003). (Measures such as providing a 'menu of contracts' and performing an individual risk rating before a contract is signed also help reduce defaults.) Options for organizing farmers include self-help groups, farmer groups, farmer associations and cooperatives, especially new generation cooperatives.[6] A recent National Bank for Agriculture and Rural Development (NABARD) initiative in Gujarat to link 1800 farmers' clubs to corporate buyers of agricultural produce is a welcome step (Thakkar, 2007). Innovative ways to provide financing to small producers is also needed (Schwentesius and Gomez, 2002). Competition between agribusiness firms may be useful: contract farming in gherkins in Karnataka (India) was successful due to the fact that more than two dozen companies operated in the state; competition forced them to offer better terms to smallholder farmers.

Role of the state

The state and others should help organize contract growers into groups for their inclusion into value chains and for collective negotiation with contracting agencies.[7] However, for a number of reasons contract farming is best left to the company and the growers (Singh, 2005). State-sponsored contract farming in Punjab did not achieve its aim of diversifying from wheat/paddy rotation. The programme did not take into account the selection of crops for contracting, development of effective contract enforcement and dispute resolution systems, limiting fiscal risks to the state government, limiting the number of parties in a contractual arrangement and developing farmers' organizations capable of contracting with sponsors (World Bank, 2003). There have also been instances of corruption and malpractice due to conflicts of interest among implementing agencies and lack of monitoring (Singh, 2005). The Government of Punjab used to reimburse extension costs to contract farming agencies, irrespective of the size of the holding of the contract growers. Similarly, the Ministry of Food Processing Industries used to provide incentives for procuring from contract farming (reimbursement of 5 per cent of the value of raw materials) without regard to whether small/marginal farmers were involved.

In contrast, the AM Todd contract farming system for producing mint (with no involvement of the state) was successful due to the nature of the crop, clear contract terms, assured returns to growers by competitive prices and the commitment of the company. The state should rather encourage the organization of producers into producer companies under the new provision in this regard under the Indian Companies Act.

Regulation of supermarket chains to control or mitigate their market power is a potential tool for ensuring the presence of small growers in value chains. However, regulations do not ultimately change the economic forces that drive the procurement systems of the supermarkets. These changes and the conditions they impose on growers will have to be met if the growers are to share in high-growth opportunities offered by supermarkets. It is crucial that government and donor agencies help small farmers and entrepreneurs make the investments in equipment, management, technology, commercial practice (including product planning), market information and the development of strong and efficient organizations to meet those requirements.

The functioning of traditional markets (APMC) needs to be improved to enhance their cost efficiency so that producers and consumers can realize better prices. The amended APMC Act allows for the setting up of private markets; it is also necessary to require an open auction system, improve buyer competition in markets, provide better facilities such as cold storage and improve farmers' access to market information (Gandhi and Namboodiri, 2005). These markets are important to small farmers and even a significant proportion of medium and large farmers, who still depend on them; they also serve as the main competitors to contract farming and can help to improve the terms offered to contract growers.

Role of NGOs

There is a role for NGOs to intervene in contract situations as intermediaries to protect the interests of farmers and rural communities. NGOs can also play a role in information provision and in monitoring contracts. Intermediation is needed in agro-processing, credit, market access, information and technology to enable small farmers to reap the enhanced competitive benefits offered by freer markets.

Annex Table 14.1 *A comparative profile of contract farming operations of McCain Foods in Gujarat and Frito-Lay in Punjab*

	McCain	Frito-Lay
Type	World's largest producer of French fries, accounting for one third of world total; operates in 110 countries, with 55 plants and 20,000 employees	Subsidiary of PepsiCo, which has operations in 150 countries and runs three fast-food chains. Accounts for two-thirds of PepsiCo's revenues and is the largest snack company in the world
No. of farmers	145	250 contract farmers (total incl. non-contract: 800)
Contracted acreage	700	1700 (500 under contracts)
Average holding size (acres)	19	63
Average area under contract per grower (acres)	4	16.29
Nature of contract	Acreage but minimum quantity (multiplication ratio of 1:8)	Acreage and minimum quantity
Pricing formula	Contract A purchase price Rs*360/bag of 81.33kg (fixed price)	Contract B purchase price band of Rs320–380/bag on basis of prevailing market rate. Otherwise, rate between Rs320 and 380. Fixed price for every 10 days of delivery from 20 Nov. to 31 Dec., ranging from Rs*5.25 to 4.80/kg. Rejected potato, Rs0.5/kg.
Input supply	Gunny bags at cost, to be deducted on delivery of produce; seeds only in case of its own varieties	Seeds to some, at part or full payment
Technical services	Free of cost	Free of cost
Quality	40mm size; machinery damaged produce not >1%; hollow produce not >1%; no rotten potatoes. Only up to 1% green and heat-affected potatoes; common scab not to exceed 1%; no ill-shaped	The minimum QC standards for total potato defects (TPoD)<=15 & solids >=16, both inclusive undersize max 3% and oversize max 5%. The tolerances on undersize (45 mm)/oversize (85mm) specified. Only < 3% undersize potato acceptable with 'zero payout'. External (total 10%) and

	potatoes; black-eyed, infected potato not >1% in weight; no mixed variety of potato; potato gunny bags not to contain dust, waste or any other matter; potato sprouts not > 5mm long; minimum 19% solid matter in potato needed; no potato tuber moth-infested potatoes; and specific gravity should not < 1.075. If difference of >2% in size, machine damaged proportion, mixed varieties and specific gravity, reduces the price	internal defect (total 5%) maximum limits for each defect specified in % of the lot. Incentives for higher % solids and lower % TPoD
Delivery	At cold store, before March	At company plant at Channo
Payment	Within 15 days after delivery	Within 15 days after delivery
Major markets	Domestic institutional and retail sales	India and export to neighbouring countries
Crop failure	Attributed to carelessness by farmer	No compensation or responsibility
Penal clauses	Company can file a complaint against growers who renege on contract terms	No

Note: *Rs=Rupees (39 Rupees = US$1).

Sources: based on primary evidence, contract agreements and company interviews

Conclusions

Because of the high production costs and high market risks involved in diversifying into higher value crops, very few of the small farmers in the regions studied were able to do so. In order to avoid the exclusion of small and marginal farmers from such opportunities, it is important that policies facilitate their inclusion into the contract farming projects, stipulating a certain minimum percentage, as is the case with micro-irrigation schemes that subsidize irrigation equipment.

Contract farming across crops and regions in India is likely to spread due to food supermarket chain growth; international trade and quality issues like sanitary and phytosanitary (SPS) measures; government promotion of organic, fair and ethical trade; and banking and input industry impetus in the presence of a farming crisis and reverse tenancy. While there are concerns about the ability of small farms to survive in the changing environment of agribusiness, there are still opportunities for them to exploit. Perhaps the most promising route is by exploitation of economies of scale through networking or clustering and alliances such as contract farming (Kirsten and Sartorius, 2002).

The experience of contract farming across the globe suggests that if there are sufficient mechanisms to monitor and use contracts for development, they can certainly lead to improved conditions for all parties involved – including small and marginal farmers. Important conditions for successful partnering between agribusiness firms and small producers include increased competition for procurement instead of monopsony, guaranteed markets for farmers' produce, effective repayment mechanisms, market information for farmers to effectively bargain with companies, large volumes of transactions through groups of farmers and no alternative sources of raw material for firms (Kirsten and Sartorius, 2002).

In Gujarat and Punjab, contract farming can be a powerful tool for linking smallholders with new markets. Without intervening directly, the state can play an enabling role by supporting regulatory and institutional mechanisms to facilitate contract farming in a way that is accessible to and equitable towards smallholders.

Notes

1   The author would like to sincerely thank Prabhu Pingali and Ellen McCullough of the FAO, Rome for their very elaborate and serious comments on the draft of this chapter and the overall support during the course of the study on which the chapter is based. He would also like to thank Jayesh Talati, Alka Swami, Yamuna Pillai and Perwinder Singh Bhatia for their support in data collection and processing.

2   These policies are also being aggressively pursued through the National Horticulture Mission, the National Agriculture Innovation Project of the World Bank and the United States–India Knowledge Initiative (Witsoe, 2006).

3   The contract farming system of Frito-Lay in other areas is based on intermediaries: local traders in Maharashtra, farmers' associations in Karnataka and micro-finance institutions in Jharkhand. About 90 per cent of its contract farmers in Punjab grow other crops (often basmati and/or maize) under contract, in addition to potatoes.

4   Frito-Lay's figures are that 30 per cent of its growers are holders of less than 10 acres (semi-medium), 40 per cent of 10–20 acres (medium) and 30 per cent more than 20 acres each (large or very large).

5   Only 2.2 per cent are members of any farmer association and only 4.8 per cent of farming households have a member belonging to a self-help group (SHG). In Punjab the numbers are only 0.3 per cent and 1.5 per cent respectively (Witsoe, 2006).

6   New-generation cooperatives (NGCs) are voluntary, market-oriented, responsive to members, self-governed and have limited membership; grower members have contractual equity (Singh, 2004; Hazell, 2005).

7   It is important to recognize that there may be difficulties in enforcing collective actions due to group heterogeneity, agency resistance to such actions and the absence of any legal authority with such groups (Glover, 1987).

References

Acharya, S. S. (2006) 'Risks in agriculture: Some issues', *Agricultural Economics Research Review*, vol 19, no 1, pp1–9

Barghouti, S., Kane, S., Sorby, K. and Ali, M. (2004) 'Agricultural diversification for the rural poor – guidelines for practitioners', ARD Discussion Paper No. 1, World Bank, Washington, DC

Bingen, J., Serrano, A. and Howard, J. (2003) 'Linking farmers to markets: Different approaches to human capital development', *Food Policy*, vol 28, pp405–419

Chengappa, P. G., Achoth, L., Rashmi, K., Degga, V., Reddy, B. and Joshi, P. K. (2005) 'Emergence of organised retail chains in India during post liberalization era', paper presented at the South Asia Regional Conference, Globalization of Agriculture in South Asia: Has it made a Difference to Rural Livelihoods?, Hyderabad, India, 20–25 March

CII and McKinsey & Co. Inc. (1997) *Food and Agriculture Integrated Development Action (FAIDA) – modernising the Indian food chain*, Confederation of Indian Industry (CII) and McKinsey & Co. Inc.

Cygnus (2007) *Food Processing India*, Cygnus Business Consulting and Research, Hyderabad

Gandhi, V. P. and Koshy, A. (2006) 'Wheat marketing and its efficiency in India', IIMA Working Paper No. 2006-09-03, Indian Institute of Management, Ahmedabad (IIMA), Ahmedabad, September

Gandhi, V. P. and Namboodiri, N. V. (2005) 'Fruit and vegetable marketing and its efficiency in India: A study of wholesale markets in the Ahmedabad area', in J. Sulaiman, F. M. Arshad and M. N. Shamsudin (eds) *New Challenges Facing Asian Agriculture Under Globalization*, vol 2, pp520–538, Proceedings of the Asian Society of Agricultural Economists (ASAE) Conference, 2002, Kuala Lumpur, Malaysia

Gill, S. S. (2005) 'Diversification of Punjab agriculture: A faulty design and bureaucratic apathy', mimeo

Glover, D. (1987) 'Increasing the benefits to smallholders from contract farming: Problems for farmers' organizations and policy makers', *World Development*, vol 15, no 4, pp441–448

Government of India (GoI) (2003) *Contract Farming Agreement and its Model Specifications*, Ministry of Agriculture, Dept of Agriculture and Co-operation, New Delhi

Gujarat, Government of (2006) 'Gujarat agriculture at a glance', presentation made at the National Conference on Kharif Campaign, Agriculture and Co-operation Department, Government of Gujarat, Gandhinagar

Gulati, A. and Mullen, K. (2003) 'Indian agriculture in the 1990s and after', Stanford Centre for International Development (SCID), Stanford

Haque, T. (2000) 'Contractual arrangements in land and labour markets in rural India', *Indian Journal of Agricultural Economics*, vol 55, no 3, pp233–252

Hazell, P. B. R. (2005) 'Is there a future for small farms?', in D. Colman and N. Vink (eds) *Reshaping Agriculture's Contributions to Society*, Proceedings of the 25th International Conference of Agricultural Economists (ICAE), 16–22 August, Blackwell, US, pp93–101

International Food Policy Research Institute (IFPRI) (2006a) 'Agricultural diversification in the Punjab: Trends, constraints and policy options', IFPRI South Asia Office, New Delhi

IFPRI (2006b) 'Withering Punjab agriculture: Can it regain its leadership?', draft, IFPRI South Asia Office, New Delhi

Jha, D. (2001) 'Agricultural research and small farms', presidential address at 60th Annual Convocation of the Indian Society of Agricultural Economics (ISAE), Kalyani, West Bengal, 22–24 January

Key, N. and Runsten, D. (1999) 'Contract farming, smallholders and rural development in Latin America: The organization of agroprocessing firms and scale of outgrower production', *World Development*, vol 27, no 2, pp381–401

Kirsten, J. and Sartorius, K. (2002) 'Linking agribusiness and small-scale farmers in developing countries: Is there a new role for contract farming?', *Development Southern Africa*, vol 19, no 4, pp503–529

Kumar, P. (2006) 'Contract farming through agribusiness firms and state corporation: A case study in Punjab', *Economic and Political Weekly*, vol 52, no 30, ppA5367–5375

Landes, R. and Gulati, A. (2004) 'Farm sector performance and reform agenda', *Economic and Political Weekly*, vol 39, no 32, pp3611–3619

Mittal, S. (2007) 'Can horticulture be a success story for India?', ICRIER Working Paper No. 197, International Council for Research on International Economic Relations (ICRIER), New Delhi

Mitra, S. and Sarkar, A. (2003) 'Relative profitability from production and trade – a study of selected potato markets in West Bengal', *Economic and Political Weekly*, vol 38, no 44, pp4694–4699

Ornberg, L. (2003) 'Farmers' choice: Contract farming, agricultural change and modernization in northern Thailand', paper presented at the 3rd International Convention of Asia Scholars (ICAS3), Singapore, 19–22 August

Pingali, P. and Khwaja, Y. (2004) 'Globalization of Indian diets and the transformation of food supply systems', *Indian Journal of Agricultural Marketing*, vol 18, no 1, pp26–49

Punjab, Government of (2005) *Statistical Abstract of Punjab, 2004*, Economic Advisor, Government of Punjab, Chandigarh

Reardon, T. and Berdegue, J. (2002) 'The rapid rise of supermarkets in Latin America: Challenges and opportunities for development', *Development Policy Review*, vol 20, no 4, pp371–388

Sako, M. (1992) *Prices, Quality and Trust: Inter-firm Relations in Britain and Japan*, Cambridge University Press, Cambridge

Schwentesius, R. and Gomez, M. A. (2002) 'Supermarkets in Mexico: Impacts on horticulture systems', *Development Policy Review*, vol 20, no 4, pp487–502

Sen, S. and Raju, S. (2006): 'Globalization and expanding markets for cut-flowers: Who benefits?', *Economic and Political Weekly*, 30 June, pp2725–2731

Sengupta, A. and Kundu, S. (2006) 'Scale efficiency of Indian farmers: A non-parametric approach', *Indian Journal of Agricultural Economics*, vol 61, no 4, pp677–687

Sharma, V. P. (2007a) 'Managing price risk in Indian agriculture: Can futures markets help?', in R. H. Dholakia (ed.) *Frontiers of Agricultural Development in Gujarat*, Centre for Management in Agriculture (CMA), Indian Institute of Management (IIM), Ahmedabad, pp201–214

Sharma, V. P. (2007b) 'India's agrarian crisis and smallholder producers' participation in new farm supply chain initiatives: A case study of contract farming', IIMA Working Paper No. 2007-08-01, August, Indian Institute of Management, Ahmedabad

Sherasiya, R. A. (2007) 'Agricultural performance in Gujarat', presented at the workshop on 'Frontiers of Agricultural Development in Gujarat' organized by Dr I. G. Patel Memorial Trust (Silver Jubilee of Gujarat Economic Association (GEA) Trust) and Centre for Management of Agriculture (CMA), Indian Institute of Management Ahmedabad (IIM) at IIMA, 24 February

Simmons, P., Winters, P. and Patrick, I. (2005) 'An analysis of contract farming in east Java, Bali and Lombok, Indonesia', *Agricultural Economics*, vol 33, pp513–525

Singh, B. and Singh, K. (1996) 'Future requirements of cold storage facility in Punjab', *Indian Journal of Agricultural Marketing*, vol 10, no 3, pp42–51

Singh, K., Chahal, S. S. and Kaur, P. (1996) 'An economic analysis of potato marketing in Punjab', *Indian Journal of Agricultural Marketing*, vol 10, no 3, pp34–41

Singh, N. K. (2007): 'Hot potato: You can't say no to this sugar-free tuber', *Indian Express*, 13 April, Ahmedabad

Singh, S. (2002) 'Contracting out solutions: Political economy of contract farming in the Indian Punjab', *World Development*, vol 30, no 9, pp1621–1638

Singh, S. (2004) 'The new generation co-operative: Theory, practice and relevance', *The Co-operator*, vol 42, no 5, pp229–230

Singh, S. (2005) 'Role of the state in contract farming in Thailand: Experience and lessons', *ASEAN Economic Bulletin*, vol 22, no 2, pp 217–228

Srinivas, N. N. (2005) 'Field test: You reap what you sow', *The Economic Times*, Ahmedabad, 30 March

Stokes, S. E. (2006) 'The dilemma of contracting: risk management or risky business?', June [online] http://flaginc.org/topics/pubs/arts/CLE_SES.pdf, last accessed 17 October 2007

Thakkar, M. (2007) 'Farmers' clubs to feed retailers, food chains', *The Economic Times*, 16 February, Ahmedabad, p3

Tomek, W. G. and Peterson, H. H. (2001) 'Risk management in agricultural markets: A review', *The Journal of Futures Markets*, vol 21, no 10, pp953–985

Tripathi, R. S., Singh, R. and Singh, S. (2005) 'Contract farming in potato production: An alternative for managing risk and uncertainty', *Agricultural Economic Research Review*, vol 18, pp47–60

White, B. (1997) 'Agro-industry and contract farming in upland Java', *The Journal of Peasant Studies*, vol 24, no 3, pp100–136

Witsoe, J. (2006) 'India's second Green Revolution? The sociological implications of corporate-led agricultural growth', in D. Kapur (ed.), *India in Transition: Economics and Politics of Change*, Centre for the Advanced Study of India, Philadelphia

Wolf, S., Hueth, B. and Ligon, E. (2001) 'Policing mechanisms in agricultural contracts', *Rural Sociology*, vol 66, no 3, pp359–381

World Bank (2003) 'Revitalising Punjab's agriculture', Rural Development Unit, South Asia Region, World Bank, Washington, DC

Chapter 15

Marketing China's Fruit: Are Small, Poor Farmers being Excluded from the Supply Chain?

Jikun Huang, Yunhua Wu and Scott Rozelle

Introduction

China's agricultural and food markets have become substantially more efficient and competitive during the past several decades, after nearly 30 years of reform (Park et al, 2002). Markets also have become highly integrated across space (Huang et al, 2004). While there is no absolute proof about what explains the performance of markets, China's food economy has a number of characteristics that are consistent with well-functioning markets: few regulations, easy entry and literally thousands of traders in every market (Rozelle and Huang, 2007).

Several recent studies on the emergence of modern supply chains have shown that both downstream and midstream segments of the marketing chain in China have also evolved dramatically (Bi et al, 2004; Hu et al, 2004; Goldman and Vanhonacker, 2006; Huang et al, 2007). For example, in the downstream segment, the supermarket revolution arrived in China in the early 1990s and has been spreading as fast as or faster than anywhere in the world (Hu et al, 2004). There have also been changes in the midstream segment; wholesale markets have emerged and have evolved steadily (Dong et al, 2006; Wang et al, 2006).

What is the impact of these shifts on participation by farmers in the newly emerging sectors? Internationally, in recent years there has been a debate on the impacts of rapid changes in food marketing chains. Many scholars and policy makers have been concerned about the rise of supermarkets and other new marketing institutions on small farmers in developing countries, with some arguing that there could be serious distributional impacts. For example, there are case studies in Latin America, central and eastern Europe, Mexico, Brazil and Kenya that suggest that it is the rich, large farmers that benefit from the rise of demand for fruit and vegetables and the emergence of supermarkets (Schwentesius and Manuel, 2002; Berdegue et al, 2005; Reardon and Timmer, 2007). Because of the high transaction costs involved in purchasing agricultural products from millions of small farmers and difficulties in monitoring quality and food safety, it is often assumed that supermarkets and their agents will turn to larger and better-off farmers. As a consequence, the rise of demand for horticultural and other high-value commodities in the consumption basket of consumers and the concomitant rise in supermarkets have created concern among the international community about the possible adverse consequences on small farms and poor farmers (Reardon and Timmer, 2007).

The empirical evidence on the impact of supermarket emergence (and the rise of other marketing chain participants) on the participation and welfare of farmers in China is mixed. Studies based on supermarket or processor surveys often show that new supermarket chains and specialized suppliers could be engines of food product market expansion and have a significant, although ambiguous, impact on small farmers; some studies have shown positive effects while others have shown negative effects (e.g. Zuo and Zhang, 2003; Hu et al, 2004; Hu et al, 2006). But other studies, based on one large household survey conducted in Greater Beijing, found that although there have been significant changes in the downstream segments of horticultural and dairy marketing chains, these shifts have not penetrated into the upstream segments (Dong et al, 2006; Wang et al, 2006; Wu et al, 2007). While the work from Greater Beijing is convincing, given the study's limited focus geographically, there is still a question about whether or not the findings can be applied to other areas of China, especially to production areas (Beijing is unusual in that it is a mega-consumption centre where most foods are not produced locally).

The overall goal of this chapter is to increase our understanding of the impacts of shifts in marketing chains on producers in developing country food economies. More specifically, we are interested in whether or not the evolution of China's fruit supply chain is helping or hurting small farms by allowing small/poor farmers easy or limited access to growing fruit markets. In this chapter we pursue three specific objectives. First, we trace shifts in supply chain activities over time. Second, we describe how different types of farmers, small and large, are participating. Finally, we use multivariate analysis to try to isolate the determinants of participation, focusing on the effect of farm size and wealth (measured in terms of assets).

To achieve these objectives, we first narrowed our geographic focus to the Shandong province and our commodity focus to fresh fruits, particularly grapes and apples. We justify these selections in the following section. Within the key subsectors, our research focused on a subset of issues. Who (or what type of farmer) is producing fruit as the market expands? What are the observed marketing choices by farmers and how have these marketing choices changed over time?

Have the changes in the downstream segments penetrated into the upstream segments and affected how farmers market their fruit? What are the major determinants of the marketing choices of farmers? And, most importantly, have small and poor farmers been excluded from China's marketing chains?

In the next section, we discuss the study's sampling methodology and data collection. Then we analyse farmers' marketing choices and major factors that may correlate with marketing choices. Next we present two separate multivariate econometric models to explain marketing choices and interpret the results. We conclude the study with policy recommendations.

Data sources and sampling measures

Selection of commodities

We selected fruit commodities as this is the single most dynamic sub-sector in Chinese agriculture. During the 1990s, the area planted to fruit increased from 5.2 to 8.9 million hectares (NBSC, 2007). During this time, the share of fruit area in total cropped area also rose significantly, from 2.3 per cent to 5.7 per cent (one of the highest orchard shares in the world). After 2000, similar trends continued (NBSC, 2007). Production even increased much more than area expanded, due to rising yields. In 1990, total fruit production was only 18.7 million tons; by 2006 it had increased to 172.4 million tons. We selected apples and grapes as the focus of our analysis for three reasons. First, the production of apples and grapes are the number one and number six most prevalent fruits in the entire fruit economy of China respectively. Hence, in some ways, these crops are representative of more than just Shandong Province (the study area). Second, the production of both apples and grapes has increased significantly in the past 15 years. Between 1990 and 2006 apple production in China increased by more than 6 times (from 4.3 to 26.1 million tons); grape production rose even more, by a factor of 7.3, from 0.86 to 6.3 million tons (NBSC, 2007). Growth patterns differ between apples and grapes, allowing for an interesting comparison between them. Apples expanded most rapidly in the early period and have levelled off in recent years; grapes, on the other hand, have continued to experience rapid growth during the entire period after 1990.

What factors have been behind these growth patterns? While it is beyond the scope of this paper to empirically analyse the determinants of fruit production trends, one factor is the emergence of competing fruits, the demand for which has risen as incomes have increased. Second, shifting extension policies might have played a role. During the 1980s China's agricultural officials began to promote apple production (through expending apple orchard area), allowing farmers to shift from the production of other crops (e.g. grains, fibres and oilseeds) to apples and by introducing new varieties (Zhang, 2005). This promotion programme led to a staggering increase in apple production by nearly four times between 1990 and 1996. The share of apples in total fruit production rose from 23 to 37 per cent in China during these seven years (NBSC, 2007). The sharp rise in production in such a short period of time, however, led to a fall in the price of apples. For example, between 1994 and 1997, the price of one of the major varieties, Hongfushi, dropped from 3.6–4.0 yuan/kg to 1.8–2.0 yuan/kg; the price of Guoguang, another major variety, dropped from 1.4–1.6 yuan/kg to 0.8–1.0 yuan/kg (with US$1 = 8.6 yuan in 1994 and 8.3 yuan in 1997) (Ji and Yue, 1999).

We choose Shandong province as the study site for two reasons. First, among China's 31 provinces, Shandong is the largest in terms of fruit production. In the past 15 years, the province accounted for about 10 per cent of the nation's fruit area, with even larger shares in apples (21 per cent) and grapes (13 per cent) (NSBC, 2007). Because of higher than average provincial yields, Shandong produced 28 per cent of the nation's apples and 14 per cent of its grapes in 2005 (NSBC, 2007). Such high output makes Shandong the largest apple producer and third largest grape producer among China's provinces. Historically, Shandong has been a market leader for apples, fruits and other commodities (Rozelle et al, 2002). In recent years the province is perceived as having dynamic markets with institutions that are often replicated in other regions.

Sampling framework

The data for this study come from a stratified random survey in Shandong province. This survey is a representative sample of apple and grape growing villages in the province. The first step in conducting the survey involved creating two sampling frames of county-level apple production and grape production. Based on the rankings in terms of apple or grape area per farm population, we divided all counties into five groups: High-1, High-2, Mid-1, Mid-2 and Low. The groups accounted for about 10 per cent, 15 per cent, 20 per cent, 25 per cent and 30 per cent of rural farm population respectively, within the sampling population. One county was randomly selected from each of the above five groups. Hence, in total, there are five sample counties for each commodity. The farm population in each set of counties provided data for our weighting system, which was used to create point estimates for the provincial averages of each of our variables.

The rest of the sampling (for towns and villages) proceeded on a basis similar to that used for selecting counties. The number of towns, however, differed by the type of county. Specifically, in each of the two high production counties, five townships were selected (two high production townships, two medium and one low). In each of the two medium production counties, three townships were selected (one high production township, one medium and one low). In the low production county, only two townships were selected (one high production township, one low). In total for each commodity, the survey teams visited 18 townships (10+6+2). We followed a similar approach to choose villages within each township. In total for each commodity, we interviewed farmers in 35 villages (22 in high production counties, 10 in medium production counties and 3 in low production counties) from 18 townships in 5 counties. The population shares for all townships and villages were collected.

The last step of the sampling process involved selecting the sample house-holds within the sample villages. Both the apple and grape household sampling procedures were similar, but here we use apples as an illustration. In most of the 35 apple villages, we divided all the households into two groups: households with apple production and those without apple production. Then we randomly selected seven apple-producing households and three non-apple-producing households in each village. In all the villages, we obtained estimates of the total number of apple-producing and non-apple-producing households which were used in the weighting system.

There were some deviations from the methodology, however. In some villages, there were fewer than seven apple producers in total. In these cases, we selected all apple households and three or four non-apple-producing households. In some villages there were almost no non-apple-producing households. In this case, we randomly selected ten apple-producing households. After choosing the sample households in this way, we interviewed 340 households and ended up with 338 valid sample households (because questionnaires from two households were not complete). In total, 279 households in the sample are apple-producing house-holds and 59 are non-apple-producing households. In the case of grapes, we interviewed 330 households. We ended up with 329 valid sample households. Of this total, 232 are grape-producing households and 97 are non-grape-producing households.

Creating weights for the analysis

To generate statistics that can be considered representative for the entire popula-tion of Shandong (and for use in the weighed regression analysis), we needed to create a weighting system. Our system required data on the number of apple or fruit farms or households that produce and do not produce apples/grapes. To do so, we collected the area planted to apples and grapes and the size of the farming population for all counties, all townships within the sample counties and on all villages within the sample townships. With these data, we constructed farm population-based weights to create point estimates of our variables that are provincially representative for all farmers who sell apples or grapes in the markets.

To create the weights, we begin by noting that the weight for hth household with apple (or grape) marketing from the kth village of the jth township of the ith county, P_{ijkh}, is defined as:

$$P_{ijkh} = Z_i \times Z_{ij} \times Z_{ijk} \times Z_{ijkh} \tag{1}$$

where Z_i is the weight for the ith type of county and its value corresponds to the share that the apple (or grape) farmers from the ith type of county accounts for in all apple (or grape) farmers in Shandong. The symbol, Z_{ij}, is the weight for the jth township in the ith county and its value corresponds to the share that the apple (or grape) farmers from the jth type of township accounts for in total apple (or grape) farmers in the ith county. Similarly, Z_{ijk} is the weight for the kth village of the jth township in the ith county and its value corresponds to the share that the apple (or grape) farmers in the kth type of village accounts for in total apple (or grape) farmers in the jth township of the ith county. Finally, Z_{ijkh} is the reciprocal number of sample farmers who sold apples (or grapes) during the study period in the kth village of the jth township of the ith county.

The production and marketing of apples and grapes in Shandong

In this section we examine production and marketing trends in our sample households in Shandong province, first looking at production trends and then marketing trends. In the analysis of marketing, after describing trends in marketing patterns, we examine cross tabulations of marketing patterns by farm size and value of assets (or wealth).

Household apple and grape production

Unlike the large fruit orchards and plantations that characterize fruit production in some countries, fruit production in China (or more precisely Shandong province) is dominated by small farms. This system is partly a result of the nature of land tenure in China. All households have land contracted from their villages with use rights for 30 years. Every farm family in a village was given land. In China's densely populated villages, this means that, on average, household farm size in our sample was only 4.4–5.1mu (0.29–0.24 hectares, Table 15.1, row 3). Among all households surveyed, the largest farm size was only 30mu (or 2ha) in the apple-producing villages and 40mu (2.7ha) in the grape-producing villages (Annex Table 15.1).

Similar to the trends in apple and grape production at the national level, fruit production has increased since 2001. Moreover, the growth in grapes has exceeded the growth in apples (probably because rapid growth in apple production occurred in the late 1990s, before our survey). In grape-producing villages, among the 329 households surveyed, 200 households planted grape in 2001 (Table 15.1, rows 1–2). The number rose to 232 in 2006, an increase of 16 per cent during the 5-year study period. In addition to the rise in farmer participation rate in apple production (which was only marginal), the increase in apple production also (and mainly) came from the rise in average apple area per farm, from 2.7mu to 2.9mu between 2001 and 2006 (0.18–0.19ha, Table 15.2). Despite the small size of Shandong fruit farms, in fruit production villages, on average, farmers allocated about half of their total cultivated area to maize, wheat, cotton oilseed, vegetables and other crops (Table 15.2, last column).

Table 15.1 shows that except for farm size and off-farm employment, all other household characteristics are similar between apple-producing (or grape-producing) and non-apple-producing (or non-grape-producing) households. There is no significant difference when comparing household size, the size of the

Table 15.1 *Characteristics of the sample households in Shandong Province, 2001 and 2006*

	Apple-producing villages			Grape-producing villages		
	Average	Apple-producing households	Non-apple-producing households	Average	Grape-producing households	Non-grape-producing households
Number of observations						
2001	338	276	62	329	200	129
2006	338	279	59	329	232	97
Households (2006 data)						
Household cultivated land (mu)	4.4	5.2	3.5	5.1	6.4	4.7
Population (number)	3.4	3.3	3.6	3.5	3.7	3.4
Head age (years)	53	52	54	54	52	55
Head education (years)	7.3	7.4	7.3	7.4	7.4	7.4
Size of labour force (number)	2.8	2.6	2.9	2.7	2.8	2.7
Off-farm labour share (%)	41	30	54	45	39	46
Per capita asset in 2001 (yuan)	5065	4622	5510	6415	5908	6721

Notes: All numbers are weighted averages. 15mu = 1 hectare.

family labour force, the age of the household head or the education level of the household head. There are two notable differences in the descriptive statistics between apple- and grape-producing and non-apple- and non-grape-producing households. On average, households with larger sizes of farms are associated with larger areas of fruit production. However, these are descriptive statistics that

Table 15.2 *Cultivated area of apple- and grape-producing households in Shandong Province, 2001 and 2006*

Year	Sample	Cultivated sown area (mu)			
		Total	Fruit	Apple/grape	Other crops
Apple-producing households					
2001	276	6.2	3.2	2.7	3.0
2006	279	6.5	3.8	2.9	2.6
Average	555	6.4	3.5	2.8	2.8
Grape-producing households					
2001	200	8.6	4.1	2.3	4.5
2006	232	8.5	4.4	2.3	4.1
Average	432	8.6	4.2	2.3	4.3

Notes: All numbers are weighted averages. 'Other crops' mainly include maize, wheat, cotton, peanut and vegetables.

do not control for other factors. In fact, using the same survey data, Huang et al (2007) show that, after controlling for other factors, farm size is not a statistically significant determinant of a farmer's decision to participate in apple or grape production. Based on this result, it is concluded that small farmers are not being excluded from the opportunity to engage in fruit production in China on the basis of size.

The other difference between apple-/grape-producing households and non-apple-/non-grape-producing households is with regards to their participation in the off-farm labour market. Huang et al (2007) also show that households' labour allocation decisions, to both off-farm employment and to apple or grape production, involve trade-offs. Moving into fruit production leads to lower levels of participation off the farm; likewise, decisions to shift family members into off-farm employment reduces the likelihood and intensity of fruit production. This implies that for households that are not able to participate in off-farm employment, whether poor or rich, the expansion of Chinese fruit markets provides new employment opportunities for engaging in and expanding fruit production. This difference also appears in Table 15.1 (rows 7 and 8).

Household apple and grape marketing choices

Marketing channels

One of the most important findings of the survey perhaps relates to the nature of the sales transaction between apple-producing and grape-producing households and their buyers. Our survey of fruit marketing behaviour shows that most fruit, in particular apples, move through traditional supply channels and that there is little penetration of the new entrants (e.g. supermarkets, Table 15.3) that are emerging prominently in the downstream segment in the marketing channels. In the case of apples, during the sample period apple-producing households sold over 90 per cent of their apples in traditional channels (columns 2 and 3). Brokers (or small, itinerant traders that visit villages and procure apples directly from farmers) account for between 20 and 25 per cent of sales between 2001 and 2006. Farmers sold nearly 70 per cent of their apples to small-scale traders who then sold produce in wholesale markets.

Only a small share of apples was marketed to processors or other modern supply chain agents (Table 15.3, columns 4 and 5). Modern channels, which mainly include processing firms and specialized suppliers, together accounted for only 7 per cent in 2001.[1] Our data do show a slight upward trend between 2001 and 2006, although by the end of our sample period, total sales to agents from modern market channels only reached 11.2 per cent.[2] Hence, in the case of apples, despite major restructuring in the downstream and midstream segments of fruit markets, for now these shifts have not significantly affected farm procurement.

The case of grapes is somewhat different than that of apples. The share of grape-producing households selling to wholesalers accounted for only 27.2 per cent of sales. While much less than the case of apples, the total share of grape-

Table 15.3 *Marketing channels of apple- and grape-producing households in Shandong Province, 2001 and 2006*

		Shares by marketing channels (%)				
	Sample size[a]	Brokers[b]	Wholesalers	Processing firms	Other modern channels[c]	Total
Apple-producing hhs						
2001	263	23.8	69.2	2.6	4.4	100
2006	275	21.9	67.0	3.3	7.9	100
Average	—	23.1	68.4	2.8	5.7	100
Grape-producing hhs						
2001	151	30.0	28.4	31.4	10.1	100
2006	224	25.5	26.1	30.2	18.2	100
Average	—	27.7	27.2	30.8	14.3	100
All villages						
2001	414	25.8	56.1	11.9	6.3	100
2006	499	23.8	48.2	15.6	12.6	100
Average	—	24.8	52.7	13.5	9.0	100

Notes: All numbers are weighted averages. a The numbers of sample households are slightly less than those for the apple- and grape-producing production households presented in Tables 15.1 and 15.2 because there were a few very small fruit farms that did not sell any of their output (i.e. they produced for home consumption only). b The numbers under the 'broker' category also include farmers that directly sold their fruit to consumers in local periodic and wet markets. c The other modern channels for apples include special suppliers (3.2 per cent in 2001 and 5.9 per cent in 2006), restaurants (0.7 per cent in 2001 and 0.2 per cent in 2006) and export companies (0.4 per cent in 2001 and 1.8 per cent in 2006). The other modern channels for grapes include special suppliers (10.0 per cent in 2001 and 18.1 per cent in 2006), restaurants (0.1 per cent in both 2001 and 2006) and supermarkets (0.00 per cent in 2001 and 0.02 per cent in 2006).

producing households that sold their grapes to small traders (brokers and wholesalers) was still high and exceeded half of all sales.[3] This is also similar to the findings of a community-level marketing analysis study in Shandong (Huang et al, 2006).

A significant, and growing, share of grape-producing households sold their grapes to processors and other agents from modern marketing channels. Data from the grape-producing villages show that actors in the midstream segments of the modern supply chains do reach down to the farm gate. Processing firms procure more grapes than any other type of buyer (30.8 per cent), although the share did not increase between the beginning and end of our survey period. Although only a relatively small share of grape-producing households sells grapes to specialized suppliers (which are typically procurement agents from large wineries), the share has risen between 2001 and 2006 (from 10.1 to 18.2 per cent). Interestingly, this pattern of marketing is different from Greater Beijing where no penetration of modern chains at all (even in grape-producing villages) was found in horticulture-producing villages (Dong et al, 2006; Wang et al, 2006).

Modern supply chains maintain low levels of penetration, but a slight rise in their share was nevertheless observed. There are several explanations for the emergence of vertical integration in China's fruit markets. Processing is more common in the fruit sector than the vegetable sector. The largest share of sales into modern channels by grape-producing households is mainly to buyers from local wineries. In all counties that had significant portions of grape sales into modern supply chains, local wineries were present. There were no apple processing facilities (e.g. apple juice factories) in any of the sample counties.

Newly introduced storage technologies also affected the way farmers marketed their produce. Firms themselves accounted for most of the rise in sales in modern marketing channels by sending out buyers to purchase grapes for placement into cold storage. There were a rising number of buyers from supply firms that were investing in cold-storage facilities around northern China. These specialized suppliers often procured directly from fruit farmers, performed sorting and grading activities, and then delivered the higher quality fruit into cold storage. Produce was then resold by the cold-storage firm when prices were higher or during the Spring Festival. Buyers who were procuring for large, regional and national wineries, on the other hand, were stagnant between 2001 and 2006.

The question is, what are the full implications of the changes in procurement practices that were observed between 2001 and 2006? On one hand, there has been a change in farmers' points of sale, from small, traditional brokers and buyers that resell in local, traditional fresh markets or regional ones through other brokers. On the other hand, there was not much difference between traditional brokers and those that purchased as agents for cold storage facilities. According to our interviews with both types of agents, they all worked in very small, typically family-run and operated firms. The terms and conditions of the sales were the same (all done on a spot basis, with payments made in cash). Almost all transactions between farmers and specialized suppliers were conducted without contracts. Hence, if we consider the cold-storage agents to be traditional traders because of their lack of coordination with farmers, then there was no significant trend in farmers selling to modern channels, despite increased sales to local processors (wineries). Furthermore, the only difference between apples (and tomatoes and cucumbers (see Huang et al, 2007) is the fact that many grape-producing households produce for local wineries. Even in the case of grapes, where there is a growing processing sector, it is difficult to find the effects of rapid changes in the downstream and midstream segments of the supply chain at the farm gate.

Consistent with this interpretation is the fact that, despite the rise of supermarkets in urban areas, there is no evidence that the impacts have penetrated to the village level. In fact, there were zero purchases by agents of supermarkets in our apple-producing villages. There was also zero purchasing by agents of supermarkets in our grape-producing villages.

Table 15.4 *Household size, wealth and marketing channels in apple-producing villages in Shandong Province, 2001 and 2006*

	Sample size[a]	Brokers[b]	Wholesalers	Processing firms	Other modern channels[c]	Total
				Shares by marketing channels (%)		
Household cultivated land in 2001						
< 4 mu	149	26.2	70.9	1.7	1.2	100
4–7 mu	247	13.9	72.2	3.2	10.8	100
7 mu	142	34.1	62.8	2.0	1.0	100
Per capita assets in 2001						
< 4000 yuan	296	22.4	64.6	2.7	10.4	100
4000–7000 yuan	104	20.1	74.5	3.0	2.4	100
> 7000 yuan	138	25.2	67.3	3.3	4.2	100

Notes: All numbers are weighted averages. See notes for Table 15.3 for key to a, b and c.

Who is selling into traditional and modern supply channels?

In this sub-section we examine differences in the characteristics of apple-producing and grape-producing households that sell their apples and grapes into traditional and modern supply chains (Tables 15.4 and 15.5). In the first set of rows of each table we look at the size of farm (comparing how small and large farms market their apples and grapes). In the second set of rows, we look at farm assets (comparing how poor and rich farmers market their apples and grapes).

According to our data, there is no evidence that small apple-producing households are relegated to traditional supply chains or excluded from modern supply chains (Table 15.4, row 1). There is no clear linear relationship between farm size

Table 15.5 *Household size, wealth and marketing channels in grape-producing villages in Shandong Province, 2001 and 2006*

	Sample size[a]	Brokers[b]	Wholesalers	Processing firms	Other modern channels[c]	Total
				Shares by marketing channels (%)		
Household cultivated land in 2001						
< 4 mu	80	56.0	19.4	17.9	6.6	100
4–7 mu	136	54.7	20.7	18.2	6.4	100
7 mu	159	47.5	30.2	15.8	6.6	100
Per capita assets in 2001						
< 4000 yuan	142	55.3	30.5	10.1	4.0	100
4000–7000 yuan	76	35.3	24.2	24.5	16.0	100
> 7000 yuan	157	57.0	12.6	22.1	8.3	100

Notes: All numbers are weighted averages. See notes for Table 15.3 for key to a, b and c.

and share of farmers selling to brokers, with 26.7 per cent of those in the lowest tercile (<4 mu, <0.27 ha) selling to brokers, 13.9 per cent in the middle tercile (4–7mu, 0.27–0.47ha), and 34.1 per cent in the upper tercile (>7mu, >0.47ha). The same relationship holds between farm size and other marketing channels (buyers in wholesale markets, processors and others). There is no discernible relationship between farm size category and marketing channels.

The same is true with respect to the relationship between household wealth and choice of the marketing channel within apple-producing households (Table 15.4, rows 4–6). Farmers with lower levels of assets and those with higher levels of assets participate similarly in the channel for brokers and wholesale market buyers. The same is true for participation in modern markets. Our data confirm that small and poor apple-producing households are not being relegated to traditional marketing channels. Although there has been limited activity between apple-producing households and modern supply chain agents, small and poor households are not being excluded.

The same conclusion holds for grape-producing households (Table 15.5). There is a slight positive correlation between farm size category of grape-producing households and the likelihood of selling to brokers, but a negative correlation between farm size category and the likelihood of selling to buyers in wholesale markets. There is no evidence of small farmers participating less in processing or other modern supply chains. Wealth level has a similar relationship to marketing as farm size. In the case of all categories of sales to traditional and modern supply chains, there is no clear relationship between level of wealth and marketing activity. Taken together, our descriptive statistics for both apple-producing and grape-producing households are consistent with the conclusion that small, poor farmers in China have equal access to all forms of marketing.

Prices and marketing channels

It is often thought that a clear impact of point of sale on the welfare of farmers can be examined, in part, through the prices received by farmers. In this sub-section we examine differences in the prices received by farmers that are operating in different marketing channels. To do so, we compute average prices by marketing channel and these are reported in Table 15.6.

Overall, marketing channel impacts farm-gate prices differently for apples and for grapes. In the case of apples, the results are consistent with the idea that

Table 15.6 *Procurement prices by marketing channels in Shandong Province, 2006 (in yuan/kg)*

| | Marketing channels based on the first buyers | | | |
	Brokers	Wholesalers	Processing firms	Other modern channels
Apples	1.64	1.91	2.31	2.26
Grapes	2.44	2.71	1.93	2.16

Note: See Table 15.3 for definitions of the marketing channels.

participation in modern marketing channels benefits farmers because they receive a higher price for their output (Table 15.6, row 1). Farm-gate apple prices received from brokers (1.64 yuan/kg at the time of the survey, US$1 was equal to 7.97 yuan) and wholesalers (1.91 yuan/kg) are below prices from processors (2.31 yuan/kg) and agents working in the modern marketing chain (2.26 yuan/kg). Such evidence suggests that those who can sell outside of traditional marketing channels are earning higher unit prices for their produce. While average apple prices were lower for those selling in traditional channels, grape-producing households that sell to processing firms (1.91 yuan/kg) and agents from modern supply chains (2.16 yuan/kg) actually receive a lower price (Table 15.6, columns 3 and 4). At least in our sample, those households that sell to non-traditional channels in the grape economy are earning lower unit prices.

The main issue to understand in interpreting these prices is what they mean for participation in modern supply chains. Why are farmers earning higher prices in non-traditional chains for apples and in traditional chains for grapes? Findings from our field work, while illuminating, also show the limitations of using price as a metric for understanding the welfare impacts of point of sale. According to interviews, differences in price patterns arise from the quality of products marketed through each of the channels. In the case of apples, agents from the modern supply chains focused on procuring larger and higher quality apples since they were often bound for the export market (mostly to Russia and eastern and central Europe). The quality of apples being sold in domestic markets was lower on average. When the one trader that we interviewed who participated in both the domestic and export market was asked about the quality of apples and their prices in each of the chains in which he operated, he replied that the price difference was explainable entirely by quality. He claimed that if an apple that received a higher price in the export channel was sold in the domestic market, in most cases it would receive a higher than average price for the domestic market.

A similar quality impact was observed in the grape market. While almost all grapes in the traditional markets were for direct consumption (and were typically of a variety that was lower yielding and received a relatively high price), those sold in the non-traditional channels were lower quality wine grapes for processing. This difference in varieties explains why the processor's price is the lowest.

Is participation in modern marketing chains a reliable way to increase income through higher prices? The evidence in Table 15.6 clearly shows not. It may be that when non-traditional channels emerge, farm households can benefit from access to new opportunities, but one interpretation of our data is that the main benefit of alternative channels is not necessarily that they offer a higher price. Price differences may primarily reflect differences in the inherent quality of the product being sold. Modern marketing may be a gateway to commodities that are higher than average quality and therefore bring higher than average prices. This is the case in our apple sample. In our grape sample, however, the non-traditional channels emerged as a marketing pathway for a commodity that is inherently lower quality and lower priced. Hence, marketing impacts should not be inferred from price alone.

Multivariate analysis of the farm size, wealth and marketing choices

While interesting, it is important to remember that the descriptive results at best suggest the underlying relationship between two variables. It could be that many other factors confound the relationship. Therefore, in this section, we undertake multivariate analysis to analyse the determinants of marketing choice, with a focus on the effects of farm size and wealth, *ceteris paribus*.

Our model of the determinants of the marketing choices, M_{ijt}, of our apple-producing and grape-producing households is specified as:

$$M_{ijt} = f \text{ (Farm Size}_{it-n}, \text{Asset}_{it-n}, \text{Incentive}_{it}, \text{Household}_{it},$$
$$\text{Other Control Variables}_j) \tag{2}$$

where, M_{ijt} is a vector of the marketing choices of the ith farmer from the jth village in year t (in either 2001 or 2006). In the regression, we divide the farmer's marketing choices into three channels (small broker, buyers in the wholesale market and agents from the modern supply channels). As in the discussion above, modern channels include sales to processors, special suppliers and others (which equals the sum of columns 4 and 5 in Table 15.3).

Farm Size and Asset are the variables of interest and are the same variables as presented in Tables 15.4 and 15.5. Farm Size is measured as total area cultivated by the household (in mu, or 0.067ha) in the base year (where $t–n = 2001$). Assets are measured as per capita assets in consumer durables and housing, in yuan, in the year 2001.

The Incentive variable stands for a matrix made up of two terms. The first term is the distance of the village from the nearest county road (measured in km). This is a proxy for farm-gate prices since they should vary mainly according to transport costs.[4] The second term in the Incentive matrix is the share of house-hold labour working off the farm in 2001 (measured in per cent). This variable approximates the household's forgone income, or opportunity cost, from engaging in fruit production. We assume that the larger the share of a household's labour that is allocated off the farm, the higher the opportunity cost.

The model also contains a set of variables that seek to account for a number of household characteristics. In our model, Household characteristics include the age of the household head (in years) and the education level of the household head (in years of educational attainment). We also include a number of other village-level Control Variables. In total there are eight Control Variables, including: (a) the average land area of the typical apple-producing (grape-producing) household in the village in 2001; (b) whether or not the village has a farmer association (a dummy variable equals 1 if the village has a farmer association, otherwise it equals 0); (c) the distance of the village from the nearest wet market (km); (d) the distance of the village from the nearest wholesale market (km); (e) the number of years that has elapsed since the nearest wholesale market was established (years); (f) the existence of sale tax in the local periodic market (a dummy variable equals 1 if there is such a tax, otherwise it equals 0); (g) whether or not the local government regulates fruit marketing (measured as a dummy variable which equals 1 if there are any local government regulations on where the farmers can and cannot sell their fruit marketing during the past 5 years (between 2001 and 2006), otherwise it equals 0; and (h) the number of fruit processing firms in the county.

The model in equation (2) is estimated in two ways: OLS and Tobit. The results of the OLS estimation are reported because we can run a weighted regression using the population weights described in the sampling section. While the Tobit model in some respects is more appropriate than OLS, since there are many zero values in the independent variables, we cannot estimate Tobit with our weights.

Multivariate results

Both regression models performed well (Tables 15.7 and 15.8). The Adjusted R-square, a measure of goodness of fit of the weighted OLS models (both tables, columns 1–3) ranged from 0.15 to 0.40, levels that are sufficiently high for cross-section regressions. The estimated coefficients of many control variables (Incentive, Household and Other Control Variables) were of the expected sign and significant. For example, in the apple marketing regression, the sign on the road distance variable was positive in the Broker equation and negative in the Wholesaler equation. As is observed in Wang et al (2006), when roads are poor, small brokers are able to go into fairly remote areas and procure higher valued crops, such as fruit. Farmers themselves, however, appear to find it relatively difficult to get to wholesale markets. Likewise, when taxes are charged in the local periodic market, apple- and grape-producing farmers are more reluctant to sell their output there (included in the broker's category) and opt for alternatives.

The most important results, however, are found in the coefficients of variables of interest: Farm Size and Assets per capita (Tables 15.7 and 15.8, rows 1 and 2). In both sets of regressions, for apple-producing and grape-producing households, the coefficients on the Farm Size variable are insignificant. This is true for both model specifications and for all channel equations (Broker, Wholesaler and Modern marketing channel). Consistent with the descriptive statistics, there is no measurable systematic relationship between farm size and choice of marketing channel. One interpretation of this result is that in Shandong province apple and grape markets, there are no constraints that limit smallholders from entering modern supply chains and keep them in traditional broker chains and wholesale markets.

The same general results are found for wealth (Tables 15.7 and 15.8, row 2). Assets per capita variables in all of the regressions models are insignificant. This is true when model specification is either weighted OLS or Tobit. It is true for apple-producing and grape-producing households. It is true in the Broker, Wholesaler and Modern supply chain equations. As suggested by the descriptive statistics,

Table 15.7 Determinants of apple marketing channels in Shandong Province, 2001 and 2006

	Broker (1)	OLS (w/ weight) Wholesaler (2)	Modern (3)	Broker (4)	Tobit (w/o weight) Wholesaler (5)	Modern (6)
Farm size and assets:						
Cultivated land in 2001 (mu)	1.17 (0.90)	−0.67 (0.75)	−0.50 (0.35)	−0.77 (1.52)	0.17 (0.57)	−0.74 (0.69)
Per capita assets in 2001 (10,000 yuan)	2.90 (3.96)	−0.30 (3.64)	−2.60 (1.86)	0.25 (8.25)	3.13 (3.54)	2.14 (3.91)
Proxy for incentives:						
Distance to county road (km)	4.40 (1.58)***	−6.97 (1.71)***	2.57 (1.20)**	10.87 (3.92)***	−5.44 (1.55)***	−0.16 (1.79)
Off-farm labour share in 2001 (%)	−0.00 (0.07)	−0.18 (0.08)**	0.19 (0.05)***	−0.02 (0.18)	−0.14 (0.07)*	0.10 (0.08)
Household characteristics:						
Age of HH head (years)	−0.35 (0.26)	−0.06 (0.28)	0.41 (0.17)**	−0.15 (0.60)	−0.10 (0.24)	0.28 (0.28)
Education of HH head (years)	−0.58 (0.92)	−0.54 (0.97)	1.12 (0.50)**	−3.30 (2.30)	1.00 (0.96)	2.68 (1.10)**
Village control variables:						
Village per household apple areat-6 (mu)	−5.75 (2.42)**	3.93 (2.18)*	1.82 (1.02)*	−11.78 (4.73)**	2.73 (1.88)	0.87 (2.14)
Farmer association (yes=1;no=0)	30.87 (7.18)***	−25.50 (7.18)***	−5.38 (2.55)**	53.85 (15.20)***	−25.82 (6.28)***	−1.40 (7.00)
Distance to wet market (km)	−1.18 (0.33)***	1.12 (0.32)***	0.06 (0.14)	−2.81 (0.82)***	1.14 (0.33)***	0.30 (0.37)
Distance to wholesale market (km)	0.01 (0.12)	0.07 (0.13)	−0.08 (0.09)	0.14 (0.34)	−0.08 (0.14)	−0.25 (0.16)
Number of years elapsed since establishment of wholesale market	−0.01 (0.16)	0.35 (0.20)*	−0.34 (0.16)**	0.45 (0.48)	0.02 (0.18)	−0.02 (0.21)
Sale tax in periodic market (yes=1;no=0)	−21.57 (6.47)***	17.19 (6.61)***	4.39 (3.22)	−75.69 (16.72)***	23.22 (6.69)***	−2.49 (7.28)
Regulations on marketing (yes=1;no=0)	0.09 (6.53)	6.74 (6.36)	−6.83 (2.50)***	42.32 (14.65)***	−14.66 (5.99)**	−21.79 (7.53)***
Constant	57.23 (18.52)***	64.35 (20.29)***	−21.58 (10.21)**	47.48 (45.03)	50.57 (18.51)***	−47.12 (20.96)**
Observations	538	538	538	538	538	538
R-squared	0.16	0.15	0.17			

Notes: All numbers in parentheses are robust standard errors. ***, ** and * represent statistically significance at 1%, 5% and 10%, respectively. Apple modern channels include special suppliers, processing firms, restaurants and export companies.

Table 15.8 *Determinants of grape marketing channels in Shandong Province, 2001 and 2006*

	Broker (1)	OLS (w/ weight) Wholesaler (2)	Modern (3)	Broker (4)	Tobit (w/o weight) Wholesaler (5)	Modern (6)
Farm size and assets:						
Cultivated land in 2001 (mu)	-0.48 (0.57)	0.31 (0.61)	0.17 (0.46)	0.01 (1.26)	-0.20 (1.16)	1.12 (0.96)
Per capita assets in 2001 (10,000 yuan)	0.14 (2.93)	-1.22 (1.02)	1.09 (2.99)	-1.85 (4.51)	3.80 (5.32)	1.87 (3.44)
Proxy for incentives:						
Distance to county road (km)	-1.39 (1.12)	-0.03 (0.85)	1.42 (0.90)	-1.67 (1.92)	-2.79 (1.85)	2.01 (1.57)
Off-farm labour share in 2001 (%)	-0.20 (0.09)**	0.06 (0.09)	0.14 (0.07)**	-0.05 (0.21)	-0.12 (0.21)	0.03 (0.16)
Household characteristics:						
Age of HH head (years)	0.12 (0.32)	-0.24 (0.28)	0.12 (0.20)	1.22 (0.77)	-1.85 (0.78)**	0.39 (0.59)
Education of HH head (years)	-0.51 (1.01)	0.50 (1.11)	0.01 (0.90)	2.45 (2.70)	-1.67 (2.72)	1.42 (2.12)
Village control variables:						
Village per household grape area-6 (mu)	-7.15 (2.95)**	3.99 (2.38)*	3.16 (2.25)	-12.39 (6.82)*	17.11 (6.65)**	1.03 (4.91)
Farmer association (yes=1;no=0) (13.38)***	8.74 (7.40)	-29.29 (5.44)***	20.55 (7.87)***	-6.53 (18.39)	-107.30 (22.54)***	50.54
Distance to wet market (km)	-0.93 (0.47)**	-0.73 (0.47)	1.67 (0.38)***	-2.18 (0.99)**	-1.68 (0.94)*	3.45 (0.87)***
Distance to wholesale market (km)	0.22 (0.52)	1.25 (0.41)***	-1.47 (0.31)***	1.70 (1.00)*	2.22 (1.01)**	-3.79 (0.94)***
Number of years elapsed since establishment of wholesale market	-0.11 (0.23)	0.03 (0.17)	0.08 (0.16)	0.13 (0.48)	0.07 (0.51)	-0.41 (0.40)
Sale tax in periodic market (yes=1;no=0) (20.75)***	-70.12 (10.95)***	-7.58 (7.54)	77.70 (11.16)***	-104.27 (24.92)***	-31.23 (28.61)	94.23
Regulations on marketing (yes=1;no=0) (10.23)***	-24.58 (5.88)***	3.16 (6.56)	21.42 (5.96)***	-35.76 (12.82)***	-2.71 (12.96)	30.16
Number of wine and other grape processing firms in county capital	-11.01 (1.63)***	2.49 (1.52)	8.52 (1.30)***	-19.38 (3.61)***	-0.04 (3.30)	12.42 (2.74)***
Constant (44.76)***	160.85 (23.55)***	25.37 (19.95)	-86.22 (17.78)***	66.01 (54.39)	96.21 (57.20)*	-166.59
Observations	375	375	375	375	375	375
R-squared	0.40	0.19	0.39			

Notes: All numbers in parentheses are robust standard errors. ***, ** and * represent statistically significance at 1%, 5% and 10%, respectively. Grape modern channels include special suppliers, processing firms, restaurants and supermarkets.

our regression results confirm that poor apple- and grape-producing households in Shandong Province are not being contained in traditional channels any more than households with higher assets. Likewise, access to modern supply chains is wealth neutral; poorer farmers appear to have equal access.

Conclusions

Although upstream segments of the marketing chain have evolved dramatically in the past 20 years, there is little evidence that impacts have directly reached the farm gate. As is found in other farm-level studies that sample randomly, and correct for sample selection bias, most farmers are selling their apples and grapes into traditional marketing channels. Small brokers and wholesalers procure nearly 90 per cent of apples and well over half of grapes. Despite the rise of supermarkets, no farmers were found to sell to them directly.

On the other hand, midstream changes in modern marketing chains did reach the farm gate in the fruit sector, which is different from our earlier findings in the vegetable market (Wang et al, 2006). This is particularly true for grapes. There was a significant and somewhat growing trend of the shares of farmers selling their grapes to processors and other agents from modern marketing channels.

However, we find that modern channels are remarkably neutral in terms of farm size and wealth. There is no evidence, in either the descriptive statistics or the multivariate analysis, that small farmers are being denied access to the modern supply chains where those chains exist. The same is true for the poor. It seems plausible that, in a market economy like that for fruit, in which there is little regulation, easy entry, and tens of thousands of traders, buyers go to those who can produce at lowest cost. This group includes poor, small farmers, who typically can be expected to have lower opportunity costs on their time.

In such an environment there are a number of priorities for policy makers. First, continued hands-off management of markets is appropriate. Markets at all levels are competitive and food is being provided to the cities in an efficient and inexpensive way. Smallholder farmers are participating. Second, when a market is dominated by many small agents, both in traditional and marketing channels, there is a big challenge in meeting the growing demand for food safety. Evidence from many other countries shows that policies focused on producing safer pesticides may help to improve the safety of the marketing system. Regulation on the production and import side of the pesticide industry may be the best way to clean up fruit production.

Annex Table 15.1 *Description of major variables used in the models of the determinants of the marketing channels of apple- and grape-producing households and their impacts on farmers in Shandong Province, 2001 and 2006*

	Apples			Grapes		
	Mean	Min.	Max.	Mean	Min.	Max.
Brokers (%)	22.6	0.0	100	52.8	0.0	100
Wholesalers (%)	67.0	0.0	100	22.2	0.0	100
Modern channel (%)	10.5	0.0	100	25.0	0.0	100
Net income in 2006 (yuan/mu)	3132	−689	10,864	3041	−2030	11,116
Incentives:						
Distance from county road (km)	1.7	0.0	5.0	3.1	0.0	30.0
Off-farm labour share in 2001 (%)	25.6	0.0	100	33.2	0.0	100
Farm size and assets:						
Cultivated land in 2001 (mu)	5.4	0.9	30.0	6.5	0.5	40.0
Per capita assets in 2001 (10,000 yuan)	0.53	0.01	3.83	0.76	0.02	16.31
Farm household head:						
Age (years)	48.4	22.0	77.0	49.7	22.0	75.0
Education (years)	7.6	0.0	13.0	7.0	0.0	15.0
Village Control Variables:						
Village per household apple or grape area t-6 (mu)	1.3	0.0	4.2	0.7	0.0	4.3
Farmer association (yes=1; no=0)	14.0	0.0	100	32.6	0.0	100
Distance from wet market (km)	6.9	0.0	50.0	7.3	0.0	40.0
Distance from wholesale market (km)	13.9	0.0	65.0	10.5	0.0	36.0
Years of establishment of the nearest wholesale market	1988	1949	2005	1990	1949	2003
Sale tax in periodic market during past 5 years (yes=1; no=0)	80.1	0.0	100	76.7	0.0	100
Regulations on marketing during past 5 years (yes=1; no=0)	12.1	0.0	100	49.0	0.0	100
Number of wine and other grape processing firms in county seat			?	2.1	0.0	5.0

Note: All figures were in 2001 and 2006 except for those with the year specified.

Notes

1   2.6 per cent plus 4.4 per cent, Table 15.3, row 1.
2   3.3 per cent plus 7.9 per cent, Table 15.3, row 2.
3   55 per cent or 27.7 per cent plus 27.2 per cent, Table 15.3, row 6.
4   We use this variable because the regression is run mainly using cross-sectional household data.

References

Berdegue, J. A., Balsevich, F., Flores, L. and Reardon, T. (2005) 'Central American supermarkets private standards of quality and safety in procurement of fresh fruits and vegetables', *Food Policy*, vol 30, no 3, pp254–269

Bi, X., Dong, X., Huang, J., Hu, D. and Rozelle, S. (2004) 'Securing small producer participation in restructured national and regional agri-food systems, China country project report on "Regoverning Markets"', Center for Chinese Agricultural Policy, Chinese Academy of Sciences, Beijing

Dong, X., Wang, H., Huang, J., Rozelle, S. and Reardon, T. (2006) 'Small traders and small farmers: The small engines driving China's giant boom in horticulture', Working Paper, Center for Chinese Agriculture Policy, Chinese Academy of Science, Beijing

Goldman, A. and Vanhonacker, W. (2006) 'The food retail system in China: Strategic dilemmas and lessons for retail international/modernization', a paper presented in the Global Retail Conference, 17–18 July, University of Surrey, UK

Hu, D., Fred, G. and Reardon, T. (2006) 'New way about supermarket+processing firm+farmers', *Agricultural Economic Problems*, vol 1, pp36–39

Hu, D., Reardon, T., Rozelle, S., Timmer, P. and Wang, H. (2004) 'The emergence of supermarkets with Chinese characteristics: Challenges and opportunities for China's agricultural development', *Development Policy Review*, vol 22, pp557–586

Huang, J., Rozelle, S. and Chang, M. (2004) 'The nature of distortions to agricultural incentives in China and implications of WTO accession', *World Bank Economic Review*, vol 18, no 1, pp59–84

Huang, J., Rozelle, S., Dong, X., Wu, Y., Huang, Z., Niu, X. and Zhi, H. (2006) 'Small farmers and agri-food market restructuring: The case of the fruit sector in China', a Project Report Submitted to Agricultural Development Economics Division, Food and Agriculture Organization of the UN, Rome

Huang, J., Wu, Y. and Rozelle, S. (2007) 'Moving off the farm and intensifying agricultural production: Linkages in China's rural labour markets', Working Paper, Center for Chinese Agricultural Policy, Chinese Academy of Sciences

Ji, Y. and Yue, F. (1999) 'Current situation and development of apple production and marketing in China', *Journal of Shandong Agriculture and Management College*, vol 4, pp14–16

National Bureau of Statistics of China (NSBC) (2007) *China Statistics Yearbook*, China Statistics Press, Beijing

Park, A., Jin, H., Rozelle, S. and Huang, J. (2002) 'Market emergence and transition: Arbitrage, transition costs, and autarky in China's grain market', *American Journal of Agricultural Economics*, vol 84, no 1, Febuary, pp67–82

Reardon, T. and Timmer, C. (2007) 'Transformation of markets for agricultural output in developing countries since 1950: How has thinking changed?' in R. E. Evenson and P.

Pingali (eds), *Handbook of Agricultural Economics, Agricultural Development: Farmers, Farm Production and Farm Markets*, Elsevier Press, Amsterdam, pp2808-2855

Rozelle, S. and Huang, J. (2007) 'The marketization of rural China: Gain or pain for China's 200 million farm families?', Paper presented at the conference Growing Pains: Tensions and Opportunity in China's Transformation, Stanford University, Stanford, CA, 2–3 November

Rozelle, S., Huang, J. and Benziger, V. (2002) 'Continuity and change in China's rural periodic markets', *China Journal*, vol 49, no 1, pp89–115

Schwentesius, R. and Manuel, A. G. (2002) 'Supermarkets in Mexico: Impacts on horticulture systems', *Development Policy Review*, vol 20, no 4, pp487–502

Wang, H., Dong, X., Huang, J., Rozelle, S. and Reardon, T. (2006) 'Producing and procuring horticultural crops with Chinese characteristics: Why small farmers are thriving and supermarkets are absent in rural China', the 26th Conference Paper of the International Association of Agricultural Economists, 14–19 August

Wu, Y., Huang, J., Rozelle, S. and Yang, Z. (2007) 'The rise of dairy processing firms and farmers participations in dairy production in China', *Issues in Agricultural Economy*, vol 336, no 12, pp62–69 (in Chinese)

Zhang, X. (2005) 'Apple production situation, problem and development in China', *Orange and Subtropical Fruits Information*, vol 21, no 6, pp1–3

Zuo, R. J. and Zhang L. J. (2003) 'The impact of agricultural supermarket chain on the agricultural industry chains', *Rural Economy*, vol 3, pp31–32

Chapter 16

Supermarkets and Small Farmers: The Case of Fresh Vegetables in Honduras

Madelon Meijer, Iván Rodriguez, Mark Lundy and Jon Hellin

Introduction

Purpose of the study

Various studies have described the trends in the 'supermarket revolution' (see for example Reardon and Berdegue, 2002; Hu et al, 2004; Berdegue et al, 2007) and have pointed out that changes in the global agricultural economy present both opportunities and challenges to rural producers. With expanding urban populations and changes in dietary habits, trade liberalization and spreading technological innovations, value chains are being restructured to remain competitive. Changes include greater vertical integration and a shift from exclusive reliance on spot markets toward the use of specialized wholesalers, the proliferation of private quality and safety standards, and increased private enforcement of public standards (Pingali et al, 2005; Gulati et al, 2007).

In 2005, the International Center for Tropical Agriculture (CIAT), with the support of the Food and Agriculture Organization of the United Nations (FAO) and in collaboration with a development agency, undertook a series of supply chain analyses focusing on how changes in markets affect smallholder vegetable producers in Honduras. The focus of the study was on improving chain governance for those farmers already active in vertically integrated chains and involved three parts:

1   a desk study on the relative rate of expansion of supermarkets and the effects that their purchasing practices have on markets for specific vegetable crops and, in particular key entry barriers that limit smallholder participation in these markets;

2   a participatory review of the supply chain for cucumbers, bell peppers, tomatoes, broccoli, potatoes and lettuce, focusing on price terms, margins, transaction costs, logistical and storage needs, and quality standards;

3   the identification of strategies to facilitate the participation of smallholder producers in vegetable supply chains linked to supermarkets – bearing in mind the entry barriers mentioned above.

During the course of the study, farmer typologies were identified and further explored and additional information was found on alternative marketing channels.

Background on Honduras

Honduras is the second largest country in Central America (after Nicaragua), comprising about 112,000 square kilometres. About 80 per cent of the country's land area consists of interior highlands or hillside areas, with the remaining 20 per cent classified as lowland valleys. Within the interior highlands, numerous flat-floored valleys are mainly used for extensive livestock operations. Hillside areas are dominated by subsistence agriculture (largely maize and beans) and staple food production and are characterized by small land holdings, low levels of technology and low productivity. Mountains and heavy rainfall make much of the region particularly vulnerable to soil degradation, especially when more marginal lands are brought into production and fallow periods are shortened (Lutz et al, 1994; Stonich, 1995).

Honduras is a very poor country, with low life expectancy rates and low literacy rates. Fifty-four per cent of the population lives in rural areas, although migration away from the countryside is increasing (Table 16.1). The inequitable distribution of land in Honduras has traditionally forced smallholder farmers onto steeplands. This trend increased after the Second World War, commensurate with the growth of agricultural export crops and a high population growth rate of 3.2 per cent per annum (Leonard, 1987, p38). In the 1950s and 1960s parts of Honduras were for the first time drawn into national and international markets. There was a growth in non-traditional agricultural exports such as cotton, sugar and beef (Durham, 1979, p117; Stonich and DeWalt, 1989; Stonich, 1995). Honduras typifies the worldwide problem of inequalities in land distribution and associated land degradation in steeplands (Leonard, 1987).

Honduras has a very small open economy, with the US as its most important trade partner. It is highly vulnerable to changes in international market conditions, notably coffee, and to natural disasters such as Hurricane Mitch, which had devastating effects in 1998. There are few tools for risk management and the capacity to respond to adverse shocks is very limited; remittances from abroad play a vital role in offsetting the effects of shocks. The country has had a substan-

Table 16.1 *Key country features of Honduras, 2005*

	Honduras	Latin America and Caribbean	World Lower middle income
Population (millions)	7.2	551	2,475
Population growth (%/year)	2.2	1.3	1.0
Surface area (000km²)	112	20,418	39,946
Urban population (% of total population)	46	78	49
GNI (US$ billions)	8.0	2,210	4,746
GNI per capita (US$)	1,120	4,008	1,918
GNI per capita (PPP)	2,900	8,111	6,313
GDP growth (%/year)	4.0	4.4	6.9
GDP per capita growth (%/year)	1.8	3.1	5.9
Agriculture (% GDP)	13.9		
Literacy (% adults)	80	90	89
Life expectancy (years)	68	72	70

Source: World Bank, Development Economics, Development Data Group (DECDG)

tial part of its debt cancelled,[1] freeing funds for poverty reduction. However, it remains low on the Human Development Index, which includes indicators on education, health and income per capita: in 2004 the index was 0.683, making it 117th out of 177 countries (UNDP, 2006). The lack of opportunities for economic development in the rural areas has led to high levels of emigration to the US. Export processing free zones (*maquiladoras*) have been set up, especially in the north of the country, while scarce financial services in the rural areas limit the opportunities for agricultural investment. With respect to agricultural trade, both exports and imports have increased since 2003, after a strong drop in exports after Hurricane Mitch. Processed agricultural imports have increased steadily since 1991, reflecting the changing dietary habits for (semi-)processed products, the growing demand for which is not met by the local agroindustrial sector (Figure 16.1).

The first supermarket chain in Honduras (the locally owned *La Colonia*) started operating in 1976, the second chain in 1988 and the third chain in 1995. During the 1990s more chains entered and consolidation took place, with Wal-Mart Central America now holding 35 out of 51 stores in the country. Total supermarket sales were US$267 million in 2004, an estimated 25 per cent of the food market. Fifty-seven per cent of the ownership of supermarket chains is in foreign hands (Table 16.2). Initial sector growth was accomplished by opening more selling points and, to a lesser degree, by incrementing sales per selling point. In order to continue growing, supermarkets now use strategies for choosing sites and sales formats according to specific target populations (from discount stores for the low socio-economic strata to membership shops with mainly imported

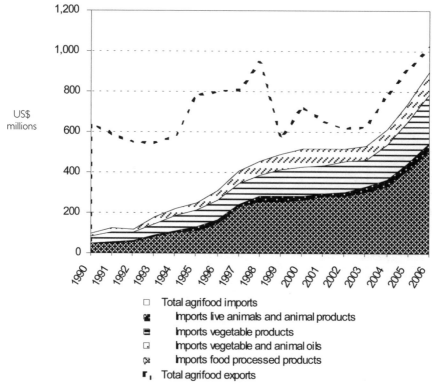

Note: FOB = free on board; CIF = cost, insurance and freight.

Source: Agropyme, 2006

Figure 16.1 *Imports and exports of the agriculture and livestock sectors in Honduras, 1990–2005 (imports in CIF, exports in FOB)*

products for the higher socio-economic classes). In addition, targeted temporary promotions are used to compete with traditional marketing channels (such as 'fresh Wednesdays' or 'farmer Thursdays'). This search for increased sales per outlet, reflected in lower prices, implies increasing competition with traditional channels. Its impact on suppliers further up the chain, in particular on small producers, is discussed later in the chapter.

The vegetable sector in Honduras operates within a context defined by public policies. These include the Poverty Reduction Strategy Paper (PRSP) and the State Policy for the Food Sector and Rural Areas of Honduras 2003–2021, including sanitary and phytosanitary rules and the Law for Small and Medium Enterprises. The horticultural agri-food chain in particular has been identified as a promising avenue for increasing the competitiveness of the agricultural sector, and a horticulture committee has been set up in which the private sector and producers are involved.[2]

In addition, Honduras is signatory of the Central American Free Trade Agreements (CAFTA) with the US (now called DR-CAFTA following inclusion

Table 16.2 *Characteristics of the main supermarket chains in Honduras, 2004*

	Owner (nationality)	Sales/year (US$ millions)	No. of outlets	Location
La Colonia	Local	63	11	Tegucigalpa
Junior	Local	46	1	San Pedro Sula
Price Smart	USA	48	2	Tegucigalpa and San Pedro Sula
Despensa Familiar	Guatemala, Costa Rica and the Netherlands (CARHCO)	25	22	Tegucigalpa, San Pedro Sula, Comayagua, Choluteca
Comisariato Los Andes	Local	20	1	San Pedro Sula
Paiz	Guatemala, Costa Rica and the Netherlands (CARHCO)	14	5	Tegucigalpa and San Pedro Sula
Stock	Local	12	3	Tegucigalpa
Mas x Menos	Local	10	2	Tegucigalpa and Choluteca
Yip	Local	9	1	Tegucigalpa
Colonial	Local	9	1	San Pedro Sula
La Económica	Local	9	1	San Pedro Sula
ELDON	Local	2	1	Roatán
TOTAL		267	51	

Note: a Now Wal-Mart Centroamérica.

Source: USDA, 2004

of the Dominican Republic). Initially, actors from the horticultural agri-food chain felt that the approval of CAFTA was a step forward in terms of competitiveness. However, CAFTA also opens the door for potential agricultural imports – including vegetables – from neighbouring countries and the US itself. While the full impact of CAFTA remains to be seen, this treaty, more than any national-level policy, will define the future for many horticultural producers in the region.

Methodology

The study methodology drew heavily on previous work in participatory value chain analysis (in particular, a field guide developed by Ruralter (Van der Heyden and Camacho, 2004)). Various aspects of the supply chains were analysed, including market conditions, the history of the chain, relationships between the actors, and the policy environment, using workshops, focus groups, participant observation and semi-structured interviews with key actors. Critical points, competitive advantages and strategic actions to improve the functioning of the supply chain were also analysed. For the final phase it was paramount that the key value chain actors participated in the process; therefore substantial time was invested in developing links and building trust with key actors along the supply chains. The research process was linked explicitly to the technical secretariat assigned to the horticultural sector by the Ministry of Agriculture, which convened and chaired many of the meetings in collaboration with researchers.

Description of the vegetable chain in Honduras

Using the market map as a conceptual framework (see Hellin et al, 2005), the value chains are analysed using three interrelated spheres: direct actors in the chain (those actors that actually own the product at some stage in the process, add value and sell it on); business development services that support the chain to work more efficiently (such as technical advice and financial services); and the enabling environment, which encompasses policies and the rules and regulations as set out by local, regional and national governments.

In hillside environments, vegetable production benefits from a lower incidence of pest and disease and slightly improved access to year-round water supplies and, as a result, can be less expensive than other environments. Vegetable production also occurs in lower lying valleys, but these regions were not included in the current study principally because producers there tend to be large-scale commercial operators.

Value chain actors

There are several channels for selling produce. The more traditional market channel is comprised principally of networks of informal traders that link areas of vegetable production with regional and national markets. This market channel is characterized by cash payments, limited quality demands and significant levels of social capital between actors. The tendency is to sell the final product in urban wholesale markets (e.g. wet markets) or traditional retail, although some products are also sold to smaller supermarkets. The main wet markets are in the capital, Tegucigalpa, and the main commercial city, San Pedro Sula, in the north of the country. The weekly market *El Estadio* in Tegucigalpa is the biggest, with 835 stalls. Some traditional traders have developed the necessary skills and knowledge to sell a portion of their produce to specialized wholesalers and, in some cases, to supermarkets and restaurants directly. This channel represents a midpoint between the traditional system and the modern retail system.

The board of directors of the wet market in Tegucigalpa does not perceive supermarkets as a major competitor, but producers identify two major impacts of supermarkets on the retail sector: (1) a diminished number of clients and (2) difficulty in sourcing sufficient supply during critical periods such as June/July, given that producers sell the best quality to the supermarkets and the remainder to the wet market. Data on sales volumes for 11 types of vegetables during June

Table 16.3 *Principal characteristics of small-scale vegetable producers in Honduras*

Variables	Unorganized small producers	Small producers in formal organizations	Independent producers with secure markets
Access to technology			
Inputs (seeds, fertilizers and pesticides)	Low	Medium	Medium
Use of seed beds or greenhouses	Low	Medium	Low
Irrigation	Low	Appropriate	Appropriate
Market access conditions			
Packing houses	No	Yes	No
Transport from the field to the packing house	Cannot pay costs	Can pay local transportation	Owns vehicle
Market information	No access	Limited access, limited knowledge	Good access, good knowledge
Price conditions	Low and instable prices	Good and stable prices	Good and stable prices
Use of quality standards	No	Yes	Yes
Type of packaging	Sacks	Plastic trays	Plastic trays
Technical assistance			
Production	No access, limited knowledge	Access, good knowledge	No access but good knowledge based on experience
Business organization	No access, limited knowledge	Access, good knowledge	No access but good knowledge based on experience
Resources used			
Land	Own land, small parcels	Own and rented	Own and rented, production in partnership with others
Labour	Family	Mostly family with some outside help.	Some family but principally hired labours
Capital, inputs	Informal lenders	Personal capital and credit	Personal capital and credit

Source: Lundy et al, 2006

Table 16.4 *Producer organizations included in the study*

Organization	No. of farmers	Annual sales, 2006 (US$)	Products	Market channels
APROHFI	110	310,000*	Carrots, lettuce, broccoli, potatoes	Specialized wholesalers, supermarkets, restaurants, wholesale markets
COHORSIL	285	205,000*	Tomatoes, bell peppers	Specialized wholesalers, supermarkets, wholesale markets and local markets

Note: * Annual sales based on monthly average data from field work in Honduras and El Salvador.
Source: Based on Agropyme, 2005

2005 showed the same amount of vegetables being sold in wet markets as in supermarkets.

The types of organization within the modern retail system range from formal associations to the 'lead farmer' model, wherein one farmer is a lead producer and associates him or herself with (a small group of) other producers to achieve required volumes, quality and consistency. Producers in the modern system are then linked into specialized wholesalers and/or directly into supermarkets, restaurants and hotels. A certain degree of competition exists between formal farmer

---

Box 16.1 The farmers' cooperative Cohorsil

Cohorsil is a farmers' cooperative founded in Siguatepeque, Honduras, in 1980. During the 1980s and 1990s, the cooperative started three businesses: agricultural inputs commercialization, coffee processing services and coffee commercialization services. However, in 2000 the price of coffee plummeted and farmers were losing money on production. With support from the Swiss non-governmental organization (NGO) Swisscontact, Cohorsil developed a business plan oriented toward helping members move into production of fresh vegetables for high value and less risky markets (such as agro-industry, export and supermarkets). To make this move, farmers needed a wide range of new services, and Cohorsil got involved in providing many of them. It supplies directly, for a fee, seedlings produced in greenhouses, new inputs, warehouse and packaging facilities and marketing services. Cohorsil also forms partnerships with private suppliers offering specialized services such as international market linkages and certifications. Cohorsil negotiates with private suppliers on behalf of its members for services such as pesticide residues and soil analysis, technical assistance, design and installation of drip irrigation systems, transportation and legal services.

Payment for such services is made sometimes by Cohorsil and sometimes directly by members. Some farms have been certified; gradually more farmers are being connected with new clients and producing new products in a profitable way. Cohorsil now has five branches serving 285 members and more than 4200 non-members in 17 villages.

Box 16.2 The farmers' association APROHFI

APROHFI is a Lenca ethnic group farmer association, founded in 2002 as the 'exit strategy' of an agriculture diversification project developed by the Honduran Foundation for Research in Agriculture (FHIA). It includes 110 small farmers (men and women) dedicated to 18 crops. APROHFI has successfully established commercial relationships with supermarkets, restaurants, hotels and specialized suppliers in San Pedro Sula, the second-largest city in Honduras.

Production is scheduled according to demand; many innovations have taken place in the production, packaging and commercialization areas. Many of them are co-financed by NGOs such as Technoserve and Swisscontact. It took four years to make the business self-sufficient; now annual turnover is US$310,000 and the association has an exclusive contract to sell fresh vegetables to Pizza Hut in Honduras. This relationship challenges the association and its members to fulfil new quality standards and more frequent deliveries for a wider variety of products.

organizations and some of the more progressive traders as both seek to sort, pack and, in some cases, add value to the horticultural products they sell.

For the purposes of this study, producers in the chain were subdivided into three categories:

1   unorganized small producers;
2   small producers organized into producer associations;[3]
3   independent producers with a secure market.

The third category was included upon discovery of a distinct business model promoted by the specialized wholesaler Hortifruti, part of Wal-Mart Central America, which develops business networks around a lead farmer; this chapter focuses on the second and third categories. The principal characteristics of the types of small vegetable producer in Honduras are shown in Table 16.3.

Table 16.4 shows the limited number of smallholder horticultural producers engaged with producer organizations in Honduras: the combined membership includes 395 producers, which constitutes less than 5 per cent of a total of 18,000 horticultural producers. This merits further attention, given that support for producer organizations is frequently seen to facilitate access of smallholder producers to markets; this is discussed further later in the chapter.

The main specialized procurement firm in Honduras is Hortifruti, which operates all over Central America as a specialist agency for Wal-Mart Central America, which owns the largest chain of retailing stores in the region (and one of the largest in Latin America): 363 sales points by mid-2005, annual sales of US$2 billion and 22,550 employees (Gonzalez-Vega et al, 2006).

Hortifruti is the main supplier of agricultural produce for the network of retailing stores, with processing plants in Costa Rica, Nicaragua and Honduras.

Table 16.5 *Changes in the demand for 16 vegetables by three specialized wholesalers*

Specialized wholesaler (coverage)	Yearly volumes (pounds)[a] 2002[b]	2006[c]	% change, 2002–2006	% average yearly increment
Hortifruti (national)	1,669,200	15,289,872	816	74
Ebenezer (San Pedro Sula)	2,719,600	10,688,028	293	41
La Colonia (Tegucigalpa)	5,252,000	7,457,840	42	9

Notes: a Vegetables used to calculate this volume include: potatoes, onions, bell peppers, carrots, lettuce, cabbage, beets, broccoli, pataste (a type of squash), cauliflower, cassava, peas, romaine lettuce, escarole lettuce and cucumbers.

b Data generated by Agropyme in 2002 through interviews with purchasing managers. At the time, La Colonia had not yet developed a consolidated purchasing system..

c Estimated volume based on first semester sales data (January to June 2006).

Source: Agropyme, 2006

To guarantee the highest quality products, Hortifruti has gradually developed relationships with small and medium local producers, which the corporation typically supplies with quality seed and packing materials and some technical assistance during sowing, harvesting and post-harvest activities. In most cases, there are no formal written contracts, but the continuation of a mutually beneficial and stable relationship over time has resulted in informal or implicit contractual arrangements. In addition, Hortifruti sometimes purchases on a seasonal basis from other growers with whom it maintains looser ties (Gonzalez-Vega et al, 2006).

A core pool of about 45 preferred producers enjoy longer-term contractual arrangements. These lead farmers are mainly selected for their willingness and capacity to innovate and deliver exactly according to Hortifruti's requirements. They do not necessarily own big farms, but they must possess sufficient fixed assets, including trucks (although some of them share or pool the use of trucks), and be able to deliver quality produce directly to the Hortifruti plant in Tegucigalpa. In order to meet volume requirements, some of the lead farmers also procure produce from neighbouring farmers who are able to meet the quality standards. This implicit delegation of the sorting and procurement of certain commodities saves Hortifruti some search costs, while the lead farmers who deliver to Hortifruti have incentives to carefully select and closely monitor their associates (Gonzalez-Vega et al, 2006).

The small lead farmers have an average of 4 hectares under irrigation, a good network of local associates (three to five on average) who complement the required volumes and access to finance and technical assistance, backed by the contract with Hortifruti. The associate producers interviewed have an ongoing relationship with the lead farmer and on average dedicate 2.6 hectares cultivated exclusively for the lead farmer. They do not own packing and other facilities. The relationship is usually based on family ties or long-standing friendships.

The lead farmers/producers are price takers with no negotiating power, but they perceive strong benefits in complying with the requirements of Hortifruti. These benefits include: (1) a secure market outlet; (2) secure payment with short delay; and (3) technical and financial assistance facilitated by Hortifruti. Hortifruti facilitates access to technical assistance programmes financed by international cooperation, but does not provide technical support to its preferred suppliers. It does have a supervisor who monitors the production operations, whose annual costs are being covered by the producer (approximately US$1000 per farmer for the first year, then reduced to half that amount, because visits become monthly instead of twice a month).

Small producers organized in producer associations were the initial focus of the study and two were found to be supplying Hortifruti on a preferred supplier basis. Hortifruti, however, prefers to deal with individual suppliers (the lead farmers) because decision-making processes in the producer organizations are complicated, reducing the chance of speedy negotiations, and traceability is easier with individual suppliers.

Pricing arrangements between Hortifruti and its suppliers can take one of three forms:

1   price bands, where a minimum and maximum price are agreed upon, depending on the season;
2   a fixed price throughout the year;
3   the market price.

Which of these three arrangements is used is decided by the store managers and can change according to the season. The price-band modality is used with the preferred suppliers with whom a relationship of at least one year has been established and is applied to the high-rotation products (such as potatoes, onions, tomatoes and lettuce). The fixed-price modality tends to be applied to scarce produce of low rotation, such as spinach. The market price is offered to new providers or spot purchases.

Markets

The fresh vegetable subsector in Honduras represents US$132.5 million per year;[4] 37 per cent of this value is added at the farm level. Production is managed by 18,000 small farmers on 11,800 hectares of land.[5] According to Hortifruti, its estimated market share in 2006 was 4 per cent of the fresh vegetables sub-sector in Honduras, for a total sales value of US$5.2 million per year. As seen in Table 16.5, Hortifruti enjoyed a growth rate in volume of over 70 per cent per year since 2002.

The vegetable crops included in the study are highly dynamic. Tomatoes were considered to be a high-risk crop for smallholders,[6] and according to the general manger of Cohorsil, only medium to large producers with significant access to capital could produce them successfully. Demand for tomatoes in Honduras is 114 metric tons (mt) per week. Supermarkets account for 28.5mt of that total (25 per cent) (Agropyme, 2005). With regard to bell peppers, 95mt are consumed weekly, with 23.5mt (21 per cent) sold by supermarkets (Agropyme, 2005).

Most vegetables, such as tomatoes and bell peppers, are sold individually but there is an increasing tendency for specialized wholesalers and producer organizations to explore the possibility of selling pre-packaged trays of both products. In addition there are attempts to brand these products. The grades and standards applied by supermarkets to them vary depending on, among other factors, the availability of the product in the market, the relationship with the supplier and the going price. Interviews with producer organizations confirmed the view that supermarkets actively adjust their grades and standards to their own benefit.

Enabling environment and business development services

As mentioned earlier, it is likely that the signing of CAFTA, more than any national-level policy, will define the future for many horticultural producers in the region. While this study did not analyse the details of the treaty, it is clear that in order to take advantage of the potential export opportunities, and to compete with an increase in high-quality imports, producers need to comply with required quality standards. Small producers and enterprises are often at a disadvantage because frequently they are not able to certify their produce. Thus it will be extremely important to provide accessible business development services such as information about and access to certification bodies, technical assistance and market intelligence that will facilitate small producers' linkages to these more demanding markets.

Farmers are also likely to need better access to credit; the financial system in Honduras is rather underdeveloped. There are 16 banks in Honduras, with assets of US$5.3 billion as of the end of 2004 (Gonzalez-Vega et al, 2006). There is a state-owned agricultural development bank, BANADESA, which has collapsed several times during its history and which has achieved only limited outreach. Severe political intrusion in financial markets, including recent legislation pardoning loans, has had a serious impact on the country's culture of repayment. Moreover, major problems with property rights have limited farmers' ability to offer their land as collateral. Furthermore, there are significant regulatory asymmetries in Honduras, which penalize those financial intermediaries willing to offer their services in the rural areas, even when the associated risks are not necessarily excessive. Few financial NGOs operate in the rural areas and even fewer provide loans for agricultural purposes (Gonzalez-Vega et al, 2006).

Although regulations are in place with respect to sanitary and phytosanitary requirements, they are seldom implemented; as a result, private standards (as established by the supermarket chains) determine the market. No regulating mechanisms are in place that moderate the commercial practices that affect small producers in particular. These include, for example, late payments, which in some cases exceed 60 days (in effect forcing producers to provide credit to the chains);

rejection of produce with no verification mechanisms; and penalties for poor product quality levied at the moment of delivery.

Analysis

One main question addressed by this study is whether, and how, small farmers can take advantage of the opportunities offered by dynamic markets. The investment costs required (in both financial and human capital) are high and appear to increase as the system evolves. Lack of access to financing represents one of the main barriers for small farmers and buyers to enter the new value chains. Lead farmers have a very difficult time getting funding to build packing houses or cold-storage facilities as they are neither creditworthy nor the target of traditional development assistance.[7]

Perhaps more important for small farmers entering the new value chains than their access to credit, risk management tools and insurance programmes are such personal attributes as skills, attitudes and experience. A crucial condition for being able to participate in dynamic value chains is the ability to innovate. Successful farmers (and farmer organizations) that have managed to benefit from emerging market opportunities will eventually meet competition from other farmers and organizations; the front-runners must innovate continually to remain competitive (Berdegue, 2002). This assumes that participating in the more dynamic chain makes the producer better off. (Those farmers able to meet the requirements of new-style retailers may still prefer to supply the traditional channels.) As shown below, the margins of producers participating in the new chains do appear to be substantially higher than they would be through other channels. Another advantage is more stable prices. In Central America, a number of studies have identified exceptionally wide fluctuations in the prices of agricultural products throughout the year, due to insufficient storage facilities and lack of access to marketing credit (as described by Gonzalez-Vega et al, 2006). Willingness to participate in the new chains is increased if there is sustained demand throughout the year and broader opportunities for diversification, which lower the risks faced by participating farmers (Gonzalez-Vega et al, 2006).

Below we present an economic analysis of stages of the value chain, a rapid gap analysis of market channels and what small farmers can offer and a brief comparison of two organizational models.

Economic analysis

Here economic analysis is used to look at the margins, costs and benefits at different stages of the chain, paying particular attention to the margins of the producer organizations. The analysis focuses on the distribution of returns on investment among actors along the supply chain and the differences between marketing channels (Table 16.6). In general terms, the chain dynamics during the period of study showed a relative proximity of prices among different chain actors active in

Table 16.6 *Distribution of final consumer price among supermarket supply chain actors in Honduras*

Variables	Tomato	Bell pepper	Potato	Broccoli	Lettuce	Carrots	Average
			Products (%)				
Production costs	15	22	24	15	17	17	18
Farm to packing shed transportation costs	4	12	1	4	6	1	5
Net farmer income for sale to producers' organization	20	0	24	14	18	12	14
Transportation costs to Tegucigalpa or San Pedro Sula	2	2	1	4	5	1	2
Net producer organization income for sale to specialized wholesaler in Tegucigalpa or San Pedro Sula	4	3	3	1	2	5	3
Gross profit for specialized wholesaler for sale to supermarket	25	32	16	32	22	33	27
Gross profit for supermarket	30	30	30	30	30	30	30
Retail price paid by final consumer	100	100	100	100	100	100	100

Source: Lundy et al, 2006

diverse market channels. The local trader who buys at the field level is competing with the producer organization, while the specialized wholesaler/supermarket channel competes with the traditional wholesaler in urban centres. Despite the apparent competition, the demands of each commercial channel vary in terms of quality and consistency. Wholesalers who specialize are able to demand higher prices from supermarkets for similar products due principally to their investment in refrigeration, adherence to grades and standards and consistent supply. While there is no clear shift to exclusive use of specialized wholesalers, our data indicate that there is a tendency for the supermarkets in Honduras to move in this direction.

According to these data, 30 per cent of the final consumer price is gross income for the supermarket, 27 per cent gross margin for the dedicated wholesaler, 7 per cent transport costs, and 18 per cent production costs. The producer receives 14 per cent when s/he sells to an association and the association itself receives a margin of 3 per cent. The preceding data should be treated with caution because it was not possible during the study to ascertain with confidence the net margins for supermarkets and specialized wholesalers; the apparent lion's share of the final consumer price that they appear to receive may not be entirely accurate due to such factors as product perishability. During participatory workshops, supermarket buyers noted that spoilage of 8–10 per cent for tomatoes and peppers was considered average (Lundy et al, 2006).

It is interesting to highlight the relatively low level of producer organization participation in the final consumer price (3 per cent). When researchers reflected on these results with members of the supply chains, the question was raised of the economic viability of existing producer organization models. The combination of relatively low product volumes plus low margins means that many of the farmer organizations require ongoing subsidies to cover operational costs, despite significant support from donor and development agencies over long periods of time. The rationale behind this model is to maximize benefits to participating farm families. However, a model that is inherently unsustainable at the organizational level may not be the best way to achieve this objective over time.

Gap analysis/entry barriers

We used a rapid gap analysis to set out the requirements of demanding market channels versus what small farmers generally can offer individually. The procurement practices of the supermarket chains, which impose various standards of quality and performance, differ dramatically from the way transactions take place through traditional marketing channels. The new institutional buyers enter into long-term informal contractual relationships with new specialized wholesalers or enterprising agricultural producers involving a complex series of commitments and standards of performance, which frequently require costly and risky investments by the producer (Gonzalez-Vega et al, 2006, pp20–21). Hortifruti's produce standards cover appearance; degree of development; cleanliness; physical aspect and colour; damage from insects, disease or equipment; water content; smell; texture; firmness; ripeness; size; and tolerance to packing. Additional standards of traceability have also been implemented, with a bar code assigned for each farmer's produce. These efforts have ensured compliance with strict privately developed food safety and quality standards, equivalent to those adopted by the European good agricultural practices scheme GLOBALGAP, the Food and Drug Administration (FDA) of the US and the internationally recognized Codex Alimentarius (Gonzalez-Vega et al, 2006).

Other supermarket procurement agents apply standards according to their own criteria, without previous communication to the suppliers. This affects the relationship at the moment of delivering the produce, where the subjectivity of the storehouse managers leads to disagreement with the suppliers on product quality, with possible reductions in price for poor quality or extra charges for possible storage losses.

In order for the producers to comply with Hortifruti's standards, they need to invest in selection, cleaning and packing facilities. They must also train workers in harvesting and post-harvest techniques. Good agricultural and good manufacturing practices are being promoted, but could still be greatly improved. To reduce the financial pressure these investments require, Hortifruti has facilitated access through a financial institution to credit at preferential rates, under the condition that the producer can show a contract with Hortifruti; the sums owed to the bank are subtracted weekly from delivery payments.

The main entry barriers for producers to supply Hortifruti include: (1) the trial period, which serves to select providers that possess the attitudes that Hortifruti appreciates in a commercial relationship (described below); (2) acquiring the knowledge and making the investments necessary to be able to implement good agricultural and good manufacturing practices; and (3) meeting volume targets on time. Producers able to overcome these entry barriers can access the network of Wal-Mart stores via Hortifruti. For many producers and producer organizations, this market is attractive because it demands far more produce than they currently grow.

The trial period lasts six months, during which time Hortifruti assesses the producers' leadership skills, their attitude toward establishing a commercial relationship, speed of decision-making and ability to meet required volumes, quality and delivery times. Hortifruti tends to initiate trial periods during times of high prices, so that producers are more likely to comply with the quality requirements. After this period, producers taken into the preferred supplier scheme are either assigned bigger volumes of the same products or encouraged to diversify into different products. Producers can negotiate a more stable price, either through price bands or fixed prices, depending on the type of product. Hortifruti's current strategy is to focus on its current providers and only when volume requirements are not being met does it invest time in screening new preferred suppliers.

Complying with the volumes and delivery periods is directly related to producers' geographic location, access to technology and finance, transport facilities and access to qualified technical assistance. Given the strict requirements set out above, it is very difficult for individual small producers to become listed as preferred suppliers to Hortifruti, despite its perceived advantages. The best chances are as associated providers to lead farmers or through producer organizations.

Comparison of different organizational models

In order to compare net margins earned by producers delivering to their producer organizations, with lead farmers and their associates, basic costs were registered during the 2006 growing season (Table 16.7). Again, the data need to be treated with caution, as they cover only one growing season and a very limited number of producers. However, they do suggest that producers benefit by participating in contractual arrangements. They also seem to indicate that supplying Hortifruti individually gives slightly higher margins than supplying through association with a lead farmer. In the lead farmer model, the preferred supplier covers production costs exclusive of labour and the associated producer provides labour costs. The data also show that one producer incurred substantial losses; this is explained by the producer giving priority to complying with required volumes despite substantial overspending on production costs (in this case heavy use of pesticides to combat pests).

When the lead farmer and producer organization models are compared using key variables,[8] some interesting results are found. First, the cost to link to dynamic

Table 16.7 *Net margins of four lead farmers and their associate producers supplying Hortifruti*

Producer	Product	Production modality			Differential margin between own production and shared production (%)	Relation input and transport costs/labour costs
		Own	Shared			
		Net margin, lead farmer	Net margin, associated provider[a]	Net margin, lead farmer[b]		
'A'	Tomato	53%				2.4
'B'	Cabbage	34%	66%	−81%	114	1.7
'C'	Lettuce	73%	86%	58%	15	3.4
	Cucumber	57%	79%	22%	35	3.0
'D'	Squash	71%	79%	58%	13	1.7
	Kidney bean	85%	88%	79%	6	1.5

Notes: a Gross income paid by the dedicated supplier minus labour costs, divided by the gross income.

b (Gross income of the dedicated supplier minus gross income of the associated producer) minus (inputs and transportation costs) divided by the (gross income of the dedicated supplier minus gross income of the associate producer).

Source: Agropyme, 2006

markets in the lead farmer model is higher than for the two producer associations for individual farmers, but lower by land area (Table 16.8).

The data indicate that as farm size grows, per hectare costs of organization, technical assistance, sorting and packing fall, creating economies of scale. In the lead farmer model, most costs are variable costs associated with marketing and working capital. Fixed costs such as irrigation, warehouse facilities and organization are tightly linked to market demand. In the farmer organizations, however, fixed costs are higher and used in an inefficient fashion (Agropyme, 2006, p39).

A second point of comparison is who assumes the costs of the organizational models. The lead farmer model responds to market needs and, as such, most investments come from the lead farmers themselves. For the farmer organizations, international donor support continues to be important (Table 16.9).

Table 16.8 *Costs of linking farmers to dynamic markets, by organizational model*

Organizational model	Average cost per farmer (US$)	Average cost per manzana (US$)
Lead farmer	4544	905
Farmer organization (APROHFI)	3912	5585
Farmer organization (Cohorsil)	3631	1452

Note: 1 *manzana* = 2.47 hectares.

Source: Agropyme, 2006

Table 16.9 *Funding sources for organizational models*

Organizational model	Funding source (%)		Individual
	External donor	Hortifruti /Association	producer
Lead farmer	12.2	5.3	82.5
Farmer organization (APROHFI)	84.3	9.1	6.5
Farmer organization (Cohorsil)	56.5	19.9	23.6

Source: Agropyme, 2006

The rationale behind significant donor support for the farmer organization model is that of social inclusion. In APROHFI, for example, the majority of farmers are members of the Lenca ethnic group and have small land holdings and high levels of household poverty. The use of public funds to subsidize organizations ranges from a high of US$3299 per farmer for APROHFI to a low of US$553 in the lead farmer model. This disparity has implications for the design of development interventions and the targeted use of public subsidies, discussed below.

Discussion

Within policy, research and development agendas, there is growing interest in making markets work for the poor. Featuring high on the development agendas is enhancing farmers' access to markets through the production of high-value agricultural products such as vegetables. One of the findings from research in Honduras is that smallholder farmers' access to high-value vegetable markets is limited and that obvious models and approaches are largely elusive. Despite significant investments of time and financial resources, existing producer organizations encompass significantly less than 5 per cent of total horticultural producers in Honduras. Only if these subsidies provided market access to a larger percentage of smallholders would there would be a case for continuing public sector or donor support.

Possible causes identified for the limited inclusion are: limited business skills within existing producer organizations; non-replicable organizational models for linking smallholders to dynamic markets (for example, too costly in terms of time and financial resources, with limited benefits); and general uncertainty about the benefits that smallholders can expect from the supermarket channel (Lundy et al, 2006). In addition to the issue of organizational reach, there are significant issues of business viability to be addressed. Many of these organizations cannot cover their costs through their activities and thus rely on ongoing subsidies to stay in the market (see Table 16.6).

The findings in Honduras are mirrored in neighbouring Nicaragua, where Berdegue et al (2007) calculated that through donors' new 'business linkages' programmes in horticulture, some NGOs had project budgets per farmer that were eight times what the Ministry of Agriculture had available to spend per farmer. It is likely, therefore, that these programmes will continue to serve a limited number of elite small and medium farmers. Governments are unlikely to be able to replicate them and thus they will probably not be sustainable in the longer term (Reardon and Flores, 2006).

This chapter highlights the need to identify alternative forms for smallholder organizations that might achieve similar social and economic returns for farmers at a lower overall cost. A promising avenue to explore in this regard is the lead farmer model currently under development by the private sector and the existing models of informal collective action in marketing that function around traders. Prior to recommending the lead farmer model as the solution, however, additional work is needed to gain greater insight into the equity implications of this model. Key issues include a greater understanding of the role that farmers play in their communities and how much benefit from market linkages accrues to these actors as opposed to other producers in their networks. The data presented in this chapter, while illustrative, are far from definitive.

A second related issue is the use of public funds. The significant variation between linkage costs per farmer and per area cultivated found in Honduras would seem to imply that efficiency gains in the use of targeted subsidies are indeed possible. With the help of further research it should be possible to increase market linkage programme coverage for roughly the same per farmer cost as current interventions. Governmental, non-governmental and donor agencies would be advised to review these issues in the design and implementation of new market linkage efforts in Honduras and elsewhere.

A study of access to markets for farmer organizations could learn from existing models, draw out key insights and engage commercial actors to develop adapted versions of effective models that permit both market access and improved smallholder equity. Such a process of co-development based on shared learning would appear to be appropriate for future action-research projects in the field – and an important area of innovation within more traditional market linkage projects and programmes. Further work is needed to balance the private sector need for supplier development with social goals of inclusion, equity and sustainable management of natural resources. The end product of this work should be improved business models that provide development paths for rural producers and their organizations in dynamic market channels through the provision of high-quality products.

Notes

1   The amount of debt cancelled reached US$200 million per year as of 2006, to be disbursed through the poverty reduction strategy paper (PRSP) framework. However, the process for project approval has been perceived as excessively bureaucratic.
2   Non-organized small producers are not represented on this committee.
3   Based on two case studies: APRHOFI (Asociación de Productores de Hortalizas y Frutas de Intibucá) and Cohorsil (Cooperativa de Horticultores de Siguatepeque

Limitada). These were the only two producer organizations found to be supplying supermarkets in a consistent fashion.

4   Honduras Central Bank (www.bch.hn).
5   Estimates made by the farmer training programme of the Millennium Challenge Corporation.
6   According to members of the supply chain analysis steering committee.
7   How the rise of supermarkets influences the development of the financial sector has been described by Gonzalez-Vega et al (2006).
8   Variables incorporated into the comparison include organization, technical assistance, warehouse facilities, packing, marketing costs, drip irrigation, working capital and research costs. To standardize the comparison, data for the first two years of each system were used.

References

Agropyme (2005) 'Analisis de la cadena de valor para tomate de mesa, chile dulce, broccoli, lechuga, zanahoria y papa producida por pequeños productores, con enfoque en la comercialización a través de supermercados', Agropyme, Swiss Agency for Development and Cooperation (COSUDE) and Swisscontact, Tegucigalpa

Agropyme (2006) 'Innovaciones organizacionales de pequeños productores de vegetales para participar en canales de comercialización dinámicos en Honduras', report for the Regoverning Markets Programme, Agropyme, COSUDE, and Swisscontact, Tegucigalpa

Berdegue, J. (2002) 'Learning to beat Cochrane's treadmill. Public policy, markets and social learning in Chile's small-scale agriculture', in C. Leeuwis and R. Pyburn (eds) *Wheelbarrows Full of Frogs: Social learning in rural resource management*, Agricultural University of Wageningen, Wageningen, The Netherlands

Berdegue, J., Reardon, T., Balsevich, F., Flores, L. and Hernández, R. A. (2007) 'Supermarkets and small horticultural product farmers in Central America', in J. F. M. Swinnen (ed.) *Global Supply Chains, Standards and the Poor: How the Globalization of Food Systems and Standards Affects Rural Development and Poverty*, CABI, Wallingford, UK, pp135–144

Durham, W. H. (1979) *Scarcity and Survival in Central America: Ecological Origins of the Soccer War*, Stanford University Press, Stanford, CA

Gonzalez-Vega, C., Chalmers, G., Quiros, R. and Rodriguez-Meza, J. (2006) 'Hortifruti in Central America: A case study about the influence of supermarkets on the development and evolution of creditworthiness among small and medium agricultural producers', Microreport no. 57, Prepared for USAID, Rural and Agricultural Finance Initiative, Rural Finance Program, Ohio State University, Columbus, OH

Gulati, A., Minot, N., Delgado, C. and Bora, S. (2007) 'Growth in high-value agriculture in Asia and the emergence of vertical links with farmers', in J. F. M. Swinnen (ed.) *Global Supply Chains, Standards and the Poor: How the Globalization of Food Systems and Standards Affects Rural Development and Poverty*, CABI, Wallingford, UK, pp91–108

Hellin, J., Griffith, A. and Albu, M. (2005) 'Mapping the market: Market-literacy for agricultural research and policy to tackle rural poverty in Africa', in F. Rl. Almond and E. D. Hainsworth (eds) *Beyond Agriculture – Making Markets Work for the Poor*, Natural Resources International Limited, Aylesford, Kent and Practical Action, Bourton-on-Dunsmore, Warwickshire, UK, pp109–148

Hu, D., Reardon, R., Rozelle, S., Timmer, P. and Wang, H. (2004) 'The emergence of supermarkets with Chinese characteristics: Challenges and opportunities for China's agricultural development', *Development Policy Review*, vol 22, no 5, pp557–586

Leonard, H. J. (1987) *Natural Resources and Economic Development in Central America: A Regional Environmental Profile*, International Institute for Environment and Development, Washington, DC

Lundy, M., Banegas, R., Centeno, L., Rodriguez, I., Alfaro, M., Hernandez, S. and Cruz, J. A. (2006) 'Assessing small-holder participation in value chains: The case of vegetables in Honduras and El Salvador', FAO, Rome

Lutz, E., Pagiola, S. and Reiche, C. (1994) 'The costs and benefits of soil conservation: The farmers' viewpoint', *The World Bank Research Observer*, vol 9, no 2, pp273–295

Pingali, P., Khwaja, Y. and Meijer, M. (2005) 'Commercializing small farms: Reducing transaction costs', ESA Working Paper No. 05–08, Agricultural and Development Economics Division, FAO, Rome

Reardon, T. and Berdegue, J. (2002) 'The rapid rise of supermarkets in Latin America: Challenges and opportunities for development', *Development Policy Review*, vol 20, no 4, pp371–388

Reardon, T. and Flores, L. (2006) '"Customized Competitiveness" strategies for horticultural exporters: Central America focus with lessons from and for other regions', Viewpoint Article, *Food Policy*, vol 31, no 6, pp483–503

Stonich, S. (1995) 'Development, rural impoverishment and environmental destruction in Honduras', in Painter, M. and Durham, W. H. (eds) *The Social Causes of Environmental Destruction in Latin America*, The University of Michigan Press, Michigan, MI

Stonich, S. and DeWalt, B. (1989). 'The political economy of agricultural growth and rural transformation in Honduras and Mexico', in S. Smith and E. Reeves (eds) *Human Systems Ecology: Studies in the Integration of Political Economy, Adaptation, and Socionatural Regions*, Westview Press, Boulder, CO, pp202–230

UNDP (2006) 'Informe nacional sobre desarrollo humano Honduras: Hacia la expansión della ciudanía', UNDP Honduras, Tegucigalpa

USDA (2004) 'Foreign Agricultural Service, Honduras Market Development Reports', Retail Food Sector, prepared by Ana Gomez, Agricultural Specialist

Van der Heyden, D. and Camacho, P. (2004) 'Guia metodológica para el análisis de cadenas productivas', Ruralter, Quito

Chapter 17

Impact of International Food Safety Standards on Smallholders: Evidence from Three Cases

Clare Narrod, Devesh Roy, Belem Avendaño
and Julius Okello

Introduction

Food safety has received heightened attention in the developed as well as in developing countries because of: an increased demand for safe food by households with rapidly rising incomes; technological improvements in measuring contaminants; a more diverse group of exporters; and increased media and consumer attention to the risks of food-borne illnesses and the dangers associated with recent food scares. Examples include Salmonella in cantaloupe and pesticide residues in green beans and grapes. In response, food retailers and food service firms in developed countries have created private protocols relating to pesticide residues, field and packing house operations and traceability. Likewise, governments in both developed and developing countries have responded with both mandatory and voluntary programmes for food safety. The increased food safety standards can potentially exclude small farmers who face four problems: (1) how to produce safe food; (2) how to be recognized as producing safe food; (3) how to identify cost-effective technologies for reducing risk; and (4) how to be competitive with larger producers (Narrod et al, 2005).

Food safety standards could very easily create differentiation among small farmers. This chapter uses case studies to assess the impact of food safety standards on smallholder producers of different crops in three countries: cantaloupe in Mexico, green beans in Kenya and grapes in India. All three cases had substantial smallholder participation prior to the introduction of increased international food safety standards (IFSS) and provide a good opportunity to assess the standards' impact on smallholder participation in the markets.

In the case of Mexico we looked at the effect on smallholder cantaloupe producers when increased food safety standards were applied to all exports. Cantaloupe was exported to the US until food safety concerns between 2000 and 2002 resulted in a ban on imports from all Mexican sources in 2002. Later, the US opened the market to selected firms with Mexican and US government approval, but US firms began demanding good agricultural practices (GAPs) and good manufacturing practices (GMPs) to minimize microbial contamination in fresh produce. During the interim period many smallholders found other domestic market outlets. The ban resulted (at least in the short term) in a two-tier system with larger farmers catering to the export markets and smallholders either selling to domestic markets or switching to honeydew melons, papaya or other products. At the time of writing it was too soon to gauge the longer-term impact.

In the case of grape exports from India, we compared the effects on smallholder income of accessing the more discerning markets with high food safety standards versus not accessing them. Mahagrapes, a marketing partner to farmer cooperatives, started exporting grapes to Europe in the early 1990s. During the first few years, the cooperatives faced extremely high rates of rejection by European markets (at times greater than 80 per cent). Within three years, nearly half of the cooperatives had parted ways with Mahagrapes to focus again on domestic markets; only a select set of smallholders retained access to the export markets.

In the case of Kenya, green beans exported to the European supermarkets were pre-cut and pre-packed, a process that required large investments to coordinate supply and upgrade hygienic conditions at farms or packing houses. The product had to meet EU public standards and, more importantly, the private standards of the retailers (for example the British Retail Consortium (BRC)). The private standards were usually more stringent than the public ones, requiring mechanisms such as third party certification and traceability in addition to restrictions on pesticide usage and the maintenance of hygiene standards. The effect of such stringent standards was to screen out many smallholders from export markets. A select group of smallholders continued to access the market even with very stringent standards, while other smallholders switched to the canning sector or to those wholesale export chains with less stringent standards.

We argue that in analysing the impact of IFSS on smallholders, there needs to be a distinction between short- and long-term impacts and between effects on smallholders who had institutional support and those who did not. These distinctions are important; much of the literature considers only the short-run impact, overestimating the impact on smallholders (see for example Muwanga, 2007). When smallholders are faced with stringent requirements in the export markets, their coping strategies differ depending on the options available to them, which determine the overall impact of IFSS on their livelihoods. In India and Mexico, the absence of an intermediate market confined small farmers to the lowest-end, unorganized domestic markets or forced them to switch products (with high impact). In Kenya on the other hand, green bean producers unable to meet IFSS could switch to supplying the canning industry or the wholesale export chains, which cushioned the effects of IFSS being introduced.

It is possible that over the long run more smallholders and associated firms will be able to meet increased IFSS standards, as in the Indian and Kenyan cases and a number of other cases of small farmers participating successfully in high-value markets. Such an outcome, we argue, is dependent largely on the provision of adequate institutional support to the smallholders, customized to their needs (see Narrod et al, 2007).

Cantaloupe exports from Mexico

The impact of salmonella outbreaks on exports

Mexican cantaloupe exports have been associated with food-borne disease outbreaks on various occasions.[1] In 1989/1990, an outbreak of Salmonella Chester was detected in fresh-cut cantaloupe in salad bars in several states in the US, resulting in two deaths. In 1991, outbreaks of Salmonella Poona in states in the US and Canada were traced back to cantaloupe originating from Texas or Mexico. In 1997 Mexican cantaloupe was identified as the source of an outbreak of Salmonella Saphra; investigations concluded that contamination had occurred either during production or harvesting and that the lack of refrigeration at the distributor level had contributed to its spread. In 1998, outbreaks of Salmonella Oranienburg associated with Mexican cantaloupe were detected in Ontario, Canada. In 2000 outbreaks of Salmonella Poona in eight states in the US were traced back to Mexican cantaloupe. In 2002 outbreaks of Salmonella associated with Mexican cantaloupe were found to originate in the states of Guerrero and Sonora. The outbreaks between 1997 and 2002 associated with the Salmonella pathogen led the US Food and Drug Administration (FDA) to issue an import alert, followed by a total ban in 2002.

The ban severely affected Mexican cantaloupe exports to the US, which fell from US$72 million in 1999 to just US$2.7 million in 2003 (USDA, 2006) and resulted in Mexico losing much of its market share to Guatemala, Costa Rica and Honduras. By 2004, Mexico accounted for only 2.7 per cent of the imports to the US market, while Guatemala had taken over 38 per cent of the market. At the same time, the area under cantaloupe plantation in Mexico declined to 5909 hectares (24 per cent of the total land area formerly dedicated to cantaloupe). The ban was lifted eventually, but imports to the US were allowed only under certain conditions. After a series of negotiations between the Mexican and US governments, in October 2003 Mexican cantaloupe was allowed to enter the US provided that the product met the terms of the 'Programme of federal recognition requirements for production, harvest, packaging, processing and transport of cantaloupe' (the 'NOM-EM-038-FITO') imposed by the Mexican government.

As expected, the US import ban on Mexican cantaloupe led to market reallocation away from Mexico in the short run, which affected smallholders'
participation in the export market.

Smallholder cantaloupe producers

Before the outbreaks of Salmonella, exporting cantaloupe was a good source of
income for smallholders from the Mexican states of Guerrero, Colima, Durango,
Michoacán, Oaxaca and Sonora. After the outbreaks, production of cantaloupe
for export was concentrated primarily in Sonora. Although the outbreaks were
associated only with production in Guerrero, where sanitary conditions in
cantaloupe production were poor, the effect of the Salmonella outbreak affected
all producers in terms of lost export sales, low prices and forgone income, which
led them to reduce the land area cultivated with cantaloupe.

In order to determine the impact of these changes on small growers, a small-
farm survey was conducted at harvest time in Colima, Mexico, where growers had
produced cantaloupe since 1980 (Avendaño et al, forthcoming) and had been
export-oriented. Colima is a state neighbouring Guerrero, where growers were
implicated in several Salmonella outbreaks. In January 2007, questionnaires were
given to 17 cantaloupe growers, three growers with packing facilities and a
grower/packing/shipper exporter, none of whom had ever been affected by food
safety problems. A vast majority of growers in Colima are small-scale producers
working on *ejidal* (communally held) property; 24 per cent of the sampled growers
started production with only 1–3 hectares of area planted with cantaloupe. During
the period 2000–2004 the number of growers increased by 59 per cent; for 53 per
cent of the growers, the area planted rose from 1–3 to 4–6 hectares. However, the
organization of production/marketing changed significantly due to the food safety
shock in the US market (the principal destination) and the consequent set of strict
rules requiring the adoption of good agricultural practices (GAPs) by the producers and good manufacturing practices (GMPs) by the packers.[2]

The compliance process associated with exporting cantaloupes

To demonstrate conformity with food safety standards, the grower or a firm needs
to follow a sequence of steps to comply with the new regulations (Figure 17.1).
The main source of information about regulations for most Mexican growers is
the government, through a department in the Secretariat of Agriculture and Rural
Development (SENASICA).

Growers or firms need to identify and interpret new requirements, including
whether production falls under the scope of the regulation and how it affects the
company's products. This helps to determine the investments that will be needed
and the costs that will be incurred for compliance, which might include water
usage (such as water treatment, ice plants, structures for water run-off, medical
and hygiene facilities). One of the most important costs associated with food
safety, which is often underplayed, is investment in worker education and training.
Obtaining certification verified by a third party implies constant monitoring in
order to be prepared for audits.

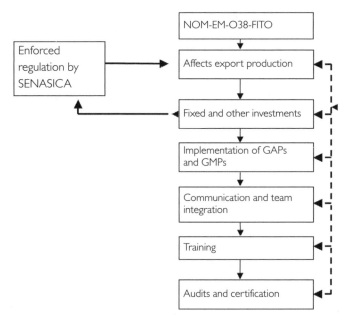

Source: Adapted from Henson and Heasman (1998)

Figure 17.1 *Compliance process for a Mexican export-oriented cantaloupe firm*

Standards involve both conditions on the farm and the packaging process; the latter is extremely important because it determines the shelf life of the product through post-harvest treatment. Packaging is done either by the producer or a fruit packer, during which time the quality of the product is monitored. If the product is rejected, it can either be redirected (directly or through an agent) to the domestic market for fresh consumption or to the processing industry. Certification of the packaging process for export is guided by the regulation NOM-EM-038-FITO-2002, which enforces the implementation of proper agricultural practices and management for the production and packaging of cantaloupe and requires approval by a government department (SENASICA-SAGARPA). In addition, each product distributor requires private certification. After packaging, shipping cantaloupes requires maintaining the cold chain. The cold-storage facility must comply with government practices. It is easier for many of the large growers to comply with higher standards because they own their packaging facilities.

The use of clean water is central to maintaining food safety, and GAPs require periodic analyses of water that take into account microbial counts. Most (88 per cent) of the growers interviewed in Colima used water from rivers, where it is difficult to maintain water quality. There was no consistent testing of water for microbiological and pesticides residues. Only 59 per cent of the small cantaloupe growers reported ever having their water tested, and then only when costs were borne by a firm.

Only 12 per cent of the respondents said they had been affected indirectly because of price reductions after the Salmonella outbreaks. Of the small cantaloupe growers surveyed 71 per cent did not have knowledge of the implications of GAPs. Lack of information was cited by 41 per cent of the farmers as the main reason for not implementing food safety, while 12 per cent were informed but thought that there was no need, given that they were not aiming to export. Only 29 per cent of growers argued that they were implementing a food safety programme – and many of them thought that the proper use of pesticides qualified as a complete food safety programme. Surprisingly, 88 per cent of the small growers said they were not concerned with food safety issues, mainly because they were linked indirectly to the market through intermediaries.

It is important when growing cantaloupe to carry out soil analysis to determine the quality of the soil and the volume of soil enhancers needed. The GAPs programme requires evidence of such analysis and producer documentation on previous uses of the land. Hygienic facilities on farms and in packing facilities are also indispensable for a food safety programme. The norm for sanitation was to have portable toilets on farms to use during plantation and harvest. But with a reallocation of export and institutional markets away from smallholders, buyers no longer demand such facilities from them, and only 24 per cent of the smallholders had been required to provide them. For 94 per cent of the small growers, toilet facilities were not even in the vicinity; they were most often more than half an hour away. This is a critical constraint for small growers trying to comply with GAPs and GMPs.

Larger farms

There are few larger export-oriented cantaloupe farms in Colima. One of the two medium-sized farms turned toward exporting honeydew melon because the product was not subject to strict IFSS and exports of it continued, although returns on honeydew melon are lower than for cantaloupe. Production and packing activities for the larger farms were integrated, with two large farms/firms, which had a long history of cantaloupe production, obtaining SENASICA certification and regaining access to the North American market in 2007. The firms comply with the extensive requirements of GAPs and GMPs, conducting regular soil and water tests, keeping registers on land use, fencing plantation area, and using well water that is tested every month during production for microbiological contamination. They have also invested in osmosis plants to guarantee water quality and have toilet facilities on-farm with running water, wash stations and soap and paper. Prior to harvest and packing all workers are given hygiene maintenance training. All processes are documented and made available for clients and official visits (usually from government representatives from SENASICA or FDA), which usually occur three times during preparation, harvest and packing.

Costs of compliance with IFSS

The requirements to be met along the supply chain determine the compliance costs and differ depending on the target market. The compliance requirements are strictest for international markets, followed by domestic institutional markets. The highest costs associated with investing in food safety programmes are the facilities, with additional costs for worker training and overheads. At the high end, the costs to obtain certification are US$850 per hour of the time of the company employee carrying out the audit (Avendaño et al, forthcoming). The time required varies based on farm size. Most certification programmes are carried out by American companies such as Primus Labs, which inspects and certifies 68 per cent of the fruit and vegetable firms in northwest Mexico. A survey in 2006 showed that the fixed costs for establishing a packing facility that meets the international standards for fresh produce averages US$1.5 million, in addition to US$27,500 in expenses related to food safety certification; maintaining the cold chain for produce such as ice plants costs between US$400 and US$800,000 depending on capacity. Third-party certification averages US$3000 per farm, US$2000 per packing facility and US$10,000 for associated training and major audits, depending on the size of the operation.

The effects of food safety requirements for cantaloupe have been directly reflected in both the fixed and the variable costs of production. Taking as a benchmark the cost increases incurred for other crops owing to compliance with GAPs and GMPs, the variable cost of production is likely to increase by 20 per cent (Avendaño et al, 2006). Because cantaloupe producers in Mexico are not organized into farmer groups (and among the farmers surveyed, only 12 per cent of respondents reported producing under contract), such compliance costs are uneconomical for them.

Kenya green bean exports and the imposition of the IFSS

Exporters of green beans from Kenya must conform to an array of food safety standards. Along with the public and private standards in the European markets, some home-grown food safety standards have emerged for horticultural crops, especially for export markets (Freidberg, 2003). These include KenyaGAP, the code of conduct of the Fresh Produce Exporters Association of Kenya (FPEAK) and the Horticultural Ethical Business Initiative (HEBI), which deals with labour issues, as does the Ethical Trading Initiative (ETI). At least three leading Kenyan exporters (Vegpro Ltd, Homegrown (Kenya) Ltd and Kenya Horticultural Exporters Ltd) have developed their own codes of practice that encompass hygiene, pesticide usage and traceability. These standards are high, vary across the supply chains based on target markets and determine whether smallholders can participate in the chains. Table 17.1 summarizes the various foreign and domestic food safety standards that affect growers of green beans in Kenya.

There are four marketing outlets available to the farmers: European supermarket chains, wholesale export chains, the canning industry and domestic markets.

Table 17.1 *Standards for green bean exporters in Kenya*

Foreign standards	Domestic standards
British Retail Consortium	Kenya Bureau of Standards
GLOBALGAP	HCDA code of practices
Ethical Trading Initiative (UK)	KenyaGAP initiative
HACCP (hazard analysis critical control point)	Horticultural ethical trading
Nature's Choice (Tesco/UK)	Company/exporter code of practices
	Other public sanitary standards

Source: Okello et al (2007)

The UK supermarket chain has the most stringent IFSS (Singh, 2002; Jaffee, 2004; Henson et al, 2005); these include restrictions on the type and quality of inputs used in production, and on pests and diseases prohibited in the UK. Green beans marketed through this chain must be third-party certified as meeting standards such as those set by GLOBALGAP and the BRC and (in most cases) food safety protocols set by the retailers. The beans must also be accompanied by a phytosanitary certificate issued by a competent authority guaranteeing absence of prohibited pests and, more importantly, they must follow a traceability system.

Handling and hygiene practices during harvesting, grading and packing of green beans sold through the supermarket chain are closely coordinated. The exporters have adopted the hazard analysis critical control point (HACCP) and GAPs and have extended these practices to the farm level. The growers are required to have toilets, pesticide storage units and hand-washing facilities available on the farm or in the grading shed. Leading exporters also monitor closely the quality of irrigation water and soils used for growing the beans, often testing the water and soil twice a year for pathogens (especially forms of E. coli and Salmonella).

The exporters require that farmers keep records of the type and quality of inputs used. Duplicate copies of these records accompany the beans to the exporter's processing facility (pack house). The farmers keep their own records individually or collectively. The EU importers monitor the exporters and expect that the exporters will in turn monitor their green bean growers. In general, the relationship between the importers and the retailers is informal. There are typically no formal contracts because of the need for flexibility that allows orders to be changed, even at the last minute, depending on market circumstances. Flexibility in supply is essential because major supermarket stores tend to avoid direct price competition, opting instead, for example, to reduce a bean order when a competitor has beans on sale. Such decisions could be communicated to an exporter just hours before a shipment is scheduled to leave, and the exporter is expected to change the order accordingly. Conversely, an exporter could experience a sudden, last-minute increase in the size of an order. An exporter's inability to adjust to such changes could lead to its being removed from the list of preferred suppliers, or could jeopardize chances for future contract renewal. To allow for the necessary flexibility, exporters often have their outgrowers plant more beans than needed for their regular buyers and then sell the surplus to other markets.

The relationship between a UK importer and an overseas exporter usually involves formal contracts that are renewed as long as the exporter does not grossly violate the IFSS. The exporters, especially those supplying to EU supermarkets, monitor their growers through a team of well-trained field assistants. However, some EU importers are extending their monitoring to the farm level through regular visits for inspection of the use, storage and disposal of pesticides, and the hygiene level on the farm and in the farm-level packing and holding facilities.

The most careful control of pathogen contamination occurs in the exporters' pack houses. Leading exporters in Kenya have invested in state-of-the-art equipment for washing beans with chlorinated water and chilling them before packing. The workers wear special clothes and rubber boots in the pack house and are required to wash their hands at regular intervals or during shift changes in order to avoid cross-contaminating beans with pathogens.

One leading export company randomly takes swabs from workers' hands and tests them for pathogens. If a swab tests positive for pathogens, the worker is penalized. All containers used at various stages of processing are colour-coded to avoid mixing and cross-contamination. In addition to requiring strict adherence to hygiene during processing, some companies pack and attach bar codes under temperature-controlled conditions. (High-care pre-packed beans are sorted, chopped, arranged into trays and pallets and bar-coded.) The EU importers' warehouses that repackage and bar-code beans for their supermarket clients function under similar conditions.

Green beans from most small- and medium-scale farmers feed into the wholesale chain. In general, exporters selling exclusively to the wholesale markets do not require farmers to comply with foreign private food safety standards and traceability. They do demand some physical attributes (e.g. on size, spot-free produce), consistency in volume and conformity with EU public standards. However, monitoring and coordination are generally not as close in this supply chain.

Beans marketed through domestic channels are processed or sold fresh. The chain for domestic consumption is the least coordinated of the three for now, although that is changing. Some exporters sell rejects and/or leftovers of the export channel to a central warehouse (for example Fresh'n'Juicy), which packages the beans and distributes them to major supermarket chains (such as Nakumatt). These domestic retail outlets buy other domestically traded vegetables directly from farmers, but there is no evidence that they purchase green beans directly from farmers.

Kenya cans green beans for export to France and the canning industry is another outlet for small farmers of green beans. Canners of green beans in Kenya source most of their supplies from smallholders. The market for canned beans does not demand compliance with private IFSS. The only IFSS the processors need to meet is the pesticide residue limits. The firms undertake the sourcing, storage and application of pesticides to guard against violation of the limits.

Effects of standards on small actors in the green bean supply chain

With the imposition of IFSS, the supply chains in Kenyan green beans (especially for the supermarkets) have become more tightly coordinated. A tightly coordinated supply chain works against the smallholder in three ways; through information asymmetry and transaction costs, organizational constraints, and regulatory failure (Rich and Narrod, 2005). Information asymmetry makes it harder for smallholders to guarantee food safety without costly third-party certification or close monitoring. It is more expensive for exporters to monitor numerous smallholders. In addition, it is typically not economical for smallholders to establish the quality management systems essential for assuring food safety. Finally, smallholders tend to be geographically dispersed, thus increasing the cost of coordination.

In the case of Kenyan green beans, the exact number of smallholders marginalized by IFSS is unknown, but summary evidence suggests that more than half of the small outgrowers in Kenya were dropped *immediately* following imposition of IFSS (see Okello et al, 2007). Consequently, while in the 1980s over 60 per cent of green beans in Kenya were produced by smallholders, by 2003 this share had dropped to about 30 per cent (Kimenye, 1993; Jaffee, 2004).

Continued participation of smallholders in the green bean supply chains with high standards

The loss of smallholder participation arises from the prohibitive costs of aligning production with IFSS requirements and demonstrating compliance. The main costs of compliance include investments in the required facilities, the cost of switching from toxic to less toxic pesticides, changes in productivity arising from the adjustments and the costs of establishing traceability. The costs of demonstrating compliance with IFSS include investment in training and quality assessment manuals and the costs of pre-audit and certification. The investments also vary depending on how much experience farmers have with IFSS (i.e. how much they have learned by doing).

Table 17.2 compares the typical costs of IFSS compliance for a smallholder farmer group (15 members), an individual smallholder farmer and a large-scale farmer producing beans under contract for UK export. The individual cases were selected as representative of their categories. The data were obtained from records and supplemented by discussions with farmers, group leaders and one of the certification companies in Kenya.

Table 17.2 shows that when the smallholders work together as a group, the cost of compliance per unit of income is significantly lower. The reduction in costs has to be balanced with the risk that expanding the group size would lower the monitoring standards (if monitoring resources remain the same), because more

Table 17.2 *Costs and incomes associated with IFSS compliance and certification by grower type, 2006 (in Kenya shillings; 74 Kenya shillings=US$1 at time of survey)*

Certification	105,890	94,540	94,540
Total IFSS investment costs	438,954	228,190	311,340
Cost per farmer	29,264	N/A	N/A
Total income over investment period	11,120,000	336,000	1,248,000
Year 1 income	3,600,000	96,000	384,000
Year 2 income	7,520,000	240,000	864,000
Cost of compliance as % of total income	4	68	24
Pre-audit (1)	132,000	56,750	32,000

Cost item	Farmer group	Small farmer	Large farmer
Grading shed	59,800	20,000	34,000
Charcoal cooler	41,000	5,400	32,000
Toilet[a]	5,000	–	7,000
Pesticide storage unit	24,450	8,000	37,000
Disposal pit[a]	1,000	–	1,000
Needs assessments, manuals	24,750	21,500	31,000
Analyses (soil, water, MRL)	45,064	40,000	41,800

Note: a The small farmers' plots are assumed to be close enough to their homes that there is no need for a separate toilet and pesticide disposal pit; many exporters allow this.

Source: Okello et al (2007)

members would have to be supervised. There is moreover greater ease in free-riding as group size increases. In all cases, the incomes earned in the second year are substantially higher than those in the first year. This could be because the farmers: (1) increased their production and sales volumes once they obtained GLOBALGAP certification (allowing more reliable access to the export market); (2) achieved better prices through access to the premium markets; and/or (3) learned how to cope with the standards. (See Henson et al (2005) for evidence of learning curves in dealing with food safety.)

In response to IFSS, most smallholders in Kenya who could not meet the standards adopted coping strategies such as switching target markets or products, but some of them, who received institutional support, continued to participate in high-value agricultural markets. Narrod et al (2007) describe the successful participation of the smallholders owing to a combination of collective action and public–private partnerships.

Contract farming, in particular, has helped smallholders by facilitating their access to inputs (e.g. information and credit) and thus mitigating the costs of compliance. Contract farming allows smallholders access to technical information regarding pesticide usage, hygiene requirements and agronomic practices (including integrated pest management) that facilitate compliance with IFSS. They also receive quality seeds (and in some cases protective clothing) under interlinked credit arrangements. Contract production of green beans enables buyers to monitor and enforce IFSS compliance (at lower transaction costs) under a longer-term relationship.

Many small farmers in Kenya have been linked with exporters through small-holder outgrower schemes. Green bean farmer groups existed even prior to the IFSS, mainly for the purpose of marketing (finding buyers and negotiating better prices for members). Beginning in the late 1990s with the imposition of the IFSS, exporters began transforming the way these smallholder groups operated (Jaffee, 2004). The groups were reorganized and their size was reduced from as high as 350 farmers per group to fewer than 30 farmers. The farmers were then trained on the new quality parameters, the IFSS and the necessary production practices. They were then subjected to close monitoring under more formal contracts than under the previous procurement arrangements. Some exporters supervised group members individually and penalized them for violation of practices. However, most supervised the group as a whole and penalized all members for violations (Okello, 2005). Typically, the exporters provided group members with technical information essential for meeting the pesticide usage and hygiene requirements of IFSS, along with loaned seeds.

Leading exporters prefer working with farmers in organizations because it is cheaper to train farmers as a group. The group leaders undergo training; they are then able to act as trainers themselves as well as monitoring and enforcing IFSS compliance. Some exporters require farmer organizations to hire their own technical assistants who can quickly respond to problems with hygiene, pests and disease.

The organization must have a grading shed with a toilet in the vicinity, a cement floor and washable tables, a charcoal cooler and a facility for hand-washing. A strategy used by some leading exporters in Kenya is to have the producer organization hire a technical assistant and a clerk. The technical assistant enforces compliance with pesticide residue requirements by members, conducts occasional field visits with the exporter's agronomist as part of the training and keeps records for all members regarding the type, amount and date of pesticides used. The clerk enforces compliance with hygiene requirements within the grading shed.

A good traceability system includes records of crop, produce and pesticide stock movements. Producer organizations have met the high human capital needs of establishing traceability by jointly hiring field technical assistants and depot/grading shed clerks to compile the records required under IFSS. Each producer organization is allocated a number by its buyer (exporter) and every farmer within the organization is allocated a number for each plot, which must accompany all of her/his produce. Labels for the plots denote the name, variety of crop and date of planting.

Through producer organizations, smallholders make jointly the investments needed to comply with the IFSS, such as cold storage and grading facilities, toilets and pesticide storage units, technical assistants and grading shed clerks. The organizations also conduct training for members and facilitate farmer-to-farmer monitoring in the absence of the exporter's field technical assistant. They invite experts to train farmers on GAPs, especially the observance of pre-harvest intervals following pesticide application, integrated pest management, packer hygiene and maintenance of a functional traceability system.

Several public–private partnerships have been active in Kenya to help maintain smallholder access to markets. Such partnerships focus on providing information, financial support and capacity building (e.g. training for smallholder group leaders), including for audits and certification for GLOBALGAP compliance. Donors and non-governmental organizations (NGOs) have also jointly established Africa's only indigenous certification company, aimed at reducing the cost of GLOBALGAP and making it more accessible to smallholders. Several partnerships have provided support for post-harvest facilities, geographically targeting areas with large numbers of smallholders. For example, the Government of Kenya, in partnership with the Japanese International Cooperation Agency, owns cold-storage facilities in areas that grow fresh vegetables. The government, the Kenya Plant Health Inspectorate Service and USAID have worked together to develop regulatory and pest control mechanisms. Several NGOs in Kenya train smallholders in food safety requirements.

Other coping strategies of green bean smallholders

One of the strategies used by green bean farmers who switch markets has been to reorient production towards the domestic canning industry. In 2000, only a few hundred farmers grew beans for the canning industry, but by 2004, 20,000 smallholder farmers were growing beans for one of Kenya's leading green bean canners, with 3000 having attained GLOBALGAP certification.[3] In canning, the processing companies undertake the production practices that must comply with IFSS, thereby eliminating the information asymmetry problems faced by the fresh produce exporters. The companies employ pesticide spray operators for their outgrowers. Farmers are not involved in sorting, grading or storage; they harvest produce and drop it off at company-designated collection points. Thus, the farmers do not need to invest in the facilities required by the fresh export market. However, canning companies pay up to 25 per cent less than the price farmers get for fresh beans for export.

There are five canning companies currently operating in Kenya. The companies produce some beans on their own farms, but the bulk of the canned beans are sourced from small- and medium-scale outgrowers. Some of these canners have a long history of working with smallholders. One company dominated green bean processing in the mid-1990s, with an outgrower scheme involving 30,000 smallholders in western Kenya and parts of the Rift Valley (Jaffee and Bintein, 1996). The current canned bean industry leader has established an outgrower base including 20,000 smallholders spread over the traditional and emerging green bean growing areas of Kenya.

Grape exports from India and the impact of IFSS

India is dominated by smallholders: in 2001 82 per cent of landholdings were under 2 hectares (Roy and Thorat, forthcoming). India is the third leading producer of fruits and vegetables in the world (after China and the EU), contributing 9 per cent of world fruit production and 14 per cent of world vegetable production in 2005 (FAO, 2005). India is a relatively small horticultural exporter, with only a 2.3 per cent share in world horticultural trade in 2004, a figure disproportionate to its share in global production. The smallholder base for agriculture in India imposes limits on the number of farmers capable of adopting more sophisticated farm practices and undertaking the necessary investments to meet more stringent food quality and safety requirements (Umali-Deininger and Sur, 2006).

One of the few successful stories of Indian participation in western export markets is that of Mahagrapes, a marketing partner to a group of cooperatives that came into existence in 1991. Several government agencies supported its establishment including federal agencies such as the National Cooperative Development Corporation, the National Horticultural Board and the Agricultural and Processed Food Products Export Development Authority. State agencies that also helped establish Mahagrapes included the Government of Maharashtra's Department of Cooperation and the Maharashtra State Agriculture Marketing Board.

Exports started in 1991. In the beginning, Mahagrapes had 29 grape-growing farmer cooperatives as members but within the first three years the number was reduced to 16 as a result of high rates of consignment rejections in the European markets. In the second year, a large consignment was rejected, with losses of 20 million rupees (about US$771,000). Many cooperatives left Mahagrapes to concentrate on the domestic market or look for alternative marketing arrangements.

In the early years of exports, consignment rejection was as high as 80 per cent. Consignment rejections occurred primarily because of imperfect under-standing of market requirements, from seed quality to harvest and post-harvest care and packaging practices. The government stepped in with soft loans to the cooperatives to help set up a pre-cooling and cold storage infrastructure. Mahagrapes claims that rejection rates declined from less than 10 per cent after 1995 to a negligible rate of less than 1 per cent after 2001. However, fruit quality and sanitary and phytosanitary measures, and the methods used to ascertain them, change year to year, and Mahagrapes needs to keep abreast of the changing requirements so as to amend regularly their own production, processing, storing and testing methods. For instance a consignment to the Netherlands was rejected because the method employed in India for testing chemical residues differed from that used in the Netherlands.

Other product attributes that can be the basis for rejection are berry size, fruit colour, bunch weight, blemishes, bag weight (minimum/maximum), stem colour, shrivelled berry, split berry, sulphur dioxide (SO_2) damage, and berry waste pest damage, shattered berry, chill damage, temperature, residue, taints and odour, packing quality and average weight. Since the introduction of Regulation EC No. 1148/2001, which required all fresh produce arriving in the EU as of 1 July 2002 to undergo an ISO 9000-style inspection to verify conformity with marketing standards, Mahagrapes has learned how to minimize potential problems, and rejection rates have decreased substantially.

Over time, the small farmers working with Mahagrapes have built up the capacity to meet stringent food safety standards for export to the developed countries (in Europe) and Mahagrapes has helped farmers in several ways and has been active in all three stages of the compliance process: information (creating a knowledge base about market requirements and disseminating to farmers); decision and implementation.[4]

In the implementation stage, Mahagrapes provides materials and technical help along with infrastructural support to facilitate the implementation of the standards. It provides farmers with packaging material that complies with international norms (such as plastic bags and palettes imported from Spain). Special SO_2 sheets are imported from China and are used to cover the grapes before they are sealed in corrugated cardboard boxes. Bruising or other damage during transit is reduced; SO_2 gas is released after 15 days when the consignment of grapes arrives at its destination.

Acquiring a GLOBALGAP certificate individually is costly for small and medium farmers, but Mahagrapes provides each cooperative society and its member farmers with certification that they are GLOBALGAP-compliant. Individual farmers have to pay only 1200 rupees (approximately US$28) per year.

Different grape varieties are targeted to different markets, with Thompson seedless grapes planted mainly for export to European markets. The smallholders who are not able to access this market sell to export markets with less stringent standards and/or sell to the domestic markets. The Sharad seedless variety is sold mainly in the domestic market, while the Sonaka is marketed domestically and exported to the Gulf countries.

With the ability to meet the food safety standards for Thompson seedless variety and access the western markets, the small farmers working with Mahagrapes have had significant increases in their incomes (net of the costs of compliance). Drawing upon Roy and Thorat (forthcoming), below we discuss how food safety standards have led to differentiation among small grape farmers.

Differentiation among small grape farmers created by food safety standards

Roy and Thorat (forthcoming) looked at the financial gains to smallholders from accessing markets with high food safety standards. Based on a primary survey of small farmers exporting through Mahagrapes and those selling mostly to local markets, the authors assessed the gains from compliance with IFSS. The difference in earnings attributable to meeting the standards were balanced with control

Table 17.3 *Profit equation – dependent variable profit, in thousands of Rupees per acre of land (1 Rupee = US$40 approximately)*

Explanatory variables	Coefficients (t values) OLS estimates	Coefficients (t values) instrumental variable estimates
Membership (the level effect)	27.6 (2.53)**	96.36 (2.53)**
Distance from the city centre	−0.093 (−0.18)	−0.58 (−1.10)
Schooling	2.28 (0.30)	11.68 (1.59)
Age	−0.28 (−0.59)	−0.67 (−1.55)
Land	−2.39 (−4.54)***	−2.56 (−2.65)**
Experience	−1.76 (−0.87)	−2.95 (−1.15)
Experience squared	0.060 (1.10)	0.08 (1.10)
Total land* membership	−1.5 (1.2)	−3.51 (−1.29)
Grapeland* membership	2.5 (2.28)**	0.22 (0.09)
Number of observations	132	132

Note: * statistical significance at 1%; ** statistical significance at 5%; *** statistical significance at 10%.

Source: Roy and Thorat (forthcoming)

factors in the two groups of farmers, both those that could be observed and hence measured (such as farming experience) and that could not be observed (such as skills). There were no significant differences in terms of land sizes or access to transportation and communication infrastructure between farmers who met the standards for export and those who catered to the local market -- but they did differ significantly in terms of human capital. The small or medium farmers who exported to western markets had substantially more experience in farming. The costs of compliance were mitigated by the higher profits from western rather than domestic markets (Table 17.3).

Conclusions

We have discussed the impact of increased IFSS on smallholder farmers for different crops in three countries. The cantaloupe (Mexico) and green bean (Kenya) cases provided strong indications of the screening effect of the IFSS on smallholder producers supplying high-end export markets, at least in the short term. In the cantaloupe case smallholders were completely eliminated from the export market and almost all smallholders reoriented themselves toward domestic markets. In contrast, the green bean case shows a menu of coping strategies by the smallholders, ranging from switching target markets to continuing to participate in the export market under modified institutional arrangements. The production system for green beans in Kenya, as for grapes in India, has an overwhelmingly large share of smallholders; in order to meet the needs of the supply chain, buyers had to adopt innovative solutions that made it profitable to deal with smallholders.

Smallholders are affected by IFSS in other ways beyond the strong initial screening effect and milder, longer-term effects. Markets with IFSS are characterized by high costs of compliance but also high returns. As shown by the Kenyan example, over time, the capacity of small farmers to comply with IFSS and participate in high-value markets can improve, due to the provision of adequate, customized institutional support.

In the case of India's grapes, smallholders (after initial setbacks) consistently provided grapes with high food safety standards, and the IFSS-compliant small farmers earned significantly higher returns than their non-compliant counterparts. It is quite possible that those farmers most likely to cater to the exporting sector are those with higher skills (more education and experience). When farming systems are dominated by smallholders such that supply needs cannot be met without them, it might not be sufficient to analyse the group as a bloc; IFSS can lead to differentiation within groups of smallholders rather than just between large farms and smallholders.

Over time, given adequate institutional support, smallholders can cope with stringent food safety standards. Thus, policy makers have to be wary of the pessimism that is common with regard to smallholders' ability to meet stringent food safety standards. Not only is there a need to search for innovative solutions based on best practices that emerge from comparative studies, policy makers must realize the potential of differential impacts within groups of smallholders after safety standards are introduced. Policy should best be directed towards enabling the most vulnerable of smallholders. These smallholders would be the least educated, least experienced and least coordinated, horizontally and vertically.

Notes

1   The discussion here is based on Avendaño et al (forthcoming).
2   GAPs and GMPs are not foolproof: a routine sampling programme done by the FDA in October 2006 found Salmonella in Mexican cantaloupe that was to be distributed throughout the US and Canada.
3   Estimates from the Kenya Horticultural Development Project (an NGO).
4   These stages were described by Kleinwechter and Grethe (2006) with regard to how mango exporters in Peru adapted to GLOBALGAP standards.

References

Avendaño, B., Rindermann, R., Monores, S.Y. L. and Lagarda, A. M. (2006) *La Inocuidad Alimentaria en México. Las hortalizas frescas de exportación*, MAPorrua, Mexico City
Avendaño, B., Narrod, C. and Tiongco, M. (forthcoming) 'Food safety requirements in Latin American cantaloupe exports and their impact on small farmers', IFPRI Discussion Paper, IFPRI, Washington, DC
Food and Agriculture Organization of the United Nations (FAO) (2005) Agricultural data, FAOSTAT, Rome

Freidberg, S. (2003) 'The contradictions of clean: The supermarket ethical trade and African horticulture', *Gatekeeper Series*, no. 109

Henson, S. and Heasman, M. (1998) 'Food safety regulation and the firm: Understanding the compliance process', *Food Policy*, vol 23, no 1, pp9–23

Henson, S., Masakure, O. and Boselie, D. (2005) 'Private food safety and quality standards for fresh producer exporters: The case of Hortico Agrisystems, Zimbabwe', *Food Policy*, vol 30, pp371–384

Jaffee, S. (2004) 'From challenge to opportunity: Transforming Kenya's fresh vegetable trade in the context of emerging food safety and other standards in Europe', Agriculture and Rural Development Discussion Paper No. 2, World Bank, Washington, DC

Jaffee, S. M. and Bintein, G. (1996) 'French bean connection: Sustaining success in Kenyan contract farming venture', *African Rural and Urban Studies*, vol 3, pp63–99

Kimenye, L. N. (1993) 'Economics of smallholder French bean production and marketing in Kenya', PhD dissertation, Michigan State University, East Lansing, MI

Kleinwechter, U. and Grethe, H. (2006) 'The adoption of the Eurepgap Standard by mango exporters in Piura, Peru', contributed paper at the 26th Conference of the International Association of Agricultural Economists (IAAE), 12–18 August

Muwanga, K. M. (2007) 'Experiences on adjustments to private standards in key export markets. A case of East Africa', Presentation to the World Trade Organization (WTO), [online] www.wto.org/english/tratop_e/sps_e/private_standards_june07_e/muwanga_e.ppt

Narrod, C., Gulati, A., Minot, N. and Delgado, C. (2005) 'Food safety research priorities for the CGIAR' – a draft concept note from IFPRI for the Science Council, IFPRI, Washington, DC

Narrod, C., Roy, D., Rich, K., Okello, J., Avendaño, B. and Thorat, A. (2007) 'The role of public–private partnerships and collective action in ensuring smallholder participation in high value fruit and vegetable supply chains', CAPRi working paper 70, CAPRi, Washington, DC, available at http://dlc.dlib.indiana.edu/archive/00002686

Okello, J. (2005) 'Compliance with international food safety standards: The case of green bean production in Kenyan family farms', PhD Dissertation, Michigan State University, East Lansing, MI

Okello, J., Narrod, C. and Roy, D. (2007) *Food safety requirements in African green bean exports and their impact on small farmers*, IFPRI Discussion paper no. 737, IFPRI, Washington, DC, available at www.ifpri.org/PUBS/dp/ifpridp00737.asp

Rich, K. M. and Narrod, C. (2005) 'Perspectives on supply chain management of high value agriculture: The role of public–private partnerships in promoting smallholder access', draft, mimeo

Roy D. and Thorat, A. (forthcoming) 'Success in high value export markets for small farmers. The case of Mahagrapes in India', *World Development*

Singh, B. P. (2002) 'Nontraditional crop production in Africa for export', in Janick, J. and Whipkey, A. (eds) *Trends in New Crops and New Uses*, ASHA Press, Alexandria, VA

Umali-Deininger, D. and Sur, M. (2006) 'Food safety in a globalizing world: Opportunities and challenges for India', paper presented at the International Association of Agricultural Economists Conference, Gold Coast, Australia, August

United States Department of Agriculture (2006) 'FASOnline: U.S. Trade Internet System', Foreign Agriculture Service, US Department of Agriculture, Washington, DC, [online] www.fas.usda.gov/ustrade/

Index